Cognitive Internet of Things

Cognitive Internet of Things

Enabling Technologies, Platforms, and Use Cases

Pethuru Raj, Anupama C. Raman, and
Harihara Subramanian

CRC Press
Taylor & Francis Group
Boca Raton London New York

CRC Press is an imprint of the
Taylor & Francis Group, an **informa** business

AN AUERBACH BOOK

First edition published [2022]
by CRC Press
6000 Broken Sound Parkway NW, Suite 300, Boca Raton, FL 33487-2742

and by CRC Press
4 Park Square, Milton Park, Abingdon, Oxon, OX14 4RN

ISBN: 978-0-367-34825-0 (hbk)
ISBN: 978-1-032-21335-4 (pbk)
ISBN: 978-0-429-32822-0 (ebk)

DOI: 10.1201/9780429328220

Typeset in Garamond
by SPi Technologies India Pvt Ltd (Straive)

Contents

Authors

Pethuru Raj works as a chief architect at Reliance Jio Platforms Ltd. (JPL) Bangalore. Previously, he has worked in IBM Global Cloud Center of Excellence (CoE), Wipro Consulting Services (WCS), and Robert Bosch Corporate Research (CR). In total, he gained more than 20 years of IT industry experience and 8 years of research experience. He has Completed the CSIR-sponsored PhD degree at Anna University, Chennai, and continued with the UGC-sponsored postdoctoral research in the Department of Computer Science and Automation, Indian Institute of Science (IISc), Bangalore. Thereafter, he was granted two international research fellowships (JSPS and JST) to work as a research scientist for 3.5 years in two leading Japanese universities. He focuses on some of the emerging technologies such as the Internet of Things (IoT), Artificial Intelligence (AI) Model Optimization Methods, Big, Fast and Streaming Analytics, Blockchain, Digital Twins, Cloud-native Computing, Edge and Serverless Computing, Reliability Engineering, Microservices Architecture (MSA), Event-driven Architecture (EDA), and 5G.

Anupama C. Raman works as global head – Software Center of Excellence (Software Academy) in Continental Corporation. Anupama is a software engineer and has over 18 years of experience in companies which include IBM, Dell EMC, Flipkart, etc. She is a passionate technology writer and has authored several Forbes blog articles on technology topics. Anupama is also a public speaker and has spoken in several leading national and international conferences.

Harihara Subramanian works for the SABRE Corporation as a senior principal software architect. Hari has been working with software development and various software architecture concepts since 1999. He is an energetic and highly focused technology leader with a proven track record in software development, software architecture principles, and implementations. He has been an active contributor to various online and offline forums in different technologies and focuses his time on technology consulting, software development, microservices architecture (MSA), Distributed Systems, Cloud Computing, IoT, and more.

Chapter 1

Describing the Cognitive IoT Paradigm

Introduction

Once upon a time, many people used only one computer. Today, everyone has a personal computer and handheld devices. Tomorrow is brewing a completely different scenario where all these computers connect, intermingle, and understand human(s) temporal, emotional, spatial, physical requirements. Soon, all the interconnected computers build services in time with all the zeal and skill in a discreet manner.

The future Internet is about the interconnection of millions of computing machines, distributed software services and billions of interconnected items such as machines, instruments, equipment, wares, utensils, actuators, drones, robots, etc.

With the unprecedented maturity of edge and digitization technologies such as sensors, actuators, chips, tags, stickers, specks, beacons, LED lights, etc., every tangible item in our everyday environments (homes, hotels, hospitals, offices, etc.) gets transitioned into a digital object (also touted as a sentient or an intelligent thing). That is, all kinds of physical, mechanical, and electrical systems become digitized. Any digitized (or digitally enabled) artefact gets and gains the distinct capability of joining and contributing to mainstream computing.

Thus, the extreme connectivity, the deep integration, the constant data capture, the real-time data processing and analysis, the correct decision-making, and the execution in a timely and trustworthy fashion are the prime functionalities of our personal, social, and professional devices, robots, drones, and other automated machines. Therefore, the raging Internet of Things (IoT) phenomenon is proclaiming a potent, promising, and pivotal paradigm for the future.

The fast-emerging and evolving IoT idea is a strategic and highly impactful one to be collaboratively investigated, coherently worked on, decisively realized, and passionately sustained with the intelligent adoption of cutting-edge technologies,

DOI: 10.1201/9780429328220-1

lightweight processes, optimal and organized infrastructures, integrated platforms, enabling tools, pioneering patterns, and futuristic architectures.

Industry professionals and academicians are constantly looking out for appropriate use, business, and technical cases to proclaim the IoT concept's transformational value and power to the larger audience of worldwide executives, end-users, entrepreneurs, evangelists, and engineers.

A growing range of open and industry-strength standards are being formulated, framed, and polished by IoT domain experts, industry consortiums and standard bodies to make IoT more visible, viable and valuable. Governments across the world are setting up special groups intended to define pragmatic policies and procedures of IoT. These procedures help governments realize the strategic significance of citizen-centric services to ensure and enhance the people's comfort, choice, care, and convenience.

Research students, scholars, and scientists work together on path-breaking technological solutions to identify the implementation challenges and overcome them via different means.

With the steady progress of artificial intelligence (AI) methods, there is a convergence between the fast-growing IoT and AI technologies. The gist of this exciting linkage is to enable IoT devices to self-learn out of the data getting generated by various participating IoT devices (digitized objects, connected devices, cyber-physical systems (CPSs), etc.) in exhibit cognitive behaviour.

This chapter discusses several perspectives of IoT ideas, their broader spectrum, trends that set up the stage to realize and demonstrate those ideas. The necessary reasons to pursue the IoT ideas, their prickling and prime concerns, changes, and challenges associated with looking at those ideas seriously and sincerely. The challenges that we see applying those ideas extensively and expediently, near and long-term future, key benefits, security and associated risks and mitigations path. Also, we discuss the usefulness of IoT for shaking up the world with intelligent devices and its sustainability and ideas around leveraging several nearby and faraway cloud environments to capture and stock the anonymized data. The collected data then subject the collected and cleansed IoT data to extract actionable insights in time and disseminate the knowledge unveiled to the appropriate IoT devices, which in turn nourished adequately to be adaptive, articulate, and assistive services for the users.

About the Internet of Things (IoT) Conundrum

IoT is all about enabling extreme connectivity among common objects across the industry domains. All everyday items get digitized, web- and cloud-enabled. Then those digitized objects talk to each other in the vicinity and with remote ones through networking. Further on, they integrate with the Internet-held data sources, applications, services, platforms, etc. In other words, the future Internet comprises digital entities, connected devices, data sources, and microservices.

A string of promising and positive trends in the IT space have laid a strong foundation for the out-of-the-box visualization of raging IoT ideas. The prevailing trend poised towards empowering our everyday environment and all kinds of casual and cheap articles and artefacts to be IT-enabled, and networking all that artefacts in an ad hoc manner using various communication technologies on-demand basis to accomplish bigger and better things.

So, its seamless and spontaneous connectivity helps us leverage their distinct yet collective capabilities to understand the various cognitive needs (spatial, temporal, emotional, informational, transactional, operational, analytical, and physical) of the people in that particular environment. This understanding (unambiguous) helps decide, do, and deliver the identified services unobtrusively to the right people at the right time and the right place.

In the upcoming section, let's discuss in brief about potential and promises of the IoT paradigm and the key drivers for the surging popularity of the IoT paradigm, the enabling technologies, infrastructures and platforms, the prominent IoT solutions, the facilitating frameworks, accelerators and tools, the famous use cases, the brewing concerns and challenges, the research directions, etc.

Finally, you can find how the remarkable convergence of the IoT accomplishments and the advancements in the AI domain can bring forth hitherto unknown advantages for the entire human society.

The Trends and Transitions towards the IoT Era

Due to the general availability of many cutting-edge technologies and state-of-the-art tools, the IoT discipline is doing exceedingly well. Businesses have overwhelmingly embraced the IoT phenomenon. New use cases getting into formation and accentuated to boost people's confidence to leverage the IoT idea's unique competencies. Drawbacks and limitations are widely understood, and several technologically inspired solutions getting unearthed to surmount them. With broader acceptance and adoption, the IoT leverage has gone up significantly across the world with IoT researchers' concerted and coordinated efforts.

Deeper Digitization towards Smart Objects

Every tangible thing is getting digitized to realize the much-needed sensing, response, and communication capabilities so that each and everything in our midst is capable of participating and contributing to mainstream multi-device computing. There are multiple ways for empowering ordinary objects to become practical, usable, and extraordinary artefacts. The minuscule tags, stickers, chips, sensors, motes, smart dust, actuators, LED displays, etc., are the most common elements and entities for the speedy, more uncomplicated, and copious realization of intelligent objects. For a prime example, we humans are increasingly connected to the outside world for outward and inward communication through slim, sleek, handy, and trendy smartphones. The ubiquity and utility of multifaceted phones are foretelling many positives for humans in the days to unfold. Similarly, every commonly found item in our daily environments becomes digitized and become ingenious in its operations, outlooks, and outputs. The smartness derived via internal and external enhancements enables them to be elegantly and eminently constructive, cognitive, and contributive.

The maturity and stability of mesh network topology and technologies ensure these empowered and emboldened materials find and bind with other similarly enabled articles (local and remote) to leverage their unique functionalities and features to fulfil people's varying needs. Such longstanding and technological empowerment goes a long way in unearthing a host of nimbler business and IT models and services, fresh possibilities and opportunities for people and business, scores of optimization methods for swiftly heading towards the vision of people IT, solid and sharp increment in the user experience of diverse business and IT offerings, etc.

In one of their articles, John Hagel and John Seely Brown wrote, "big and marvellous shifts and transformation are happening in how things get made from scratch and how the hitherto untapped value is in the process of creation and aggregation". Digitalization technologies aren't just impacting production and manufacturing, but they're changing the physical world altogether. Our physical world is now technology-enabled by digitizing everything from books to movies to tools such as the flashlights, cameras, calculators, day planners, music players, and bus schedules that currently reside on our smartphones. The internet communication infrastructure and digital technologies are the most potent and path-breaking combination to bring forth significant and fundamental transformations in our physical world.

Due to a growing litany of praiseworthy improvisations, we have achieved a lot in the virtual/cyber world. There is never a best moment than now to embark on the modernization of the physical world. The principal transition for empowering our physical environments smart is to make ordinary things wise. The idea is to meticulously enable dumb things in our daily settings to be adept in their actions.

The era of searching our cars in the parking lots will be long gone; we are already witnessing the parked vehicle shows up on our feet on its own by locating us instead we find them. It's the magic of combining digitization and digitalization technologies. A few more examples maybe opt to quote; An individual is looking for an additional income with spare bed match with a potential tenant looking for a stay. It lets us find and modify an existing and proven design rather than create one from scratch and then use a manufacturing-grade tool to execute the strategy regardless of skill with very little invested time. Though the above examples need some level of intervention by humans, the next step is to eliminate them and make them cleverer.

Technology-enabled physical objects begin to understand clearly and take actions automatically and artistically by adapting to situations and contexts. With the maturity of CPS technologies, the effective utilization of physical assets is steadily growing. Physical machines' efficiency is achievable in many ways, like improving the "up-time", self-correcting systems for a costly device, or renting out excess capacity to external parties to generate new revenue streams and so on.

We read about the anti-skid technology or collision-avoidance features in a car. Set of components communicating with one another to take appropriate actions so rapidly; otherwise, it's impossible by humans. This type of real-time adjustment and feedback eliminates or reduces the need for human intervention. This trend has expanded into larger systems, like wind turbines and complex machinery interacting within a processing plant. Self-correction and automated load adjustment are bound to increase productivity. It's not the end, and there are far more values unlocked when information is available to humans to carry out the pattern analysis and systemic intervention.

The pavement we drive on becomes cannier with sensors that communicate traffic information; heavy earth-moving equipment becomes smarter when sensors monitor tire wear to reduce downtime risk. The materials become wise and collect and conduct information for the clothing a runner wears or the pipe that water flows through down to the collection points.

The greater goal is to pull all the data back into a human sphere to add value. Imagine a beverage company that faces fairly frequent stock-outs that cause customer dissatisfaction and loose sales. A year's worth of data shows that the stock-outs typically occur in conjunction with local and hyper-local events. Now the company has the opportunity not only to track and respond to stock-out situations faster but also to program the inventory-replenishment system to cross-check with event calendars, weather reports, and Twitter feeds to prepare. Companies' skills in tapping use data will determine the data's value, but the potential is more significant than just cost efficiency.

The Growing Device Ecosystem

The ecosystem space is fast evolving with the different advancements in miniaturization technologies. There is a challenging and rough passage from the mainframe and the pervasive PC cultures to trendy and handy, slim and sleek portables, handhelds and wearables, invisible tags, stickers, labels and chips, tiny sensors actuators, and versatile mobiles. This transformation subtly indicates the slow and ubiquitous transition from centralization to decentralization. Business workloads and fragmented IT services and their distribution across multiple computing devices to reap all the initially expressed benefits of distributed computing. Thus, the arrival of feature-rich devices has a substantial impact on software engineering.

However, this encouraging and path-breaking trend brings the difficulty and dodging issues of heterogeneity, multiplicity, and incompatibility. The greater acceptance of service engineering and science has helped to moderate the rising device complexity substantially. That is, devices are being expressed and exposed as device services to the outside world. The discrepancies and deficiencies of devices are abstracted or hidden through service application programming interfaces (APIs). Such a service-oriented integration approach has made it possible for device integration and orchestration. There are several device middleware solutions enabling device integration. All kinds of participating and contributing devices, machines, instruments, drones, equipment, and electronics in our personal as well as professional environments need to be individually as well as collectively intelligent enough to discover one another, link, access, and use to be competent and cognitive to accomplish bigger and better things for humans. Many envisioning the future spaces will be highly digitized environments with a fabulous collection of networked devices and digitized artefacts. Each is distinct in its facet, feature, and functionality.

Empowered devices will be interlinked through local and global networks transparently to achieve something substantial. This linkage opens up a wider variety of hitherto unknown possibilities. With multiple sophisticated yet complicated scenarios brewing silently and firmly, it is prudent to think about the ways and means of ably and adaptively identifying and utilizing their inherent capabilities (specific as well as generic) and capacities for arriving at a horde of people-centric and path-breaking services. As we are keenly waiting for the paradigm of "computing everywhere every time" to cherish and flourish, it is imperative to nourish and nudge any variety of participating devices to be highly agile and adaptive.

The devices need to figure out the contextual user needs proactively, pre-emptively, and purposefully by collaborating within. It will be beneficial to use these devices to correlate and corroborate to figure out the user(s)' contextual needs by dynamically connecting, complementing. At the other end, there is a litany of input and output devices such as smartphones to assist people in finishing their personal and professional assignments effectively and efficiently. Devices are becoming device ensembles and clusters through internal and external integration to be highly valuable for our everyday chores and obligations.

To summarize, there are a wider variety of machines, appliances, consumer electronics, instruments, handy computers and communicators, sophisticated specific and generic robots, multipurpose gadgets and gizmos, drones, kitchen utensils, etc. On the other side, there are resource-constrained, low-cost, low-power, miniaturized, multifaceted sensors, actuators, microcontrollers, stickers, tags, etc. However, the exciting part here is that all these are getting connected in their vicinity and the remote cloud platforms and infrastructures to acquire necessary intelligence in time to be beneficial to their owners and users.

Device-to-Device Integration

The pervasiveness of ultra-high communication (wired and wireless) technologies facilitates the critical and longstanding goal of enabling devices to seamlessly and spontaneously interact with one another to share their potentials. The communication field is going through a stream of praiseworthy transformations. There are new paradigms such as autonomic, unified, and ambient communication. The 5G communication paradigm is being adopted widely across the globe. Thus, the communication field is in line with business expectations. With the maturity and stability of adaptive communication platforms and infrastructures, many highly beneficial communications features and models arise. Even business processes coupled with communication capabilities and those more intimate and intensive processes are bound to erupt and evolve fast towards the greater fulfilment of peoples' aspirations.

The newly found ad hoc connectivity capability among many devices ranging from invisible and infinitesimal tags, smart dust, stickers, and sparkles in our daily environments to highly sophisticated machines in the manufacturing floors and hospitals has resulted in a series of new services. Several industrial domains are very optimistic and looking forward to this paradigm shift in conceptual and pragmatizing a growing array of creative and cognitive applications for their user community. Telecommunication service providers are the pivotal partners for the unprecedented success of D2D integration. A bevvy of next-generation applications is in the path of conceiving and constructing based on this grandeur transformation brought in by the D2D integration idea, as pictorially illustrated in Figure 1.1.

Several meaningful use cases and business cases intensify the gripping popularity of the idea of D2D communication. The prominent one is home integration solutions (proprietary and standardized) in plenty these days to simplify and streamline the rough and demanding tasks associated with home networking, communication, and automation, leading to innumerable intelligent homes. The newer concepts of smart meters and microgrids become prominent across the globe by heterogeneous

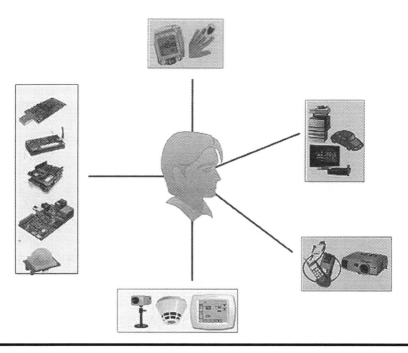

Figure 1.1 Multi-device assistance for humans.

devices' interactions. All the key and operational components of any classic cars get integrated with a centralized middleware device. Those connected devices, in turn, capture and aggregate all the usable car component state data and send them to cloud environments and get subjected to various deeper investigations. The cloud-hosted data analytics platform performs diagnosis and prognosis to extricate action-able insights in time. The knowledge discovered gets disseminated to car owners and occupants to empower them with information to plunge into remedial and repairing acts confidently and quickly. Thus, car components talk with one another for fulfilling specific process requirements. Car modules interact with a communication-enabled car middleware solution by conveying their self, surrounding, and situational data. In conjunction with real-time data analytics platforms/accelerators, the cloud infra-structures collectively contribute to the realization of autonomous cars. The idea of more profound and extreme connectivity among all kinds of devices of varying sizes, scopes, and structures produces many robust and resilient services. Those ideas get fuelled by connectivity capability, enthusiasm, and optimism among product and platform vendors, telecom companies, IT service providers, system integrators (SIs), government departments, standard bodies, research labs in academic institutions, and business organizations.

On the security side, there are a few challenging situations. With connected devices helping out in large-scale distributed computing, we will have highly versatile and integrated applications. That is, constructing and managing cross-institutional and functional applications in this sort of dynamic and device-stuffed environments get speed up with a few unpredictable possibilities. There are chances for risky interac-tions among varied services, sensors, and systems, resulting in severe complications and unwanted implications for the safety and security of human society.

Fog/Edge Device Computing

With devices stuffed with more memory and storage capacities and processing power, those devices are indeed gaining computing capability. As enunciated above, devices can form value-adding clusters that become so relevant for businesses and people. In addition to that, devices could capture, cleanse, and crunch data from various digital assets (different physical, mechanical, electrical, and electronics systems digitized methodically through edge technologies) in their environments to create insights, which are famous for their trustworthiness and timeliness. Thus, the phenomenon of edge/fog data analytics came into prominence. Increasingly the real-time data capture, storage, and processing competencies are being made possible through edge devices, devices clusters/clouds, and analytics.

Software-defined Cloud Infrastructures for the IoT Era

Cloud technologies have already been positioned and proclaimed as the highly consolidated, converged, federated, compartmentalized, shared, and automated IT environments for hosting and compactly delivering a galaxy of diverse IT solutions and business workloads. Clusters, grids, on-demand, utility, autonomic computing models, service orientation, multi-tenancy, virtualization, containerization, and many such concepts constitute cloud paradigms.

The cloud paradigm becomes an elegant and fabulous fertile ground that has inspired many out in the world to come out with several newer cloud-centric services, products, and platforms that facilitate scores of people-centric, multifaceted, and features-rich cloud applications. Besides, there have been various generic and specific innovations in the form of pragmatic processes, patterns, best practices, fundamental guidelines, metrics, etc., for moderating the rising IT complexity and enhancing IT agility, autonomy, and affordability heightened IT productivity.

Cloud and Cloud technologies had laid a stimulating and sound foundation for the grand vision of IT infrastructure optimization through seamless synchronization and connectivity. This ground-breaking evolution and elevation in the IT field have brought innumerable and insightful impacts on business and IT domains these days. Cloud technology ensures anytime, anywhere, and any device information and service access and leverage. That is, the much-anticipated fully facilitated ubiquitous service delivery with the arrival, articulation, and adoption of the mighty cloud idea. All kinds of services, applications, and data storage and processing systems are now on the verge of modernization accordingly and adroitly migrated to cloud platforms and infrastructures to reap all the originally envisioned benefits (technical, user, and business cases).

The connected vision of the cloud puzzle is to see the distinct reality with the praiseworthy advancements by IT landscapes clever adaptions of the robust and resilient cloud models. These models are primary contributors to worldwide business enterprises to achieve the venerable mission of "more with less". Thus, the cloud is the core, central, cheap, and becoming cognitive infrastructure that helps manage all kinds of business changes, concerns and challenges. With the cloud, the business entities are ready to portend and portray a brighter and fulsome future for business organizations to surge ahead and keep their edge earned in their offerings, outputs, and outlooks.

With a legion of resource-constrained, embedded, and networked devices joining in the IT landscape and with the seamless synchronization with the remote, on-demand, and elastic clouds (generic clouds such as public, private, and community or specific clouds such as storage, knowledge, science, data, sensor, device, and mobile), there abound hordes of real-time and sophisticated applications and services.

Cloud Infrastructures for Real-time Big Data Analytics

Today, the most visible and valuable trend is nonetheless the unprecedented data explosion in every business domain. As there is a convincing and significant number of machines and sensors pervasively deployed and effectively used and managed for various requirements in our everyday environments, the machine-generated data is much larger than the man-generated data. The data volume is exponentially growing with several remarkable advancements in sensors, actuators, robots, connectivity, service enablement, etc. Embedded systems getting networked locally as well as remotely are the newer attractions.

There is a substantial need to unearth new database modelling from the structured and non-structured data with data management systems such as distributed SQL, in-memory, NoSQL, and time-series databases and file systems to swiftly capture, store, and search large-scale and multi-structured data. As mentioned earlier, there are other use cases of the systems, such as the smooth transition of multi-structured data into structured data, filtering out repetitive, redundant, and routine data to have highly usable data, etc. These systems help in doing coarse-grained analytics on cleaned data. When these preprocessing activities get completed, the much-needed fine-grained data analytics get performed easily and quickly.

Big data analytics (BDA) through batch processing is one of the critical activities in the significant data era. With the arrival of path-breaking technologies and tools, the real-time analytics of big data is being made possible. The cluster and cloud computing models come in handy in quickly analysing large-scale data. With time, the value of data declines. Thus, time-sensitive data analysis becomes vital for transitioning data to information and knowledge. With billions of billions connected devices and trillions of digitized objects, the size of IoT data will grow massive and multi-structured. The BDA capability is an indispensable one for making sense and money out of IoT data.

BDA has also acquired a critical phenomenon from big data storage and management, and we can't afford to ignore it. Data across cloud, social, device, mobile, and enterprise spaces need identification and assembly to get subjected to powerful data mining, processing, and analysis tasks. The discovered knowledge has to be disseminated promptly to actuation systems and decision-makers in time to be highly beneficial for businesses, governments, financial institutions, etc. We need high affable and adorable storage appliances, real-time data analytics platforms, parallel processing methods, programming models, etc., to do proper justice for big data. The emergence of cloud environments is being touted as the finest moment in IT history. The leverage of commodity servers for big data storage and processing in an affordable manner will undoubtedly be a game-changing moment. The cloud revolution has done a lot of tangible things for big data. No SQL systems like Hadoop (MapReduce/Spark/Flink/Samza, and Hive/

HDFS) implementations, commodity servers, data appliances, and so on are the primary and dominant methods handpicked and handled to accommodate terabytes and even petabytes of incongruent data. So those churned data empower executives, entrepreneurs and engineers to make informed decisions in time and plan pragmatic action plans with all the clarity and enthusiasm. With the sustained eruption of innovative technologies, the data architecture for new-generation enterprises will go through a tectonic shift. Leading market watchers predict that big data management and intelligence will become common along with the already-established data management solutions.

There are high-performing and assuring cloud platforms and appliances by the leading infrastructure solution providers such as IBM Cloud, AWS, Microsoft Azure, Alibaba, Google, and other niche providers (Oracle, SAP, etc.) to accomplish BDA. Thus, clouds are gaining momentum with many integrated platforms for analytics, enterprise-scale applications (ERP, CRM, SCM, KM, CM, etc.), databases, data warehouses and lakes, etc. So, it is certainly a strong indication of the onset of the IoT era. Clouds will be hosting different repositories of microservices, container images for applications, middleware, databases, etc., to be easily discovered and used for the ultimate empowerment of IT-enabled businesses and people.

Cloud Infrastructures for IoT Devices

Every application is steadily mobile-enabled to enable distributed applications that can be accessed and used at vehicular speed. Mobile interfacing becoming needs mandated widely. Several mobile technologies and tools are facilitating the leverage of all kinds of application while on the move. With the explosion of smartphones, cloud-based enterprise-grade, customer-facing, and web-scale applications are being provided with mobile interfacing – several popular operating systems such as Android, iOS, KaiOS, etc., powering up smartphones. *Raspbian is the operating system (OS) overwhelmingly used in Raspberry Pi single-board computers (SBCs). Similarly, there are other Linux-derived OS solutions for various IoT devices.* Cloud connectivity is essential not only for handhelds, portables, mobiles, etc., but also for all kinds of newer input/output devices to be highly relevant to their users.

The IoT Integration Types

Digitized entities and connected devices have to be integrated with other entities locally and with cloud applications, services, and data stores. For the sake of data analytics, IoT devices ought to work with data analytics platforms hosted in cloud infrastructures as well. With machine learning (ML) and deep learning (DL) algorithms, AI libraries and frameworks are made available on cloud systems. Thus, IoT artefacts need to integrate with cloud platforms and data stores (databases, warehouses, and lakes). This section throws light on those engaging and emerging integration scenarios.

Cloud-to-Cloud (C2C) Integration

Several types of cloud service providers (CSPs) leverage diverse technologies delivering different business-centric services. Due to the enhanced heterogeneity and diversity of cloud technologies, the goal of cloud interoperability has become a tricky thing for cloud services and application developers. Cloud users too are in a dilemma. Cloud brokerage service providers, procurers, and auditors are emerging and joining the already complicated cloud ecosystem, and it may quickly lead to integration chaos without proper standardizations. There are other concerns too. Cloud consumers are very much afraid of the vendor lock-in issue as manifold barriers around cloud infrastructures and platforms are on the rise. There are a couple of well-known trends gripping the cloud landscape. Firstly, geographically distributed and differentiating clouds are being established and sustained across the globe. There are cloud centres in many regions and zones to support disaster and data recovery.

Secondly, institutions, individuals, and innovators are eyeing cloud software, platforms, and infrastructures to reap the originally postulated and pronounced benefits. That is, multiple providers are providing the same services with different SLAs and OLAs. Incidentally, business processes that span across several clouds and services of numerous clouds are emerging. This mandates for multiple cloud environments to be visited, matched, and used to build process-aware and composite data, services, and processes. All these mandates insist on the urgent need for competent federation techniques, standards, patterns, platforms, and best practices. Why is it critical? Solving specific business deliverables with cloud-managed services that needs an assurance that those services are discoverable and accessible from clusters is a dire need.

Data and application integration have to happen via cloud integration methods. Service organizations and SIs are embarking on a new fruitful journey as cloud brokerages to silken the rough edges. Cloud service brokers (CSBs) are new software solutions for cloud data, service, application, and interfaces (API and GUI) integration.

Sensor-to-Cloud (S2C) Integration

Sensors and actuators are found plentifully in many important junctions these days for achieving diversified activities. A sensor network is a group of specialized transducers to observe and record conditions at diverse locations and times. Commonly observed parameters are temperature, humidity, pressure, wind direction and speed, illumination, vibration and sound intensities, chemical concentrations, power-line voltage, pollutant levels, and vital body functions – every sensor node built with a transducer, transceiver, microcomputer, and power source. The transducer is responsible for generating electrical signals based on captured physical effects and phenomena. The transceiver can be hard-wired or wireless, receives commands from a central computer, and transmits data back to that computer. The microcomputer does process and persists the sensor output. Each sensor node draws power from the electric utility or a battery. Potential sensor networks applications include smart manufacturing for the industry 4.0 vision, intelligent homes, hotels, and hospitals, environment monitoring and video surveillance, vehicle traffic management, drones and robot control. Sensors and actuators bring in deeper automation. Most of the manual activities get automated.

As indicated above, every empowered entity in our environments integrated with IT (local and remote). With edge/fog computing becomes a necessary discipline, computing happens locally with real-time and proximate processing. The edge devices are being internally and externally enabled to form edge clouds dynamically to tackle complex localized computing and analytics needs. The implementation of traditional off-premise, on-demand, and online computing are private, public, and hybrid clouds. As sensors get into crucial places of the futuristic digital world, sensor networking with nearby sensors and far-off software applications needs to be facilitated and fast-tracked. There are frameworks and middleware platforms for enabling ad hoc networking of diverse and multifaceted sensors, and the resulting networks can produce situation-aware services.

In the recent past, wireless sensor networks (WSNs) have gained significant traction because of their potential to enable very intimate and exciting solutions in industrial automation, transportation, healthcare, and agriculture. The tremendous progress in WSN design fosters their increasingly widespread usage, which has led to immense growth in the number of nodes per deployment. The network complexity has consequently escalated. Nowadays, a city-scale WSN deployment is not a novelty anymore. This phenomenon generates lots of data of different types, and the immediate challenge is how the data can be synchronized, interpreted, and adapted for performing situation-specific needs.

Suppose we add a collection of sensor-derived data to various social networks, virtual communities, blogs, musings, business and IT data, etc. In that case, there will be fabulous and futuristic transformations in and around us. With the faster adoption of micro- and nanotechnologies, everyday things are moving towards digitally empowered to be distinctive in their actions and reactions. Thus, the impending goal is to seamlessly link digitized objects/sentient materials in our environments with cloud services (edge, private, and public).

With the arrival of CPSs, physical assets have a tie-up with cloud applications via middleware solutions, ensuring safety. Cybersystems get adequate support with streams of data and messages from different and distributed physical elements. Such an extreme and deeper connectivity and collaboration are to pump up and sustain cool, classic, and catalytic situation-aware and sensor-enabled applications.

Let's see a few IoT-specific integration scenarios in the following list

- **Multi-Sensor Fusion** – Heterogeneous, multifaceted, and distributed sensors talk to one another to create sensor mesh and networks to attend and solve complicated problems.
- **Sensor-to-Cloud (S2C) Integration** – CPSs have emerged at the intersection of the physical and virtual/cyber worlds.
- **Device-to-Device (D2D) Integration** – With the device ecosystem integration is essential.
- **Device-to-Enterprise (D2E) Integration** – To have remote and real-time monitoring, management, repair, maintenance, and to enable decision support and expert systems, ground-level heterogeneous devices have to synchronize with control-level enterprise packages such as ERP, SCM, CRM, KM, etc.
- **Device-to-Cloud (D2C) Integration** – As most enterprise systems are moving to clouds, device-to-cloud (D2C) connectivity is gaining importance.
- **Cloud-to-Cloud (C2C) Integration** – Disparate, distributed, and decentralized clouds are getting connected to provide better prospects
- **Mobile Edge Computing (MEC), Cloudlets and Edge Cloud Formation** through the clustering of heterogeneous edge/fog devices

Clouds have emerged as the centralized, compact, and capable IT infrastructure to deliver people-centric and context-aware services to users with all the desired qualities embedded. This long-term vision demands that there has to be comprehensive connectivity between clouds and the billions of minuscule sensing systems.

The IoT Reference Architectures

The raging IoT idea has been making waves these days. Every allied discipline is consciously contributing to the realization of the IoT vision. It is all about realizing smart objects, enabling them to talk to one another on a need basis to create value for humans in their daily chores. There are exceptional advancements in edge and embedded computing fields. Communication is becoming fast, highly available, efficient, adaptive, and trustworthy. Lean communication protocols and stacks and other lightweight network components (switches, routers, modems, application delivery controllers (ADCs), load balancers, network gateways, etc.) are becoming ready and refined digitized objects to find and interact with one another smoothly and in a reliable manner.

In short, the brilliant and strategic IoT concept is making the Internet even more immersive and pervasive. By enabling ubiquitous access and interaction with a wide variety of devices such as home appliances, surveillance cameras, monitoring sensors, actuators, displays, terminals, vehicles, and so on. Those devices and ubiquitous access enable a wide variety of unseen people-centric applications that implicitly use a potentially enormous amount of data. Every sector is bound to go through IoT-inspired disruptive and innovative transformations facilitating the goals of home and industrial automation, healthcare, intelligent energy management, traffic management, smart cars, etc.

The game-changing IoT domain is innately capable of bringing in several benefits in the management and optimization of public services such as transport and parking, lighting, surveillance and maintenance of public areas, preservation of cultural heritage, water and energy management, the safety of people and public assets, garbage collection, the salubrity of hospitals and schools. Furthermore, the ready availability of different types of data emitted by intelligent sensors and actuators and the real-time knowledge extraction capability go hand in hand in bringing in the much-required transparency in public administration, the greater responsibility amongst government officials, etc. Better and fool-proof service delivery systems can be in place. The co-creation of newer services and outside-in thinking will flourish, and there will be a timely awareness of city facilities and events. Therefore, the IoT paradigm is a huge booster to establish and sustain cities that are not just cities but smart cities.

A wide variety of devices, link layer technologies, and services involved in such a system make any IoT general architecture or standardization strategy challenging and complex. Let's look at the layers and components of IoT architecture as depicted in Figure 1.2.

As seen in the preceding diagram, IoT architecture primarily comprises various layers and components. Let's have a brief overview of those in the following section.

- **Information Capture** – To have context-aware and cognitive applications, it is prudent and profoundly proper that all kinds of situation/scenario information about the environment need a gleaning. As explained above, our everyday environments get stuffed with scores of digitized artefacts and IoT gateway(s). These

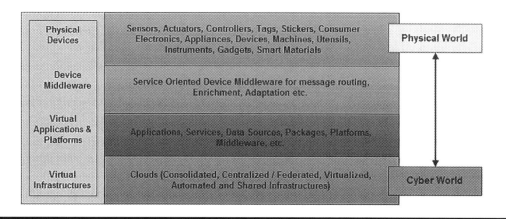

Figure 1.2   The reference architecture for the IoT.

contribute to information capture about their environments, their assets, and their status, the people therein, and the special happenings. Digitized entities such as wearables continuously monitor human physiological activities such as health status and motion patterns. The collected digital data get transmitted to data storage and processing systems (nearby and remote) for extricating precise and decisive insights towards engineering next-generation business and IT systems.

■ **Information Delivery** – Today, we have various communication technologies and network topologies to carry all sorts of collected information. The sensor networks, body area networks, car area networks, home networks, campus area networks, etc., and those networks need high bandwidth on demand. However, it no longer hinders the information delivery as 3G and 4G communication technologies provide the necessary support for the high bandwidth requirements worldwide. Also, in 2021, we are experiencing full-fledged 5G technologies and their infrastructures to meet the rising bandwidth requirements of the future. Bandwidth on demand, video on demand, ambient communication, and ad hoc networks are often-heard terms in securely delivering information to different destinations without compromising.

■ **Information Processing** – With the emergence of standardized analytics platforms, frameworks, and acceleration engines, the data analytics domain expected to grow substantially. In big data, any Hadoop implementation could filter out unwanted data to have only value-adding information. That is, transitioning multi-structured data into a structured form so that the analytical systems such as data warehouses, cubes, and marts can proceed towards fine-grained analytics is the gist of Hadoop technology. There are high-performance and purpose-specific appliances for data analytics. Real-time and streaming analytics are also maturing fast to provide real-time analytics for specific use cases. There are data mining, machine and deep learning algorithms to do diagnostic, prognostic, predictive, and prescriptive analytics. Further on, information visualization solutions are disseminating any extracted and extrapolated knowledge to the respective users in their preferred format. Thus, data collection, crunching, masking, information processing, knowledge discovery, and dissemination are in the path of simplification with noteworthy advancements in the hot IT field.

- **Applications to get smarter and wiser** – Thus, the transition from data to information and systems gaining knowledge through a plethora of mining and analytics technologies. There are widespread improvements ineffective data virtualization, synchronization, quality, and enrichment towards knowledge engineering. Once knowledge is created, corroborated, correlated, and then conveyed to appropriate software applications and people exhibit the much-wanted intelligent behaviour. That is, automated data capture and interpretation resulting in actionable intelligence goes a long way in empowering software applications to be distinct in their operations, offerings, and outputs.

Architectural and design patterns are essential for the intended success of business workloads and IT services. Service-oriented architecture (SOA), microservices architecture (MSA), and event-driven architecture (EDA) are the critical architectural styles and patterns contributing to crafting enterprise-grade and mission-critical systems.

The IoT Realization Technologies

Technologies are evolving, surviving, disappearing, making dents to the world, and so on. Many have arrived with much fanfare but could not survive the onslaughts and faded away into thin air silently without making substantial contributions to human society. Some have withstood their inherent strengths and are copiously contributing towards business augmentation, acceleration, and automation. In this section, you can find several influential technologies for IoT realization.

- **Computing paradigms** – Service, social, cluster, grid, on-demand, utility, mobile, cloud, and fog/edge computing.
- **Communication technologies** – Unified, ambient, and autonomic communication models providing standards-compliant 4G and 5G communication capabilities.
- **Context-aware technologies** – Sensing, vision, perception, and actuation technologies.
- **Middleware technologies** – Integration, intermediation, aggregation, fusion, federation, transformation, arbitration, enrichment, & composition technologies.
- **Digitization & edge technologies** – Tags, SBCs, stickers, specks, sensors, and smart dust, motes, LEDs, controllers, chips, and codes, actuators, beacons, etc., categorized under Digitization and Edge Tech.
- **Miniaturization technologies** – Micro- and nano-scale electronics product design technologies.
- **Knowledge engineering technologies** – Semantic, event capturing and processing, data mining, analytics, and dissemination technologies, machine and deep learning algorithms, natural language processing (NLP) approaches.
- **Interface technologies** – Natural & adaptive, intuitive, and informative interfacing technologies.

The following list has a brief overview of specific technologies and tools that are suitable for the broader and deeper adoptions of the IoT paradigm

- As miniaturization, instrumentation, connectivity, remote programmability/ service-enablement/APIs, sensing, vision, perception, analysis, knowledge-engineering, decision enablement, etc., can work together cohesively, these methodologies/systems/technologies take a favourite spot within the IoT landscape
- A flurry of edge technologies (sensors, stickers, specks, smart dust, codes, chips, controllers, LEDs, tags, actuators, etc.)
- Ultra-high-bandwidth communication technologies (wired as well as wireless (4G, 5G, etc.))
- The low-cost power and range communication standards: LoRa, LoRaWAN, NB-IoT, 802.11x Wi-Fi, Bluetooth Smart, ZigBee, Thread, NFC, 6LowPAN, Sigfox, Neul, etc., come under the category power and range communications standards
- Robust network topologies, Internet gateways, integration and orchestration frameworks, and transport protocols (MQTT, UPnP, CoAP, XMPP, REST, OPC, etc.) for communicating data and event messages
- A variety of IoT application enablement platforms (AEPs) with application building, deployment and delivery, data and process integration, application performance management, security, orchestration, and messaging capabilities
- A bevvy of IoT data analytics platforms for extracting timely and actionable insights out of IoT data
- Edge/fog analytics through Edge Clouds
- Software-defined Federated Clouds
- Cloud-native computing
- Edge/fog computing

Though there are many technology choices, the good news is that several of them are erupting as path-breaking technology and facilitate the intended IoT tasks better and better. In the current era, the focus was on technologies to co-exist, complement each other, and form technology clusters to solve hard-to-crack problems which weren't quickly solvable a few years back. The much-discussed and dissected cloud technology represents a wiser collection of several enterprise-scale, mission-critical, and accomplished technologies. That is, the prevailing trend is to leverage potential technologies individually or collectively as per evolving needs.

Having commendable advancements in infrastructure optimization and process excellence besides a dazzling array of state-of-the-art platforms (development, debugging, delivery, deployment, orchestration, brokerage, compliance, etc.), the right technologies need to be understood and used rightfully to realize the IoT vision.

There are many names such as the Internet of Everything (IoE) (promoted by Cisco), the Industrial Internet (GE), the Internet of Important Things, etc. All the Internet-centric technologies are bound to converge to emit out spectacular and scintillating applications for humankind. The bountiful and beautiful result is that strategically sound synchronization between the physical and the virtual worlds. Digitization is bound to grip each and everything in this world. With digitalization technologies and tools sprucing up fast, the terms (connectivity and cognition) are discussed and discoursed in greater detail in the upcoming sections.

The IoT Implications

The resultant applications are a growing collection of intelligent and interactive workspaces; the environments include smart homes or aware homes and smart offices. For instance, the Japan Railways (JR) sets up railway stations to enhance travellers' convenience, choice, and comfort. A keen environment typically comprises a fluctuating array of infinitesimal electronic gizmos that perceive the context, act, and react based on the happenings and events. Further on, they achieve seamless mobility, interoperability, and connectivity among the participating devices of the environment. The stationed and positioned devices can also connect and collaborate with any other devices entering the ecosystem

The unique characteristics of these devices are self-organizing, self-adapting, self-repairing, and self-optimizing, self-configuring, and self-recovering. These devices are fail-safe and bounce back to the original state in case of malfunction, severe obstructions, disturbances, and disasters and capable of automatically forming insightful wireless ad hoc networks with others in the vicinity perceive, conceive, and concretize situation-specific services. IDC, one of the leading market researchers and watchers, has come out with the following opportunities for businesses in the years ahead.

- **New business models and capabilities** – The IoT will help enterprising businesses creating value streams for customers, speeding up time to market, and respond more rapidly to customer needs from uncharted territories. New and premium services can be built and delivered to fulfil customer delight. The more accurate, timely, and situation-aware realization happens through the accumulation of connected devices and digitized items.
- **Real-time information on mission-critical systems** – Enterprises can capture more data about processes and products more quickly. The captured data gets subjected to various investigations to bring forth timely and relevant insights, which, in turn, produces knowledge-filled services.
- **Diversification of revenue streams** – The IoT can help companies make and monetize additional services on top of traditional lines of business. Event-driven, insights-driven, people-centric, and physical services are not only to business services but also to people. In short, the prevailing IT tends to people IT. More intelligent systems, networks, and environments can be implemented and sustained.
- **Deeper visibility** – The IoT will make enterprises see inside into their business easier, including tracking and tracing from one end of the supply chain to the other, which can lower the cost of doing business in far-flung locales. Harsh and risky environments, unmotorable pathways, tunnels, expressways, bridges, buildings, and other critical establishments can be minutely monitored, measured, and managed.
- **Efficient, intelligent operations** – Access to information from autonomous endpoints will allow organizations to make on-the-fly decisions on pricing, logistics, and sales and support deployment.

Precisely speaking, the extreme connectivity of essential things is to bring a paradigm shift in the way people live, work, socialize, prognosis, decide, act, and react. Viable and venerable business models are in the process of concertedly enabling product vendors, IT and telecommunication services providers, cloud providers, SIs, end-users, and national governments to team up together for the knowledge era.

The IoT-inspired Industrial Applications

As enunciated elsewhere, the IoT domain is surging due to the five intriguing trends in the IT field. Therefore, the IoT conundrum has a captivating and cognitive impact on every human in this increasingly connected world.

1. Digitization and Digitalization
2. Distribution and Decentralization
3. Industrialization
4. Compartmentalization and Commoditization
5. Consumerization

You can find a few well-known and widely articulated applications through the modernizations mentioned above. It is a foregone conclusion that new and upcoming technologies would bring renewed perspectives and bring forth provisions for overcoming complexities and original foretasting applications that are transformative, innovative and disruptive. In this section and the ones to come, we have enlisted many existing services transitioning and turning more creative and intelligent. Also, altogether newer applications from the ground up are being crafted.

Connected Applications

In an extended enterprise scenario, all functional divisions are interconnected via the cloud-hosted middleware suite. The cloud takes the prime spot in any integrated environment as their standard services are network-accessible and deployable in their platforms. At the same time, only a few specific functionalities need at the edges (edge computing). The CSB plays a stellar role in streamlining and simplifying the complex integration hurdles and hitches, as Figure 1.3 shows.

Cloud integration appliances and solutions are in plenty to effortlessly ensure data flows across clouds (private, public, and edge). In short, CSBs are very relevant for distributed computing. Cloud interoperability as a cloud computing characteristic is vital for the success of the IoT concepts. Both generic and specific clouds need integration and cohesiveness to fulfil the unique demands of any IoT applications, and hence cloud integration is essential for the projected success. There are integration appliances, middleware, service repository, and scores of tools for enabling cloud connectivity and interactions. Like SIs, we will hear more about cloud integrators/brokers in the days to emerge for producing and providing scores of next generations connected applications to people.

Structural Health of Buildings

The proper maintenance of the historical and cultural buildings of a city requires the continuous monitoring and measurement of the actual health parameters of each

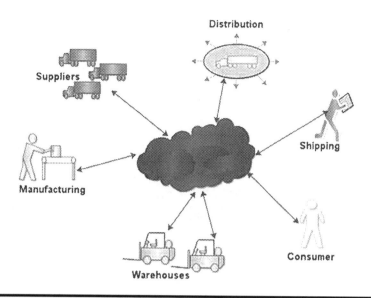

Figure 1.3   Cloud is the central environment for next-generation connected applications.

building and the identification of the areas that are vulnerable for any easy prey. The urban IoT may set up a distributed database for capturing and storing the sensor readings of buildings. Building-specific sensors such as vibration and deformation sensors monitor and record the building stress in the recent past. Atmospheric agent sensors in the surrounding areas monitor pollution levels, and temperature and humidity sensors employ a complete environmental condition characterization.

This database reduces the need for expensive periodic structural testing done by human operators and allows targeted and proactive maintenance and restoration activities. Also, it's possible to combine vibration and seismic readings to study better and understand the impact of light earthquakes on city buildings. This database may become publicly accessible to make the citizens aware of the care taken in preserving the city historical heritage. The practical realization of this service requires installing and maintaining specific sensors in the buildings and surrounding areas. These sensors have to collectively collect, corroborate, and correlate with extracting insights in synchronization with a cloud-based cyber application.

Smartness Overloaded Industries

Smart Energy

Energy has become a scarce commodity, and hence its preservation is very much obligatory. More energy consumption means more heat dissipation into our fragile environment, with efficient usage of precious power energy. The world's immediate attention is global warming, and with IoT-enabled devices, environmental degradation kept in check and kept minimized to move towards achieving ecological sustainability.

Making the electricity consumption meters more intelligent to ensure accurate measurements help consumers decode and plan efficient energy savings strategies.

The advanced metering infrastructure (AMI) is an active and ongoing research area to generate solutions for energy efficiency.

Smart Healthcare

There are many specific instruments and equipment for measuring and managing several health parameters of humans. With connected devices, the automation of several manual activities is a reality. Similarly, healthcare applications are comprehensive with incredible insights and integrated to enhance the quality of healthcare delivery sharply. Thus, digital elements along with connected devices and CPSs contribute immensely to next-generation healthcare services. IoT solutions can trigger a reminder to the patient and their family members and the doctor if any emergency arises from any abnormality in any health readings.

Smarter Homes

Energy efficiency, home security, remote operations, and resource management are attributes of intelligent homes with the sophisticated home networking, integration, automation, safety, and control systems available in the market. Multifaceted sensors connect HVAC devices and their controllers with edge/fog clouds faraway and collaborate to provide sophisticated services to homeowners and occupants all the time.

Smart Cargo Handling

IoT solutions are being manufactured and embedded into various storage/handling containers, including cargo containers, money and document bags, and nuclear waste drums. The real-time location of the container, their handlings through motion sensors, sensing whether the container is open or in close, and the motion sensors prevent any possible security and theft risks also increase the recovery capability of stolen or lost material with the gathered data.

Smart Traffic Management

Ground-level sensors, advanced cameras, and other traffic monitoring solutions can collectively provide real-time road traffic information to vehicles' drivers via automobile GPS devices to enable them to contemplate and better alternatives. This is achieved through proximate data processing and real-time data analytics solutions that are running on edge device clouds. In conjunction with batch processing/BDA at remote cloud servers, accurate information helps derive, deliver, and convey indication to drivers of oncoming vehicles in time to avoid traffic congestion.

Smart Inventory and Replenishment Management

Retail stores are destined to be keen and innovative with their operations, subsequently integrating the IoT idea. Robots can help customers to spot their preferred items quickly. Robots can also identify empty shelves and intimate mall managers to arrange the refilled and place in their respective locations on time. Hypermarkets deliver them to customer homes through drones. Understanding the shoppers' behavioural patterns can give shop owners a range of premium services with zeal and clarity. Identity and classification of employees entering the warehouse for the safety of articles at malls are some of the potential implementations of the IoT ecosystem.

Smart Cash Payments

Connected credit/debit card readers provide encrypted data transmission capability. This facility brings forth a stream of benefits for customers at the transaction and ticketing counters in hyper malls, hotels, movie theatres, food joints, etc. Retailing becomes a smooth affair without standing in the queue for cash payment. The seamless connectivity between tags, tag readers, cash cards, merchant banks, retailers, etc., goes a long way in considerably enhancing the customer experience.

Smart Tracking

IoT solutions allow parents to track their children very precisely sitting from the office. These advanced solutions empower caregivers and doctors to remotely track those with disabilities and people who are independently living, disease-stricken, debilitated, and bed-ridden. Managers can monitor their employees performing duties in rough and challenging places. Mainly working in oil wells, fighting a forest fire, helping in disaster-struck areas, battling in war zones, hiking in the mountains, etc., are to immensely benefit through such kinds of technological innovations.

The connected vending machine can convey the details such as the number of empty bins and bottles inside to suppliers in real-time and how many more are needed to fill up the vending machine. The information shared helps suppliers in many ways. Instead of sending an entire truck, suppliers can send only the items required, indeed a sharp improvement over the current practice.

Smart Displays

All kinds of machines such as ATMs, vending machines, television sets, security video cameras, signposts, dashboards, etc., can be intertwined together at strategic locations. With such intimate integration through an intelligent IoT middleware solution, customized video and static images can be dispatched to these machines to flash time-sensitive and preferred details. A hungry person could order his pizzas on his mobile phone. Interestingly he or she can see the pizza details and pictures in the larger screen attached with any one of these machines. Or connected projectors can show the images on a white wall to give a clear vision.

Smart Asset Management

Every industry has its own set of specific assets. For example, hospitals may have many scanning machines, a dazzling array of healthcare-specific equipment, blood glucose and ECG monitors, robots for assisting surgeons, bedside LEDs, beacons, displays, and other diagnostic instruments. The real challenge lies in finding them in an emergency where every minute is critical, not just trace them. Still, upkeep, management, monitoring, inventory, security, etc., are also super important tasks. An advanced IoT solution sharply reduces the time consumed by employees to pinpoint the assets' exact location, considerably increments their utilization, and provides the ability to share high-value assets between departments and facilities. With every purchase, the new equipment needs to integrate with existing hospital environment assets. The integration is a sheer reality with the remote cloud platforms via an IoT middleware, remote monitoring, repairing, and management. Through the connectivity established with cloud-hosted healthcare applications, every machine could update and upload its data to the centralized and cyber applications; thereby, several activities get automated fully by avoiding manual intervention, interpretation, and instruction.

Air Quality

It is well-known that nations worldwide have set inappropriate mechanisms to arrest the threatening climate change. There are attempts through a host of ways to cut down greenhouse gas emission into our fragile environment, to enforce energy preservation, and subsequently to decrement heat dissipation so that the global objective of sustainability realization can happen sooner than later. To such an extent, the IoT capability provides the means to monitor the air quality in all kinds of crowded areas and joints such as open-air stadiums, parks and playgrounds, etc. Besides, IoT communication can facilitate health applications on joggers' devices to capture and transmit data to remotely held applications and data sources. In this way, people can always find the healthiest path for outdoor activities can always be on (continuously connected) to their preferred personal training application or trainer. The realization of such a service requires the deployment of that air quality and pollution sensors across the city, and the sensor data has to be made publicly available to citizens.

Noise Monitoring

Noise can be seen as a form of acoustic pollution as much as carbon oxide (CO) is for air. An urban IoT can offer a noise-monitoring service to measure the amount of noise produced at any given hour in particular areas. Besides building a space-time map of the noise pollution in the area, this service can also enforce the safety of people and public properties employing sound-detection algorithms that can recognize, for instance, the noise of glass crashes or brawls. This service can remarkably improve both the quietness of the nights in the city and the confidence of public establishment owners. However, installing sound detectors or environmental microphones is bound to face strong opposition. It needs many regulations to ensure these sensors and devices are not penetrating the security and privacy of individuals, not more than what is necessary for the accomplishments of the tasks.

Smart Parking

This facility is being given based on road sensors and intelligent displays that direct motorists along the best path for parking in the city. The benefits are many. It helps drivers to find a parking slot quickly. Thereby, there is less CO emission from the car and subdued traffic snarl. The smart-parking service integration with the urban IoT infrastructure gets needed visibility through widespread advertisements. Further on, through short-range communication technologies, it is possible to remotely verify whether vehicles are parked appropriate and in the correct slots allocated for them. Intelligent parking stands out when it comes to disabled parking as it's all about seamless, genuine, fully assisted parking for disabled parking.

Professionals and experts are exploring, experimenting, and expounding an increasing array of value-added business and use cases for various industry segments to keep the momentum in the IoT space intact. That is, connectivity and software-inspired empowerment are next-generation evolution in the machine space. There is no doubt that there will be more IT automation for all kinds of dumb and dormant systems.

How to Make IoT Environments Intelligent?

Any IoT environment comprises scores of networked, resource-constrained, and intensive, and embedded systems. Precisely speaking, it is all about the combination of digitized elements and connected devices. IoT artefacts are not individually intelligent, but the charter is to make them separately and collectively wise. The promising methods are enumerated as below.

1. The **Internet of Agents (IoA)** is to empower each digital object to be adaptive, articulate, reactive, and cognitive by mapping a software agent for each of the participating digital elements.
2. Through realizing **digital services** (every digital object and connected device is expressed and exposed as a service) and through service orchestration and choreography, next-generation digital applications can be crafted out of many different and distributed digital services.
3. The concept of **Digital Twin/virtual object** is also maturing and stabilizing to empower digital objects to be intelligent and innovative.
4. The proven and potential **IoT data analytics at edge and cloud levels** are the prominent and dominant aspects of knowledge discovery and dissemination. The captured knowledge loops back to devices to exhibit adaptive behaviour.
5. The application of **artificial intelligence (AI)** technologies (machine and deep learning algorithms, computer vision methods, NLP capabilities, etc.) leads to the realization of more intelligent systems, services, and solutions.
6. The new concept of **smart contracts** through the blockbuster blockchain technology leads to sophisticated and decentralized applications.

There are enabling platforms, databases, and middleware solutions for data preprocessing, storage, processing, analytics, and mining. Further on, there are frameworks, libraries, languages, etc., for empowering systems, networks, and environments to self-learn and be adaptive in their decisions, deals, and deeds.

1. With big data and streaming, we make use of digital data for diagnostic and deterministic insights. Batch processing is the standard mechanism to extract insights out of big data. There are streaming engines to emit viable information out of streaming data in real time.
2. Machine and deep learning algorithms gain a lot of recognition and respect to extricate, predictive, prescriptive, and personalized insights in time.
3. There are varied database management solutions such as SQL, NoSQL, and NewSQL databases, data warehouses and lakes for digital data analytics.
4. There are in-memory databases for real-time analytics and actuation.
5. There are data virtualization solutions for data integration from distributed and disparate data sources. Also, there are knowledge visualization tools in the form of report-generation tools, displays and dashboards, etc., to give a 360-degree view of any system under monitoring and investigation. Also, several formats, such as maps, charts, graphs, etc., can visualize information to different people.
6. There are parallel data processing and analytics platforms (Spark, Storm, Samza, Flink, etc.) on cloud environments.
7. There are event stores such as Kafka for processing and stocking millions of event messages per second.
8. There are machine and deep learning platforms, frameworks, and libraries for accelerating and automating analytics (cognitive analytics).
9. Fog or edge data analytics is gaining speed with many lightweight data analytics platforms capable of running on fog/edge device clouds.

Thus, IoT data gets duly captured, cleansed, and crunched to generate actionable insights in time. The discovered knowledge gets looped back to IoT devices to behave differently based on changing situations and needs. As indicated above, the challenge before us is to produce cognitive systems and environments. There are cognition-enablement frameworks to simplify the realization of cognitive applications. AI is the primary domain for transitioning any IoT system to be cognitive in its actions and reactions. Let us plunge into what is AI and how it facilitates building cognitive services and solutions.

Connectivity + Cognition Leads to Smarter Environments

There are multiple definitions for AI. The idea is to find ways to empower business workloads, IT services, digitized entities, and connected devices accordingly to manifest in humans' "cognitive" functions. It is all about making our everyday devices to simulate human intelligence. ML, NLP, DL, etc., are the few essential technologies in the AI domain. Conceptually, there is no significant difference between cognitive computing and AI. Cognitive computing assists in realizing self-learning systems that use data mining, data crunching, pattern recognition, and NLP and imitates the way the human brain works. We have talked about the concept of IoT in detail in this chapter. In short, the gist of the IoT paradigm is all about connectivity. That is, digitizing typical articles in our midst and connecting them with other digitized assets as well as with remotely held, cloud-hosted, and service-oriented applications.

With the association of fast-evolving cognitive computing, all kinds of digitized objects are cognition-enabled to showcase intelligent behaviour. Thus, it boils down to two essential things: connectivity and cognition. With the coupling and clubbing together the inspiring aspects of IoT and cognitive computing, we will be soon stuffed, safeguarded, surrounded, and sandwiched with intelligent IoT devices. Our everyday environments (personal, social, professional, etc.) will become cognition-enabled IoT devices. As we have seen in the preceding sections, there are many newer and enhanced industrial use cases on IoT. Now, we envisage better and bigger use cases for the indomitable convergence of IoT and cognitive computing.

IoT devices individually and collectively generate a massive amount of multi-structured data through their interactions and collaborations. Typically, big data go through pipelines where generated data garnered and transmitted to cloud platforms for investigations and insights as part of batch processing techniques and tools. The idea is to uncover hidden patterns and other usable insights such as strategically sound associations, fresh possibilities and opportunities, any impending risks, and urgent tasks, etc., in the IoT data getting produced and procured – precisely speaking, IoT devices' data (state) and their interaction data to discover and disseminate knowledge. The information acquired can be given to ponder about the next course of actions. Even IoT devices get the developed knowledge directly to be adaptive in their obligations and assignments. In short, we are heading towards the days of data-driven insights and insights-driven decisions/deeds/deals. There is a greater awareness about the indisputable fact that data encompass hidden knowledge. The processes to move data to information and expertise are maturing and stabilizing fast with the ready availability of intelligent technologies.

Thus, data analytics in an automated manner will be the game-changer for the arising era of knowledge-driven services to businesses and human society.

Characterizing Cognitive Systems and Environments

There is a paradigm shift in computing with the advent of cognitive computing. We come across an assortment of business cases, and hence there is surging popularity for this computing model. Many longstanding goals are achievable to greater satisfaction through the correct usage of cognitive computing technologies and tools. A variety of currently running applications and services gets augmented, accelerated, and automated by applying this unique and trend-setting computing paradigm. The business impacts and implications of this original technology are more significant and felt widely across. A set of industry challenges and concerns get addressed through this unique idea.

The world moves from tabulating systems to programmable systems and now widely tending towards cognitive systems, data transfer to information and knowledge. That is, we are aspiring to build and sustain intelligent cities, counties, and countries. It is no longer about replacing man with the machine but rather augment devices with adequate intelligence. Machine intelligence is the new buzzword in the IT industry.

Cognitive systems are capable of self-learning, reasoning, and interacting with human beings. With multiple data sources, plans are being enabled to self-learn and adapt. Machine and deep learning algorithms can crunch big data to spit out useful information without any interpretation and involvement of human resources. Cognitive systems designs are context-aware and make sense of complex, unpredictable, and unstructured data. With big data, cognitive systems are becoming more pragmatic and functional. They can read text and visualize images and videos. They can hear and understand natural speeches and exhibit intelligent behaviour. And they interpret data, organize it, and offer sensible explanations for it. In summary, Cognitive systems can read, write, speak, see, hear, and learn, and they are already on the emerging path.

IBM Watson is a prime example of live cognitive systems, and it's a successful system in cancer prognosis and medication prescription. Other well-known examples include brain-machine interfaces, humanoid robots, intelligent drones, cognitive and sensory prostheses, software and robotic assistants, self-driving cars, autonomous weapons, etc. With the cognitive computing model, there are programming languages and frameworks to quickly build and deploy cognitive systems. Cloud environments are evolving as a one-stop IT solution for all kinds of business automation needs. Cognition-enablement platforms are available as PaaS (platform as a service) to streamline and speed up constructing cognitive applications. Future is cognitive, and solution to any complicated AI problems through sophisticated cognitive systems soon a reality.

As widely seen, cognitive computing has impacted decisively various industry verticals, including travel, sports, entertainment, fitness, health, and wellness. Cognitive systems and devices have laid down a stimulating and sparkling foundation for setting up and sustaining cognitive environments.

Building Cognitive Systems and Services

Our current systems ought to be programmed precisely to empower them to perform what we want. That is, we need to supply both logic and data. If we wrongly program or give incorrect input data, then the system output would also be wrong. Envisioning all kinds of situations and inputs and coding accordingly is a tough assignment. That is, in the beginning, everything is fixed by itself. Dynamically bringing in and incorporating changes does not go out well with the current software engineering. Formally written rules play an essential role in transitioning input into valuable output. Another noteworthy point here is that currently running programmable computers primarily work with structured data. In other words, envisioning every turn and twist and accommodating them in software programs are a tough job. They are simply incapable of processing qualitative data. If there is an unpredictable input, then the system is going to be in a dilemma. This inflexibility comes as a barrier in elegantly addressing some of the crucial requirements of the increasingly connected world. It is not an exaggerated statement to say that our present-day computers are just dumb. They just do as per the program logic, nothing more, nothing less. These systems have been deterministic. But the future seems to be bright. We are excited about the faster stability of newer technologies that ultimately can lead to cognitive systems.

As articulated above, cognitive systems can self-learn from a large amount of raw data emanating from multiple sources, reason with purpose and interact with humans naturally and intelligently. They need not be explicitly programmed. We just feed data, and they learn automatically from data to come out with new evidence-based theories and reasons. They just uncover hidden patterns in input data to be self-reliant. Cognitive systems are probabilistic and can work well with multi-structured data.

Further on, more data means more precision in decision-making and actuation. The widely known expert and recommendation systems are the basic cognitive systems. In short, the unique and distinguished human intelligence gets into machines and devices through a host of sophisticated technologies. It's important to note that the cognitive systems are not here to replace human thoughts or actions, but they can participate, assist, and augment people in our everyday decisions, deals, and deeds.

Setting up and sustaining cognitive systems are beset with numerous challenges and concerns. Academicians, researchers, IT practitioners, and even commoners are working in unison to surmount the intriguing challenges in producing cognitive systems and devices. Most CSPs, such as AWS, Microsoft Azure, IBM Cloud, Google Cloud, etc., are giving cognitive application development toolkits. IBM Watson, the hugely popular cognitive platform, is being expressed and exposed as a service across multiple cloud providers. There are independent software vendors and SIs such as TCS, Infosys, Wipro, HCL, etc. They are also focussing on the AI domain deeply to produce cognitive applications. Correspondingly cloud infrastructure modules are advancing to realize next-generation cognitive services.

Envisioning Cognitive Edge Devices

As described above, edge devices evolve with computing capabilities and analytics platforms inbuilt to fulfil edge analytics. Thus, the futuristic aspects of edge computing and analytics are on the steady path of realization. Further on, edge device clusters and clouds are being established to do large-scale data storage and processing in a fault-tolerant fashion. Now, machine and deep learning algorithms with lightweight libraries and frameworks are being run in edge devices to automate predictive analytics. With significant technological advancements, the capture of sensor/actuator data, storage, albeit temporarily, and analytics in real time through the leverage of one or more resource-intensive devices (sometimes touted as fog devices) are garnering the attention of business executives and IT professionals. Deployment of AI algorithms in edge clusters leads to the realization of cognitive edge devices and their services. Below, you can find why the real-time analytics is swiftly and smoothly accomplished at edge clusters.

1. **Volume and Velocity** – As part of 3Vs of big data, volume and velocity are about ingesting, processing, and storing vast amounts of real-time data, gathering, and making them ready to process.
2. **Security** – Location of the devices in sensitive environments is crucial. Control vital systems or send private data from the devices need careful consideration. Unlike humans, machines can't simply type the password, so new paradigms need strict authentication and access control implementation.
3. **Bandwidth** – If devices constantly send the sensor and video data, it will hog the Internet and cost a fortune. Therefore, edge analytics approaches must achieve scale and lower response time by having clear and well-planned deployment strategies.

4. **Real-time Data Capture** – Storage, processing, analytics, knowledge discovery, decision-making, and actuation are other analytical criteria for edge devices.
5. **Less Latency and Faster Response** – Indeed, the analytics results need a far superior response for super-fast reflection of cognitive abilities.
6. **Context-Awareness capability** – The devices need to be aware of the contexts and act according to the context, without which the results and actions may be futile.
7. **Combining real-time data with historical state** – There are analytics solutions that handle batch processing well and a few tools that also can process streams without historical context. It is challenging to analyse streams and combine them with historical data in real time.
8. **Power consumption** – Cloud computing is energy-hungry, and that is a concern for a low-carbon economy.
9. **Data obesity** – In a traditional cloud approach, a massive amount of untreated data are pumped blindly into the cloud that is supposed to have magical algorithms written by data scientists. This vision is not the best efficient, and it is pragmatic to pre-treat data at a local level and limit the cloud processes at the strict minimum.

Thus, accelerated automated analytics at cloud servers and edge devices through the readily available technologies, tools, and resource-intensive devices are getting momentum. The predictive analytics capability is thriving, and our everyday devices are all set to be self-learning and adapting as per changing contexts. Further on, cognitive device services are being containerized and composed to produce cognitive applications and environments. With containerization-enablement platforms (Docker) and orchestration platforms (Kubernetes), forming a homogeneous edge cloud from heterogeneous devices is expedited. Thus, making our environments (homes, hospitals, hotels, etc.) cognitive is accentuated and accelerated with the help of sophisticated technologies.

Conclusion

The IoT concepts, technology, devices, and ecosystems steadily conquered the minds of researchers and engineers to the point of becoming one of the most transformative IT domains. In this chapter, we have explained the nitty-gritty of the IoT technology paradigm along with some of its famous industrial use cases. The IoT idea is continuously penetrating and permeating into every suitable business vertical. The IoT realization technologies are stabilizing fast, so many IoT-enablement platforms are being released to the market. There is a steady proliferation of varieties of SBCs, etc. Resultantly the IoT adoption is simply mesmerizing across the globe. New IoT use cases are being unearthed and published to enhance confidence in this new technology. Enterprising businesses broadly embrace this trend-setting technology in a big way. With more innovations and specific use cases, people will start using IoT devices and their people-centric services. Now there is a shift.

With zillions of IoT devices being deployed in our everyday environments, the direct output is the humungous amount of poly-structured data emanating from

IoT devices and environments. The delectable advancements in the AI space can squeeze personalized, predictive, and prescriptive insights out of IoT big data quickly in an automated manner. The data insights get supplied back to IoT devices to be intelligent. Empowered IoT devices can contribute to realizing cognitive services and applications. Thus, we are destined towards the era of cognitive systems and solutions.

References

An Information Technology (IT) Portal. http://www.peterindia.net, 2013.

Chen, Min, "Towards smart city: M2M communications with software agent intelligence" *Multimedia Tools Applications* vol. 67, 167–178, 2013.

Elmangoush, Asma, Hakan Coskun, Sebastian Wahle, and Thomas Magedanz, "*Design Aspects for a Reference M2M Communication Platform for Smart Cities*," *9th International Conference on Innovations in Information Technology* 2013.

Gelenbe, Erol and Fang-Jing Wu, "Future Research on Cyber-Physical Emergency Management Systems" *Future Internet*, 2013.

Hancke, Gerhard P., Bruno de Carvalho e Silva, and Gerhard P. Hancke Jr., "The Role of Advanced Sensing in Smart Cities", *Sensors* 2013.

Hassan, Mohammad Mehedi, Biao Song, and Eui-Nam Huh, "*A Framework of Sensor-Cloud Integration Opportunities and Challenges*", *ICUIMC*, 2009.

Jin, Jiong, Jayavardhana Gubbi, Tie Luo and Marimuthu Palaniswami, "*Network Architecture and QoS Issues in the Internet of Things for a Smart City*" *International Symposium on Communications and Information Technologies (ISCIT)*, 2012.

Pawar, Satish Phakade, Smart City with Internet of Things (sensor networks) and Big Data, Institute of Business Management & Research (IBMR), Chichwad, Pune, 2013.

Perera, Charith, Arkady Zaslavsky, Peter Christen, and Dimitrios Georgakopoulos, "*Sensing as a Service Model for Smart Cities Supported by Internet of Things*" *Transactions on Transactions on Emerging Telecommunications Technologies* 2014.

Raj, Pethuru, *Cloud Enterprise Architecture*, CRC Press, USA 2012.

The Sensor Cloud the Homeland Security, http://www.mistralsolutions.com/hs-downloads/tech-briefs/nov11-article3.html, 2011.

Vicini, Sauro, Sara Bellini, and Alberto Sanna, "*How to Co-Create Internet of Things-enabled Services for Smarter Cities*" *SMART 2012: The First International Conference on Smart Systems, Devices and Technologies* 2012.

Zanella, Andrea and Lorenzo Vangelista, "Internet of Things for Smart Cities" *IEEE Internet of Things Journal* vol. 1, no. 1, 2014.

Chapter 2

Demystifying the Cognitive Computing Paradigm

Introduction

Lately, the information and communication technologies (ICT) space is fascinated with a lot of appreciable growth. A dazzling array of innovative, disruptive, and transformative technologies and tools in computing, communication, sensing, perception, vision, knowledge discovery, visualization, decision-making, and actuation are hitting the market these days to bring in a slew of more in-depth automation.

Briefing the Next-generation Technologies

There are several other pioneering technologies in the enviable ICT space.

- **Consumerization – Extended Device Ecosystem** – Trendy and handy, slim and sleek mobile, wearable, implantable and portable devices (instrumented, interconnected, and intelligent devices)
- **Sentient & Smart Materials** – Attaching scores of digitization/edge technologies (invisible, calm, tiny, and disposable sensors and actuators, LEDs, stickers, tags, labels, motes, dots and dust, beacons, specks, codes, chips, controllers, etc.)
- **Extreme, Deeper Connectivity and Networking Standards** – 5G cellular communication for the IoT era, Wi-Fi 802.11 ax, etc.
- **Commoditization and Industrialization – Infrastructure Optimization & Elasticity** – Programmable, consolidated, converged, adaptive, automated, shared, QoS-enabling, green and lean IT infrastructures
- **Compartmentalisation through Virtualization and Containerization** through hypervisors for virtualized workloads and the docker platform for productive and portable workloads

DOI: 10.1201/9780429328220-2

- **Middleware Solutions** (intermediation, aggregation, dissemination, arbitration, enrichment, collaboration, delivery, management, governance, brokering, identity and security)
- **In-Memory & In-Database Data Processing Appliances for** big, fast, and streaming data analytics
- **Process Innovation and Architecture Assimilation** (SOA, EDA, SCA, MDA, ROA, WOA, MSA, etc.)
- **New Kind of Data Sources, Databases and Data Warehouses** (SQL (clustered, analytical, and parallel), NoSQL, NewSQL, and hybrid models)
- **A Bevy of Pioneering Technologies** (virtualization, miniaturization, integration, composition, sensing, vision, perception, mobility, knowledge engineering, visualization, etc.)
- **New Computing Paradigms** (edge/fog, cognitive, and cloud-native computing)
- **Natural, Intuitive, and Informative Interfaces/Simple (web 1.0), social (web 2.0), semantic (web 3.0) and smart (web 4.0)**
- **Artificial, Ambient and Augmented Intelligence** for predictive, prescriptive, personalized, and cognitive insights
- **Blockchain Technology for Digital Security**
- **Augmented and Virtual Reality (AR & VR)**
- **Programming Languages** (Golang, Scala, RUST, Ballerina, Kotlin, Dart, Node.js, etc.) and low-code platforms

The Internet of Things (IoT) paradigm is establishing and sustaining the dreamt connected world. Any ordinary and casual thing in our daily environments gets digitized to join mainstream computing. All kinds of physical, mechanical, electrical, and electronics systems are digitized to enable them to find one another seamlessly and spontaneously in the vicinity and interact purposefully towards fulfilling modern business processes and goals. Further, ground-level devices, machinery, instruments, equipment, and utilities getting integrated with cloud-hosted and remotely held cyber applications, services, and databases to be adequately and astutely enabled to exhibit adaptive behaviour. Thus, the connectivity and integration bring in the much-desired intelligence for hardware modules and software components.

Artificial Intelligence (AI)

Next in line is none other than the widely discoursed and deliberated AI paradigm. **Artificial intelligence (AI)** is the field dealing with many advanced technologies and tools to make our everyday systems intelligent. Machine learning (ML) is one such pioneering technology contributing immensely to the AI field's enormous success. ML deals with several algorithms bringing massive success by enabling machines to self-learn without getting programmed explicitly. Today we write data ingestion, storage, manipulation, analysis, and display logic and aggregate them as an application to be deployed in computers to do the intended tasks. We need to feed in data and the code to do the data processing to get the intended results. But ML is quite different. ML enables computer systems to learn from the data and produce relevant results automatically and artistically. Precisely speaking, ML is a subfield of AI, and it provides any IT system and business application the ability to learn and improve from experience automatically.

Deep learning (DL) is another popular field in the AI space. DL is ML done through neural networks (NNs). The NN algorithms that can learn non-linear relations between data have significantly augmented several tasks. Especially computer vision (CV) requirements are in the process of automation through path-breaking DL algorithms. Though AI is a known concept, it has redeemed itself due to several distinct IT space advancements in the recent past.

1. Now we have several breakthrough ML and DL algorithms. DL algorithms need an enormous amount of discrete data to bring forth accurate information. ML algorithms primarily leverage supervised and unsupervised techniques to do feature extraction and engineering. But DL methods, which are predominantly NNs-centric, are the automatic feature extractors learning important relations in data themselves

2. The amount of multi-structured data getting generated and analysed is becoming massive. We are heading towards the world of trillions of digital entities, billions of connected devices, and millions of software services. Thus, the amount of interaction, operational, transactional, and analytical data is exponentially growing. We live in a world that generates around 2.5 quintillion bytes of data per day. This data generation rate is bound to go up in the days to come. The number of mobile, fixed, portable, nomadic, implantable, handheld, and wearable devices already exceeded the number of people on the planet. Also, a study indicates that 90% of the total data we have across the world got generated only in the last two years. The amount of untapped data across all industry verticals is and startlingly tremendous. Fortunately, we have a litany of automated data lifecycle management tools to collect, cleanse, and crunch data in time to extricate actionable insights. We have cloud storage solutions to stock big data affordably. Thus, the emergence of cloud computing co-existence with integrated data analytics platforms and ML/DL algorithms' scores foretells brighter days for the data-driven AI era.

3. Graphical processing units (GPUs) empower us to run powerful models on big data in a reasonable amount of time. GPUs are famous for embedding hundreds of cores and suitable for parallel processing. The GPUs are becoming affordable due to a series of technology innovations, and hence there is the widespread usage of GPUs for big data analytics (BDA). The computing and storage costs have come down sharply. GPU's compute abilities are increasing, whereas the cost per FLOP for GPUs decreases year by year.

4. Another innovation is tensor processing units (TPUs) – ML has achieved many breakthroughs. ML algorithms are producing a paradigm shift for institutions, individuals, and innovators. Having realized this vast and growing demand, Google has purposefully built the TPU to facilitate further disruptions. Cloud TPU is the custom-designed ML ASIC that powers Google products like translate, photos, search, assistant, and gmail.

5. There are concerted and collaborative research endeavours initiated towards unearthing original AI approaches and algorithms that, in turn, solve process and data-intensive problems efficiently. A lot of time, talent, and treasure are focusing on AI technologies and tools. Face recognition, object detection, text summary, machine intelligence, speech-to-text translation, etc., are the prominent and dominant application areas for the AI field's continued popularity.

All these above factors are still in play and will continuously stimulate the AI world to realize path-breaking inventions bound to bring tectonic changes in peoples' lives. Many believe that AI is the future of human society.

With zillions of devices and software services interacting in synchronous and asynchronous fashions, a tremendous amount of data gets produced for Data virtualization, integration, ingestion, processing, and analysis tools for transitioning data to insights. There are batch and stream-processing methods. There are integrated platforms for performing big and real-time data analytics. There are deterministic and diagnostic analytics procedures widely leveraged across multiple industry verticals to extract actionable intelligence. With the faster maturity yet the stability of the ML and DL algorithms (these disciplines come under the AI domain), the longstanding goal of predictive, prescriptive, and personalized analytics is to see the neat reality.

Several business verticals embrace the AI techniques and tips to crunch big and real-time data to uncover beneficial patterns and associations. It articulates fresh opportunities and possibilities and finds impending risks and other valuable knowledge in time. CV, natural language processing (NLP), artificial neural networks (ANNs), and other prominent subdomains under the AI domain automate several manual tasks. Also, predictive insights will become the new normal for the world with substantial advancements in AI. Systems will become more intelligent and sophisticated. Knowledge is the core and central tenet for all kinds of enterprise-grade systems soon. AI is all about the various technologies and tools to make our computers, communicators, and other digital assistants intelligent in their decisions, deals, and deeds, i.e., simulating human-like intelligence in our everyday machines and systems is the guiding principle behind the enormous success of the AI paradigm.

Business behemoths worldwide have started to embrace this enigmatic technology to be competitive and predictive in the knowledge-driven market. Retail and online stores extensively use this technology to strategize, plan, and execute various things with utmost clarity and confidence. Banks and other service providers get considerably boosted through this AI movement. The sharp increase in different and distributed data sources, connected entities, purposeful interactions, etc., leads to a massive amount of multi-structured data. The integrated data analytics platforms and their ready availability help collect, ingestion, storage, processing, mining, and analytics, thus squeezing actionable insights into data heaps. Businesses started to give premium, path-breaking, and people-centric services through the information insights emitted by data analytics, mining, and learning technologies and tools. The intelligent and humanoid robots (AI-enabled) came as a boon for performing various physical services.

Amazon's cashier-less Go stores is a game-changer. We need not stand in a queue. We can pick up our items and leave the store with the collected goods. The Amazon account gets charged, and we get the receipt. Amazon uses a combination of AI and data pulled from multiple sensors to ensure that customers charged only for the picked items.

Business applications and IT services are intelligent in their actions and reactions. They must be compassionate and responsive. Further on, our everyday devices and machines must be made canny. AI is widely accepted as the way forward to make our systems clever in their tasks.

Data collection, ingestion, processing, storage, analytics, mining, learning, and visualization are the essential technologies in bringing knowledge out of data heaps.

There are integrated platforms for more in-depth data analytics. Worldwide business behemoths and organizations are keenly strategizing to have data analytics capability in place to fulfil the widely expressed needs of "data-driven insights and insights-driven decision-making and action".

Software-defined Cloud Environments

Now, we move to talk about competent IT infrastructures for data analytics. With cloudification, currently, running applications are being cloud-enabled. That is, monolithic and massive applications get dismantled into a group of microservices. Cloud-based application development is also happening with the availability of cloud-hosted platforms. Nowadays, with the maturity of a few strategic technologies, cloud-native application development is gaining momentum. Cloud-native computing brings many distinct advantages for data and process-intensive business applications.

Cloud native computing – microservices architecture (MSA)-based services, containerization of those services, container orchestration platforms with CI/CD (continuous integration/continuous deployment), resiliency with service mesh all made cloud native computing popular and a widely accepted paradigm of Agile software world.

Cognitive computing is getting a place in the futuristic technological domain and pushing investments with all the talents, treasures, and time. This chapter is to untangle and articulate this computing paradigm in detail. With the faster stability of several technologies mentioned above, cognitive computing days every time are not too far away.

Defining Cognitive Computing

It is all about establishing and sustaining all kinds of business applications and IT services to perform and provide cognitive capabilities innately. Typically, human cognitive competencies include learning from data and experiences, reasoning with evidence, proposing new hypotheses, interacting with the environments and people intelligently, etc. Simulating these unique characteristics in our software applications and everyday electronics is the goal of cognitive computing.

Simply speaking, the ensuing cognitive era is to have proven techniques and tools to empower our professional, social, and personal software systems and devices to mimic the functioning of the human brain and improve human decision-making.

Several cognitive computing products, processes, patterns, platforms, and procedures simplify and streamline cognitive systems' methodology. Big enterprises invest heavily in bringing forth integrated development environments, frameworks, accelerators, specialized engines, and toolkits to swiftly and smartly build and deploy cognitive systems. There are industry-specific cognitive systems in the form of expert and recommendation systems.

Take a real-world humanoid robot. This robot's main functionality is to give the best and timely advice to empower people to make correct decisions faster. Today, we make decisions based on our past experiences and intuition. But the future belongs to the prospering idea of "data-driven insights and insights-driven decisions".

The recent robots are capable of traversing through thousands of individual's experiences and their results instantly. Quickly analysing the factual details, intelligent robots can develop actionable insights, contributing handsomely to making timely tactical and strategical decisions. Thus, a large amount of experience data (facts and figures), analysing, learning, and reasoning algorithms and powerful computers constitute a combination for cognitive computing's intended success.

As depicted in the Figure 2.1, cognitive computing represents the new-generation self-learning systems that can utilize ML models to mimic how the human brain works. Eventually, this technology is bound to facilitate the automated IT model creation capable of solving problems without human assistance.

The Distinct Attributes of Cognitive Systems

Business workloads and IT services, and all kinds of edge/fog devices are transitioning to be cognitive in their actions and reactions. Cognitive technologies are being part of everyday devices under cloud environments (public, private, hybrid, and edge); device middleware solutions (IoT gateways/brokers/smartphones, etc.) are moving towards more and more cognitive. Cognitive applications are not, therefore, ordinary or typical applications. The widely insisted properties of cognitive computing systems (hardware and software) as listed below.

- **Adaptive** – Cognitive systems can intelligently learn from their environment and the associated systems. There can be multiple data-generating systems constantly feeding data to one or more sub-systems. Cognitive systems are inherently capable of making sense out of the data received and adapting their behaviour accordingly. Precisely speaking, cognitive applications are capable of ingesting and integrating information from multiple systems (collocated and remotely located). Integrated systems get data dynamically in real time regardless of ambiguity and unpredictability and master over time.
- **Iterative** – They must aid in precisely defining a problem by asking questions or finding additional source input when a situation seems inadequate. Cognitive applications are generally iterative. With iteration, the accuracy of decisions is on the higher side.
- **Stateful** – Cognitive systems must remember and recollect previous interactions/sessions/transactions in a process and return information suitable for the specific application as and when needed.
- **Context-aware** – They can decisively and deftly understand the prevailing situation. They must arrive at the context information by aggregating the latest details from various context-sensitive elements such as meaning (semantics), syntax (grammar), time, location, mood, etc., to answer correctly.
- **Interactive** – They must interact with people and machines naturally. Speech recognition (SR) is one such phenomenon where voice interfaces get attached to devices. Such seamless interactions allow users to make explicit their requirements comfortably

Figure 2.1   Cognitive Computing Properties.
Source: Maruti Techlabs.

These are their unique characteristics, and they deviate significantly from today's business and IT systems. Intelligence is the core and central aspect of cognitive systems.

Machines are enabled to be intelligent through self-learning. ML and DL algorithms facilitate the learning. NLP helps to understand conversational languages and respond accordingly. Pattern recognition helps in uncovering and visualizing valuable patterns in data volumes. Cognitive systems running on parallel and supercomputers can churn a large and growing information repository to come out with correct answers for various questions. Doctors treating cancer patients can put forth specific and sophisticated questions to cognitive systems to better medication recommendations to their patients.

We keep hearing and learning more about Siri, Alexa, Google Assistant, and Cortana. What are they? They are, in fact, good examples of digital persona assistants.

Many exciting virtual assistants are evolving in the market; Dr AI by HealthTap is a cognitive solution. It helps physicians connect patients on finding the prioritized list of symptoms gleaned from a hundred thousand plus physicians' knowledge and several thousands of anonymized patient profiles with the individual patient's profile.

Some enterprise-grade use cases are fraud detection using ML and predicting oil spills in oil and gas production cycle. While computers are faster at calculations than humans for decades, they have also failed to accomplish tasks that humans take for granted. For example, understanding the natural language or recognizing unique objects in an image or video is a simple thing for humans. Thus, cognitive technology bias towards positioning it as the one that makes such a new class of problems realized. Cognitive systems can fluently respond to complex situations characterized by ambiguity and create far-reaching impacts on our everyday works and walks.

Cognitive Computing Technologies

The scope of cognitive computing is engagement, decision, and discovery, as IBM's study report. These three capabilities are related to the ways people think and demonstrate their cognitive abilities in everyday life.

■ Engagement – Cognitive systems generally deal with big data (structured, semi-structured, and unstructured). Cognitive systems have the inherent ability to extract deep domain insights from big data and provide expert assistance in time. The models built by these systems include the contextual relationships between various system entities, and these models result in forming viable hypotheses and arguments. These specialized and sophisticated systems can reconcile ambiguous and even self-contradictory data. Thus, these systems can establish and engage in deep and decisive dialogue with humans. The chatbots are a well-known example of an engagement model. Many of the AI-centric chatbots are pre-trained with domain knowledge for quick adoption in different business-specific applications.

■ Decision – Decisions made by cognitive systems continually evolve based on new information, outcomes, and actions. These systems models built using reinforcement learning and the autonomous decision-making of any systems depends on its ability to trace why it took that decision and its ability to change its response's confidence score. A widespread use case of this model is the use of IBM Watson in healthcare. The system can collate and analyse patients' data, including his/her history and diagnosis of the past and present. The solution cites recommendations on its ability to understand the meaning and analyse queries in the context of medical data with its complexity and natural language, including doctors' notes, patient records, medical annotations, and clinical data feedback. As the AI solution learns, it becomes increasingly more accurate. Providing decision-support capabilities and reducing paperwork allows clinicians to spend more time with patients.

■ Discovery – This involves finding insights and understanding a vast amount of information. These models build on DL and unsupervised ML. With the generation and capture of big data, there is a clear need for systems that help exploit information more effectively than humans. The Louisiana State University (LSU) solution of Cognitive Information Management (CIM) shell is well-known among the cognitive world. It employs distributed intelligent agents in the model, and they collect streaming data, like text and video, to create interactive sensing, inspection, and visualization. Eventually, the visualizations provide real-time monitoring and analysis. The CIM shell not just stops at sending alerts but also reconfigures the fly and isolates a critical event that fixes the failures.

IT systems and software applications typically do not think and act. No longer it's a true statement! They are empowered through a stream of cognitive technologies and tools to do things that only humans can do in their everyday lives. It is now possible to incorporate human perceptual skills, such as recognizing handwriting or identifying faces, finding objects in images, etc. Systems and software are becoming part (embodied) of human cognitive skills such as learning from data heaps, reasoning with evidence, uncovering useful and usable patterns, interacting with people naturally through human-machine interfaces (HMIs), proposing newer theories, etc. Knowledge discovery, context-awareness, and decision-making with clarity and confidence, act with sensitivity and sagacity, etc., are the unique competencies of cognitive systems. Technologies that can perform the tasks mentioned above (typically associated with human intelligence) are cognitive technologies.

Cognitive technologies have been evolving over decades. There are mental application development toolkits and platforms. IBM Watson is the first and widely known platform to produce cognitive systems across multiple industry verticals. Other product vendors and cloud service providers are also showing extra interest and bringing out mental toolkits. Lightbend, the provider of the world's leading reactive application development platform, has aligned with IBM to help advance the development of cloud-native cognitive solutions. There are impressive outcomes with CV, NLP, SR, and robotics. Self-driving cars extensively use CV being provided by DL algorithms. Precisely speaking, cognitive technologies enhance and extend the power and spread of information and communication technologies.

Cognitive systems have the inherent potential to enable business establishments to break prevailing trade-offs between speed, cost, and quality. In the years ahead, we can elegantly and excitedly expect various positive impacts of cognitive technologies on organizations to grow noticeably.

Cognitive Computing: The Industry Use Cases

Cognitive computing is getting more focus from many industries, including homeland security, agriculture, automotive electronics and avionics, financial services, social utilities, healthcare, infotainment, oil and gas, power and utilities, real estate and retail, logistics and travel, hospitality, etc. The prominent application areas were broad and included research, sales, promotion campaign, and customer service.

Experts believe that cognitive technologies' growing applications fall into three main categories: **product, process, or insight**. Products and solutions are embedded and empowered with cognitive capabilities to understand users' tactical, spatial, temporal, and situational needs, produce, and provide appropriate services to them in time in a discreet manner. Process applications embed pioneering technologies in their workflows to automate, augment, and accelerate operations. Insightful and intelligent applications natively use cognitive technologies to uncover valuable and usable patterns, beneficial associations, actionable intelligence, impending dangers, risks and threats, and fresh possibilities and opportunities. The knowledge discovered gets disseminated in time to consider and execute tactical, operational, and strategical decisions across an organization.

Products and Services Become Smarter with Cognitive Technologies

Organizations can embed path-breaking cognitive technologies to substantially increase the value of their products or services by making them multifaceted, robust, resilient, versatile, and intelligent. A well-known example of the excessive use of cognitive technology is the Netflix online movie rental service's recommendation feature. This added facility uses ML algorithms to predict which movies a customer will like. This capability accounts for as much as 75% of Netflix usage. A more recent example is that eBay uses machine translation to enable users who search in Russian to discover English-language listings that match. Recommendation and expert systems can be built and used with the faster maturity and stability of ML algorithms. Web-scale corporates immensely leverage the advancements in the AI space to bring forth pioneering services and use cases to their loyal and royal customers and consumers.

CV through DL algorithms and self-driving/autonomous cars are all set to be a glorious reality sooner than later. Automakers are increasingly depending on the crucial advancements being unearthed in the DL space to conceive and concretize several path-breaking and hitherto unheard use cases.

General Motors (GM) is exploring using CV methods to make some of its vehicles safer. The CV solutions help determine whether the driver is spending enough time looking at the road ahead or the rear-view mirror. Audi integrates SR technology into some cars to naturally enable drivers to converse with infotainment and navigation systems.

Medical imaging technology is bound to see a sharp improvement in the days to come. CV capabilities intrinsically enable radiologists to pinpoint specific areas of mammograms effectively and efficiently diagnose breast cancer. The medical imaging system automatically analyses mammogram images and outlines suspicious areas to indicate potential abnormalities.

The pizza delivery chain Dominos has introduced a new function in its mobile application that lets customers place orders by voice, intends to increase revenue by making ordering anytime, anywhere on any device. Those who order in such a comfortable and convenient manner tend to purchase more frequently.

The Associated Press (AP) has implemented a natural language-generation software that automatically generates corporate earnings stories and leads AP to publish ten times more business stories than earlier. AP's scale and improve the quality of its business news coverage is phenomenal with its NLP and cognitive abilities systems.

Creating New Product Categories

We discussed how existing products, solutions, and services gain noteworthy intelligence through cognitive technologies and tools. It is now possible to bring entirely new products and services through the intelligent leverage of proven and potential cognitive computing methods. Cognitive systems and services open more unique markets, vistas, and avenues and unearth fresh ways and means for achieving more significant revenues. The Roomba robotic vacuum cleaner has come out with a new category and spawned several competitors. Google Now can anticipate one's need for information and provide it before being asked. Crewless aerial vehicles, robotic pack animals, and robotic caregivers for the elderly or infirm are prominent domains to get advanced and adventurous products through the power of cognitive technologies. We are going to get bombarded with cognitive systems and environments in the years to unfurl. Industry verticals are keen on embracing cognitive competencies to be dominant in the cut-throat competitive market.

Automation and Orchestration of Processes through Cognitive Technologies

With business applications becoming complicated, distributed, and multifaceted, process-centric problem resolution acquires special significance. There are business process mark-up languages (BPML), business process management platforms, and other related solutions. Process components such as notified activities/jobs getting into shape through formalized process/workflows. Control and data flow from one process component to another happen in a controlled and configured manner. Process automation is the most incredible thing to do. Also, now the new concept of process orchestration is catching up fast. Cognitive technologies are facilitating automation. Resultantly the work gets done faster, cheaper, and better. Service providers automate the process tasks, whereas customers benefit immeasurably through automation.

In the manual labour process, labourers use various toolsets to finish work fast with ease. Cognitive technologies automate any work in two ways. Firstly, they can assist and augment professionals to complete any assigned task quickly and easily. For instance, healthcare decision-support and expert systems typically propose diagnoses, suggest medical treatments, or recommend patients for clinical trials. They have an automated reading and filtering of news and bulletin data to highlight any influencing information that helps with a financial advisor's view of an asset class or stock. Cognitive technologies may eliminate some lower-end jobs. For example, automated voice response systems are to replace human customer service agents for first-tier customer support. Driverless mining trucks are to reduce risks to human drivers and cut labour costs.

By using proven cognitive technologies, the Hong Kong subway system carries over five million passengers daily. It boasts a 99.9 percentage on-time record that emphasizes the sharp improvement of quality and its efficiency. In a typical week, ten thousands of workers carry out as good as 2000 plus activities across its engineering system to keep running it all smooth. The Hong Kong subway system operator had embraced cognitive technologies to automate and optimize these engineering works' planning. Encoding rules of thumb learned by experts over multiple years of experience and constraints like regulations about maximum noise levels allowed at night, the schedules, etc. The system employs a "genetic algorithm" that pits many solutions to the same problem against each other to find the best one. This optimization algorithm produces an optimal engineering schedule automatically and saves two days of planning work per week.

Government Transparency and Campaign Finance Commission of State of Georgia must process 40,000 campaign finance disclosures pages per month. Most of them are handwritten. There came an automated handwriting-recognition solution to keep up with the workload and crowdsourced human review to ensure quality.

Cincinnati Children's Hospital Medical Centre is deciding clinical trial for the patients using NLP to read free-form clinical notes and ML to refine the list of terms extracted from them. A well-intended study proved that the above clinical trial process of finding clinical trial eligibility for the patients has increased its efficiency to 450% and reduced the workload by 92%.

Cognitive Technologies Enable the Transition of Data to Information and Knowledge

This is the third category of applications facilitated through cognitive technology. The transformation of data to processed information and gathered knowledge is the business world's widely articulated need. We have enormous data getting processed through batch processing. With the availability of powerful computers, big data gets subjected to various investigations through real-time data processing methods. Thus, the real-time analytics of big data gains prominence with the ready availability of competent data analytics platforms, accelerators, and specialized engines.

Natural language processing (NLP) techniques have made it easy to analyse large volumes of unstructured textual information. That is, text-to-speech (TTS) and speech-to-text (automated speech recognition (ASR)) capabilities achieved through the praiseworthy accomplishments in the NLP space. That is, creating information from unstructured data heaps is being accelerated and automated through NLP methods. ML algorithms can help in drawing actionable conclusions from large and complex data sets. They also contribute to making correct predictions out of operational data. Business organizations leverage cognitive technologies to generate insights out of data. The knowledge discovered and disseminated can help reduce costs, produce premium services, improve efficiency, increase revenues, and guarantee customer delight.

Stevia First, a biotech startup with developed intellectual property (IP) covering the production of a naturally derived sugar substitute, is vigorously exploring a range of cognitive technologies to generate valuable and usable insights. One promising application is none other than optimizing its industrial processes. The company has a breakthrough mechanism (smart search) to determine the optimal parameters for the volume of raw materials and process time to boost the production process's cost efficiency.

Intel is beneficially using ML algorithms to improve sales prospects and revenue generation. One approach is to automatically classify customers using a predictive algorithm into categories likely to have similar needs or buying patterns. This categorization helps Intel to formulate winning schemes to target the identified types to penetrate further.

To improve market and mind shares, Allstate, the USA insurance company, has embarked on a project to understand its esteemed customers' views correctly and concisely. The various comments, complaints, concerns, and compliments expressed by its users on social media are being systematically captured, cleansed, and crunched to understand their feelings in greater detail. This technology-enabled solution empowers Allstate to prioritize and prescribe additional customer-centric solutions and services.

Similarly, BBVA Compass bank extensively uses a social media sentiment monitoring mechanism to track and understand what consumers feel about the bank and its various offerings. The mechanism involves native incorporation of NLP technology, automatically identifies important information, salient topics of consumer chatter and the sentiments around those topics. The extricated insights finally influence the bank's decisions on setting fees and offering consumer perks and how customer service representatives should respond to particular customer inquiries about services and fees.

Aetna and GNS Healthcare have teamed up to use ML and other analytic techniques to improve patients' health and reduce the cost of caring for them. Their analyses focused on metabolic syndrome, a condition that significantly increases the risk of stroke, diabetes, and heart disease. The team came up with the model using claims and biometric data from 37,000 Aetna members that predict the risk of developing metabolic syndrome and the probability of developing any of the five conditions associated with the disorder. The models can also determine which medical interventions are most likely to improve an individual's health outlook.

The usage patterns vary based on the problem at hand and the expressed strength of cognitive technologies associated with knowledge discovery needs and dissemination towards producing and sustaining innovative and disruptive ideas and propositions. Data volumes are collected from different and distributed sources and subjected to various investigations to unearth hidden patterns, usable insights, fresh possibilities, and opportunities. Thus, the widely talked IT and business transformation receives a substantial boost with cognitive technologies' smart leverage. Cognitive technologies could be the real game-changer, and IT's future soon. The second famous cognitive paradigm contribution is the remarkable and rewarding optimization of business and IT operations. Process excellence is the grand reality of the cognitive era; Other benefits include achieving predictive and prescriptive maintenance of industry assets, and forecasting can be accurate, etc. Augmenting and assisting humans in taking correct and futuristic decisions, deals, and deeds, automating the repetitive tasks, guaranteeing customer delight, etc., are other categories of activities getting enormous support from the advancements in the cognitive computing space.

If we think cognitive technologies are the solution to every problem, then it's not. Organizations must evaluate the business, technical, and user implications for using cognitive technologies safely and strategically. There are several enabling frameworks, integrated platforms, accelerating libraries, and toolsets to simplify and streamline the development and deployment of well-intended cognitive applications. Several industries have been seriously exploring and evaluating cognitive computing to be ahead of their competitors. There are expert opinions and suggestions that organizations must look across their business processes, their product offerings, and their markets to examine and understand where the use of cognitive technologies may be viable, valuable, and vital. The clear articulation of tactical and strategical advantages is a must and accentuated to exemplify the cognitive paradigm's distinctions and nullify any kind of impending risks.

Thus, with the systematic application of cognitive technologies, business processes and products are bound to gain a paradigm shift. Also, squeeze actionable and timely insights out of data. The knowledge discovered can be disseminated to humans, business workloads, IT systems, and services to exhibit intelligent behaviour.

Real-world Cognitive Computing Applications

Every industry is trying to be more competent in its operations, offerings, and outputs through the deft usage of proven and promising AI concepts. As we near the promised cognitive era, cognitive applications are bound to be standard and widely made available. There are several everyday use cases of cognitive computing.

- Speech recognition
- Sentiment analysis
- Face recognition
- Object detection
- Risk assessment
- Fraud detection
- Behavioural recommendations
- Recommender and expert systems
- Question and answer systems

Below list are a few of the most popular cloud-hosted cognitive services platforms.

- IBM Watson
- Microsoft Cognitive Services
- Google's DeepMind
- Amazon's Cognitive Services (includes Alexa)
- SparkCognition
- Numenta

Cognitive computing simulates and stimulates human cognition. This new computing paradigm allows and discreetly helps humans make the best use of all kinds of experiences, history details, evidence, facts, and figures to take precise and perfect decisions in time. Cognitive computing comes in handy for humans in their everyday activities without replacing human efforts. Precisely speaking, cognitive computing contributes immensely in assisting humans in their daily assignments.

The cognitive era can bring in radical and rapid technological transformation. This movement's impetus is to result in trailblazing and transformative cognitive systems that understand unstructured data, a reason to form hypotheses, learn from experiences, and interact with humans naturally. From data to information and knowledge process must be fully automated to arrive at disruptive and deft systems.

The Strategic Implications of Cognitive Computing

Cognitive computing aims to create skilled business workloads and ICT systems that simulate human cognitive skills efficiently and effortlessly. Cognitive systems are famous for grinding through mountains of data to automate the abstraction of insights and report any discovered knowledge through attached dashboards in real time and near real time. With the ready availability of cloud infrastructures, cognitive platforms and applications can be optimally and universally made available to end-users in a risk-free and rewarding fashion. Fresh and fast deployment models of cognitive software solutions have brought in ways and means of giving cognitive capabilities as a collection of managed and hosted services.

When used in the finance domain, cognitive technologies working alongside the existing ERP systems and robotics can upend operational finance and bring about unprecedented agility and transparency to the processes. As enunciated above, there can be a few meaningful impacts of cognitive computing in the years to unfurl.

The Widespread Usage of Cognitive Systems

There will be a more significant number of cognitive systems in our everyday environments such as homes, offices, manufacturing floors, hotels, warehouses, construction areas, retail stores, etc. Humanoid robots are becoming pervasive and persuasive with the machine and deep learning algorithms' continued maturity and stability, ANNs, pattern recognition, and NLP methods. Intelligent and mobile robots are beneficial to people in their obligations. We will see more and more virtual assistants and conversational bots in human-less grocery stores, conference halls, automated eateries, and autonomous cars. Thus far, the IT landscape's different advancements have resulted in information, transaction, analytical, and commercial services. Henceforth, we can safely expect game-changing services such as physical, context-aware, and people-centric services accomplished through cognitive systems in the years ahead.

With advanced chatbots paradigms, repetitive and straightforward questions get answered by AI-enabled chatbots in a human-like conversational style. Service organizations such as B2C e-commerce service providers and product vendors extensively use chatbots to answer various questions and clarify doubts expressed by their prospective customers. Support teams also utilize chatbots to respond to their users' repeated questions. Their usage is steadily growing as the recent chatbots are being sagaciously enabled through promising cognitive technologies to deliver various information services to business partners, employees, customers, and consumers with all the clarity and confidence. Cognitive systems can naturally interact with humans. All the latest machines are fit with HMI capability to interact with their operators and users spontaneously. Thus, cognitive systems are to do things without much intervention, interpretation, and involvement of humans. The data accumulation with the exponential rise of distributed data sources extricated from actionable insights empowers our everyday systems with the right and relevant intelligence.

Precisely speaking, with cognitive systems abound in and around us, we get technical assistance to all our activities and needs.

Edge Computing

As articulated elsewhere, there will be 50+ billion connected devices in the years to come as per the leading market watchers and analysts. The exponential growth of connected devices demands higher bandwidth. These embedded, networked, and edge devices are growing with more memory and storage capacities and higher processing capability. The future 5G networking is capable of handling many such devices in particular environments. The device density is bound to go up sharply as we are heading towards more intelligent environments in our daily walks and works.

Increasingly edge devices are being clustered to accomplish faster/parallel data processing to guarantee real-time data analytics. The responses must be quick. Any vehicles on the road must communicate very fast. Not only that, but they also must talk to their nearby ICT infrastructures. Capturing and transmitting data to faraway clouds to be processed is not a correct approach for the increasingly real-time world. Thus, edge device(s) need to perform superior computing. Therefore, processing logic and resources are embedded in edge devices to make edge/fog computing ubiquitous. The processed data then gets into cloud storage. This arrangement also helps to filter out redundant and repetitive data at the source itself. Thus, the new concept of edge or fog computing gains prominence as a machine and deep learning algorithms are being stuffed in edge devices to be cognitive in their deliveries. The vision of "intelligence at the edge" is gaining momentum with several implementation technologies' and continuous availability. There are AI libraries such as portering TensorFlow in edge devices. Robots at various locations such as eating joints, entertainment plazas, supermarkets, railway stations, etc., are being empowered through cognitive technologies.

Serverless Computing

This is a new computing model gaining many market and mind shares these days. Certain functions need lightweight, short, and quick infrastructure modules. These functions get activated based on some events (business, technical, and user). Developers can just focus on application-building without worrying about setting up appropriate infrastructure to run the application as per the changing loads. Infrastructure service providers must set up and sustain infrastructure modules (virtual machines and containers) to run such functions effectively with automation. Largest number of containers created to perform serverless function will be in a matter of seconds. Thus, scheduling optimal infrastructure resources and scaling them up and out as per the load variation are automated with the availability of intelligent technologies and tools. Especially containerization plays out a very vital role in shaping up this fast-emerging concept of serverless computing. Thus, there is a new buzzword, "Function as a Service", sweeping the cloud IT. With edge devices joining in mainstream computing, any event from distributed devices and people can activate the appropriate functions to process the event data/message to arrive at a timely and intelligent conclusion. IoT edge devices and gateways intensify with cognitive technologies to be process-aware, people-centric, situation-aware, insights-filled, service-oriented, event-driven, etc.

Enhanced Cognitive Capability with Big Data

We all know that when we have a large dataset to train and test machine and deep learning models, the output is more accurate. There are data lakes and oceans to feed enough data to these algorithms to serve society in a better and bigger manner. The emergence of affordable cloud storage facilities also serves the knowledge-discovery purpose. As indicated above, the extra and enormous computing power brought in by GPUs and TPUs can handle DL algorithms with ease.

With the rapid growth of data sources, the amount of data getting generated is tremendous. With the availability of path-breaking computing, networking, and storage technologies, more data gets processed, analysed, and mined. The steady stream of powerful learning algorithms contributes immensely to extricate actionable insights out of data heaps. Data mining is the process of turning mere data into information, and knowledge is maturing and stabilizing fast. Thus, companies worldwide desperately need to collect and crunch all kinds of internal and external data to add insights to their business workloads and IT services. There are data virtualization and knowledge visualization solutions. Data ingestion, transformation, storage, and access becomes more manageable, faster, and cheaper. Today roughly one percentage of the total data is subjected to a variety of investigations. With the enabling products, platforms, processes, patterns, and procedures in place, the amount of data getting analysed goes up remarkably in the days to come.

Cognitive systems are the next-generation intelligent systems that are empowered adequately to analyse, interpret, reason, and learn innately. The aim is to augment human intelligence substantially and sagaciously. Cognitive systems do some tasks without any interpretation, involvement, and instruction of human resources. They can understand the context behind the content. That is, cognitive computing is taking BDA from data-driven to value-driven. It is, therefore, confirmed that with the onslaught of trailblazing technologies, the impacts of cognitive systems for commoners are going to rise considerably.

Cognitive Intelligence (CI)

We have explained about AI before. AI represents a collection of pioneering technologies and tools for embedding human-like intelligence in computers, communicators, sensors, actuators, appliances, instruments, machinery, equipment, and toolkits to exhibit intelligent behaviour. In addition to such devices, software applications and IT systems must acquire this extra and exotic intelligence to be distinctly different. Cognitive intelligence (CI) is a new breed of commercial AI for businesses to meet the more complex demands. One such need is to have modern human-machine interactions. Primarily, this monitors how traditional AI processes data, filling in gaps and identifying misinterpretations. A CI platform's goal is to complete tasks without any human interpretation and involvement, quickly understand and process unexpected or unfamiliar external inputs, and adjust its response accordingly. There are several applications for this domain, as articulated below.

Cognitive Intelligence (CI) Applications – Some unique capabilities are being introduced and sustained through CI approaches.

Smart IoT – As discussed above, the IoT phenomenon is for transitioning everyday and simple things in our midst into digitised objects. That is, all kinds of physical, mechanical, and electrical systems in our everyday environments get systematically digitized. These digital entities can purposefully interact with one another in the neighbourhood to share their unique capabilities. Further on, electronics devices, embedded systems, and single-board computers (SBCs) need increased instrumentation to be well interconnected. The era of connected devices is flourishing with proper nourishment from original equipment manufacturers (OEMs). Thus, it is forecast that there will be billions of connected devices and trillions of digitized elements in the years to come. Besides, enterprise-scale cloud-native applications will be composed of hundreds of polyglot microservices. There will be millions of software services to realize software applications (operational, transactional, analytical, visualization, etc.) in minutes. However, empowering digitized objects and connected devices to be intrinsically intelligent in their operations and outputs are strategic goals. Finding, binding, and interacting with one another and with cloud-hosted cyber applications and services is a must with necessary supplied parameters. Such comprehensive connectivity, along with other measures, brings much-needed intelligence.

For example, there are requirements as follows. Swarms of drones or any remote facilities filled with intelligent sensors and actuators need to coordinate to accomplish more significant tasks. AI agents can give multitudes of devices the situational awareness capability and work together to solve problems. An oil rig in the oceanic with thousands of sensors must have a faster Internet to communicate sensor data streams to faraway cloud applications and databases to facilitate cloud-based IoT data analytics capability. Therefore, embedded and edge devices must be networked and given suitable intelligence internally and externally to enable them to prognosis dangerous problems proactively and pre-emptively to prevent any untoward incident or accident.

Thus, robots, factory machines, earthmovers, MRI instruments, drones, rovers on Mars, fleets of ships, super-tankers, and such fabulous IoT devices have to be meticulously connected, tracked, and coordinated through the power of AI. IoT and cognitive technologies convergence results in unheard and unexplored use cases and CI to achieve IoT's intended success.

AI-Enabled Cybersecurity – With deeper connectivity in place, cyberattacks will also increase and bound to happen. This rise in cyberattacks will result in an explosion of network penetrations, distinctly sophisticated social engineering attacks, the release of intelligent computer viruses like wildfire are bound to happen. The conventional security mechanisms fail miserably here. Hence, there is an insistence to smartly leverage the AI domain's various accomplishments to extract security insights in time so that corrective and countermeasures can be taken by security experts even systems automatically to thwart any cyberattack. Thus, AI takes the way forward to secure our data stores, hardware, and software systems.

Cognitive Analytics in Healthcare – Now, advanced and automated healthcare data analytics throws deeper insights into doctors, surgeons, nurses, and other healthcare service providers. Cognitive agents are bound to drive hitherto unheard advancements in genomics research, drug discovery, diagnostics, and population health. The technology implements human-like reasoning software functions that perform deductive, inductive, and abductive analysis for life sciences applications. These cognitive applications act as an enabler to experts and help them assess hypothetical discovery scenarios, detect health anomalies, classify diagnostic results, and discover associations between seemingly unrelated health information sources.

Intent-Based Natural Language Processing (NLP) – Data scientists must move from essential ML techniques such as classification to more holistic ANNs to capture humans' intent precisely. Simple word-matching is no longer serving the greater purpose. For instance, if I say, "I want to book a Doctor appointment", the bot can refer to the nearest doctors based on my location. The bot can look through my search history to guide a specific doctor based on multiple parameters. CI is to help businesses to be more analytical in their decisions.

Thus, the realization of advanced functionalities through CI is possible and brings deeper automation across business processes.

Cognitive Computing Strategy: The Best Practices

Having understood the strategic implications, enterprises are keenly evaluating and embracing the cognitive paradigm. Several cognitive technologies are emerging to speed up the realization of cognitive systems. Cognitive platforms and products are being built and released into the market to develop and run cognitive applications that can run on cloud infrastructures. Cognitive applications are more and more available as a service through clouds. Real-world use cases and applications are being unearthed and popularized for conveying the need for cognitive computing capabilities. As business houses are strategizing and planning, a well-intended way forward is to have a data-driven scheme to derive the flourishing cognitive phenomenon's maximum benefit. Institutions feel the need for cognitive solutions and services to assist business ably. Also, IT professionals and their primary role lies in insightfully interpreting data from different and distributed sources to supply the right and relevant knowledge. Thus, human empowerment is the goal. Here are the steps to consider before moving towards a cognitive computing platform.

■ **Focus on Data Sources and Systems** – As enunciated above, the cognitive journey must begin with the correct data and data management systems to be successful. Every enterprise has its own set of internal and external data sources, and most of it or almost every bit of it has something useful for enterprises. Employees, customers, business partners, and geographical data are some of the enterprise data sources hugely facilitating business direction and destination. Data, when crunched, emits out actionable insights.

Cognitive applications increasingly draw different types of digital data from multiple sources. Also, they aggregate sensory inputs such as visual, gestural, and auditory data. It processes the collected and cleansed information by comparing it to the set of data it already knows. With more data, it learns more. With that, the prediction accuracy goes up.

- **Design enterprise systems to support data generation** – Some of the widely used automation systems across enterprises are
  - Enterprise resource planning (ERP)
  - Customer relationship management (CRM)
  - Supply chain management (SCM)
  - Knowledge management (KM)
  - IoT-enablement and analytics platforms etc.

  Enterprises need enterprise-scale businesses and IT systems to run their business operations comfortably, and these systems produce a massive amount of multi-structured data. They must be captured and fed into cognitive systems to generate insights in time. With IoT-inspired digital entities and connected devices producing a lot of data individually and collectively, cognitive systems lead to enterprise success. Data is the new fuel and asset for worldwide businesses. Cognitive systems play a strategic role in knowledge discovery and dissemination.

- **Understand KPIs influencing business processes** – There is an exponential growth of data in the connected era. Also, there is a grand realization that the two paradigm shifts (data-driven insights and insights-driven decisions) are essential for sustaining business growth. Therefore, the role and responsibility of cognitive systems are bound to grow considerably in the days ahead. Hence, it is crucial to identify the correct set of KPIs for the enterprise and its processes. Identifying and understanding KPIs in light of a cognitive solution goes a long way in achieving process excellence.

  Cognitive applications use many of the latest technological innovations and inventions, such as DL algorithms and NNs, data mining, NLP, and pattern recognition.

- **Setup an elastic IT infrastructure to store and maintain data** – Cloud infrastructures are the optimized and organized IT infrastructure for hosting and running applications and data storage. Most large and medium enterprises already have robust IT infrastructure that stores data. As inscribed above, data is the base for cognitive systems. In short, we need appropriate infra for setting up and sustaining cognitive solutions, which have become an essential tool for digital innovation, disruption, and transformation. With the pervasiveness of cloud environments (public, private, edge, and their various combinations), the cognitive era is to commence and shine.

Thus, cognition-enablement approaches by business executives and IT teams getting momentum more than ever, and with the pertinent technologies are in place, we can confidently expect the cognitive days sooner than later.

Cognitive Application Platforms

As indicated above, there are several enabling frameworks and platforms to adopt and adapt the cognitive paradigm. This section focuses on a couple of acclaimed stages and their various contributions.

mAdvisor is a patent-pending AI and cognitive computing platform that helps enterprises to translate raw data into expressive insights and descriptions without any manual intervention. So the enterprises can cut the analytics timelines from many days to minutes with mAdvisor.

mAdvisor employs cognitive technologies like ML, machine reasoning, DL, natural language generation, NLP, and expert rules systems, thereby enabling enterprises to identify fresh revenue streams and enhance customer experience and productivity. Other widely indicated use cases are

- **Text Analytics** – It is all about mining text documents to extract correct context and insights. Text documents include Web 1.0 simple websites, Web 2.0 social websites, e-mails, research publications, white papers, internal memos, review comments, etc. The idea is to uncover valuable associations and discover usable patterns. Text analytics confirms about meeting the business metrics and indicates whether the expectations met or not. Further on, predicting outcomes can be automated through analytics on text files.
- **Speech Analytics** – Phone interactions of customers and public speeches of important people are made available or subject to various investigations to extricate some valuable outcomes for society's betterment. Cognitive applications can intrinsically acquire, analyse, and help synthesize voice data from different data sources like contact centre recordings.
- **Computer vision** – This is a popular application of cognitive computing. We have images and videos from multiple sources these days in large quantities. Cognitive systems can store, process, and analyse images for diverse applications such as predictive maintenance of essential assets, autonomous cars, ambient assisted living, robots-assisted surgery, face recognition, counterfeit product detection, etc.
- **IoT & Sensor Data Analytics** – We are to have zillions of digitized objects, sensor-attached assets, and connected devices in our everyday locations. All kinds of physical, mechanical, electrical, and electronic systems are increasingly digitized and connected within. These connections and linked systems can quickly and voluntarily share their unique capabilities and status data with others in the vicinity and with remote ones through one or other networks. Assets and their surroundings' data can be minutely captured, cleansed, and crunched to squeeze out valuable and usable information in time. The insights extracted go a long way in identifying any visible deviations and deficiencies, pinpointing performance issues, health conditions, external and internal attacks, detecting anomalies/outliers, slowdown/breakdown, etc. Increasingly real-time analytics of device, log, operational, security, and performance data is being made possible with the help of edge computing capability, accomplished by forming dynamic and ad hoc edge clouds. Edge analytics is the future undoubtedly with the faster maturity and stability of edge computing technologies and tools. Machine and deep learning algorithms are being directly deployed in edge/fog devices to gather data diversity. Devices automatically learn and act based on real-time predictive and prescriptive insights.
- **IBM Watson** – Without any iota of doubt, this solution is the famous and fabulous cognitive platform. IBM Watson has laid down a stimulating foundation for the flourish of the cognitive computing model. It invariably leverages

ground-breaking technological innovations such as NLP, machine and deep learning, pattern recognition, knowledge representation, data mining, knowledge discovery and dissemination, etc.

Below points hint at the typical sequence of Watsons when it gets the input

- Watson ingests questions or inputs in natural language mode
- Instantaneously search its information repository for an answer to the question posed
- Develops newer hypotheses on its own
- Substantiates the theory through compelling pieces of evidence
- Generates appropriate responses in time and delivers them in natural language mode.

There are several scenarios and needs across industry verticals for such cognitive platforms.

Note: IBM Watson is hugely popular in the healthcare domain. This platform collates the entire gamut of knowledge around a medical condition, such as patient history, research papers, best practices, symptoms, diagnostic tools, and more. It then analyses all the information and recommends sync with the patient's changing condition. It is humanly impossible for any doctor to possess such a vast amount of healthcare information. Doctors may leverage such insights to adopt evidence-based treatment options considering all factors, including the individual patient's presentation and history. As you may note, this phenomenon is a significant upgrade from the present scenario where the doctors make educated guesswork, based on grossly incomplete information, with the decision based on the doctor's limited range of knowledge.

Cognitive computing applications are also making their indelible mark in multiple domains. An excellent real-life example is Hilton Hotel's Connie, the first concierge robot, which helps visitors with hotel information, local attractions, etc. It recognizes questions posed in natural language and answers accordingly. Cognitive computing started to deliver a positive return on investment (RoI). Enterprises have already achieved more considerable successes by smartly applying this futuristic technology. For instance, a packaged goods company using cognitive computing to automatically resolve customer problems, pre-empting customers' usual practice of raising a ticket, could achieve a 30% reduction in tickets.

- **Watson Assistant** – There are several surveys and statistics to illustrate what consumers want these days. A study reveals that 73% of US consumers indicated that "valuing their time" is the utmost important thing a brand can do. If a business is not meeting these high expectations, then it is bound to suffer. A staggering 91% of unsatisfied customers will not return if they don't feel each interaction is efficient or tailored to their needs.

  Like Watson Assistant, conversational AI can quickly and efficiently automate customer service processes by retaining fickle customers and improving the employee experience and boosting businesses' bottom line.

■ **IBM Watson Discovery** is IBM's AI search engine that specializes in extracting answers from complex business documents. This product has received the highest scores possible in the information ingestion, intent intelligence, relevancy intelligence, and tuning tools criteria as per the Forrester report. These distinguished capabilities offer companies augmented AI to significantly improve the quality of enterprise search results, enabling more thoughtful decision-making.

Data of 2.5 quintillion bytes produced every day. The volume continues to grow; many businesses will have to have an automated solution to assist their employees and royal customers in finding the right information, making correct decisions, and completing tasks faster. With a cognitive search solution like Watson Discovery, any business can boost human intelligence using varied *AI technologies* by effortlessly sorting through a staggering amount of data to find specific information quickly.

■ **IBM Watson Talent** – Hiring and harnessing the right people creates substantial business value for any enterprising adventure. Also, it is no secret that possessing an army of smart-working professionals is a crucial and competitive advantage for any ambitious business. To effectively plan for both talent acquisition and skilling, we need an AI-backed talent management solution to fulfil human resources' varying expectations. IBM Watson Talent is a modular and easy-to-use talent management solution for acquiring, retaining, and building people towards reaching organizations' goals.

■ **IBM Watson Media solution** is to infuse the much-needed AI competencies into media workflow or video library. This technological empowerment helps media service providers to look out for viable opportunities for significantly improving viewer engagement, video data analytics, and to make money out of media resources. The IBM Watson web site is informative and inspiring.

Watson Marketing is an AI-powered digital marketing platform to help teams work smarter and deliver their customers' experiences.

IBM RegTech, or regulatory technology, is applying innovative competencies and techniques to help financial institutions better meet their regulatory monitoring, reporting, compliance, and risk management needs. In today's increasingly complex regulatory environment, financial institutions should deliver greater transparency to enhance and preserve client and stakeholder trust.

IBM Watson IoT Platform is a managed and cloud-hosted service designed to make sense out of IoT data. As indicated above, we will have billions of connected devices and trillions of digitized objects in the years to unfold. The data getting generated when these entities interact with one another in a purpose-specific manner will be staggering. Making sense and money out of the exponentially growing data heaps is being pronounced an enormous opportunity for society hitherto unheard of services conceived and concretized. Fresh possibilities can be visualized and realized through collecting and analysing IoT data in real time. Context-aware and cognitive applications can be built and deployed for augmenting and assisting people in their daily works and walks.

By introducing the much-needed automation in data analytics through cognitive computing technologies, enterprises worldwide envision exciting days ahead.

Cognitive platforms such as the Watson IoT Platform simplify and streamline extracting actionable insights from IoT data collections in an automated manner. Additional add-on services such as Blockchain and analytic services enable organizations to capture and explore data for devices, equipment, and machines and discover insights that can drive better decision-making.

Microsoft Cognitive Services: With a set of APIs, SDKs, and cognitive services from Microsoft, developers can make their applications more intelligent, and they can plug and play smart features – such as sentiments and emotions detection, vision and speech recognition, knowledge, search, and language understanding – into their applications.

CognitiveScale was founded by former members of the IBM Watson team. It is cognitive cloud software for any enterprise. Augmented intelligence platform from CognitiveScale delivers insights-as-a-service and fast-tracks the creation of cognitive applications in travel, retail, healthcare, and financial services. They all help businesses make sense from "dark data" – messy, disparate, third-party data and drive actionable insights and continuous learning.

SparkCognition is an AI-powered cyber-physical software for the safety, security, and reliability of information technology (IT), Industrial Internet of Things (IIoT), and operational technology (OT). The technology is more inclined towards manufacturing. It can harness real-time sensor data and learn continuously from those sensors to find and mitigate risks and prevent policies to intervene and avert disasters.

Companies like Qualcomm, Intel, and other leading technology companies take steps to integrate cognitive solutions into their applications designed for specialized industries. Uber, the famous car rental company, is researching many AI technologies and acquired Geometric Intelligence and Otto, an autonomous truck and transportation startup. Gamalon, an AI enthusiastic company, took Bayesian Program Synthesis (probabilistic programs for auto data model) as the base and developed novel AI techniques that accelerate ML to 100x level. All it required was just a few pieces to train the system to achieve the same accuracy levels as NNs.

Numerous product vendors are showing immense interest in bringing forth a slew of next-generation cognitive toolkits, accelerators, specialized engines, frameworks, and platforms for realizing several sophisticated services and applications. Experts are profoundly analysing the current business challenges and drawbacks. And, they are evaluating the success rate and ratio of leveraging cognitive computing methods to surmount those downsides. Therefore, a clarion call for freshly approached tools for making cognitive computing penetrative, pervasive, and persuasive.

Artificial Intelligence (AI) vs Cognitive Computing

What is cognitive computing? In a simple term, computers learning and imitating the human thought process is cognitive computing. Cognitive computing does learn by studying patterns and suggests humans take relevant action based on its understanding. In AI, the system takes full control of a process and takes steps to complete a task or avoid a scenario using a pre-defined algorithm. Cognitive computing serves as an assistant instead of the one finishing the job. In a way, cognitive computing provides humans with the power of faster and more accurate data analysis without worrying about any wrong decisions from the ML system. Cognitive computing endows humans with superior grade precision of research and study while ensuring everything is in their control. An example could be an AI-backed system that would decide treatment for a patient without consultation with a human doctor. Simultaneously, cognitive computing would supplement the human diagnosis with its own set of data and analysis, which improves the quality of decision and adds a human touch to critical processes.

There are a few crucial differences between AI and cognitive computing systems, though cognitive computing is a precise subset of AI. The objective of cognitive computing is solely to help humans making their decisions using human-like cognition. AI does not try to mimic human thoughts. Instead, a sound AI system collects best-in-class algorithms for neatly and nicely solving a given problem. Cognitive systems do not replace humans and instead support humans in their decisions. Cognitive computing does not impose decisions on humans but rather supplements our decision-making task. A typical and true AI may instead be making all the decisions that could sometimes supersede human-thinking capabilities.

On the other hand, a cognitive system would recommend the best course of actions based on clear pieces of evidence-based recommendations. The Figure 2.2 illustrates the differences between AI and Cognitive Computing.

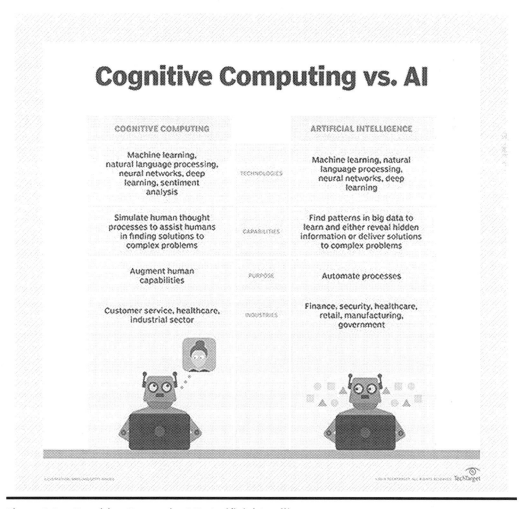

Figure 2.2   Cognitive Computing VS. Artificial Intelligence

Advantages of Cognitive Computing

In the process automation field, the modern computing system moves towards revolutionizing the current and legacy systems by analysing and processing large amounts of volumetric data. Cognitive computing helps employ a computing system for relevant real-life system. Cognitive computing simplifies the following

- **Accurate Data Analysis** – Cognitive systems are highly efficient in collecting, juxtaposing, and cross-referencing information to analyse a situation effectively. IBM Watson helps physicians collect and analyse data from various sources. The data sources could be patients' previous medical reports, published medical journals, diagnostic tools data, anonymized past data from the medical fraternity. These systems thereby assisting physicians in providing a data-backed treatment recommendation benefit both patients and doctors. Cognitive computing robotic process automation speeds up data analysis and helps doctors to take quick and informed decisions.
- **Leaner & More Efficient Business Processes** – Cognitive computing can analyse emerging patterns, spot business opportunities, and take care of critical process-centric issues for near real time and real time. With a vast amount of data examinations, a cognitive computing system such as Watson can simplify many processes, reduce risk, and trigger swift actions according to changing circumstances. This process prepares businesses to streamline a proper response to uncontrollable factors; simultaneously, it helps create lean business processes.
- **Improved Customer Interaction** – To enhance customer interactions by implementing robotic process automation, the technology may come in handy. As cognitive computing made it possible to provide relevant and only relevant information specific to contexts and valuable information to the customers, it takes customer experience to the next level and engages them with a business forever.

One of the critical distinctions between AI and cognitive platforms is that you want the AI system to do something for you. Another side, the cognitive platform is instead you turn to for collaboration or assistance. The cognitive platforms and applications range from medicine to customer service, and it's a great boon to the medical industry. Doctors can use these cognitive systems to assist them in diagnosing patients. Utilizing only the doctors' ability to analyse a patient's medical history against every medical textbook ever written, identifying possible diseases is humanly impossible. The doctor might never have considered, or even he/she knew about it.

The essential distinction between AI systems and CI is that we wanted the AI system to do something for us. But a cognitive platform is something we turn to for collaboration or assistance. These applications for cognitive platforms range from medicine to customer service. It's a great boon to the medical industry, and doctors can use these systems to assist them in diagnosing patients. Utilizing only the doctors ability to analyse a patient's medical history against every medical textbook ever written, identifying possible diseases is humanly impossible. The doctor might never have considered or even know about it. Businesses can use it to incorporate all kinds of risk factors into a decision before providing a company with a recommendation about an investment or a location to build a new satellite office. The possibilities for this technology in the future are enormous, and no industry will be left untouched by it in the next decade.

Financial services are the most likely industry we'll witness these systems make significant advances. As we go into the exponential growth of raw data across all the economic sectors, there are more ways to make money that may not seem possible to humans who have no way to process and analyse the petabytes of data stored in the cloud. These sorts of enormous data processing are precisely what these platforms intended for, and if any industry that is willing to invest in this will be financial services firms for sure.

Like healthcare, the law firms may also be willing to gain significantly from this technology. With the millions of case law pages that attorneys must sift through when preparing lawsuits – or when defending a client from one – a whole army of paralegals could not provide the kind of analysis and assistance that this platform could provide.

Law firms poised for significant gain with cognitive and AI technology for lawsuite filings as the lawyers need to go through millions of pages when preparing lawsuits or even defend their clients. AI will provide the kind of analysis and assistance that an army of paralegals workforce may take days to develop manual analysis.

Consumer service will see an enormous benefit from these systems, both in retail and corporate communications. Retail outlets use AIs to act as shopping assistants for their customers, and this trend accelerates once AI technology becomes more widespread. Chatbots long crossed the rudimentary form of these kinds of computing and servicing basic customer service inquiries. As they become more sophisticated, they eventually replace entire human call centres for any conventional query and routing only the most unconventional customer service issues to a human agent.

Real-estate businesses may employ the systems to incorporate any risks into a mitigated decision-based design before suggesting a company with an endorsement about a venture or a location to commence a new satellite office. The future and possibilities associated with cognitive technology are enormous, and no industry will be left untouched by it in the next decade.

Conclusion

We have explained the essentials of cognitive computing in this chapter. Also, we have illustrated how this fresh computing model will be a massive game-changer for the IT industry and worldwide businesses. There is an overwhelmingly agreed view on this computing phenomenon and its ability to bring in a series of breakthrough changes to IT and IT services. Cognitive computing is undoubtedly the way and immediate future for IT to be a forerunner for producing the promised knowledge-driven society. Businesses can gain a bevy of innovations and disruptions in their interactions with their customers, consumers, and clients through this unique paradigm. The widely discussed and deliberated digital transformation needs, fully and fabulously fulfilled goals can be through the rational and sincere usage of the accentuated tenets and cognitive computing traits. Several pioneering cognitive computing use cases across multiple industry verticals are etched in this chapter to boost this enigmatic computing idea's confidence succulently. Academicians and practitioners are teaming up together to unearth both evolutionary and revolutionary concepts and products to make way for the cognitive era. Precisely speaking, cognitive computing is riveting and rewarding indeed.

References

https://www.forbes.com/sites/bernardmarr/2016/03/23/what-everyone-should-know-about-cognitive-computing

https://www.cloudflare.com/en-in/learning/serverless/what-is-serverless/

https://research.aimultiple.com/chatbot-intent/

https://www.marlabs.com/platforms/cognitive-computing-AI-ML-platform/

https://analyticsindiamag.com/how-to-implement-intent-recognition-with-bert/

https://www.ibm.com/watson

Chapter 3

The Cognitive IoT:
The Platforms, Technologies,
and Their Use Cases

Introduction

IoT platform is a multi-layered technology platform which is used to manage and interconnect devices which are part of the IoT ecosystem. This platform helps to bring all the objects online and helps to establish interconnectivity among the devices. All the services which are necessary to enable communication amongst these devices are offered by the platform. In short, IoT platform is a software platform which connects various components of IoT ecosystem like edge hardware, access points, and data networks to the user applications.

Cognitive IoT platform is the convergence of cognitive computing technologies with the data collected from connected devices which are part of a typical IoT ecosystem. First, we examine the architecture of a generic IoT platform. Then we examine how it is augmented with cognitive IoT capabilities.

Chapter Organization

This chapter is organized into basically three parts as depicted in the following Figure 3.1:

DOI: 10.1201/9780429328220-3

Figure 3.1   Chapter Organization

Generic Architecture of IoT Platform

Generic four-stage architecture of IoT platform is depicted in the following Figure 3.2:
Following are the four stages in the architecture:

■ Stage 1 contains sensors and actuators
Stage 1 which contains sensors and actuators deals with the collection of data from various sources. Some of the prominent sources of IoT data are the following:
– Smartwatches
– Smart home systems
– Smart grids
– Smart transportation systems
Stage 2: Internet gateways and data acquisition systems

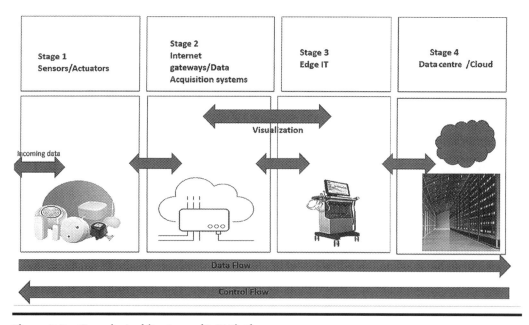

Figure 3.2   Generic Architecture of IoT Platform

– Stage 2 contains internet gateways and data acquisition systems. Data which comes in from different systems will be of different forms, most of them will be in analogue form. This data needs to be converted into digital form. This is done by the gateways.

Stage 3 contains edge information technology (IT) systems. These systems mainly perform analytical functions. They do analysis of the data and the results of data analysis are presented in the form of dashboards for visualization purposes.

Stage 4 comprises cloud and data centre. From the data which is collected from various sources, only certain kinds of data need analysis, others just need to be stored for use later or even as a part of compliance process. These types of data are stored in cloud systems or sent to data centres for storage in some form of storage media.

Generic Architecture of Cognitive IoT Platform (CIoT)

The generic architecture of cognitive IoT platform is depicted in the following Figure 3.3. CIoT is the convergence of cognitive computing technologies with the data collected from connected devices which are part of a typical IoT ecosystem. Consequently, the evolution of ubiquitous computing leads to heterogeneous infrastructure challenges.

Through the objective context, a generic IoT architecture handles the challenges which emerge in context awareness by producing a smart and cognitive system which has the capabilities to achieve user requirement. Cognitive IoT merges intelligence into the physical objects which are present in the physical world. In order to achieve

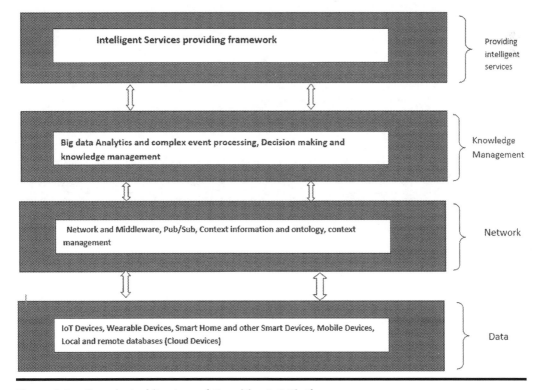

Figure 3.3   Generic Architecture of Cognitive IoT Platform

this, the data generated by IoT devices and web data are passed through a context management middleware which senses it. The objective context of the architecture is used for the external intelligence of service. The subjective context is used to enhance the existing services to fit some specific spatial-temporal situations. Big data management provides a high level of data quality and accessibility for big data analytics. An intelligent service is required to ensure the monitoring and control of the system.

Data Flow in a Cognitive IoT-Based Architecture

IoT produces huge amount of data. This in turn increases the volume, variety, and velocity of data which is being generated daily which in turn leads to information explosion. Another aspect to be mentioned here is that the data comes from a huge number of diverse sources and hence will be in various formats and it will be a combination of structured and semi-structured data.

Hence, it is very essential to define a process of data flow to process the data from various input sources, process it, and transfer it to output sources. This architecture is depicted in the following Figure 3.4:

The various components of data flow are the following:

- Data source
- Data collection
- ETL
- Business analytics
- Service

Data Source: Data comes into cognitive IoT system from diverse sources. So, it needs to be processed in order to extract meaningful insights and expected results.

Data Collection: As depicted in the following Figure 3.5 the process of data collection is also known as data acquisition. Data needs to be collected from different

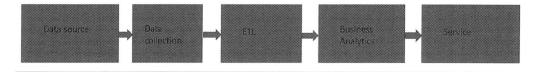

Figure 3.4   IoT Data Flow Components

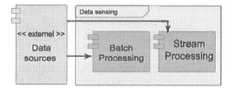

Figure 3.5   Data Collection

types of sensory devices in a timely manner and should be made available for processing at a right point in time. Hence, there are two subcomponents for collection of data; they are:

■ Batch processing: This subcomponent is used to collect data at rest
■ Stream processing: This subcomponent is used to collect data in motion

Extract, transform, and Load (ETL): This is done by the business intelligence system (BI). It involves manipulation and processing of data from diverse sources in order to convert it into a single format and store it in a repository. The process of ETL involves the following key steps as depicted in the following Figure 3.6:

- **Data ingestion:** This involves transforming the collected data from the input source to the output source.
- **Data Storage:** This involves storing the collected data in a data store which has good storage capacity.
- **Data Wrangling:** This involves mapping of raw data into another format which helps in processing and analysis of output data.
- **Business analytics:** The business analytics will further process data to make it ready for data modelling. Business analytics helps managers to view and other desired outputs in the form of dashboards.

In the next section, we will discuss the architecture and functionalities of some of the major IoT platforms which are available in the market today.

Cognitive Capabilities Offered by IoT Platforms

Cognitive capabilities offered by IoT platforms can be grouped into three main categories; they are the following:

Discovery: Finding hidden insights, useful patterns/connections in the vast amounts of available information.
Engagement: Offering new forms of interactions between IoT ecosystem and things. This in turn changes the way humans and systems interact, extending the user's capabilities.
Decision: Providing evidence-based decision-making capabilities.

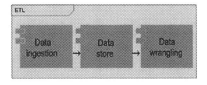

Figure 3.6   Data Collection

Classification of Cognitive Capabilities Offered by IoT Platforms

Cognitive capabilities offered by IoT platforms can be grouped into two broad categories based on the end users of the products; they are the following:

- Cognitive capabilities for consumer market
- Cognitive capabilities for enterprise market

Cognitive Capabilities for Consumer Market

This segment is targeted to end users. Here the cognitive technologies are used to generate new ways of creating value for end consumers thereby removing their pain points and enhancing their daily experiences. Some of the prominent consumer cognitive products include personal assistants, wearable devices, home automation, and so on. These products are very user-friendly and often respond to voice commands from the end user. These products also collect data about the user from Internet, personal email, calendar, devices, contacts, and other electronic gadgets that the consumer uses to perform tasks daily. Some of the popular examples in this category are the following:

- Amazon Echo
- Apple Siri
- Google Search

Cognitive Capabilities for Enterprise Market

Large vendors that offer enterprise cognitive IoT platforms and services include a broad range of solutions and tools in their portfolio. Most of the vendors deliver their services and tools on the Internet through cloud-based platforms which in turn offer scalability, accessibility, and flexible billing options. AI-based algorithms and services are used across diverse industries, from healthcare to automobile to finance to insurance. Vendors that provide enterprise cognitive services focus on offering core cognitive capabilities to their enterprise customers using technologies like:

- Artificial intelligence (AI) algorithms to specific industry solutions.
- Natural language processing (NLP) and machine learning (ML).
- Question-answering (QA) technologies provide the foundation for several core cognitive capabilities that are provided by enterprise cognitive services.

The above core capabilities are used by organizations to build cognitive solutions for their enterprise customers/markets.

Core cognitive services available on the market include these examples:

- Conversation services text mining
- Information extraction
- Text analytics

- Machine translation
- Computer vision
- Image recognition
- Speech recognition.

Prominent Cognitive IoT Platforms

Some of the prominent players who offer cognitive IoT services on their cloud platforms for enterprise customers are the following:

- Google Cloud IoT Platform
- IBM Watson Platform
- Amazon AWS IoT Core
- Microsoft Azure IoT Suite

Each of these platforms will be discussed in detail in this chapter.

Google Cloud IoT Platform

The architecture of Google Cloud IoT platform is given in the diagram below. The main components of the architecture are the following:

- Google Cloud IoT Core
- Cloud IoT Edge

These two components are explained below.

Google Cloud IoT Core

It is a fully managed service for securely connecting and managing a global network of devices. Cloud IoT Core is a serverless component. Because of this, it has the capability to support huge number of connected devices without the need for any server provisioning and configuration. Data from millions of devices can be ingested by Cloud IoT Core for processing by other fully managed services which are running on GCP. Cloud IoT Core provides acts like a gateway into the Google Cloud Platform.

Cloud IoT Edge

Cloud IoT Edge component basically contains a set of software packages and services. These are responsible for providing edge-based capabilities to the Linux-based devices which are connected to the cloud platform. These edge-based capabilities offer capabilities to the devices to run and apply ML-based models at the data source. The device in this context can refer to anything ranging from medical devices to robotic devices to wind turbines and so on, where it makes sense to apply ML for deriving predictions based on data.

Reference Architecture for Google Cloud IoT Platform

The reference architecture of Google Cloud IoT Platform as seen in the following Figure 3.7:

The main components about the reference architecture are explained below:

(1) Telemetry input data – This typically is a measurement value which is detected by relevant sensors This value could be a temperature reading, pressure reading, decibel reading, distance reading, etc. This data is transmitted by the device to Cloud IoT Core using MQTT. Since the devices transmit data using MQTT, they send data to the same global endpoint.

(2) Data which is received by Cloud IoT Core is then sent to Cloud Pub/Sub. Cloud Pub/Sub is Google Cloud Platform's fully managed message queue and event broker. Data which is received by Cloud IoT Core is sent via the broker as messages to Cloud Pub/Sub which in turn sends the data to a queue as a notification topic. Topics which are received by Cloud Pub/Sub are stored for seven days. This data can also be accessed immediately by other services as per their need.

(3) Processing from Cloud IoT Core or from Cloud Pub/Sub can take any number of different paths. Dataflow can be added to historical data held on Google Cloud Storage, Google BigQuery, or in Cloud Bigtable. Google BigQuery can be used for ad hoc analysis or Cloud Data Studio can be used for visualization.

(4) If any predictions are needed, they can be done using Cloud Machine Learning (ML) Engine to train and refine ML models using the anonymized data stored in buckets on Google Cloud Storage.

(5) Cloud Functions is an execution environment for single-purpose functions that can respond to events. Several functions can work together to quickly evaluate the data values which are present in the message to calculate values in real time.

(6) Updates to the refined ML models are compiled using the TensorFlow Lite tools and sent to the device by Cloud IoT Core.

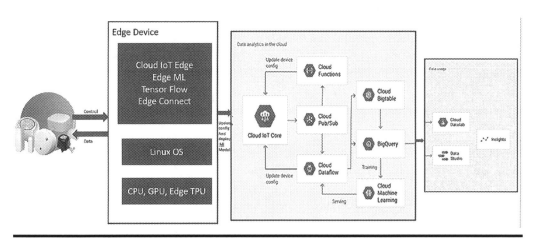

Figure 3.7   Reference Architecture - Google Cloud IoT Platform

Some of the key features of Google Cloud IoT Platform are the following:

■ It has multi-layered secure architecture
■ It has features which help in improving operational efficiency. Some of the possible use cases are predictive maintenance for assets and other equipment, smart city components like smart buildings etc.
■ It has good machine learning capabilities
■ It offers support for a wide range of embedded operating systems
■ It has location intelligence capabilities

IBM Watson IoT Platform

The architecture of IBM IoT platform is depicted in the IBM Watson IoT platform (Figure 3.8) with, the various components of the IBM Watson IoT platform are the following:

■ Analytics
■ Connect
■ Risk management
■ Information management
■ IBM Bluemix open standards and services

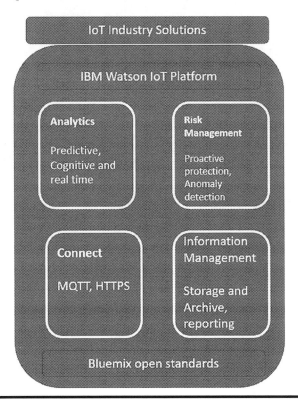

Figure 3.8   IBM Watson Overview

IBM Watson IoT Platform – Connect: This component helps to manage devices, networks, and gateways.

IBM Watson IoT Platform – Information Management: This component helps to integrate information which are both in structured and unstructured formats, from the ecosystem around us.

IBM Watson IoT Platform – Analytics: This component helps to gain insights from information which is received using real-time, predictive, and cognitive analytics

IBM Watson IoT Platform – Risk Management: This component ensured that you leverage the right information from the right sources. This component also ensures that the right type of software runs on the information.

IBM Bluemix Open Standards: IBM Bluemix standards and APIs provide the following core capabilities in addition to a host of other capabilities:

- Runtime environment for the apps choosing any language at runtime
- DevOps development toolkit which provides monitoring, deployment, and logging tools to the developer
- Lot of APIs: Some of the key APIs are natural language processing, machine learning, text analytics, video and image analytics.
- Provisions to connect to on-premise systems, public and private clouds.

The various steps involved in **the device connectivity and management function** of IBM Watson IoT Platform – are summarized in the following Figure 3.9:

The following Watson APIs which offer cognitive service are currently available as part of the platform:

Language:
– Conversation
– Document Conversion
– Language Translator
– Natural Language Classifier
– Natural Language Understanding
– Personality Insights
– Retrieve and Rank
– Tone Analyser

Speech:
– Speech to Text
– Text to Speech

Vision:
– Visual Recognition

Data Insights:
– Discovery
– Discovery News

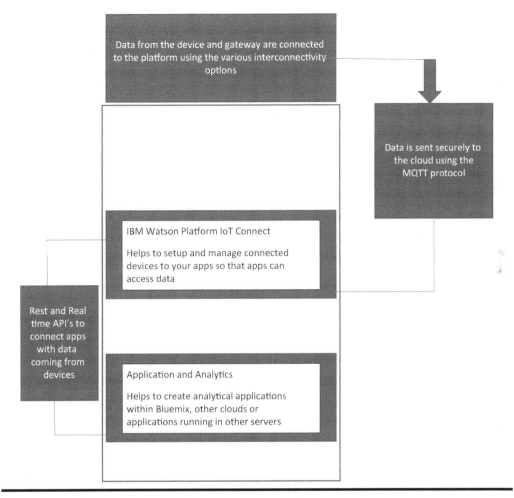

Figure 3.9   Cognitive Services of IBM Watson

INTERESTING COGNITIVE USE CASE OF IBM WATSON

IBM Watson Education

With Watson Education, teachers and students together can transform the individualized learning experience throughout their lifelong learning journey. Solutions and apps that have analytical and cognitive capabilities help teachers learn about their students holistically. This helps the teachers to shape and drive personalized learning suited to each person, assisted by technology that understands, reasons, learns, and interacts. Students are offered personalized constructs that make learning easier and much more meaningful for them. Educators and students build relationships and hubs of collaboration, exchanging and growing expertise to create new possibilities in education that help shape a better future for everyone.

Architecture of Amazon Web Services IoT (AWS IoT)

AWS IoT architecture consists of the key components which are depicted in the following Figure 3.10:

Each of the components present in the architecture and some additional services are explained in this section.

Alexa Voice Service (AVS): The Integration of AVS to AWS IoT helps to leverage Alexa Voice feature to any connected device. This also helps the developers to offload computationally intensive audio tasks from device to the cloud.

Custom Authentication Service: Custom authorizers can be defined in the AWS IoT architecture and these authorizers help us to manage our own authentication and authorization strategy by creating a custom authentication service and a lambda function.

Device gateway: This component helps the devices to communicate securely and efficiently with AWS IoT components.

Device Provisioning Service: This service allows us to provision devices as per the template defined for AWS IoT. This template defines the resources that are required for provisioning your device. The main fields present in the template are the following:
  – A thing
  – A certificate
  – One or more policies

A thing is an entry in the registry which contains the various attributes that are used to describe a device which is connected to the IoT system. The devices

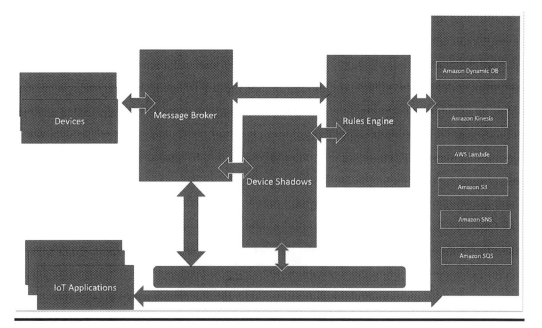

Figure 3.10   AWS IOT Reference Architecture

which are connected use a certificate-based authenticate system to connect with AWS IoT. Policies which are configured determine the list of operations a device can perform in AWS IoT. The templates contain variables that are replaced by values in a dictionary (map). It is possible to use the same template to provision multiple devices by passing different values for template variables in the dictionary.

Device shadow: This is a JSON document which is used to store and retrieve current state information for a specific device.

Device Shadow service: This service provides persistent representations of each device in the whole of AWS Cloud. This helps us to publish updated state information to a device's shadow. This device shadow can synchronize its state with its original device when it connects.

Group registry: Groups follow a parent-child structure. Several devices can be categorized into a group. The groups in turn can contain other groups. Any action performed on the parent group will get applied automatically to its child groups as well. Similarly, permissions given to a group will be applied to all the devices in the group as well as its child group.

Jobs service: This allows you to define a set of remote operations that are sent to and executed on one or more devices connected to AWS IoT. For example, you can define a job that instructs a set of devices to download and install application or firmware updates, reboot, rotate certificates, or perform remote troubleshooting operations. To create a job, you specify a description of the remote operations to be performed and a list of targets that should perform them. The targets can be individual devices, groups, or both.

Message broker: Message broker provides a secure mechanism for devices and AWS IoT applications to publish and receive messages from each other. You can use either the MQTT protocol directly or MQTT over WebSocket to publish and subscribe. You can use the HTTP REST interface to publish.

Registry: It organizes the resources which are associated with each device in the AWS Cloud. It is possible to register our devices and associate them with up to three custom attributes for each. It is also possible to associate certificates and MQTT client IDs with each device. This improves the ability to manage and troubleshoot the devices.

Rules engine: It provides message processing and integration capability with other AWS services. We can use an SQL-based language to select data from message payloads. We can then process and send the data to other services, such as Amazon S3, Amazon DynamoDB, and AWS Lambda. If it is required to republish messages to other subscribers, a message broker can be used.

Security and Identity service: This service takes care of security in the AWS Cloud. It is necessary for the devices to keep their credentials safe so that they can securely send data to the message broker. The message broker in turn uses AWS security features to send data securely to devices or other AWS services.

Following Table 3.1 lists out various AWS services with which the AWS IoT integrates directly:

Table 3.1 AWS Services Integration of IoT

Name of the service	Description of functionality
Amazon Simple Storage Service	Provides scalable storage in the AWS Cloud
Amazon DynamoDB	Provides managed NoSQL databases
Amazon Kinesis	Enables real-time processing of streaming data at a massive scale
AWS Lambda	Runs code on virtual servers from Amazon EC2 in response to events
Amazon Simple Notification Service	Sends or receives notifications
Amazon Simple Queue Service	Stores data in a queue to be retrieved by applications

Working of AWS IoT

AWS IoT provides capability for internet-connected devices to connect to the AWS Cloud. It also enables applications in the cloud to connect and interact with internet-connected devices. Common IoT applications have options to either collect and process telemetry directly from devices or enable users to control a device remotely. The state of each device which is connected to AWS IoT ecosystem is captured and stored in a device shadow. The Device Shadow service is responsible for managing the device shadows by responding to requests involving retrieval or updation of device state data.

The Device Shadow service facilitates communication to and from applications to devices. The communication between a device and AWS IoT is secured through X.509 certificates. AWS IoT can generate its own certificate, or it is possible for you to use your own certificate as well. When a device communicates with AWS IoT, it presents the certificate to AWS IoT as a credential. All devices that connect to AWS IoT should have an entry in the registry.

The registry stores information about a device and the certificates that are used by the device to secure communication with AWS IoT. You can create rules that define one or more actions to perform based on the data in a message. For example, you can insert, update, or query a DynamoDB table or invoke a Lambda function. Rules use expressions to filter messages. When a rule matches a message, the rules engine triggers the action using the selected properties. Rules also contain an IAM role that grants AWS IoT permission to the AWS resources used to perform the action.

Microsoft Azure IoT Architecture

Microsoft Azure IoT Architecture basically uses three terminologies; they are the following:

- Things
- Insights
- Actions

These terminologies are depicted with the help of the terminology diagram which is depicted in the following Figure 3.11:

Microsoft Azure IoT Reference Architecture

The reference architecture of Microsoft Azure IoT System is depicted below:
At the core, an IoT application consists of the following subsystems:

(1) Devices (and/or on-premise edge gateways): These devices have the capability to securely register with the cloud, and the various connectivity options which are supported by the Azure platform. This in turn will enable sending and receiving data from the cloud.

(2) Cloud gateway service/hub: This is used to securely accept that data from the IoT devices. This will also offer device management capabilities.

(3) Stream processors: These processors consume the data from the cloud gateway. They are also used to integrate data with business processes and store them in appropriate storage devices.

(4) User interface: This is used to visualize telemetry data and facilitate device management.

(5) All these components are depicted in the following Figure 3.12:

Figure 3.11   Terminologies Diagram

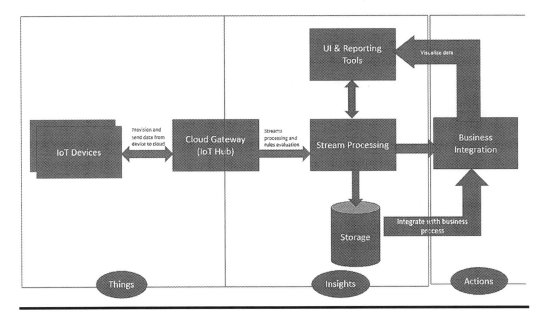

Figure 3.12   Azure IoT Reference Architecture

The Cloud Gateway offers a cloud hub. This cloud hub offers following capabilities:

■ Secure connectivity,
■ Telemetry and
■ Event ingestion
■ Device management (including command and control)

Azure IoT hub is mostly used as the cloud gateway in the architecture. The maximum number of devices supported by the IoT hub at any point in time is five. IoT hub also provides an entity store which can store the metadata of various devices connected to it.

In case if large number of devices need to be supported/connected, it is better to use Azure IoT Hub Device Provisioning Service (DPS). DPS offers scalability by supporting assignment and registration of large number of devices. As mentioned before, stream processing helps to process large streams of data records and evaluates rules for those streams. For stream processing, it is better to use Azure Stream Analytics. This is recommended in scenarios where complex rule processing is needed for large number of applications. For simple rules processing, it is better to use Azure IoT Hub Routes.

Business process integration implies execution of actions based on insights which are gained from device telemetry data which is gained during stream processing. The different types of messages which are integrated are informational messages, alarms, email or SMS, data from CRM, and more. The recommended component for business process integration is Azure Functions and Logic Apps. Data can be divided into warm path (data that is required to be available for reporting and visualization immediately from devices) and cold path (data that is stored longer term and used for batch processing). It is recommended to use Azure Cosmos DB for warm path storage and Azure Blob Storage for cold storage. For applications with real-time reporting needs, it is recommended to use Azure Time Series Insights.

The user interface for an IoT application can be delivered on different types of devices. They can also be delivered in native applications and browsers. Applications which are recommended for reporting and UI across IoT systems are the following:

■ Power BI
■ TSI Explorer
■ native applications
■ custom web UI applications

OpenMTC

The OpenMTC platform is a prototype implementation of an IoT/M2M middleware aiming to provide a standard-compliant platform for IoT services. The architecture of OpenMTC platform is depicted in the following Figure 3.13:

OpenMTC collects data from various sensors and actuators which could belong to different vertical domains. After data collection, data is aggregated and forwarded to applications. The final step is mediation instruction to end devices in order to trigger event-based control.

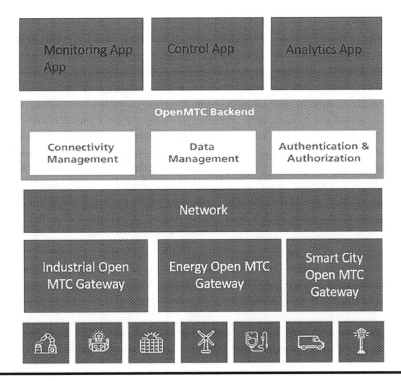

Figure 3.13   Open MTC

The integration middleware aggregates data from multiple gateways that could be assigned to various application domains.

With the help of REST APIs, application developers can access data from various devices, without being concerned about the underlying technology specifications of devices connected to the gateways.

Gateways contain technology-specific protocol adapters. This will help to retrieve the data from various devices running in various domains using different protocols and store them in an oneM2M-compliant data model. Connectivity between the gateways and the backend could be either local networks, the Internet, or operator-managed networks, as oneM2M specifies network agnostic interfaces.

OpenMTC software is written in Python and has the capability to be used on different hardware platforms (e.g. x86; ARM).

How to Get Started with OpenMTC

1. Start by cloning the OpenMTC repository to your project folder:
   ```
   $ git clone https://github.com/openMTC/openMTC.git
   $ cd openMTC
   ```
2. Build an OpenMTC gateway image:
   ```
   $ ./create-binary-docker gateway
   ```
3. Run the gateway Docker image:
   ```
   $ docker run -d --name gateway  -p 0.0.0.0:8000:8000  \
           -e "LOGGING_LEVEL=DEBUG"    openmtc/gateway -vv
   ```
4. **CONGRATS!** You are now running your own OpenMTC platform now.

Summary

IoT platform is a multi-layered technology platform which is used to manage and interconnect devices which are part of the IoT ecosystem. Cognitive IoT platform is the convergence of cognitive computing technologies with the data collected from connected devices which are part of a typical IoT ecosystem.

In the first part of the chapter, generic four-stage architecture of IoT platform was discussed. Later on, the cognitive features and the generic architecture of cognitive IoT platform were discussed. Cognitive IoT products cater to two different types of markets, they are:

- End-user market
- Enterprise market

End-user cognitive IoT products focus on solving the daily pain points of the customers. Enterprise cognitive IoT products offer a combination of AI, ML, and deep learning capabilities to offer lot of specialized features needed by enterprise customers.

The last section of the chapter focuses on explaining the key cognitive cloud-based IoT platforms which are available in the market. They are the following:

- Google Cloud IoT Platform
- IBM Watson Platform
- Amazon AWS IoT Core
- Microsoft Azure IoT Suite

References

https://www.softwaretestinghelp.com/best-iot-platforms/

Building Cognitive Applications with IBM Watson Services: Volume 1 Getting Started Red Book publications from IBM

https://services.google.com/fh/files/misc/iot_partner_quickstart1.0.pdf

https://www.openmtc.org/

https://docs.aws.amazon.com/iot/latest/developerguide/iot-dg.pdf

23rd International Conference on Knowledge-Based and Intelligent Information & Engineering, A New Architecture for Cognitive Internet of Things and Big Data

# Chapter 4

Delineating the Key Capabilities of Cognitive Cloud Environments

Introduction

The cloud journey thus far has been fascinating and inspiring. Software-defined cloud environments are becoming common now. With container-enablement and orchestration platforms becoming matured and stabilized, we see the movement towards establishing and sustaining containerized cloud environments. With serverless, the server management tasks are being done by cloud service providers so that developers just focus on incorporating business capabilities. There are other noteworthy innovations and deeper automation through a bevy of pioneering technologies in the cloud space. What next? With the surging popularity of artificial intelligence (AI) algorithms, cloud enthusiasts and experts are trying to empower cloud assets and applications to exhibit intelligent or cognitive behaviours in their functionalities. That is, we are heading towards cognitive cloud environments powered by a host of path-breaking AI techniques. In this chapter, we talk about cognitive computing and its impacts on society. Further on, we discuss the unique features, functionalities, and facilities of clouds with cognitive ability in this chapter.

AI for Deeper Data Analytics and Decisive Automation

We are now entering into the third era of computing. Realistically speaking, it is undoubtedly the cognitive computing era. This new and unique computing paradigm can fundamentally change the way humans work with machines and devices. In the past, users have to code every small thing using a programming language to enable machines to understand and act accordingly. Digital systems in our midst empowered through cognition-enablement technologies with the emergence of cognitive

DOI: 10.1201/9780429328220-4

computing intrinsically and tools to understand any changing context accurately, learn iteratively, reason with evidence, propose new theses, and act intelligently. Also, natural language processing (NLP) (speech recognition and synthesis) capabilities enable machines to understand humans' instructions and take their everyday life to the next best level with clarity and confidence. Natural interfaces have become the new normal for human beings and devices to connect, communicate, and collaborate meaningfully. The widespread adoption of the machine and deep learning algorithms and toolkits has brought in a sea change in our handhelds, wearables, implantable, portables, mobiles, etc. These AI-enabled devices assist humans in their daily assignments.

With the data analytics domain growing rapidly and radically, the problematic transition from data to information and knowledge is getting speeded up and simplified. Many distinct improvements and improvisations are getting unearthed and articulated in the data analytics space. There are pioneering algorithms, approaches, platforms, procedures, patterns, and best practices to streamline the task associating with knowledge discovery and dissemination. Practically speaking, a variety of breakthrough methods came up in the last few years towards data production, collection, integration, ingestion, storage, processing, analytics, mining, and visualization. The fields of data science, engineering, and management have acquired special significance due to the tremendous technological growth in data generation and analytics.

AI, comprising machine and deep learning (ML/DL) algorithms, computer vision (CV), and NLP, is emerging as the pioneering one for making sense out of data heaps. Besides IT systems, electronic devices and digitized objects also join mainstream computing. With this movement, zillions of digitized entities, connected devices, and business applications produce a massive amount of multi-structured data. The knowledge extracted from data goes a long way in empowering people, business workloads, and IT services to be intelligent and insightful in their actions. The insights programmatically captured empower all kinds of devices in our home, office, and manufacturing environments to be cognitive in their service deliveries.

The idea is to provide actionable intelligence in time to personal, social, and professional devices, machines, instruments, equipment, appliances, wares, utilities, drones, robots, gears, gadgets, and gizmos intelligent in their actions and reactions. Further on, business workloads and IT services being hosted and run on enterprise and cloud servers enabled through the smart application of cognitive techniques, tricks, and tips. For edge devices to be intelligent in their operations, outputs, and offerings, data analytics and AI capabilities work together to emit trustworthy and timely insights, which get methodically looped back-to-edge devices to exhibit a kind of adaptive behaviour. In short, the arrival of versatile cognitive technology is to decisively, profoundly, and dependably impact and inspire the entire human society. Many people-centric activities are automated and augmented through the intelligence derived out of data. All sorts of operational, analytical, transactional, log, performance, health, and security data are being carefully collected and subjected to various investigations to squeeze out valuable information.

AI-induced predictive, prescriptive, personalized, and prognostic insights in conjunction with real-time insights out of streaming data contribute to intelligent devices, IT systems, networks, and environments. With edge intelligence, edge clouds are also going to be cognitive in their contributions. Edge clouds comprising fewer server machines (bare metal (BM) servers, virtual machines (VMs), and containers) can be near to users to facilitate real-time data capture, analytics, knowledge discovery, and dissemination. With connected devices (predominantly referred to as IoT devices) stuffed with more processing, memory, and storage power, several industry use cases focus on producing device clusters/clouds to achieve bigger and better tasks. Homes, manufacturing floors, hospitals, airports, entertainment plazas, eating joints, stadiums, auditoriums, malls, etc., will be stuffed with IoT devices, which can form ad hoc, purpose-specific, and dynamic clouds. Thus, edge clouds gain momentum to guarantee real-time computing applications and services, real-time insights, and edge intelligence/edge AI/on-device intelligence.

The Significance of the Cloud Paradigm

Cloud-based applications are indeed helping enterprises towards business agility, adaptivity, scalability, and affordability. The proven and potential cloud technologies and tools are being systematically used to have highly optimized and organized IT environments to support the evolving and emerging goals of business houses, academic institutions, government organizations, and establishments. The cloud paradigm has brought a seismic shift in empowering IT to achieve more with less for businesses worldwide. The cloud journey started on a positive note and is on the right track to bring in a bevy of advancements in the IT space. This trend is being categorized as IT industrialization. As we have discussed earlier, there is momentum in leveraging cloud infrastructure for running operational, transactional, analytical, and other enterprise-scale applications. These cloud deployments become simple due to well-defined and matured cloud technologies such as containerization, virtual infrastructure, orchestration, CI/CD, etc.

The virtualization of server machines has laid down a sparkling foundation for the humble origin and the growth of cloud computing. Then came a litany of powerful tools to automate many repetitive and routine tasks associated with servers and server operations. This easy availability of tools sustained the cloud journey further. Now, all kinds of systems and services are virtualized and reaping the virtualization-induced benefits. That is, we read about server, storage, and network virtualization capabilities. The virtualization concept has become a common one to hear about service, security, and data virtualization. Then came the exciting concept of containerization.

Cloud containerization or simply containers are proven to be the perfect compute resource for hosting, running and managing business workloads. Containers are lightweight and hence can guarantee native computing performance. The IT resource utilization has steadily gone up with the assimilation of containerization. There are containerization-enablement platforms to manipulate and manage containers, run comfortably inside VMs and BM servers. Also, lifecycle management platform solutions for containers came along to streamline the various lifecycle activities of containers. The best part of containers is the orchestration and deployment of multi-container applications in the cloud environment.

There are service composition and container orchestration tools to come out with composite, process-aware, and business-critical applications. The container ecosystem is growing fast to eliminate all kinds of development and deployment complexities. Managing containerized workloads is becoming simplified substantially. Resultantly, we will have containerized cloud environments in plenty in the years ahead. The faster maturity and stability of platform solutions such as Kubernetes have speeded up and simplified the adoption of containerization to reap automation and acceleration benefits.

Today many production-grade social, mobile, web, IoT, blockchain, and AI applications are being hosted and run in containerized cloud environments. With the general availability of DevOps toolsets and guidelines, application integration, delivery, deployment, monitoring, and improvement are automated, reducing the time to take software products, solutions, and services to the competitive marketplace. The faster proliferation, the remarkable convergence of microservices with containers, and the steady growth of CI/CD pipelines contribute immensely to the accelerated and frequent deployment of microservices-centric applications. Thus, the aspect of cloud-native computing begins to flourish with the following distinct developments: microservices as the efficient application building-block, containers as the optimal runtime for microservices, service composition and container orchestration platforms, and cloud infrastructures (public, private, and edge).

Thus, the cloudification phenomenon has become the prime strategy for enterprising businesses to steer theirs in the right direction. Translate data into insights so that business houses, government agencies, independent software vendors (ISVs), system integrators (SIs), cloud brokers, service providers and product vendors, and research labs can become insights-driven in their everyday obligations. And Cloud IT infrastructures and platforms are most sought-after for the same reasons.

Briefing Cognitive Computing

Simply speaking, cognitive computing is all about enabling our IT systems, business workloads, and myriads of input and output (I/O) devices to be self-learning and knowledge-filled to assist humans in their everyday works and walks accurately. The creation of self-learning systems was getting speeded up and simplified with the general availability of cutting-edge technologies and tools. The most prominent ones include ML and DL algorithms, pattern recognition, knowledge discovery, CV, and NLP. These technologies help to mirror the way the human brain typically works. The primary purpose of cognitive computing is to create computing systems that can solve complicated problems without constant human oversight. Cognitive computing applies sophisticated and state-of-the-art algorithms on a massive amount of structured, semi structured, and unstructured data to extricate actionable insights in time to bring forth use. These specialized systems converse in an intuitive, informative, and inspiring manner with people and machines. Cognitive computing offers the opportunity to solve some of the biggest challenges that society faces today.

This spectacular and strategic computing idea is penetrating every business vertical these days. It is smartly enabling enterprises better to serve their end users, customers, employees, and partners. Cognitive systems can deliver quick clarifications and interpretations. Cognitive computing techniques allow humans to gain usable intelligence from multi-structured data by uncovering viable patterns and anomalies.

Tasks previously performed by people, such as interpreting doctor's notes, and extracting essential data, can now be performed by cognitive systems with ease.

With the exponential growth of data, the arrival of AI algorithms, and the massive increase of computing power, data processing gets accelerated considerably to uncover and recover hidden patterns, beneficial associations, and fresh opportunities. Cognitive computing can disseminate this data to assist humans in decision making. It can weigh complex, conflicting, and changing information contextually to offer a best-fit solution. For example, a cognitive model may suggest a practical and achievable weight loss plan to manage diabetes.

Cognitive Computing: The Realization Technologies – Cognitive Computing combines different technologies to develop its **Cognitive models**.

Natural Language Processing (NLP) – Natural interfaces emerge as the prime interfacing method for having interaction between machines and humans in the vicinity. Speech recognition and synthesis are the primary components of NLP technology. With these NLP-centric capabilities embedded, cognitive systems can receive, understand, interpret, and offer feedbacks in written and spoken forms. Although this feat is challenging given the considerable variances in human communication, the astounding growth of the **NLP** technology promises a lot for future cognitive solutions. We have AI-backed chatbots and robots, voice-recognition solutions such as Apple Siri, Amazon Alexa, etc. Thus, the NLP paradigm is a prime technology for the intended success of cognitive computing.

Machine Learning (ML) – Today, we systematically teach our computers how to process any input data to produce desired outputs. That means we need to provide input data and the appropriate data processing logic. However, by smartly leveraging the various ML algorithms, we can empower our compute, communication, and IoT edge devices to self-learn from input data. That is, there is no need for explicit programming. However, ML, an exquisite part of the AI domain, is not a simple process. ML algorithms ingest more and more (training) data. It is possible to produce models based on that data, and most of the models are precise. An ML-trained model is the output generated when we train our ML algorithm with data and create predictive models.

In this big data world, ML helps immensely any industry type to make sense of data heaps. More data and training help to arrive more trained and tuned model that, in turn, gives better results. There are a few essential categories in the ML algorithms space.

- Supervised ML algorithms work well when there is a set of data that has explicitly labelled features. For example, you can create an ML application that distinguishes between millions of animals based on images and written descriptions. So, you train one or other supervised ML algorithms using the labelled data to arrive at a retrained and refined ML model. When it receives a fresh set of data like images, the obtained ML model can identify the animal from the image. Based on data and its descriptions, supervised ML algorithms can distinguish, classify, and predict.

- The next category is unsupervised ML algorithms, and it comes in handy where there is a massive amount of raw data, i.e. the data input is unlabelled. For example, Twitter, Instagram, Facebook, Snapchat, and such social media platforms deal with large amounts of unlabelled data. Understanding all that and their meaning requires sophisticated algorithms to go through the supplied data to find unique patterns or form clusters wherein specific data for a fit. So unsupervised ML algorithms perform an iterative process and analyse data without any human interpretation. One widely used application for this type of algorithms is to find spam emails. There are too many variables in legitimate and spam emails to correctly label emails. Therefore, ML algorithms through clustering and association can identify unwanted email.

■ The third category is the reinforcement ML algorithms that is a behavioural learning model. The algorithm may receive feedback from the data analysis and can guide the user to the best outcome. The reinforcement algorithm is different from other ML algorithms where the system doesn't go through the training with the sample data set. Instead, it learns through trials and errors. Therefore, a successful decision depends on the sequence of the reinforced process because it best solves the problem at hand.

Deep learning is also an ML method, but it's unique in a way that employs neural networks (NNs) in successive layers to learn from data iteratively. Deep learning is beneficial when you are trying to learn patterns from unstructured data. Deep learning (complex NNs) designs are to emulate how the human brain works. The idea here is that computers need to deal with poorly defined abstractions and problems by training models. A school-going child can easily recognize the difference between his teacher's face and the face of a security guard. In contrast, the computer must do a lot of work to figure out who is who. Complex NNs often involved in image and speech recognition and CV applications.

The prime advantage of ML algorithms and models is self-learning. That is the real automation in software engineering. ML algorithms can empower any compute device to learn from data and predict outcomes in an automated manner. Just the data is sufficient. However, making devices learning and make a prediction is not straightforward. The way forward is that data scientists have to use suitable ML algorithms, ingesting correct and cleaned data, identifying and using the best performing models. If all these elements come together well, it is worthwhile to continuously train the model using training and testing data and learning from them. The automation of this modelling process and training the model and testing lead to accurate predictions to support the intended business transformation.

Thus, several AI technologies' faster maturity and stability help to confidently and consistently build and use different cognitive systems in our daily lives and obligations. Cognitive solutions and services embed brain-like features into cloud applications, and edge devices help to delegate some of our decision-making activities and assignments. With more data, computing power, and AI algorithms, the days of automated data analytics are closer.

Characterizing Cognitive Systems

The IT domain is facing numerous challenges. Business sentiments are constantly changing, and people's expectations multiply; however, newer technologies keep coming and get widely adopted, IT budgets are being pruned consistently, etc. IT has become the critical business enabler. Today worldwide, businesses are being run on IT, and there is a tighter coupling between business and IT. IT agility, adaptivity, reliability, and versatility directly lead to business agility, adaptivity reliability, and versatility. Once, IT and IT services were seen as cost reduction and optimization, and today IT is being proclaimed as the profit centre for enterprises. This section discusses the key issues prevailing in the business and IT domains and how cognitive computing's faster maturity and stability can comprehensively solve and surmount the prickling issues.

The Key Drivers of Cognitive Computing

As we have discussed in the earlier chapters, digitization and edge technologies contribute to the realization of zillion digital entities. Their connectivity within them is phenomenal. All kinds of physical, mechanical, and electrical systems are digitized to join mainstream computing. Further on, these digitized entities join remotely held, enterprise-scale, event-driven, and service-oriented applications. That is, ordinary, casual, and cheap things in our everyday environments get integrated with the Web content, services, applications, and data sources leading to a projection of such trillions of digitized objects. That is, the future Internet will be composed of such empowered objects. This phenomenon is "the Internet of Things (IoT)". We also discussed earlier and read about the technical term "Cyber Physical Systems (CPS)" very often, CPS are materials at the ground, and they have seamless and spontaneous connectivity with cyber applications. The integration and connectivity between those systems empower physical things to share their unique capabilities and services. Conceptually IoT and CPS remain the same.

Now we come to scores of electronics and embedded devices networked with one another and web applications. Increasingly devices are instrumented to be interconnected, and indeed AI has the necessary abilities to transform connected devices smart. A forecast study claims there will be billions of connected devices in the coming years. Microservices architecture (MSA) and next-generation MSA patterns event-driven architecture (EDA) will make digitized entities, connected devices, and microservices coexist, collaborate, and generate a humungous amount of data. The aspect of information overload is bringing forth many technical challenges.

With multiple data sources emerging and enlarging, global data volumes are growing at an astounding rate. With so much information readily available, the challenge is to make sense of rapidly growing data heaps. Also, companies are trying to make money out of data.

There is an increased insistence for transitioning data into information and into knowledge to discover hidden yet actionable insights out of data. There is a greater awareness and acceptance that increasingly data-driven decisions, deals, and deeds have become the new normal. However, humans find it very difficult to process, analyse, and mine big data to extricate valuable insights as collecting, cleansing, and crunching accumulated data are not an easy task. We need path-breaking technologies and tools to simplify and streamline knowledge discovery and dissemination because the accelerated generation of insights enables business leaders and executives to make strategically sound moves and steer businesses on the right path towards the intended destination.

So, essentially, we need automated solutions to quickly garner, ingest, translate stock, and investigate an enormous amount of static and dynamic data translate to knowledge. Then the knowledge/insights supplied to IT services, business workloads, and even people wielding power to plan and execute. Fortunately, several pioneering methods to automate those mentioned above complicated yet sophisticated tasks, and these technologies are being meticulously combined and named cognitive computing.

Cognitive computing indeed the futuristic and fabulous computing paradigm and they are slicing and sorting through vast quantities of data to provide intelligent recommendations in time. However, they have a massive challenge of slicing and sorting through such voluminous data. As indicated above, cognitive systems have the inherent ability to continue to learn and get better over time with more data and feedbacks in their responses.

Having understood the power of cognitive systems, IBM invests its unique talents, treasure, and time in this promising and potential computing model to be highly suitable and relevant to their esteemed consumers and customers. Expert and recommendation systems are being built across industry verticals and demonstrated. Question and answer (Q & A) systems and chat boxes are being produced using cognitive technologies. There are industry-specific cognitive solutions. Further on, it is all about facilitating taking informed decisions in real time, uncovering hidden yet helpful patterns and insights out of data collections, giving correct answers for tricky and challenging questions quickly, getting newer propositions and theories to ponder about, etc. Thus, the unique contributions of this new computing paradigm are expanding gradually and gleefully.

The Distinct Attributes of Cognitive Computing

Cognitive computing is overwhelmingly nourished through the machine and deep learning algorithms, CV, and NLP capabilities. This fresh computing model is radically transforming the way we interact with the growing content. Our business applications and everyday devices (wearables, portables, mobiles, handhelds, implantable, etc.) are handsomely empowered to be cognitive in their actions and reactions. There is a buzzword "Intelligence at the edge". We are certain even commoner's digital life experience reaches newer heights with pervasive computing, ubiquitous sensing, unified communication, and ambient intelligence. Cognitive computing tools enable traditional computers and leave complex and context-driven problems for human imagination. Further on, experts and subject matter experts (SMEs) are ably and adroitly assisted in their professional assignments by cognitive systems in their specializations.

For sure, it's an incredible journey to acquire knowledge of the various ingredients of this popular computing model. It's not a difficult task either, as there are numerous technologies, state-of-the-art tools, lightweight frameworks, elegant programming languages, appliances and accelerators, etc., to support and sustain cognitive computing. Integrated data analytics platforms, highly optimized and organized IT infrastructures, etc., make cognitive computing deployment and data analytics for cognitive ability simulation much better prospectus. Big data processing gets accomplished in real time through powerful processors, breakthrough chipsets, and advanced algorithms. Multimedia images and multimodal gestures are immediately collected, compared, and crunched to identify any kind of outliers/anomalies. Preventive, predictive, prescriptive, and personalized insights are being extricated and extended in real time to skillfully enable machines and men to be adaptive in their decisions and deeds.

It is typically challenging to write software programs and packages to intelligently process sensory data, such as images, sound, and expressions. Therefore, the way forward is to empower our computers with artistic AI algorithms to do intelligent data processing and mining. Cognitive experts have come out with a few characteristics, as indicated below.

- Cognitive systems have to be adaptive. They must reflect the human brain's unique ability to learn, adapt, and evolve fast according to the changes in the situations and surroundings.
- Cognitive systems have to be extraordinarily dynamic and elegant in gathering and understanding needs and targets. With a series of digital disruption and transformation initiatives across the world, the futuristic cognitive systems have to adequately be empowered to gather multi-structured data from disparate and distributed data sources and subject them to various investigations to emit out information.
- Cognitive systems have to be naturally interactive with men and machines. They have to have the inherent culture, support, financial aids from business entities, government agencies to understand the context and articulate sensibly and accurately.
- Cognitive systems need to be context-sensitive. They have to understand, identify, and extract contextual elements such as syntax and semantics, time, location, process, task, goals, mood, and so on. Every cognitive system has to be self-, surroundings-, and situation-aware to assist and attend to people in their assignments.

The Potentials of Cognitive Technologies

The transition is happening now. Through digitization and edge technologies, everyday systems become digitized methodically. With the flourish of connectivity and integration technologies, we have connected devices in plenty these days. That is, the much-projected IoT era has dawned strikingly. Now the next noteworthy transition is to traverse from connected entities to cognitive artefacts. Soon we will witness our places are having scores of cameras, drones, and robots with cognitive abilities inbuilt. Cognitive cars, aircraft, and crewless aerial vehicles (UAVs) will be a reality in a few years. Various business domains are experimenting and exploring with cognitive computing projects and products. The list is expanding as days pass by. The technologies, processes, architectures, infrastructures, and data are fast maturing to realize cognitive systems that can empower and energize our everyday environments such as homes, hotels, hospitals, etc.

As long as the human imagination continuously expands, the potential use cases for cognitive systems are becoming vast, varied, versatile, and vibrant. *As a result, it is crucial to learn, understand, and evaluate where cognitive systems have viable potentials.* Cognitive computing systems will be ideal when problems are complex, information and circumstances are constantly shifting, and the outcome likely to depend on the context and prevailing situations.

It's no doubt that there will be substantial impacts of the power of big data through the Internet of Things (IoT), the faster maturity and stability of artificial intelligence (AI) algorithms, blockchain technology, and edge/fog computing on the future of humanity. As seen across nations, cognitive computing is already in use, assisting healthcare, banking, and land lease management. Cognitive applications are emerging for making assistive devices for people with disabilities (such as mobility and prosthetic devices). Its use in social services, education, transportation, public safety, the environment, and infrastructure is rising. The cognitive computing model will drastically and dextrously enhance and transform human lives. As cognitive systems continuously learn, intelligently reason, and naturally interact with humans as partners and collaborators, everything in cyberspace, geospace, space, and beyond (CGS) will likely change in the coming years.

It will further allow gathering data from men, machines, matter, and mother earth to draw intelligent predictions and prescriptions. Resultantly, humanity will see the dawn of a new age. Our handheld, portable, wearable, implantable, fixed, nomadic, and mobile devices with human-like cognitive abilities work hand in hand with humans in solving complex problems facing humanity.

Real-life Examples of Cognitive Systems

Today, cognitive computing systems touch every area of our lives, from travel, sports, and entertainment, to fitness, health, and wellness, not just our wellness but for our pets as well. In this section, we'll showcase five trailblazing companies using cognitive computing in various industries. The entrepreneurs and enterprises of today are looking for ways to leverage cognitive computing applications across industry verticals. Their business strategy models indicate some of the ways these technologies will transform our lives in the future.

VantagePoint AI

This is primarily for the finance industry. The pertinent challenges include providing accurate investment recommendations based on facts and data. Searching, buying, investing in the share market has traditionally been a guessing game for several investors. With the help of ML, investors can feel more confident in their investment decisions. VantagePoint is an investment trading software research and development (R & D) organization, and they experimented with forecasting stocks in 12 US sectors, including Energy, Financial, Healthcare, and Technology. VantagePoint helps its users to forecast stocks, futures, commodities, Forex, and ETFs up to an 86% accuracy. A patented NN algorithm predicts changes in market trend up to three days in advance and enabling traders to get in and out of trades at the right time and opportunity.

Welltok

For the healthcare industry, and there are challenges such as providing access to reliable and up-to-date information on healthcare to quote one. If erroneous health information on the Internet wasn't prevalent enough, then land in a situation where it needs to publish with new but often conflicting health research. Understandably these research results make it challenging for many health experts to find accurate answers to any medical questions.

Welltok reduces these gaps. It offers a concierge, AI-enabled tool that can instantly process vast volumes of data to answer questions and make intelligent and personalized recommendations. Welltok's Concierge chatbot built with IBM Watson Health is AI-powered and provides on-demand answers to questions related to health benefits and healthcare costs. Concierge chatbot delivers thousands of conversational responses based on consumer information. Welltok spent years training Watson technology on a few crucial topics to help provide reliable, science-based, and self-service healthcare seekings.

SparkCognition

This company builds AI solutions that unearth the insights living within its customers' data. The company is constantly innovating to create powerful technologies that allow its clients to optimize operations, predict future events, protect their assets, and accelerate their growth. Working closely with a global beverage manufacturer, the company has created and implemented AI systems that quickly address water waste and stop leaks, reducing plant-wide consumption to conserve our planet's most precious resource. Partnering with high-production offshore platform operators, the company has created AI systems that accurately predict impending asset failures, stop catastrophic disasters before they happen, save lives, protect the environment, and improve production. An exciting incident about one of the famous power generation company and its intention to identify and prevent suboptimal operations. The AI solution detected an anomaly that enabled critical event detection a month in advance, avoiding catastrophic failure and costly repairs. Unexpected asset failures and the high maintenance cost prevent crews from getting their aircraft up in the sky. SparkCognition's AI solutions anticipate mechanical asset breakdowns in advance so crew members can keep aircraft off the ground.

Expert System

Using the Cogito for the semantic search and analysis of strategic data, Eni, the energy company, improved the internal management of its knowledge assets and retrieved information significantly and provided advanced research to monitor external sources of information.

The American Society for Cell Biology (ASCB) wanted to enable its members with a value-added information service portal that enables rapid analysis and accelerates the various stages of research. Expert System's user-friendly Biopharma Navigator portal was the choice opted by ASCB. Biopharma Navigator collects and aggregates information from millions of scientific publications and press releases results in biomedical researcher's interests. The portal provides a unique space for them to discover relevant signals and direct them to future research through a dashboard that utilizes a dynamic display of widgets.

Expert System and SANOFI conducted a conference in which pharmaceutical and biotech executives engaged in discussions regarding the barriers to finding missions critical information and the challenges of analysing disparate data for better decision making.

The AI company **expert.ai** and **UTWIN**, the 100% digital brokerage and management platform for insurance solutions, established a partnership to enhance UTWIN's underwriting activities by leveraging the advanced capabilities of Expert System's AI platform. This platform leverages natural language understanding to process information most entirely and accurately possible. It combines the ability to comprehend textual details with the power, flexibility, and scalability required by today's businesses while also offering relevant cost-benefit advantages.

Microsoft Cognitive Services

Businesses have to meet a requirement to review and catalogue hundreds of thousands of hours of recorded calls. It's a challenge KPMG, which used Microsoft Azure Cognitive Services, is helping financial institutions solve with AI. Microsoft Azure Cognitive Services helps in building risk analytics solutions. This solution uses AI to streamline call transcription, translation, and fraud analytics, cutting time, cost, and effort by as much as 80%.

Numenta's deep experience in theoretical neuroscience research has led to tremendous discoveries about how the brain works. It has developed a framework called the Thousand Brains Theory of Intelligence that is fundamental to advancing AI. By applying intelligence theory to existing deep learning systems, the company addresses today's bottlenecks while enabling tomorrow's applications. However, deep learning systems have demonstrated notable achievements it also facing scalability problems and can't manage them with adding more data and power. Think of an approach that human would do; The human brain typically stores and processes information in a highly sparse manner. Numenta understands sparsity, a foundational element of the Thousand Brains Theory. The company has created a technology demonstration that validates sparse networks on inference tasks can unlock **groundbreaking performance gains of more than 50x** in deep learning networks with no loss of accuracy.

DeepMind

Vision loss among the elderly is a prevalent healthcare issue. Age-related macular degeneration (AMD) is one of the common causes of blindness in the developed world. The "dry" form is relatively common among elders and over 65 and causes only mild sight loss. However, in some cases, about 15% of patients with dry AMD develop a more severe form of the disease – exudative AMD, resulting in rapid and permanent loss of sight. Predicting which patients will progress to exAMD is a considerable challenge. DeepMind has come out with an answer, and it has published a research paper.

Cognitive Computing: The Benefits

We have compiled and presented some more incredible benefits of cognitive computing through real-life use cases. Experts have envisioned the sparkling competencies of cognitive systems and explained them to as given below.

Automated Data Analytics

Without an iota of doubt, this is a big data era. Every industry type generates a massive amount of multi-structured data. For an example, take the healthcare industry. Cognitive systems can collate readings and reports from disparate sources such as medical journals, patient history, diagnostic tools, and documentation of similar lines of treatment adopted in the past. These valuable and usable details are typically anonymized and acquired from worldwide hospitals and medical care centres.

Cognitive systems can provide the physician with data-driven insights and evidence-based recommendations that can significantly enhance patient care. The point is that the cognitive model does not replace human doctors. Instead, it can reliably assist caregivers, surgeons, and specialists in making informed decisions. The big job of sifting through exponentially exploding data volumes and logically processing them happens through breakthrough cognitive systems. Such cognition-enabled tools come in handy for hospitals and clinics in contemplating the right course of diagnoses and medications for their patients in time. IBM Watson Health helps solve some of the world's most pressing health challenges through data, analytics, and AI. By combining human experts with augmented intelligence, IBM Watson Health helps health professionals and researchers around the world translate data and knowledge into insights to make more informed decisions about care in hundreds of hospitals and health organizations.

Process Optimization

Process integration and orchestration are critical factors for any business category to grow and glow. Process rationalization and simplification have been a constant and cheerful endeavour for enterprising businesses to innovate and disrupt continuously. Business processes manage complex activities while also supporting continuous awareness of business conditions to inform real-time decision making, which requires a seamless partnership between humans and the machine environments they operate.

Business process management (BPM) experts study, recognize, manage, optimize, and monitor business processes that support enterprise goals. Over the years, these activities have evolved significantly to include systems that can learn at scale, employ logic and reason, and interact naturally with human beings. A cognitive process makes BPM more dynamic and probabilistic by enabling decision management systems to understand, evaluate, and comprehend business events. For instance, cognitive data management can fuel process automation via ML algorithms. Combining business processes with ML produces cognitive solutions that can enhance customer experiences. These solutions compare the data that business activity generates with data from other sources and enable dynamic and timely decision making.

For example, in a predictive maintenance process, ML algorithms to sensor data to predict whether there is an imminent breakdown. Cognitive computing helps to identify and take action based on emerging patterns. It also helps spot opportunities and uncovers issues in real time for a faster and correct response, resulting in process efficiency leading to better productivity.

Businesses will be able to ingest and process a massive amount of poly-structured data, monitor their operations and workflow, and quickly make the right decisions. Further on, businesses can learn from, adapt to, and even predict strategically sound changes. Precisely speaking, cognitive systems can learn continuously to bring in better accuracy in their decisions, answers, predictions, and prescriptions.

Cognitive automation leverages emerging technologies such as NLP, text analytics, data mining, and ML. The integration of different AI capabilities with robotic process automation (RPA) helps organizations extend automation to complex processes. It also takes not only structured data but also unstructured data into consideration. Unstructured information such as customer conversations and interactions can be easily analysed, processed, and structured into data helpful in deeper analytics such as predictive analytics. Cognitive automation creates new efficiencies and, at the same time, improves the quality of business as well. Organizations in every industry keep and drive cognitive automation at the core of their digital and business transformation strategies.

The advantages of cognitive automation include improved compliance and business quality, operational scalability at a better level, reduced turnaround, and impeccable lower error rates leading to a positive impact on business flexibility and employee efficiency.

Better Level of Customer Interactions

Companies is starting to realize the benefits of integrating cognitive technologies into their business processes. They have the potential to enhance customer experiences as well as lessen operational costs, enabling enterprises to drive efficiency. The customer experience (CX) has always been at the centre stage of every company's growth strategy. Cognitive technologies have evolved tremendously in the recent past, driving a significant transformation to online and offline customer experiences.

Natural interfaces are everywhere. Especially human-machine interaction (HMI) must be through speech, gestures, emotions, facial expressions, etc. HMI has become an exciting domain of study and research. Cognitive chatbots and robots are enabling enthralling experience for customers.

Cognitive Assistants Automate Customer Care

Unlike touch-tone and IVR systems, cognitive assistants simulate live agents. They mimic how the human brain works by mining data, recognizing patterns, and learning from experience. They offer personalized interaction through natural languages. They are emotionally intelligent. They detect sentiment and respond appropriately to tone of voice. They know from experience and improve over time. Cognitive assistants are also fast, accurate, and versatile. They become experts and scale the expertise of live agents by repeated training. They tailor interactions based on call history, purchase history, and other data to establish patterns of care.

Deeper Human Engagement and Personalization

Cognitive systems can take all data available to have personal and context-aware interactions with humans. Our web interactions, commercial transactions history, sensor data from our everyday places (homes, offices, hospitals, hotels, cities, etc.), and other value-adding data get meticulously collected, cleansed, and crunched by cognitive applications to generate personalized and predictive insights in time. By continuously collecting data and learning from them, cognitive systems gain the inherent capability to be faithful and trustworthy servant to us.

Enhanced Expertise and Knowledge Processing

By leveraging cognitive systems, humans will keep pace with the explosion of data. Any amount of data can get collected and transitioned to information and knowledge, and then the projected knowledge become decisive assistance of cognitive systems. Men find it time-consuming and tedious to make sense of big data. Still, the complexity associated with knowledge discovery and dissemination gets greatly simplified with cognitive platforms. Cognitive systems become an always-on companion that professionals can use to access and process all of the latest information quickly.

Products and Services to Sense and Think

The cognition system transitions ordinary assets to excellent articles. Cognitive products are capable of sensing, reasoning, and learning about their users and their surroundings. Cognitive systems to identify patterns develop hypotheses from vast mountains of data. This capability will help companies accelerate R&D and innovation in fields like pharmaceuticals, materials science, and even mobile start-ups. A few products to quote on sense and think are self-driving cars, robots, drones, smart homes, hotels, etc.

These advantages indicate the massive potential that cognitive computing intrinsically possesses. Embracing at an early stage will help the business experiment and personalize cognitive computing's tremendous power to deliver incredible gains to your business.

The Prominent Use Cases of Cognitive Computing

Cognitive computing refers to a pack of AI technologies to empower our simple machines to mimic human understanding of the environment. We have discussed various use cases across chapters, and we discuss two more prominent use cases here in this section. These use cases bring an immense level of contextualization and intelligence to business processes. Cognitive computing has brought the power of AI models to enterprises across the globe, and they help in better decisions and at a lightning pace. Combined with the cloud managed services and infrastructure, the cognitive computing becomes more accessible and easy to implement. While the strategic contributions of this computing model are well understood, industries and organizations are keenly strategizing and planning to have the cognitive capability.

This section throws some light on the various domains surging ahead with this futuristic technology.

- **Financial services** – With a large amount of data pouring in from multiple sources, investment managers have a tough job at hand. They must quickly take correct and competent decisions on when and where to invest clients' funds in a highly volatile yet profitable stock market. Cognitive computing can provide relevant and reliable investment recommendations to financial and fund managers by swiftly going through tens of millions of pages of documents. Cognitive systems can rapidly explore available market intelligence, risk profiles, and economic profile data to make correct decisions.
- **Healthcare industry** – This is another popular domain wherein the irresistible cognitive computing model is showing glimmering glimpses. Several stakeholders (doctors, surgeons, research scientists, insurers, patients, nurses, OEMs, etc.) find this unique technology beneficial to bring profound advancements in delivering technologically advanced care in the healthcare industry. Research papers published in the past five or six decades in the medical field have enormous insights. By examining and use of those insights, cognitive computers swiftly recommend correct medical analyses and answers. The medical field is ready for a massive shift and immensely benefit from all advancements in cognitive computing.

Several other business verticals are embracing this illustrious technology to be constructive and competitive in their obligations. Any domain stuffed with a tremendous amount of data can benefit immeasurably through the aspect of cognition enablement. In the big data era, real-time knowledge discovery and dissemination become possible through cognitive systems. All the industrial applications need this paradigm shift to be adaptive, agile, and adept. Several practical use cases have emerged and raised significant enthusiasm amongst business executives, enterprise architects, and academic professors.

Tending towards Cognitive Analytics

Many businesses started to use cognitive applications to connect with their customers and other stakeholders to supply personalized recommendations and prescriptive insights. Such applications can automatically modify or enhance the already delivered recommendations as they continuously learn from new data and experiences. With a more profound and decisive understanding of users and their prevailing situation, cognitive machines can bring forth situation-aware and sophisticated services to humans, i.e. automated analytical activities through cognitive systems. The traditional analytics capability sorely misses the much-needed automation and continuous learning. For cognitive analytics, just input data is sufficient to work with and to emit out helpful information. On the other hand, conventional analytics systems need systematic instruction with detailed data to do what the system has to do with any input.

IBM Watson is the earliest manifestation of a decent cognitive computing platform. The power of this platform is getting intense focus through a host of use cases across multiple business verticals. Healthcare is the first domain, which is getting accentuated and advanced through the smart leverage of this cognitive platform solution. Several medical conditions include patient history, symptoms, allergies, research papers and guides, previous diagnoses, prescriptions and responses, best practices, side effects, and so on. The cognitive computing platform collects, collates, and correlates the entire gamut of knowledge around any medical conditions and the ability to recommend life-savings measures, prescriptions, and healthcare solutions. Due to the rapid growth of disease and medication data, information, and knowledge, it is generally impossible for human doctors to read through all to come out with sound decisions. Herein, cognitive machines come in handy in assisting and articulating the correct way to human doctors; otherwise, it's usually a highly stressful task for them.

The difference that cognitive platforms bring to medical professionals and patients is the no more guesswork and decisions based on minimal knowledge or incomplete information. There are no intuition-based choices as they are bound to go forever. But it is going to be data-driven insights and insights-driven decisions and actions. There is a technology-enabled and significant upgrade in the medical world. With the faster stability and maturity, cognitive analytics of all kinds of data is gaining prominence and dominance. The insights being made available through cognitive computing empower fresher doctors to perform as effectively as experienced ones.

Miscellaneous Applications

The other well-known cognitive computing applications are to produce improved consumer behaviour analysis, facilitate personal shopping bots, etc. Besides chatbots, there are scores of human-like and concierge robots in conference halls, hotel lobbies, and other important junctions such as airports, railway stations, etc. These cognition-enabled robots can answer our situation-specific queries and interact with us in natural languages. Drone technology through cognitive techniques and tools are now a familiar scene across industry verticals.

Cognitive search is one grandiose application of cognitive computing. Automation of repetitive and redundant tasks, business processes optimization and automation, governance, management, maintenance, security, and sustenance of IT operations happens through cognitive computing technologies. For instance, a packaged goods company has applied the power of cognitive computing to resolve customer problems automatically, which led to substantial savings. The best way forward for any enterprise to enter and embrace this path-breaking field is to start with developing and deploying a few purpose-specific cognitive systems. From the customer experiences and feedbacks, enterprise-wide adoption can begin with all the clarity and confidence.

Cognitive Clouds

A brand new application of cognitive computing, with the IT budgets, is in continuous scrutiny, prunes the IT division of business enterprises, and searches for unearthing viable IT optimization methods to achieve more with less. This optimization is achievable by bringing forth cloud solutions and services for enabling the business automation, acceleration, and augmentation goals. Combining cloud with cognitive computing allows cloud infrastructures and workloads to become better in their operations, offerings, and outputs through ingraining the various cognitive capabilities that is the crucial challenge for IT pioneers, practitioners, and pundits in the years ahead. In this section, we write about the key drivers and differentiators of next-generation cognitive clouds.

Describing the Cloud Journey

The public cloud infrastructure, edge computing, multi-cloud, joint cloud providers, serverless and several such innovations and inventions in the cloud space become a curious journey for us in the coming days. A study reveals that around 85% of software applications run in cloud environments very soon. In this section, we are to discuss the spectacular cloud journey.

Virtualized and Managed Clouds

Physical machines become software managed several VMs by partitioning. With the phenomenal acceptance of hypervisors/virtual machine monitors (VMMs) as the cloud-enabling software solution. Other automated tools such as VMWare ESXi, Microsoft Hyper-V, Oracle Virtual Box, and RedHat KVM, hypervisors are innately assisting in quick and easy provisioning and de-provisioning monitoring, measuring, management, migration, and maintenance of VMs. VMs are the new IT resource to host and manage various applications/workloads. Hardware programming through virtualization made the deployments scale exponentially. Besides creating VMs out of physical servers or boxes, the virtualization concept has improved upon a lot these days to manipulate fine-grained resources such as memory, processing, and storage to optimize resources for running software application components.

Then there came many industry-strength tools for automating and accelerating various tasks associated with the administration and operation of cloud centres. Standardized toolsets empower job/task/workflow scheduling, load balancing, workload-enablement (assessment, modernization, consolidation, and migration) to be deployed in clouds, resource provisioning and placement, cloud integration, and orchestration, configuration management, governance and security, continuous integration, delivery, and deployment by the advancements in the DevOps space, etc. OpenStack is the leading cloud management platform in transitioning traditional IT environments to large-scale public and private clouds. Hybrid clouds are the latest buzzword, and the OpenStack platform is turning out to be the key ingredient in realizing and sustaining hybrid clouds.

Cloud brokers provide a centralized and integrated dashboard that smartly activates and manages distributed cloud resources and applications for consumers. That is, brokers fulfil the long-standing goal of distributed deployment of cloud resources, but they facilitate central management. Consumers only connect and interact with the cloud broker, which brings in an assortment of automation for provisioning and arranging appropriate cloud resources out of heterogeneous cloud services. IT infrastructures had been a closed, monolithic, inflexible, and black box. With the rapid maturity of the virtualization and automation techniques and availability of IT-centric tools, present-day IT infrastructures are becoming programmable, exposable (discovery), cohesive (compose), manageable, and amenable. That is the first-generation cloud environments.

Software-defined Clouds

Not only servers but also the networking and storage solutions need segregation (compartmentalized) to enhance their functional flexibility and utilization. All the embedded intelligence on network solutions and storage appliances are meticulously abstracted and separated through standardized software controllers. The transition ensures network and storage modules becoming commoditized to be remotely activated, augmented, aggregated, replaced, and controlled. There are network and storage hypervisors to speed up the process of having software controllers. That is, hardware modules are being software defined and software-defined clouds. We, therefore, hear, read, and experience software-defined compute storage and networking capabilities. As we know, maximum automation, enhanced elasticity, policy-based manoeuvre-ability, software-enabled monitoring, visibility, controllability, security, and so on, are making software-defined clouds adoption more interesting.

Containerized Clouds

Now, there are several shifts in running cloud centres with the emergence of lightweight containers. Real-time and horizontal application scalability through containers, system portability, high availability through redundant containers, greater resource utilization, etc., are being accrued out of the containerization movement. The need and aspects of virtualization and containerization could guarantee resource availability and elasticity, application scalability, and infrastructure and workload optimization. There are two key trends. Firstly, both legacy and modern software applications are leveraging microservices architecture and ready for cloud deployment. Secondly, there is a highly beneficial convergence of containers and microservices. Due to containers' lightweight and redundant nature, the number of containers for a workload significantly increases. Thus, in a cloud environment, containers are densely populated. This increase results in operational and management complexities of containerized clouds.

The emergence of container cluster, orchestration, and management platforms such as Kubernetes help in automation to simplify and streamline the aspect of containerization. There are service mesh solutions to guarantee service resiliency, which ultimately leads to reliable systems. Serverless computing through containers makes independent functions a separately deployable unit, and hence functions emerge as the new unit of application development and deployment. Function as a service (FaaS) is a new buzzword in the cloud industry. The serverless idea is creating a lot of interest amongst computer science and IT professionals. Installing and managing Kubernetes used to be a challenging task. However, many cloud providers provide Kubernetes as a managed service, making serverless computing famous.

Thus, there are a few noteworthy advancements in the form of federated clouds and purpose-specific clouds such as device, mobile, knowledge, data, and science clouds. The cloud journey is in the right direction towards the destination of the

Intercloud. Thereby the goal of composable and cognitive businesses rafts with breakthrough inventions, innovations, and improvisations in the cloud space. Like the Internet, the era of the Intercloud is beckoning upon us.

Envisioning Cognitive Clouds

The next innovation in the cloud movement is the realization of cognitive cloud environments. There are several scenarios wherein the relevance of cognitive clouds is widely deliberated and deciphered. For the next era of knowledge-centric services, every common and casual thing must meticulously digitized and smart. Every kind of electronics must be wiser to unequivocally assist humans in being competent in their everyday decisions and deeds. These disruptions and transformations are enabling the realization of people-centric, context-aware, insights-driven, and service-oriented applications. As the cloud will be one-stop IT infrastructure for business transformation, every contributing component of the futuristic cloud environment must be innately cognitive. The infrastructure, modules, and workloads need to be incisively analytical, self-learning, intelligent decision-making, and adaptive. Their decisions and deliveries are the most sought-after requirement to have cognitive clouds. That is, cognitive clouds are bound to play a stellar role in shaping up the transition from ordinary to extraordinary organizations. Especially for the promised brighter world, the contributions of cognitive clouds are more outstanding. Let us discuss the associated terms.

1. **Cognitive computing** is a new field of research and study primarily for establishing next-generation information systems and applications that can intrinsically sense, model, train, hypothesize through evidence, think, comprehend, answer, and act. These systems are different from the traditional algorithmic computing that simply ingests and processes input data and then outputs result without understanding the data's real context. Therefore, the strategic goal of cognitive computing is to endow our everyday computing systems to be context-aware. The context details enable computing and communication systems to be creative in their operations and outputs. The idea behind cognitive computing is making the next-gen computing paradigm that copiously mimics the human brain. It binds with NLP capability. It creates models to infer and bring forth evidence-based hypotheses, learns from the experience, interacts with humans more naturally, and helps in making appropriate decisions based on what they know. In short, all the advancements in cognitive computing are to result in pioneering cognitive systems across industry verticals.

2. **Cognitive applications and services** – Cognition is being branded as the next-generation capability for industry-generic and specific applications. Different verticals vie for astutely embedding this unique feature into their systems. Applications need to have the inherent power to capture data and learn, think, and generate answers and decisions. They are hypersensitive and responsive. There are cognitive application development platforms to simplify and streamline cognitive application building and sustenance. With cognitive analytics becoming the mainstream feature, next-generation applications need to be cognitively sound and rational.

3. **Cognitive analytics** is the real-time analytics of data (big and streaming) in a cognitive fashion. Machines can learn and predict out of data heaps quickly. The devices and even deep learning algorithms are purposefully plentiful to empower every decision-enabling system and services to self-learn and express the discovered knowledge. It is about extracting insights in time to endow our everyday systems to behave deftly. The situation-awareness feature everywhere to enable software systems to exhibit a kind of intelligent behaviour. The challenging domain of cognitive analytics emerges as the foremost requirement for next-generation business and IT systems to be skillfully and spontaneously shrewd in their actions and reactions. For any system to evolve, the learning and analytics capability is the most mandated one.

4. **Cognitive platforms** are the most sought-after tool for simplifying and speeding up the realization of mental services and applications. Model-driven software development, service composition (orchestration and choreography), governance, security, policy-awareness, etc., must be facilitated by the platform. Agent-like services and service-oriented agents will be the building block for building, integrating, and delivering cognitive applications. Like OpenStack for managed clouds, we need intelligent management platform solutions for cognitive cloud environments. Also, for extricating real-time and actionable insights, the platform has to have predictive, prescriptive, and personalized analytics capabilities.

5. **Cognitive cloud infrastructures** will be the most advanced form of clouds with several hitherto unforeseen competencies. The infrastructural resources and business workloads must be intrinsically cognitive. The log, operational, scalability, performance, and security insights emitted by analytics solutions must empower cloud infra modules and applications to be intelligent in their actions and reactions.

Cognitive systems are innately more intuitive and inspiring in the sense that they are capable of self-learning, modelling, training, hypothesizing, processing, analysing, and mining poly-structured data to extricate and extrapolate actionable insights in real time. Further on, these are naturally interfacing with their users. Traditionally, we need to write different queries and applications to interact with scores of analytical systems. In contrast, cognitive systems capabilities help automate knowledge engineering, corroboration, correlation, and dissemination. Data and its real-time analytics with critical support from AI algorithms and platforms are essential to cognitive clouds' intended success.

The Need for Integrated Cognitive Platforms

As indicated above, OpenStack-like cloud management and operating platform play a vital role in bringing down the complexities of cloud centres. The realization of managed clouds is increasingly made possible with such an industry-strength and standard-compliant platform. Now for cognitive clouds, the significance of an integrated cognitive platform is bound to escalate in the days ahead. The cognitive platform intrinsically enables all kinds of cloud infrastructures to be cognitive. The platform collects all sorts of data from various cloud infrastructures, business workloads, IT services such as platforms, middleware, databases, and others, precisely learns and understands what is in store, accordingly articulates the necessary actions to be taken to the concerned in time. The insights from the cognitive platform then disseminated to IT administrators and even IT systems to empower them to ponder the best way forward and proceed with the right actions quickly. The cognition-enabled clouds provide a stream of premium and path-breaking services to clients and customers, fulfilling all the agreed non-functional requirements/the quality of services (QoS) and experiences (QoE) attributes envisioned.

The cognitive platform is etched and enriched with best-in-class cognitive techniques and tools that collectively come in handy in realizing futuristic and flexible cognitive clouds. Currently, there are various analytical platforms and services in cloud environments for big, fast, and streaming data capture, processing, analysis, and knowledge extraction. The proposed cognitive platform has to be work with these analytical engines to be a one-stop platform solution for setting up and sustaining cognitive clouds. Not only server-centric clouds but there will also be device-centric edge clouds in plenty. Edge or fog device clouds gain a lot of attention and attraction as they have the intrinsic power to facilitate real-time and real-world applications. Edge clouds will be prevalent in the days to unfurl for real-time data capture and processing and faster response of the squeezed knowledge. Precisely speaking, any cognitive platform has to be modular, versatile, and resilient enough to be accommodated not only in massive clouds but also in ad hoc, localized, and device-centric fog clouds.

Illustrating Cognitive Capabilities for Next-generation Clouds

At the infrastructural level, all kinds of resources will become cognitive because they can be elegantly elastic to fulfil the varying needs of workloads. That is, cloud infrastructures become workloads aware. The scalability, availability, reliability, and security needs of applications are taken care of automatically through a cognitive platform. They can accurately predict and prepare every participating and contributing resource for meeting the widely fluctuating demands of workloads (the variation in sizes of data to be processed and the spike in the number of users). The cognitive analytics on the log, performance, health condition, security, operational, and transactional data emits actionable insights.

Further on, resource utilization, energy consumption, heat dissipation, task and resource scheduling, and other decision-enabling data are meticulously collected and analysed to extract actionable insights in time; a Long way to empower IT resources in meeting service-level agreements (SLAs). Diagnostic and deterministic intelligence and predictive, prognostic, and prescriptive insights will emerge to automate several tasks. There are many distinctive advantages to having technologically advanced cognitive cloud environments. The key ones include preventive and predictive maintenance, optimal load-balancing, job and resource scheduling, and autoscaling besides self-configuration, diagnosing, healing, managing, and protection capabilities.

At the workloads layer, it is all about making workloads aware of the underlying infrastructures. Infrastructure modules need to be elegantly elastic enough to ensure the agreed-upon service levels between cloud providers and users. The additional resources are available on-demand, and the configuration changes have to occur automatically based on the policies and insights derived. Compute, storage, and networking modules and other prominent solutions such as cloud integrator/intermediary/broker, cloud orchestrator, cost estimator, cloud migrator, etc., need to be equipped with relevant knowledge act intelligently on time.

- **Dynamic Capacity Planning and Management** – Understanding and predicting the capacity requirements on the fly is the crucial requirement to avoid any kind of wastage of expensive IT resources. The capability of acquiring the runtime knowledge of varying capacity needs succulently empowers cloud resources management in an optimized fashion through a bevy of automated tools. Policy-centricity is a vital characteristic for operationalizing cloud centres in an efficient way. The cognitive platform is an essential module towards runtime and automated capacity planning and provisioning while ensuring high performance and heightened energy efficiency.
- **Automated Workflow and Resource Scheduling** – Business-critical applications involve well-intended workflows. Different tasks need different schedules and execute in a sequence to accomplish business goals within all the identified and indicated constraints. Resources allocation for identified errands based on evolving priorities. That is, the skilled implementation of synchronized activities is critical for the cloud idea to be sustained. Tasks enshrined in business processes methodical execution through appropriate resources within the stipulated time. Thus identifying, provisioning, and configuring the most suitable cloud infrastructures for executing microservices needs to be fully automated. The cognitive platform can do this job deftly and decisively.
- **Intelligent Workload and Resource Placement** – There are a set of VMs and containers to execute microservices and their instances. As indicated elsewhere, software solutions are rolling out as a collection of distributed microservices. The challenge is how efficiently IT resources can be discovered and allocated for executing microservices. Also, it's essential for the workloads placed in a minimum or optimum number of physical servers to cut capital and operational costs. Plus, the energy consumption has to come down, so that heat dissipation goes down subsequently. Cognitive clouds can leverage intelligent algorithms and approaches to learn and understand the situation to make accurate predictions and prescriptions. Thus, along with IT optimization, workload optimization plays a significant role in making cloud cognitive.
- **Log and Operational Analytics** – In large-scale IT environments, there will be massive log contents with transactional and operational data. They need to be carefully collected and subjected to various investigations to understand the various operational aspects of infrastructure modules and applications. The knowledge attained goes a long way in taking timely countermeasures to stop any breakdown and slowdown. The cognitive platform must have seamless and smooth integration with various analytical tools to realize cognitive clouds. Similarly, infrastructure capacity, scalability, and availability need to be fulfilled dynamically through the intense analysis of system data (historical and current).

■ **Performance & Security Analytics** – Similarly, the performance of each of the workloads can be pre-emptively understood, and this helps administrators and even systems to indulge in tuning and tweaking to claw back to the desired performance level. Security data leads to security insights that systems can leverage to take adequate steps promptly to stop any kind of security-related risks.

■ **Predictive, Prescriptive, and Personalized Analytics** – The advancements in the AI space have laid down a stimulating foundation for predictive and prescriptive insights. Now machine and deep learning techniques are leveraged with confidence to elevate the domain of predictive analytics significantly. Empowering machines to learn on their own is a kind of automated analytics.

■ **Cognitive IoT** – As we all know, the IoT discipline is the way forward for the splendid realization of the planet vision. The projected trillions of digitized assets in association with billions of connected devices and millions of microservices are the fulcrum for the next era of computing. The direct fallout of these trends and transitions is the exponential growth of data with the purposeful interactions and collaborations among various IoT sensors and devices. ML is the most appropriate way for automating the process of extracting pragmatic insights out of IoT data. Cognitive platforms such as IBM Watson have the required capacity and capability to learn, model, train, process, mine, and analyse such a heavy load of data to spit out knowledge.

■ Cloud security has been a critical barrier for institutions and individuals to embrace the fast-growing cloud phenomenon. Several algorithms and approaches are proposed and promoted to ensure the utmost security for cloud data, applications, network, and infrastructure. The combination of crypto-anchors and blockchain technology is keeping momentum for ensuring heightened cloud security. As per IBM, the crypto anchors are smaller than a grain of salt. They contain several hundred thousand transistors and will cost less than ten cents to manufacture. They can monitor, analyse, communicate, and even act on data.

■ **Insights as a Service (IaaS)** – Assembling and analysing an enormous amount of data realized through clustered and cloud resources. Performing real-time processing of big data with algorithmic and IT challenges is beset. Now with cognitive systems, analysing big data in real time is being made possible.

Cognitive Cloud Autoscaling

Cognitive autoscaling in cloud computing is more of deployment of cognitive applications in safety-critical systems, futuristic networking architectures, and virtualized resource management. Today's autoscaling solutions utilize control loops, where the observed metric values of the system in conjunction with deployment policies and determine the actions for autoscaling. The deployment policies are configuration driven, and most of the time it's pre-configured. ML-inspired solutions sharply improve autoscaling by predicting future measured values of the system. Cognitive orchestration is ML-driven orchestration where the orchestrator can handle decision making, reasoning, and problem-solving independently.

Metric value-based scaling has been a popular approach in established autoscaling solutions. Generally, autoscaling solutions perform well. However, it does have several challenges, especially during abnormal behaviour. State detection outper-forms value observation in autoscaling.

■ State detection gives a more holistic view of the state of the system, which means that we can differentiate many states, and for instance, non-availability of service due to the high demand of the service is an anomaly.
■ State detection allows pro-active and early detection of anomalies without mak-ing any assumptions about the future, and multidimensional metric data-based decisions, which is more accurate than decisions based on evaluating future values of the system.
■ Value-based autoscaling is vulnerable to many such anomalies; an example could be the measurement of errors and runtime failures.

In a recent stress test, Ericsson implemented ML-driven orchestration and proac-tively took actions based on the detected computational state before the levels of individual system metrics had significantly diverged. This action has enhanced the resource efficiency and the quality of the cloud-based services by taking the ML advantages.

Subsequently, the researchers have compared the performance of their cognitive solution against a traditional value-based autoscaling solution. As a part of this activ-ity, they conducted a ten-hour stress test on a web server autoscaled by the two solu-tions in a cloud environment. The results were on the expected lines. Their proposed cognitive autoscaling solution based on state detection performs ten times better than the value-based autoscaling solution.

Cognitive Cryptography

Cryptographic techniques are to secure information and restrict access to it. Securing the data is mainly aimed at protecting it from theft. Theft means unauthorized indi-viduals (systems) accessing information and using it when they are not intended or allowed. Every piece of information is thus subject to protection if it is confidential and critical data. Cryptographic protocols help to protect the data from unauthor-ized or accidental access. Data security is a necessary element in the operation of various information exchange processes. Here comes the class of cryptographic protocols.

■ **Data split protocols** – This class includes cryptographic protocols allowing the secret information breaks (split) between a group of n participants. Every participant receives one part of the secret (shadow). Each separate shadow is useless on its own because it contains no complete information. All portions of the secret must be combined to reconstruct the secret. Hence, to retrieve the secret information, all protocol participants must be in complete agreement.
■ **Data sharing protocols** – This group includes cryptographic protocols that allow the secret to split between a group of n participants. To retrieve the secret, m (m < n) parts of all n combine (regroup) to one. Each shadow does not contain any complete information, but to retrieve the secret (entire content),

then the required number of shadows need to be combined. In this case, to retrieve the concealed information, it is necessary for a specific group of secret trustees, the m of n participants must agree.

However, these have certain drawbacks, such as generating empty shadows and assigning them to protocol participants without knowing the contents of the shadows they receive. In the case of data sharing protocols, a kind of consent between a selected group of secret trustees is also possible, resulting in them deciding about the fate of the data they have entrusted with or without the knowledge and agreement of the remaining participants. It is necessary to introduce the ability to randomly select protocol participants who can reconstruct the secret information to eliminate those threats. Then, no participants will know whether, in the given protocol, they are appointed as a trustee deciding about the fate of the data or not. Cognitive cryptography provides an innovative mechanism to eliminate those threats.

Cognitive cryptography is to improve personal identification processes using personal information for each protocol participant. Individual biometrics sets describing the biometric features of each protocol participant contains individual's confidential information. Because of the nature of biometrics, they constitute personal, unique information that unambiguously characterizes their owner. So individual and unique nature of biometric features is very significant both from the scientific and the practical perspective to use biometrics for personal identification and verification. Thus, cognitive cryptography is a novel approach to securing data using the individual's features of each protocol participant. Personal information in individual biometrics is used during personal identification to assign biometric traits to the right person correctly. Then, assess whether the biometric features characterize the right person or whether they belong to another protocol participant or even to an unknown individual during personal verification.

After identifying the characteristic biometric features, the information is concealed by splitting it and distributing the secret data segments among the protocol participants. At this stage, protocol participants involve in biometric verification by comparing their features with the patterns stored in the base. If the biometric characteristic for the given protocol participant complies with the pattern corresponding to that participant, the verification process is successful. As a result, the protocol participant assigned with a part of the secret (shadow). Otherwise, when there is no compliance between the characteristic biometric of the recipient and the pattern stored for them, the verification process fails. The participant cannot be assigned one of the parts of the split secret (shadow).

Thus, for intelligent information management, cognitive techniques are being increasingly leveraged.

Conclusion

Cognitive systems built to learn from data and adapt their processing accordingly automatically. They extract insights from content, offer context-specific responses and guidance, and learn through iterative feedback cycles. A converged and centralized cognitive platform is the need of the hour to enable various IT modules and resources to be insightfully capable of crunching all kinds of social, personal, professional, and machine data to answer users' questions precisely naturally. The world is to see the next set of erudite applications. The service ecosystem is to grow. There will be fresh possibilities and opportunities galore to provide enhanced care, choice, comfort, convenience, and cognition to knowledge workers and commoners in their everyday lives.

With the steady growth of cognitive computing, we will have autonomic computing in place. Our IT environments, especially cloud centres, will get a lot of unique automation capabilities. We will see application-aware IT infrastructures and infrastructure-aware applications. Continuous monitoring, measurement, management, governance, orchestration, security, and maintenance of IT services and business workloads are deftly augmented. The performance engineering metrics, health checks, enhancements metrics observation are a few that get automated. Other NFRs (Non-Functional Requirements), scalability, availability, and dependability of cloud-native and enabled applications are also getting automated through the power of cognitive computing, for instance, as we discussed automated analysis of operational and log data of cloud assets earlier. The journey towards cognitive cloud environments is so far smooth and robust with the steady progress of cognitive computing.

References

https://www.expert.ai/
https://www.eni.com/en-IT/home.html
https://www.gflesch.com/applications-and-solutions/blog/cognitive-computing-examples
https://deepmind.com/
https://www.nature.com/articles/s41591-020-0867-7 (deep mind research)
https://www.vantagepointsoftware.com/
https://www.ibm.com/in-en/watson
https://welltok.com/
https://www.sparkcognition.com/
https://docs.microsoft.com/en-us/azure/cognitive-services/what-are-cognitive-services
https://numenta.com/
https://www.ericsson.com/en/blog/2020/3/autoscaling-value-state-detection-cognitive-cloud
http://iranarze.ir/wp-content/uploads/2018/04/E6656-IranArze.pdf

Machine Learning (ML) Algorithms for Enabling the Cognitive Internet of Things (CIoT)

Introduction

Machine learning (ML) algorithms solidly equip computing machines to self-learn and deliver relevant results without being explicitly programmed to do so. ML algorithms contribute to producing a problem-solving and analytical model for any problem at hand. It starts with a base analytical model. With a large amount of training and testing input data, the base model accurately represents the problem and the solution by continuous refinement. Then, when given a new set of input data is supplied, the arrived model correctly analyses, deeply understands, intelligently uncover hidden patterns and insights, and accordingly answers. The model learns from earlier computations and experiences to interpret data to determine correct and relevant responses. This complicated process intrinsically involves feature extraction/engineering and automation of analytical model-building using one or more ML algorithms.

Today every industry vertical produces big data (a massive amount of multi-structured data). There is batch and real-time processing needs getting accomplished with the ready availability of several automated tools and integrated platforms. Cloud infrastructures are being positioned and promoted as the one-stop IT solution for automating business operations affordably and adorably. With cloud storage, it is possible to accumulate and stock a tremendous amount of poly-structured data for a long duration for a lesser price. Also, public and private cloud environments deliver virtual supercomputing-like IT infrastructures (of course, for a higher price) to quickly collect and crunch big data. Distributed, parallel, and cluster computing models process high volume data crunch with ease and fast. Clusters of physical machines and virtual machines provisions facilitate real-time analytics of big data more than ever. Several service providers give cloud-based big and real-time data analytics as managed services to simplify cloud-based data analytics assignments. Streaming analytics is gaining prominence these days. Especially for creating and sustaining real-time enterprises, there is an insistence for building real-time and streaming applications. Real-time analytics plays a vital role in realizing intelligent real-time applications by supplying relevant insights in time.

Thus, on the data side, we have big data. On the infrastructure side, we have large-scale data storage and processing machines. We have integrated analytics platform solutions for doing big, fast, and streaming data analytics on the platform side. On the algorithm side, we witness several advancements. Advancements such as artificial intelligence (AI) algorithms (machine and deep learning (ML/DL), computer vision (CV), and natural language processing (NLP)), data collection, cleansing, and crunching gain and get a lot of attention and attraction.

Knowledge discovery and dissemination get a solid boost with all these transformative and trendsetting technologies and tools. Also, there are market analysts' reports forecasting that there will be zillions of IoT devices/digital entities. Thus, IoT devices and sensors consistently generate many multi-structured data to be captured and subjected to various investigations to uncover hidden patterns and valuable associations. The noteworthy point here is that the era of deterministic and diagnostic data analytics is tending towards prognostic, personalized, predictive, and prescriptive analytics through a host of competent ML and other AI algorithms.

The Emergence of Cognitive IoT Systems

We have extensively discussed the IoT phenomenon and how this new concept brings forth a slew of IoT-enabled software applications, and how business workloads and IT services strengthened through the IoT. IoT applications are becoming multifaceted by getting integrated with cloud-hosted software libraries and packages. But the real reformation is to happen when IoT applications and services get supplied with usable intelligence. IoT is the data collector and transmitter, whereas AI toolkits are knowledge discoverer and disseminator. Let us see a bit more on this below.

The world is yet to see positive disruptions through the unique marriage of the Internet of Things (IoT) with the AI paradigm, which led to coin a new term, "**cognitive IoT (CIoT)**". We will have CIoT systems, services, and solutions in plenty in the years to come. Our everyday environments with CIoT devices are getting traction, and they will exhibit innovative behaviour that helps to enhance humankind. The owners and occupants of any CIoT environment can receive context-aware, people-centric, event-driven, and knowledge-filled services in a discreet manner. This strategically sound synchronization results in intelligent and sophisticated processes that simplify and speed up the goals of ambient intelligence. This unique combination can also inject human cognition into our everyday devices, types of machinery, equipment, appliances, and instruments. Resultantly, we will have pervasive computing, adaptive communication, and ubiquitous sensing, perception, vision, and action.

Intelligence becomes ambient, and commonly found materials in our midst become sentient to join in the mainstream computing. And all kinds of electronic systems can automatically learn out of data supplied and received, adroitly answer for queries, creatively propose new theories, and substantiate the ideas with appropriate shreds of evidence, and naturally interact with humans. IBM publications quotes, autonomic computing is all about empowering machines to be self-configuring, self-diagnosing and healing, self-governing, optimizing and defending, and self-managing. Autonomy is all set and gets driven through cognition.

A CIoT system should proactively detect any failures of its system components and reconfigure itself to provide a graceful degradation through self-healing. Any fault occurring in one part of the system does not percolate or cascade into other elements to bring down the whole system. An exciting analogy is from software API design pattern called "Circuit-Breaker".

If there is a failure in the response due to a specific component, then the code understands the failure nature and still provides a meaningful response rather than erroring. Similarly, at CIoT, if there is a sensor failure, the system should explore if it can be compensated using the corresponding digital twin of the physical sensor or make a correct inference from the remaining sensor data. Similarly, when communication bandwidth is affected by an unforeseen interference source, it must explore other viable alternatives, such as if the flow can be re-routed or the data can be compressed or encoded with suitable error control codes. Systems must be self-, surroundings-, and situation-aware to be adaptive. Cognitive systems must remain innately versatile, resilient, robust, and intelligent.

CIoT systems must interact with humans and other devices through several channels and choices such as voice, gestures, movements, audio, video, etc. That is, they ought to naturally support multimedia and multimodal interactions. Augmented reality (AR), virtual reality (VR), and mixed reality (MR) techniques can produce and sustain the future interactions between people and IoT systems. CIoT systems should understand and take the human context to choose appropriate media and modality to better user experience and efficiency. We have discussed a few sample applications of CIoT systems below.

The Cognitive IoT Systems: A Few Use Cases for ML Practice

In earlier chapters, we have discussed many CIoT use cases in detail. This section covers a few more to step in a bit more specific to ML practices front. Continuous monitoring of various body vitals and biological parameters of workers working in hazardous environments and quickly responding to any abnormal events or deviations are the most sensitive and life-critical safety measures. Last year, with the fast spread of Covid-19, several purpose-specific biosensors and wearables such as smartwatches were designed and manufactured in plenty. These IoT sensors and devices automatically team up together to accomplish better and bigger things for the entire human society. These digital entities are intrinsically capable of forming ad hoc body area networks (BANs). And the worker's smartphone acts as an excellent IoT gateway for body sensors. We have discussed earlier in the introductory chapters about those physical parameters and the criticality of communicating those parameters to the spouse or the family doctor in time. Also, we have discussed the data collected and how it sent to advanced analytics/experts engines running in faraway cloud environments and ensuring the authorities gets to take measures and countermeasures in time with all the clarity and confidence.

We have been comfortable with big, fast, and streaming data analytics platforms running on clouds. However, as indicated elsewhere, we are heading towards leveraging AI tool kits such as TensorFlow to gain more out of the collected and cleansed data. That is, AI platforms facilitate predictive analytics to derive personalized, predictive, and prescriptive insights. The fire, fall, and flame detection can be pre-emptively done through cognitive analytics engines. As there are low power and cost connectivity technologies that support short- and long-range communication, sensors and actuators can be networked quickly to gather the right and relevant data. Cloud infrastructures are optimally hosting a bevy of pioneering AI platforms. Highly reliable wireless and wireline communications are in place, IoT middleware solutions are flourishing, multifaceted sensors and actuators are hitting the market, etc. So, in short, everything falls in place to realize a dazzling array of CIoT systems.

For example, the transportation and travel industry is going through powerful enablement through the bountiful usage of IoT devices to make our journey comfortable and cognitive. We are often hearing and reading about intelligent transport systems (ITS). We also incessantly talk about self-driving cars/autonomous vehicles. Optimal route identification for smooth travel towards any destination, optimal energy consumption and heat dissipation for environment sustainability, driver assistance software, intelligent parking systems, envisaging traffic conditions, congestion-avoidance methods, regulating traffic intelligently, etc., are the vital ingredients in having smart transport and travel. Precisely speaking, every business and the consumer-centric domain enhanced with the intelligent leverage of the IoT and AI.

There are several business domains leveraging the unique capabilities of CIoT systems to deliver premium and path-breaking services to their clients and customers. We talked about AI and its contributions to realizing CIoT systems. Hereafter, we focus on ML algorithms and how they support propping up next-generation cognitive systems.

Machine Learning for Cognitive IoT Systems

ML is all about algorithms that generate algorithms. As we know, algorithms are a sequence of instructions used to solve a problem. Algorithms, generally developed by hardcore programmers to unambiguously instruct computers in new tasks, are the prime building blocks of the software-defined world. Therefore, it is essential to understand that in ML, learning algorithms are not computer programmers, and instead, they create the appropriate instructions and rules. This novel approach generates the computer instructions that facilitate learning from data without new step-by-step instructions by the programmer. So, with computers, we can programme for these sorts of new, unconventional, and complicated tasks. Applications such as image recognition applications for the visually impaired or translating pictures into speech become easy and fast through ML algorithms.

*Machine learning (ML) algorithms learns target function (f) that best maps input variables (X) to an output variable (Y): **Y = f(X)**.* This function is a learning task where we want to make predictions in the future (Y) given new input variables (X) called predictive modelling or analytics. The goal is to make the most accurate predictions possible. *Machine learning is a method of data analysis that automates and builds competent analytical and answering models.* It is a fast-evolving technology that empowers the compute machines to learn, identify patterns, and make decisions from the given data with minimal human intervention. I build software that can understand images, sounds, and language and learn more about technology each day.

The primary ingredient of ML is to give data to a learning algorithm so that it gets trained. The algorithm then generates a new set of rules based on the inferences from the data. It is a way to develop a new algorithm, formally referred to as the ML model. By using different training data, the same learning algorithm can generate other ML models. For example, the same learning algorithm can teach the computer how to translate languages or predict the stock market. Inferring new instructions from data is the core strength of ML. The further strengthening of ML happens with the large volume of training data, i.e. more the data better-trained ML models.

Also, the ready availability of big data, inexpensive cloud storage appliances to persist those data drives AI and ML exponential adaption.

It is all about iterative learning over a period. With solid and sufficient understanding, machines begin to adapt to new data. Based on the patterns uncovered and decisions made during training and testing experiments, machines learn to repeat the same when supplied with new data. The accuracy of the outputs enhanced with more data and specific training. This aspect of machines' ability to learn from the existing patterns teaches and empowers computing machines to be cognitive in their assignments.

The surging popularity of AI algorithms is due to the ready availability of big data. Correspondingly we have inexpensive cloud storage appliances to stock big data.

Google car become a reality on the crux of ML. Another fascinating ML use case is relevance and recommendations. Companies like Netflix and Amazon made customer shopping/viewing experience is mind-blowing with relevance and recommendations. ML combined with linguistic rules creation to know what customers and consumers feel about various products, processes, and people. Twitter implements this application (sentiment analysis) to understand the pulse of people. The ML competency will continue to replicate across multiple business domains.

We have been writing software programs using formal languages to unambiguously tell a compute machine how to solve a problem at hand. We are steadily moving away from that. Devices are adequately empowered to solve problems independently by identifying the value-aiding patterns in data sets. It is a known fact that by deeply analysing hidden trends and patterns, it is easy to predict future problems and to pinpoint the ways and means of preventing them from occurring.

For example, a computing machine fed a series of photographs with labels something like "this is a horse", and some others labelled as "this is not a horse" as its input. After completing this unique exercise, if you show some more photographs to the same compute machine, it can quickly identify whether the new picture is of a horse or not. Every correct and incorrect guess of the computing machine is added to its memory, resulting in better-trained models and increased accuracy of prediction in the longer run. Let's get into deeper details with a few types of ML techniques in subsequent sections below.

About Machine Learning (ML) Algorithms

ML algorithms can make systems learn to perform classification, clustering, predictions, pattern recognition, etc. ML is ideal for problems such as regression, classification, clustering, and association rules determination. Learning tasks may include understanding the function that maps the input to the output. Also, they can identify and articulate any hidden structure in unlabelled data. ML algorithms help to make critical decisions in medical diagnosis, stock trading, energy load forecasting, and so on. Retailers gain insights into their customers' purchasing behaviour. Media sites such as Netflix greatly rely on ML to sift through millions of options to select a relevant song or movie recommendations for the individuals.

There are four types of ML algorithms, as depicted in the following Figure 5.1: Let us discuss each of these in detail in the subsequent sections.

Supervised ML Algorithms

Systems typically go thru various learning algorithms and statistical models on training data, eventually simplifying the complicated learning process. A measurable factor usually referred to as "Features" for the sample training data where the ML algorithm attempts to find a correlation/connection between features and labels. Labels are outputs (values) from the ML model. During the training phase and the subsequent refinement during the testing phase, this learning identifies patterns or makes decisions on new data. To understand how supervised learning works, please follow through the following Figure 5.2 and later with an example in this section.

Suppose we have a data set of different geometrical objects such as square, rectangle, triangle, and polygon. Let's train (steps below) the model for all the given shapes one by one.

- If the given shape has four sides, and all the sides are equal, then the model labels it as a **square**.
- If the given shape has three sides, then it will be labelled as a **triangle**.
- If the given shape has six equal sides, then it will be labelled as a **hexagon**.

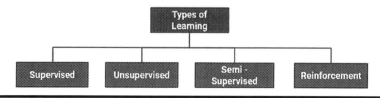

Figure 5.1 Types of Machine Learning

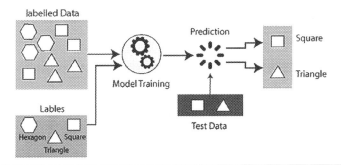

Figure 5.2   Supervised Machine Learning Algorithm Overview
Source: https://www.javatpoint.com/supervised-machine-learning.

Now, after training, we test our model using the test set, and the task of the model is to identify the shape. The machine is already trained on all types of shapes, and when it finds a new shape, it classifies the shape on the bases of a number of sides, and predicts the output.

So, the task of the trained model is to identify the shape post-training by using the test set. The machine is now ready to predict as it does have knowledge (trained) on all shapes, and when it recognizes a new shape, it classifies the shape basis of sides and predicts the output.

Types of Supervised ML Algorithms

We understand the **supervised ML** algorithms relies on labelled input data to learn a function that produces an appropriate output when given unlabelled data. Supervised learning can further be divided into two types of problems as depicted in the following Figure 5.3.

Supervised learning using algorithms like linear regression or random forest (RF) deals with regression problem such as weather forecasting, estimating life experience, and population growth prediction. Supervised learning can address classification problems such as the recognization of digits, voice, or speech. It also helps in diagnostics, identity fraud detection involving support vector machines, nearest neighbour, RF, etc.

Supervised ML aims to build a model that makes predictions based on evidence in the presence of uncertainty. We have seen that these ML algorithms are typically trained using many labelled examples in different scenarios to build a viable and sustainable model. Input is given to these algorithms along with their corresponding output/outcome during the training phase. Then, during the testing phase, a similar

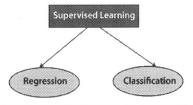

Figure 5.3   Types of Supervised ML Algorithms

input is presented without its corresponding output, and these learning algorithms must predict and specify the correct answer. If there is any discrepancy, then, again, the training phase gets restarted till the learning algorithm is turned and tuned to be reasonably accurate. Supervised learning generally uses classification and regression techniques to develop predictive models.

- **Classification techniques predict discrete responses** – Classification algorithms come in handy when the output variable needs categorical-based values. That is, there are only two classes such as Yes-No, Male-Female, True-false, etc. These techniques help identify whether an email is genuine or spam or whether a tumour is cancerous or benign. Classification algorithm predicts the outcome of a given sample when the output variable needs to be in categories. Medical imaging, speech recognition, and credit scoring are a few sample fields where these classifications algorithms play significant roles.
- **Regression techniques predict continuous responses** – Regression algorithms come into use to indicate a relationship between the input variable and the output variable, i.e. the prediction of continuous variables. These techniques predict changes in temperature or fluctuations in power demand. Regression algorithm techniques predict the outcome of a given sample when the output variable is in the form of absolute values. Electricity or power supply load forecasting and algorithmic trading are a few sample applications field for regression algorithms. Other examples include building a regression model that might process given data as an input and indicate the possible rainfall and amount of rain, the height of a person, etc.

Supervised ML algorithms solve classification or regression problems. A **classification problem** produces a discrete value as its output. For example, "likes olives on pizza" and "does not like olives on pizza" are discrete.

A **regression problem** has a real number (decimals as well) in its output. The below Table 5.1 indicates data that we could use to estimate weight against the given height.

Table 5.1 Regression Results

Height (Inches)	Weight (Pounds)
65.78	112.99
71.52	136.49
69.40	153.03
68.22	142.34
67.79	144.30
68.70	123.30
69.80	141.49
70.01	136.46
67.90	112.37

(Continued)

Table 5.1 (Continued)

Height (Inches)	Weight (Pounds)
66.78	120.67
66.49	127.45
67.62	114.14
68.30	125.61
67.12	122.46
68.28	116.09

Let's talk about dependent and independent variables, as the regression problem involves both. Dependent variables are the variables that we want to guess or predict by the algorithm, and the independent variables are variables (coefficients) that help find the dependent variables. With our example, height is the independent (as we give to find associate weight) and weight is the dependent variable (predict). Also, the row is generally referred to as an example, observation, or data point, while each column is often a predictor, dimension, independent variable, or feature.

Predicting heart attacks vulnerable and saving lives – Think of a scenario where clinicians want to predict someone's chances of getting a heart attack by analysing data from different patients. The data could be symptoms, age, weight, height, and blood pressure. They know whether the previous patients had heart attacks within a year. The key is combining the existing data into a model that predicts the chances of someone getting a heart attack, perhaps within a year. Not just prediction but also helps the clinicians necessitating the patients with precautions and saving them from heart attacks would be the goal.

In summary, supervised learning uses labelled data sets with features. These data sets then fed into the learning algorithm during the training process to work out the relationship between the selected segments and the labels. Subsequently, the learning enables the function to classify the new unlabelled data. The challenge is how to predict accurately.

Ensembling is another type of supervised learning. It enables a smooth combination of the predictions of multiple ML models that are individually weak. This blending ultimately can produce more accurate predictions on new sample data.

The Regression and Classification ML Algorithms

Linear Regression

This algorithm is a well-known approach for modelling the relationship between a dependent (predict) variable "y" and another or more independent variables denoted as "x" and expressed in a linear form. The word "Linear" indicates that the dependent variable is directly proportional to the independent variables. The independent variable needs to be constant as if x is changing (increased/decreased), then the dependent variable y changes linearly.

$$y = Mx + B$$

The preceding is a well-familiar representation of the mathematical relationship of the linear regression. Here A and B are the constant factors. Here, B is the intercept, and M is the slope of the line. Any supervised learning by using linear regression intends to find the exact value of the constants (M and B) with the help of the given data sets. Then the value of the constants will help predict the values of "y" in the future for any values of "**x**", and any ML aims to quantify this relationship. Simple linear regression involves cases where there is a single and independent variable. If there is more than one independent variable, then this process is called multiple linear regression.

Let's discuss an exciting scenario to understand the functionality better. Imagine we need to arrange a random of wood logs by their weight in ascending order. However, it's not straightforward, and there is a catch; we are not allowed to weigh the logs individually. So how do we guess it with an algorithm? If it is by our eyes, perhaps we would assume weight by some visual analysis, such as looking at the height and girth of the wooden logs. The same visual analysis can be done by our algorithms as well, and that's what linear regression is all about visual analysis in this situation. In this linear regression process, the relationship between independent and dependent variables established by fitting them to a straight and continuous line (slope, closer to the independent variable if we visualize a graph with x and y coordinates, please refer to the following Figure 5.4). Then the coefficients M and B are derived by minimizing the squared difference, the sum of the distance from data points to the regression line.

Logistic Regression

Linear regression predictions are continuous values (i.e. rainfall in centimetre), logistic regression predictions provide discrete values (i.e. whether a symptom indicates true or false for diagnosis) after applying a transformation function. A logistic regression model is a probabilistic model, i.e. the model helps to find the probability that a new instance belongs to a specific class. Since it is probability-centric, the output lies between 0 and 1. These methods are called a binary classifier, where we use the logistic regression to classify the data into two classes, a positive class and a negative class.

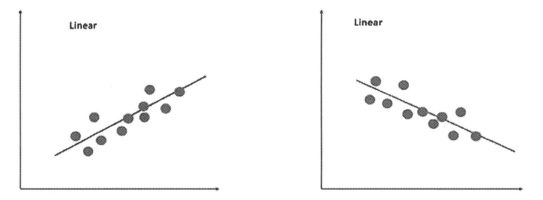

Figure 5.4   Linear Regression

Let's see a use case of classifying emails into spam and non-spam emails. We must take several labelled examples of emails and use them for training the model. After completing the derived model's training, the prediction of the class of new emails is made easy. When we feed the examples to the model, it returns a value "y". And the value of y lies in between 0 and 1 ($0 \le y \le 1$). Suppose the value arrived is 0.8. From this value, we can predict spam with an accuracy of 80%. We estimate discrete values (usually binary values like 0/1) from a set of independent variables with logistic regression. It can predict the probability of an event by fitting data to that function, which is also logit regression. With the logistic function $h(x) = 1/(1 + e^{-x})$, log transforming x, the output (y) is generated, and then the threshold is applied to force this probability into a binary classification.

Let's talk about another healthcare use case where the doctor needs to determine whether a tumour found in the patient is malignant or not. Say the default variable y is set to 1 to indicate the tumour is malignant. The x could be one of the measurements of the tumour, say the size of the tumour. As shown in the above figure, the logistic regression function transforms the value of the various instances of the data set falls into the range of 0 to 1. If the probability range crosses the threshold of 0.5 (indicated by the horizontal line), then the tumour perhaps classifies as malignant. The logistic regression $P(x) = e^{(b0 + b1x)}/(1 + e(b0 + b1x))$ transformed to $ln(p(x)/1-p(x)) = b0 + b1x$.

The goal of logistic regression is to make use of training data to find the values of b0 and b1 coefficients such that it can minimize the error between the predicted outcome and the actual outcome. Maximum likelihood estimation, a statistical method of estimating the parameters of a PD (probability distribution) by maximizing the likelihood function, helps to calculate these coefficients.

In summary, logistic regression is a classification algorithm used to assign observations to a discrete set of classes. Some examples of classification problems are Email spam or not spam, online transactions fraud or not fraud, tumour malignant or benign. Logistic regression transforms its output using the logistic sigmoid function to return a probability value.

Linear Discriminant Analysis (LDA)

Logistic regression is a type of two-class classification problem discussed earlier as a binary classification problem. For more than two classes classification, the LDA algorithm is a better-suited linear classification technique that one wants to explore. LDA is a dimensionality reduction technique. As its name implies, dimensionality reduction techniques reduce the number of dimensions or variables in a data set and LDA helps retaining as much information as possible.

The representation of LDA is simple and straightforward. LDA consists of statistical properties of your data, calculated for each class. The data includes the "mean" for each class and the variance calculated across all classes for a single input variable. Please note that the LDA technique assumes that the given data has a Gaussian distribution (bell curve), and so it's good to remove the outliers from the input data. LDA models use Bayes' theorem to estimate probabilities. They make predictions based upon the likelihood that a new input data set belongs to each class. The class with the highest chance is considered the output class, and then the LDA makes a prediction.

Decision Trees

A decision tree helps in deciding on the data item. For instance, if your friend is an investment banker, she gets to determine whether she has to give a loan to a person based on various decision-enabling parameters such as his age, occupation, and education level or deny the loan. She can quickly decide with the help of a decision tree algorithm. With decision trees, we must start the process from the root node, answer a question at each node, and take the branch corresponding to the answer. Determining or forming conclusions is quicker, easier, and accurate with decision trees as it employs a traversing technique from the root node to a leaf.

This learning algorithm works well in classifying categorical as well as continuous dependent variables. In decision trees algorithm, we split the population into two or more homogeneous sets based on the most significant attributes/independent variables. This algorithm has high interpretability, and it handles outliers and missing observations well. It is possible to have multiple decision trees working together to create a model known as ensemble trees. Ensemble trees can increase prediction and accuracy whilst decreasing overfitting to some extent with decision analysis. The decision tree representation can be as visuals for decisions and the decision-making process.

As their name, the decision trees use a structure that reflects a tree-like model of decisions. Non-terminal nodes and terminal nodes carry the input and output. Non-terminal nodes are the root nodes that represent a single input variable x and a splitting point on that variable. The terminal nodes are the leaf nodes that represent the output variable (y).

Let's discuss a scenario where we want to find potential or target customers who decide to buy a sport's car or a minivan. Various parameters influence a decision. Here in our example, as depicted in the following Figure 5.5 the primary criteria say age and marital status.

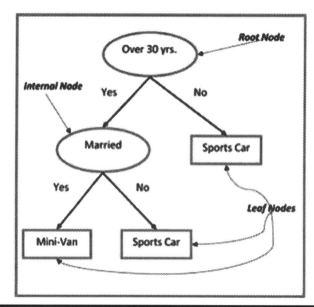

Figure 5.5   Decision Trees
Source: houseofbots.com

Precisely speaking, the feature importance is evident, and the relations are visible. This methodology is more commonly known as the learning decision tree from data. The above tree structure (diagram) represents a classification tree as the target is to classify passenger as survived or dead. Regression trees also take the classification tree structure for its representation, and they just predict continuous values like the price of a house. Decision tree algorithms are generally referred to as classification and regression trees (CART). Readers are encouraged to explore more details on various aspects of decision trees across online and offline sources.

Support Vector Machine (SVM)

This also comes under the category of supervised learning algorithms. SVM is suitable for regression and classification problems, especially where it needs to find a hyperplane in N-dimensional space that distinctly classifies the given data points. N here refers to the number of distinct features. SVM method takes the input, manipulates the given information as input, and then provides the output (classification).

As we see in the preceding Figure 5.6, we could choose as many as possible hyperplanes to classify the data points according to the classes. The objective is to find a plane with the maximum margin (the maximum distance between data points of both the classes). The margin distance maximization reinforces the data sets so that the classification of future data points can happen with more confidence and accuracy.

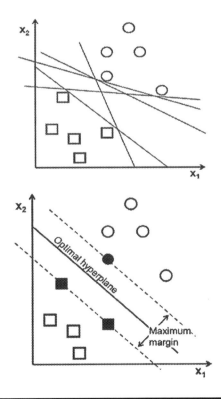

Figure 5.6 Support Vector Machine

Hyperplanes

SVM needs decision boundaries that help to differentiate the data points. Those boundaries are called hyperplanes. The data points on either side of the hyperplane segregate into different classes. Also, the dimension of the hyperplane depends on the number of features that it receives as input. A hyperplane is just a line when the number of input features is two, and it becomes a two-dimensional plane when features are three. If it exceeds three, then it is difficult to imagine the boundaries, as we see in the following Figure 5.7.

Logistic Regression and the Large Margin Intuition

In logistic regression, we squash the value within the range of [0,1] by using the sigmoid function as we consider only the output of the linear function. Then if the result of the squashed value is higher than its threshold (0.5), we assign it a label, say one (1), or if it is beyond the point, then we assign it to zero (0). But with SVM, we consider the result of the linear function. The results are higher than one (1), then assign those feature to one class, and if it is −1, then set it to another type and so on. Since the threshold values changed to 1 and −1, we reach a reinforcement range ([−1,1]) which acts as a margin as depicted in the Figure 5.8 below.

SVM is highly preferred as it produces significant accuracy with less computation power. SVM algorithms do both regression and classification. But it is widely used in classification tasks. Please visit the reference section of this book for more details and know more about the cost function and gradient updates.

Naive Bayes Algorithm

This is a classification technique based on Bayes' theorem. It's a simple mathematical formula used for calculating conditional probabilities. Conditional probability is

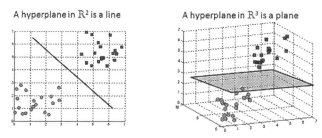

Figure 5.7   Hyperplanes

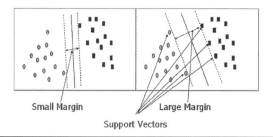

Figure 5.8   Logistic Regression and Large Margin Intuition

a measure of the likelihood of an event occurring given that another event has (by assumption, presumption, assertion, or evidence) happened.

We use Bayes' theorem and calculate the chances of an event that will occur when given the occurrence of another event that has happened already. To find the probability of a hypothesis(h) when we have prior knowledge (d), we use Bayes' theorem.

$$P(h|d) = (P(d|h)P(h)) / P(d)$$

where

P(h|d) = Posterior probability. The probability of hypothesis h is true, given the prior knowldege data d, where P(h|d) = P(d1| h) P(d2| h)....P(dn| h) P(d).
P(d|h) = Probability. The probability of data d given that hypothesis h true.
P(h) = Class prior probability. The probability of the hypothesis h true (and irrespective of the data).
P(d) = Predictor prior probability. Probability of the data occurrence (irrespective of the hypothesis).

This algorithm is perhaps "naive" because it assumes that variables are all independent of one another. The Naive Bayes model is helpful for massive data sets. Though it is straightforward, different results indicate that Naive Bayes has outperformed all the other highly sophisticated classification methods.

The model comprises two types of probabilities calculated directly from the training data:

1. The probability of each class
2. The conditional probability is given x value for every class

Once derived, the probability model makes predictions for newer data. When the data is real-valued, it is common to assume a Gaussian distribution (bell curve) to estimate probabilities easily.

It's not robust solutions that need to be always complex. In cases, simple and most straightforward solutions can also bring powerful ones, and Naïve Bayes is a simple, fast, accurate, and reliable algorithm. It works well with NLP problems. There are several materials available online, and we have given a little sample implementation in this book.

K-Nearest Neighbours (KNNs)

KNN algorithm helps in both classification and regression problems. However, it is more widely used to solve classification problems. KNN doesn't make any assumptions on underlying data, and so it's known as a non-parametric algorithm. It's also known as a lazy learner algorithm as it doesn't learn from the training set immediately; instead, it stores the data set. It acts on the stored data set at the time of classification and classifies any new instance by taking a majority vote of its k neighbours. Then the most common class gets assigned to the new incoming case. A distance

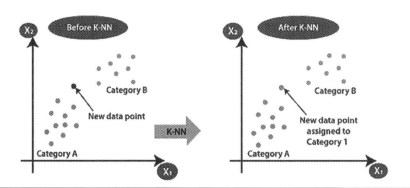

Figure 5.9   K-Nearest Neighbors (KNN)

function performs this measurement; for example, let's take a simple analogy that if we want any information about a person, we can talk to his or her friends and colleagues, and that's what exactly happens with KNN.

The things to consider before selecting KNN

- KNN is computationally expensive.
- Variables should be normalized, or else higher range variables can bias the algorithm.
- Data still needs to be pre-processed.

The KNN algorithm uses the entire data set as the training set, rather than splitting the data set into training or test set. When we expect an outcome for a new data model, the KNN algorithm will go through the entire data set and find the k-nearest instances to the new instance. Or the k number of cases similar to the new record then outputs the mean of the outcomes (for a regression problem) or the mode (most frequent class) for a classification problem. The value of k is user-specified. The similarity between instances is calculated using measures such as Euclidean distance and Hamming distance.

Suppose there are two categories, i.e. category A and category B, and we have a new data point x1 that we need to find where it lies in these categories. KNN algorithm comes in handy to see where the x1 lies and for those types of classification problems. The Figure 5.9 below vividly illustrate a sample KNN case.

The KNN works based on the below algorithm.

- **Step-1:** Choose the number K of the neighbours.
- **Step-2:** Find the Euclidean distance of K number of neighbours.
- **Step-3:** Take the K-nearest neighbours as per the calculated Euclidean distance.
- **Step-4:** Among these k neighbours, arrive at to count of data points available in each category.
- **Step-5:** Assign the new data points to the class that has the maximum number of neighbours.
- **Step-6:** Use the resultant model as your model as it's ready.

But, what happens if we have a new data point and it does need classification to the relevant category as depicted in the following Figure 5.10.

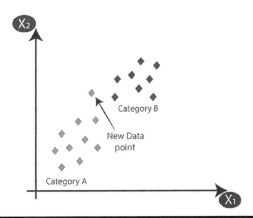

Figure 5.10 KNN plot

The Euclidean distance calculation formula is below and depicted in the following Figure 5.11.

By calculating the Euclidean distance, we got the nearest neighbours. There are three nearest neighbours in category A and two in category B, as illustrated in the Figure 5.12.

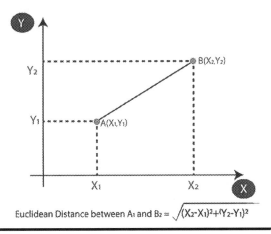

Euclidean Distance between A_1 and $B_2 = \sqrt{(X_2-X_1)^2+(Y_2-Y_1)^2}$

Figure 5.11 Euclidean Distance Algorithm

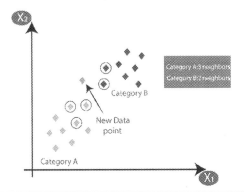

Figure 5.12 Euclidean Distance Plot

As there are three nearest neighbours from category A, this new data point must belong to category A.

KNN learns only when prediction needed, i.e. on-the-fly or just-in-time learning, but it requires a lot of memory space to store all of the data. So, it's better to update and curate the training instances over time as it helps to achieve better accuracy. Overtime training is intended to break down the distance or closeness with high dimension. However, the dimension size can also negatively affect the performance of the algorithm. This performance impact is called the curse of dimensionality. So, the suggestion is to leverage those input variables that are most relevant to predicting the output variable.

Learning Vector Quantization (LVQ)

A downside of KNN worth mentioning is that we need to use the entire training data set whenever a prediction is required. The LVQ is an artificial neural network (ANN) algorithm that allows us to choose how many training instances are needed and learn what those instances should be doing. LVQ is best suited for classification problems. It supports both binary (two-class) and multi-class classification problems based on prototype supervised learning. LVQ has two layers: the input layer and the other is the output layer. The best practice is that if you discover that KNN gives good results on your data set, then try using LVQ to reduce the memory usage.

Random Forest (RF)

Decision trees are the building blocks of the RF model. We have discussed the decision trees earlier, and we know ensemble means combining multiple hypotheses to form a better one. A forest is generally a collection of trees. An RF is a collection of decision trees, which are grown very deep, often to overfit the training data. This overfitting practice may result in high variation even with a slight change in input data. As depicted in the following Figure 5.13, RF is a culmination of several decision trees that operate as an ensemble. Decision trees are always sensitive to the specific and trained data, and they can remain error-prone to test data sets.

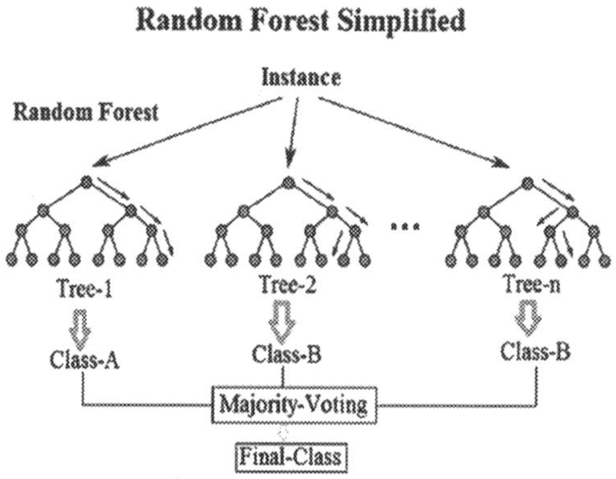

Figure 5.13   Random Forest

Each tree in the RF generates a prediction class, and with the most voted it becomes the model's prediction. The classification trees are trained based on different classification of the training data set. To classify a new item, RF puts the input vector down with each of the decision trees in the forest. As each decision tree gives a classification, the forest then chooses to have the most voted or the average of all the trees in the forest. Each decision tree evolves and helps in prediction with the steps described below:

- N is the number of cases in the training set, then N is a random sample of N. This sample will be the training set for growing the tree.
- Suppose there are M input, a number m<<M is specified such that at each node, where m are the variables selected at random of M, and the best split on this m splits the node. The value of m is kept constant for the entire splitting process.
- Each tree is grown to the most substantial extent possible, and there is no pruning that happens after that.

One of the significant advantages of the RF algorithm is that it's suitable for both classification and regression problems. The RF has almost the same hyperparameters as a decision tree or a bagging classifier. However, there's no need to combine the decision trees with a bagging classifier because we can simply use the classifier class. Another suitable use case with the RF is that any tasks that involve regression employing the algorithm's regressor of RF algorithm add additional randomness to the data model while growing the trees. Also, while splitting the node, instead of searching for the essential, it searches for the best feature from the random subsets that results in a well-diverse and better data model.

So, it's better to consider only a random subset of the features for splitting a node, and the RF picks only a random subset. With arbitrary thresholds for each feature, we can make decision trees more random and not searching or choosing the best possible thresholds.

Ensembling Methods

We have talked briefly about ensemble in the earlier section. Here in this section, we will dig deep on ensemble learning. Ensembling is a part of the ML paradigm, where multiple models called weak-learners are combined and trained to solve the same problem and get better results. It doesn't matter if the problem at hand is a classification or regression problem. What matter is the choice we make. The careful selection of the model is necessary to get better results. Be aware that our ensemble choices depend on many variables of the problem, such as the quantity of data and the dimensionality of the space, distribution hypothesis, etc. Low bias and low variance are the two most fundamental features expected for a model.

In the ensembling world, we call **weak learners** (or **base models**) models. These models are combined to bring forth complex models, which have the intrinsic money to represent real-world things more accurately. The weak learners do not provide good results because they have a high bias or too much variance. The ensemble methods are there to reduce prejudice or conflict. Here comes the concept of clubbing together multiple models to arrive at robust models.

The ensemble method combines multiple learners (classifiers) to improve results arrived by voting or averaging. Voting happens during classification, and averaging happens during regression. We discuss below the three types of ensembling algorithms, bagging, boosting, and stacking.

- **Bagging** considers homogeneous weak learners, learns them independently from each other in parallel and combines them.
- **Boosting** also considers homogeneous weak learners, learns them sequentially in a very adaptative way and combines them.
- **Stacking** or Stacked generalization ensemble involves meta-learning algorithm to learn to combine the predictions. It's a type of heterogeneous weak learners model that learns them in parallel and incorporates them by training a meta-model and predict results based on the different (more vulnerable) models' predictions.

In short, ensemble methods are the meta-algorithms that facilitate clubbing together several ML models into one robust predictive model to decrease the variance (bagging), bias (boosting), or improve the predictions (stacking).

In common, the ensemble methods use a single base learning algorithm to produce homogeneous base learners. That is, learners fall in the same type, which leads to homogeneous ensembles methods. Some methods are continuously using learners fall into the other kind, and they are heterogeneous learners, and yes, it leads to heterogeneous ensembles. For better accuracy ensemble methods than its members, the base learners must be as accurate and even as diverse as possible. In summary, the ensemble method is an ML technique that combines several base models to produce one optimal predictive model.

Bagging

This combines bootstrapping and aggregation to form one ensemble model. Bootstrapping is a statistical technique helping out in generating samples of size B, also known as bootstrap samples from initial data set size N, by randomly drawing with replacement observations B times.

One sure way to reduce the variance of an estimate is by doing the average. That is to average together multiple estimates. For example, we can train M different trees on different subsets of the data (chosen randomly with replacement) and compute the ensemble using the following formula.

$$f(x) = 1 / M \sum_{m=1}^{M} f_m(x)$$

Trees form the most efficient predictor. The following Figure 5.14 will help explain how ensembles work.

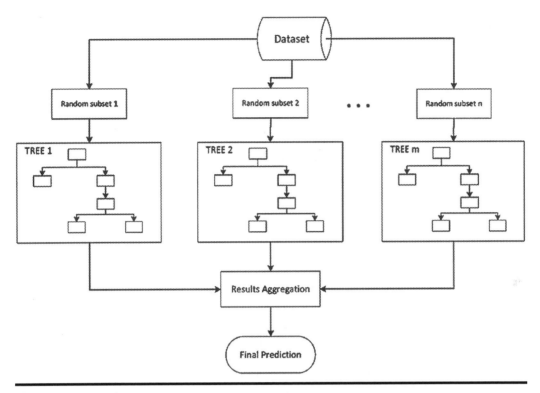

Figure 5.14   Bagging

Boosting

This is an exciting ensemble method. Boosting relies on the idea of filtering or weighting the data that train weak learners. So, each new learner gives more weight or is only acquainted with observations that the previous learners have poorly classified.

By doing this, the chosen models **learn how to predict** not just on the most common or easy observations but all kinds of data. The advantage of boosting is even if any one of the models is very bad at making predictions for some inputs, the other N-1 models will balance the results and produce better and accurate predictions almost all the time.

In bagging, each model trained independently. But in boosting, the N models are trained sequentially to take into account the success of the previous model and increase the weights of the data that the previous model had the highest error on. This error mandates the subsequent models to focus on closely observing data. Also, the **model that performs the best** on the weighted training samples become more robust as it gets a higher weight. These factors lead to a clear indication for accurate final prediction – the standard training process is listed below as steps.

1. All the data samples start with equal weights, and those data samples used to train the individual models.
2. Calculate the prediction error rate so that the training can accordingly increase the weights of those samples with a more significant error.

3. Depending on the effectiveness of the prediction of the individual model, it gets assigned with the new weights. A model that outputs good predictions will have a high amount of say (weight) in the final decision.
4. Then those weighted data is cascaded to the subsequent models, and 2) and 3) are repeated.
5. Repeat the above step 4 until we reach a certain number of models or hit error thresholds.

Once we attain a reasonably trained model, we need to subject it for predictions on new data. We always get new observation with their features, and those observations are cascaded to every one of the individual models. That is, each model can make its prediction. Then, the final global forecasts are given considering the weight of each one of these models and scaled and combined predictions.

Here are the leading boosting models.

AdaBoost (Adaptive Boosting) – This model works by the exact process described above. It is common to use decision tree stumps. Decision tree stumps are decision trees with just a root node and two leave nodes where only one feature of the data is evaluated. So, by considering only one part of our data to make predictions, each stump is a weak model. However, we can build robust and accurate ensemble models by combining many of those more inadequate models.

Gradient Boosting Machines (GBM) – GBM is a sequential training method for weak learners. GBM trains the weak learners by adding the number of estimators, but instead of adapting the weights, it tries to predict the residual errors resulted from the previous estimators. Because of this, there are no sample weights, and hence all the weak models have the same amount of say or importance. Again, decision trees are base predictors, but they are not decision tree stumps but fixed-sized trees.

eXtreme Gradient boosting – Here, too, we fit our trees to the residuals of the previous trees' predictions. However, instead of using conventional and fixed-size decision trees, XGBoost uses a different kind of trees. The ensemble is constructed from decision tree models. The trees are added one at a time to the ensemble and fit to correct the prediction errors made by the prior models, generally referred to as boosting. These models are fit using any arbitrary differentiable loss function and gradient optimization algorithm; that's why this algorithm comes under gradient boosting. Trees are built by calculating similarity scores that end up like a leaf node.

The advantage of XGBoost that it allows regularization by reducing the possible overfitting of our trees. So overall ensemble model is lean. Also, XGBoost optimization will enable us to limit the computational resources of boosted tree algorithms. Thus, it becomes a very high performance and fast algorithm in terms of time and computation.

Light Gradient Boosting Machines – LGBM are the ones for producing solid improvements for gradient boosting algorithms. Instead of using an excellent growth strategy for the decision trees like in XGBoost, it uses a leaf-wise growth strategy. This strategy achieves a higher error reduction per jump than other tree-based algorithms.

Boosting vs Bagging – In bagging, the weak learners are trained in parallel using randomness. But, in boosting, the learners are taught sequentially, as vividly illustrated with the following Figure 5.15.

In boosting, the data set is represented by the different sizes of the data points called weights so that observations that were incorrectly classified by classifier n are given more importance in the training of model $n + 1$. In bagging, the training samples are random and taken from the whole population.

Stacking

Stacking differs from bagging and boosting on two points. Stacking considers **heterogeneous weak learners** (different learning algorithms), whereas bagging and boosting assess homogeneous (weak) learners. Stacking combines the base models using a meta-model, whereas bagging and boosting connect weak learners with the help of deterministic algorithms. Thus, eventually, the stacking needs to learn many different weak learners and combine them by training a meta-model and predicting the multiple predictions that weak models return. So, there are two things here – the learners L we want to fit and the meta-model that combines L.

For instance, we can choose as weak learners a KNN classifier for the classification problem, as it involves logistic regression and an SVM with the neural network as a meta-model. Then, the neural network will take the outputs of our three weak learners as their inputs and learns to return final predictions based on them.

So, if we want to fit a stacking ensemble composed of L weak learners, we have to do the below steps.

1. Do split the training data into two folds
2. Choose weak learners L and fit them as first fold data
3. For every L (weak learners), make predictions for observations in the second fold
4. Fit the meta-model into the other fold according to its predictions made by the weak learners that come as inputs

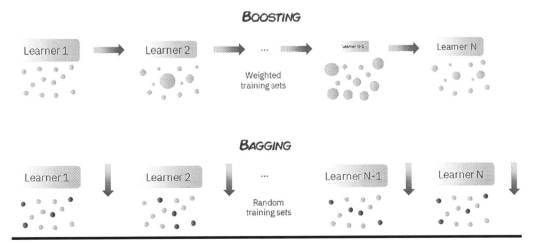

Figure 5.15   Boosting and Bagging Data models

Split of our data set into two parts leads us to have the only first half of the data to train our base models and the second half of the data for meta-model training. It's a limitation, but following a kind of "k-fold cross-training" approach can overcome this limitation. That is, all the observations can be used to train the meta-model. The prediction of the weak learners is made with instances of these weak learners trained on the k-1 folds, but it doesn't contain the considered observation. This approach can produce relevant predictions for each observation of our data set and then train our meta-model on all these predictions. Stacking helps to combine multiple classifications or regression models via a meta-classifier, or it could be a meta-regressor.

Traditionally, building an ML application consisted of taking a **single learner**, like a logistic regressor, a decision tree, SVM, or an ANN, feeding it with data, and making it perform a particular task through this data. However, rather than leveraging one model to arrive at the best/most accurate predictor, we can go for many models and take the average to bring forth the final model to ensure higher accuracy. Thus, ensemble methods involve many learners and are gaining greater attention these days.

Ensemble methods gain prominence because they can reduce the bias and variance of ML models. Ensemble methods help increase ML models' stability and performance by eliminating the dependency on a single estimator. We can see these gain and prominence in performance and stability with RF (a prominent bagging approach).

Hands-On Lab

Use Cases of Machine Learning towards Cognitive Systems

The earlier sections described several ML algorithms in detail. So, let's get some hands-on with a few of those algorithms in subsequent sections and the following few chapters.

The below section introduces readers to a development and testing environment for the example programs and uses python programming language. Readers having a fundamental understanding of python programming is prefered, and if not, do not worry as mere following the steps described in the below section gets all of us to run our sample programs quickly.

Also, please note that this is an important step and ensure you have the necessary setup in your laptop/testing environment. These steps are the fundamental steps chapter's examples, but any examples discussed in this book need this setup.

The following examples use python and pycharm IDE. So please go ahead and follow the installation guide published at https://www.jetbrains.com/help/pycharm/installation-guide.html. Creating a virtual environment is a critical step, as explained in the installation guide, as it helps us to code and runs as many samples independent as possible.

Example 5.1   Predict and generate the following three numbers for a given number sequence

Once we have the PyCharm and virtual environment setup completed, it's time to jump to our first hello world sort of example. This example is a super basic code that intends to give readers a quick understanding of what ML can do that human would do with their brain. The below ML example helps in predicting the following three numbers in the given sequence. Then we will have a couple of more examples of code for the above algorithms. Of course, predicting the tracking three numbers in the series may be a simple use case. However, the intention is to give novice users an idea of what ML is and what it can do. So, this example takes some inputs of a sequence number and predict the following three numbers according to the sequence.

Scenario 1: Given Input -> 1,2,3,4,5,6,7 Expected Output -> 8,9,10
Scenario 2: Given Input -> 3,5,7,9,11,13 Expected Output -> 15,17,19

Let's open PyCharm and create a new project as we see below steps as depicted in the following Figures 5.16-5.18.
Once the new virtual environment flow is complete, we will see in project explorer as below:

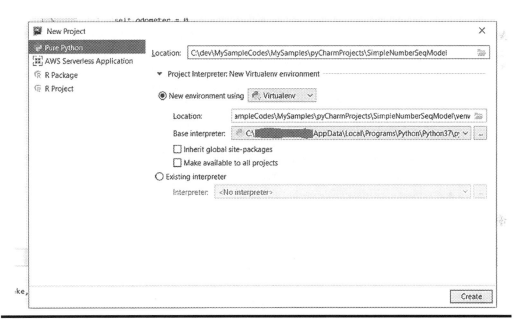

Figure 5.16   IDE - Project Create

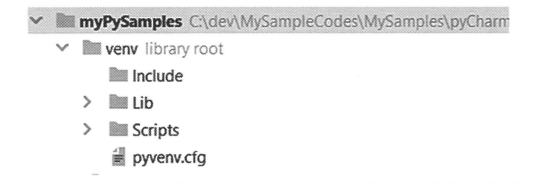

Figure 5.17   Project Structure

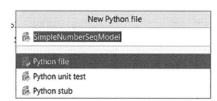

Figure 5.18 Project Structure and Sequence

Let's start writing a new python code (by left clicking on the File menu).

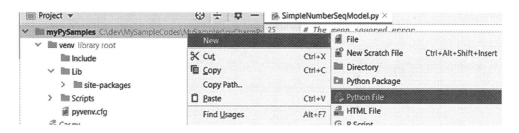

And provide a file name.

Copy the below code into the SimpleNumberSeqModel.py (and we will see more details of the code in subsequent sections).

```python
import matplotlib.pyplot as plt
import numpy as np
from sklearn import linear_model

problem = [2, 4, 6, 8, 10, 12, 14, 16]

x = []
y = []

for (xi, yi) in enumerate(problem):
  x.append([xi])
  y.append(yi)

x = np.array(x)
y = np.array(y)
# Create linear regression object
regressionObj = linear_model.LinearRegression()
regressionObj.fit(x, y)

# create the testing set
x_test = [[i] for i in range(len(x), 3 + len(x))]
print(x_test)
# The coefficients
print('Coefficients: \n', regressionObj.coef_)
# The mean squared error
print("Mean squared error: %.2f"
  % np.mean((regressionObj.predict(x) - y) ** 2))
```

```
# Explained variance score: 1 is a perfect prediction
print('Variance score: %.2f' % regressionObj.score(x, y))

# Make predictions
y_predicted = regressionObj.predict(x_test)

print("next few numbers in the series are ...")

for predicted in y_predicted:
  print(predicted)

plt.scatter(x, y, color='black')
plt.scatter(x_test, y_predicted, color='red')

plt.show()
```

save and run the code as depicted in the Figure 5.19 project flow below.

Observe the output console, and we will see the below results for the given input 1,3,5,7,9.

```
Coefficients:
 [2.]
Mean squared error: 0.00
Variance score: 1.00
next few numbers in the series are ...
11.0
13.0
15.0
```

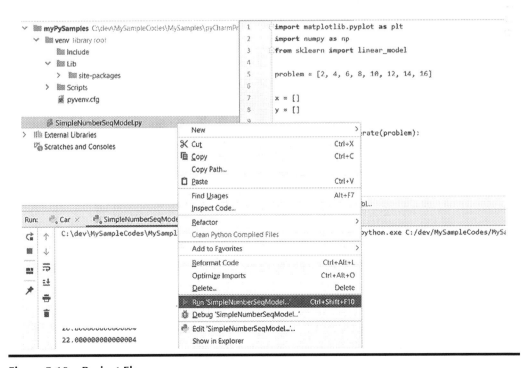

Figure 5.19   Project Flow

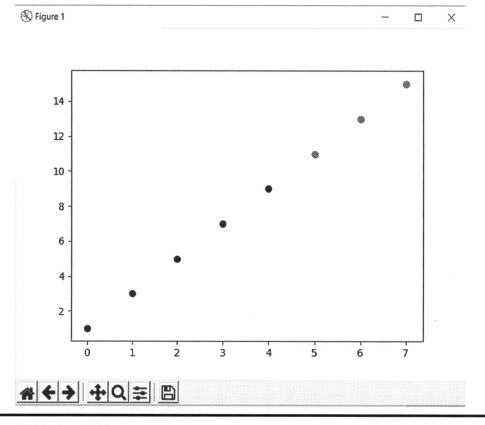

Figure 5.20   Sample Plot

And the most exciting part of this code output is it does generate and plots a simple yet cool visual graph for the given input and output as depicted in the Figure 5.20.

As we see, the dark (red when you run the program) plotted are the following three numbers of the given sequence. Let's now understand a few lines of our sample code that predict the following number in series and the code that plots the graphs.

Code Sample and Explanation

There are many python libraries such as NumPy, pandas, Matplotlib, scikit-learn, and NLTK. These examples are predominantly based on scikit-learn and using other libraries for various purposes.

Scikit is an open-source ML library that supports supervised and unsupervised learning. Scikit comes with a simple and efficient tool for predictive data analysis. It also provides various tools for model fitting, data pre-processing, model selection and evaluation, and many other utilities.

Let's understand our sample code in detail.

```
import matplotlib.pyplot as plt
matplotlib.pyplot is a collection of command style functions that simulate
graphs like MATLAB. we are using to plot our linear regression graph
```

```
import numpy as np
NumPy is open source and an entire library for scientific computing with
Python. NumPy is the most popular library that brings the computational
power of languages like C and Fortran to Python

from sklearn import linear_model
sciKit library and linear regression model

# Input Array
problem = [2, 4, 6, 8, 10, 12, 14, 16]

# for x and y coordinates
x = []
y = []

# Create linear regression object, this is where we get the linear
regression model applied to our inputs
regressionObj = linear_model.LinearRegression()
regressionObj.fit(x, y)

# create the testing set
x_test = [[i] for i in range(len(x), 3 + len(x))]
print(x_test)

# The coefficients of regression model
print('Coefficients: \n', regressionObj.coef_)

# The mean squared error
print("Mean squared error: %.2f"
      % np.mean((regressionObj.predict(x) - y) ** 2))

# explained variance score: (1 is perfect prediction)
print('Variance score: %.2f' % regressionObj.score(x, y))

# Do predictions (sci kit prediction with liner regrssion)
y_predicted = regressionObj.predict(x_test)

print("next few numbers in the series are ...")

for predicted in y_predicted:
    print(predicted)

# plot the graph
plt.scatter(x, y, color='black')
plt.scatter(x_test, y_predicted, color='red')

plt.show()
```

Linear Discriminant Analysis (LDA) Classification Example

Linear discriminant analysis or LDA is a statistical method for binary and multi-class classification; In the below example python code, we will analyse a use case where the system can predict chances of a patient as a diabetic or diabetic prone. We will use a public data set available at Kaggle – Pima – Indian diabetes database, and it consists of nine columns and more than 700 rows of data obtained from various patients (anonymous).

Table 5.2   Data Table

Pregnancies	Glucose	Blood Pressure	Skin Thickness	Insulin	BMI	Diabetes Pedigree	Age	Outcome
6	148	72	35	0	33.6	0.627	50	1
1	85	66	29	0	26.6	0.351	31	0
-		-	-	-	-	-	--	-
…	…	…	…	…	…	…	…	…

The preceding Table 5.2 provides a glimpse of the data set that we use. The first eight columns are inputs (independent variables/features). The last column is the class variable (dependent variable) which is 1 or 0; if the patient has people with diabetes, the class variable is represented as 1; otherwise, it is 0.

The following Table 5.3 provides more information on each column and its purpose, as we need to know before we jump to our code

Table 5.3

1	Number of times the patient was pregnant
2	Plasma glucose concentration two hours in an oral glucose tolerance test
3	Diastolic blood pressure (mm Hg)
4	Triceps skinfold thickness (mm)
5	Two-hour serum insulin (mu U/ml)
6	Body mass index (weight in kg/(height in m)^2)
7	Diabetes pedigree function
8	Age (years)
9	Class variable

So, our below sample code is an LDA model that predicts the class variable. That is, whether the patient has diabetes or not; is based on the observation (eight features) listed above.

```
# LDA Classification example
import pandas
from sklearn import model_selection
from sklearn.discriminant_analysis import LinearDiscriminantAnalysis

# load sample data (credits to jbrownlee)
url = "https://raw.githubusercontent.com/jbrownlee/Datasets/master/
pima-indians-diabetes.data.csv"
```

```
# define features (independent variable)
features = ['pregnencies', 'plasmaGC', 'bloodPressure', 'skinThickness',
'serumInsulinTest', 'bmi', 'pedigreeFn', 'age', 'class']
# panda data frame to populate the loaded CSV
dataframe = pandas.read_csv(url, names=features)

array = dataframe.values
X = array[:,0:8]
Y = array[:,8]

kfold = model_selection.KFold(n_splits=10)

# leverage scikit LDA
model = LinearDiscriminantAnalysis()

results = model_selection.cross_val_score(model, X, Y, cv=kfold)
sklearn_lda = LinearDiscriminantAnalysis()

X_lda_sklearn = sklearn_lda.fit_transform(X, Y)

res_mean = results.mean();
print(res_mean)
```

As per the earlier example steps, if we run the above python code, we will see our model's accuracy.

```
0.773462064251538
```

Impressive, isn't it? So, any new inputs to our model would predict whether the patient is diabetic or not. Please note that we could have written all the necessary python code ourselves for LDA. However, scikit-learn has most of the library that we can plug and play. So, we use LDA provided by scikit (from sklearn.discriminant_analysis import LinearDiscriminantAnalysis) that made our code sleek and focused more on what we need for prediction. Given the focus on CIoT of this book, we must use our pages efficient and towards IoT direction.

What's next? Go ahead and experiment with various inputs and see your model predicting the class variables.

Conclusion

The number of IoT products, solutions, and services abounding around us grows radically and rapidly for closely monitoring, guiding, and assisting us. Multiple rights and relevant IoT devices must collaborate to precisely understand our temporal, spatial, and situational needs and work out the things to be developed and delivered to people in a time in a discreet manner. IoT sensors and actuators must bestow to be context-aware and cognitive enough to fulfil varying aspirations of peoples. Towards this distinct and strategically sound empowerment, IoT device data has to be meticulously collected, cleansed, and crunched data analytics platforms and AI algorithms to extract actionable intelligence. That arrived intelligence, in turn, fed into concerned IoT devices, which, then, can easily be adaptable. Precisely, it is all about producing CIoT systems to empower people in their assignments. This chapter is specially prepared and incorporated in this book to tell all about the unique contributions of ML algorithms in realizing next-generation CIoT solutions and services.

References

http://houseofbots.com/news-detail/2289-4-top-10-machine-learning-algorithms-for-beginners

https://www.dataquest.io/blog/author/reena-shaw/

Naïve Bayes example: https://www.kdnuggets.com/2020/06/naive-bayes-algorithm-everything.html

Cost function and Gradient updates: https://towardsdatascience.com/support-vector-machine-introduction-to-machine-learning-algorithms-934a444fca47

Easy to understand examples: https://www.geeksforgeeks.org/learning-vector-quantization/

https://towardsdatascience.com/understanding-random-forest-58381e0602d2

LigthGBM performance on large data sets: https://towardsdatascience.com/what-is-boosting-in-machine-learning-2244aa196682

https://towardsdatascience.com/ensemble-methods-bagging-boosting-and-stacking-c9214a10a205

# Chapter 6

Unsupervised and Semi-supervised Machine Learning Algorithms for Cognitive IoT Systems

Introduction

Worldwide organizations are increasingly using artificial intelligence (AI) technologies and tools to initiate and implement various new capabilities. Primarily the following are the focus areas.

Data-driven Insights

We are living in the big data era. The faster adoption of digitization and edge technologies has resulted in the realization of digital entities. The connectivity and communication technologies have led to the accumulation of connected devices. Already the world is bombarded with scores of IT systems and applications. Business workloads for automation, acceleration, and augmentation of business activities are flourishing. Thus, we have these diverse and distributed digital elements, connected devices, microservices, business applications, and IT services. When these purposefully interact and collaborate, there are a massive amount of multi-structured data getting produced. Thus, data from different and geographically distributed sources are meticulously collected, cleansed, and crunched – this set of activities on raw results in knowledge extraction. The discovered knowledge gets disseminated to decision-makers and business executives to plan and execute various actions with all the clarity and confidence.

Further on, they feed the gathered knowledge from layers into networked embedded systems and this makes them intelligent in their operations, outputs, and offerings. AI is a growing collection of multifaceted algorithms, libraries, and frameworks to simplify and streamline the process of knowledge discovery out of digital data. Precisely speaking, AI, the required field of study and research, is being presented and pronounced as the critical enabler of knowledge creation out of big data.

Enhanced User Experience

As indicated at the beginning of this book, AI is generally comprising four crucial ingredients such as ML and deep learning (DL) algorithms, computer vision (CV), and natural language processing (NLP). Edge AI is a recent phenomenon providing local audio and video analytics. The NLP techniques significantly enhance user experience with AI-enabled machines, instruments, equipment, appliances, consumer electronics, gadgets, etc. Human-machine interfaces (HMI) have become the new normal. Humans can get intuitive, informative, and inspiring interfaces to calmly and cognitively interact with a host of personal and professional devices. Conversational AI is enabling the realizing intelligent chatbots to interact with enterprise applications. Customer centricity and delights fulfilled through the growing power of AI techniques and tools.

Process Automation

Automation is the ultimate target for embracing any new and promising technologies. A variety of repetitive and low-end tasks are technologically automated and accelerated. For example, robotic process automation (RPA) is a buzzword in the industry these days. Several industry verticals are using RPA to automate many simple tasks. Customer interaction is one among them. With AI getting embedded with RPA, the world can quickly expect bigger and better things. Industrial processes are rationalized, simplified, optimized, and automated. AI plays a very vital role here in bringing in excellence in business processes. Multiple orchestrated and automated computerized processes through the leverage of AI competencies. Thus, process execution is becoming deterministic, transparent, and predictable.

Thus, with the surging data volumes and the ready availability of high-performance computing facilities and large-scale data storage capacities, the mysterious AI phenomenon is gaining dominance these days to transition data to information and knowledge. Business processes become inherently intelligent to be adaptive and agile. Further on, AI-enabled systems are innately skilful in their interactions, collaborations, correlations, and corroborations.

The Emergence of Cognitive Systems

The whole world is excited about the AI paradigm. There is no doubt about that. However, designing, developing, and deploying AI solutions and services are beset with several challenges and concerns. AI systems may soon fully gain the intelligence to decide and do everything by themselves. AI systems will replace humans in decision-making and actuation in many areas where human intervention is not necessary. No human interpretation, involvement and instruction in the AI era. AI systems will have complete control over everything. There are several issues associated with AI systems. Giving 100% control to AI systems to make their own decisions and act based on the conclusions arrived has turned out to be risky and sometimes catastrophic. It needs complete and cognitive technologies and tools to realize next-generation AI systems. Delegating human power to AI systems needs some more time because of the opaqueness and the lack of trust and transparency in AI applications and services.

As an acceptable solution, the industry moves towards leveraging cognitive systems to assist and augment human beings activities in their daily works and assist them in making correct decisions. With the right choices, there are the right actions. Therefore, as a temporary solution, cognitive systems are being built and deployed extensively across industry verticals. There are machine and deep learning (ML/DL) algorithms to collect and crunch data deeply and decisively to emit out actionable insights in time. As widely known, big data produces accurate results. We have discussed the key characteristics of cognitive systems in the earlier chapters of this book.

Heading towards the Cognitive Era

Cognitive devices collectively facilitate realizing a host of next-generation cognitive applications and services such as service-oriented, event-driven, insights-driven, process-aware, and people-centric systems, networks, and environments. Several enabling technologies and tools emerge and evolve fast to arrive at such cognitive applications and environments. The other famous requirements widely articulated include the following.

1. Implementation processes ought to be optimized.
2. Appropriate IT infrastructures have to be in place.
3. Leverage flexible and futuristic architectural patterns.
4. All kinds of data getting generated have to be garnered and subjected to various deep investigations to emit actionable insights.

The first and foremost task is to transition common and cheap things in our everyday environments into digitized entities. The second thing is to realize networked embedded systems. That is, we will be surrounded and stuffed with a dazzling array of digital entities and connected devices. Then such digitized entities in a real-world environment comprising and connected devices can be quickly and elegantly refurbished to exhibit smartness in the development and delivery of its services. Let us go into the detail below.

The Realization of Digital Entities

With the voluminous production and faster proliferation of digitization and edge technologies such as implantable (microscopic sensors, microcontrollers, RFID tags, bar codes, beacons, stickers, LEDs, etc.), the journey towards the dreamt digital era is getting smoothened and speeded up. Attaching or embedding one or more edge technologies and systems can transition any concrete/tangible element into a digitized entity. By implanting one or more edge technologies onto any physical, mechanical, and electrical system in our environments (personal, social, and professional), latest technologies convert these standard systems into digitized designs.

Digital Entities Can Form Localized, Ad Hoc, and Dynamic Networks

Digitized entities gain the power to find and interact with other digitized entities in the vicinity. They create purpose-specific networks by linking up with one another in their neighbourhood to accomplish local and specific needs. Digital elements can also get integrated with web/cloud applications and databases directly or through a middleware/broker/bus/hub/gateway. These connected and digitized elements also become IoT devices, sensors, and actuators. Further, ground-level physical, mechanical, and electrical systems connected with remotely held information repository, software applications, and services with the right intelligence. This empowerment makes grounded physical systems to be highly adaptive in their actions and reactions. Therefore, the field of cyber-physical systems (CPS) has originated and pervaded into so many business domains these days. Thus, market researchers and watchers have estimated that there will be trillions of IoT devices. Therefore, the Internet of Things (IoT) fields, CPS, and cloud IT infrastructures have started to flourish.

The Explosion of Digital Data

Typically, digital artefacts generate a lot of data (state and state change, action and reaction, performance and security, log, operational and interaction). Soon we will be amid digitized objects in the days to come. These empowered devices' functional and operational capabilities are increasing externally or internally, attaching one or more digitization and edge technologies to any physical, mechanical, and electrical appliances. Their states can produce decision-enabling data by capturing and processing them meticulously.

Data to Information and Knowledge

Then, transforming the data into information and knowledge gets initiated to squeeze out valuable insights. By feeding timely and trustworthy intelligence into digital entities, the process of producing intelligent entities out of ordinary items gets speeded up. Through extensive, fast, and streaming data analytics, any digitized entity (IoT entity) becomes smart in its obligations. Robots, drones, and other electronic devices also take the same route to become cognitive in their offerings and obligations.

The Future Internet

This is the salient and standard process for transitioning ordinary objects into extraordinary assets. It is forecast that there will be trillions of such digital entities in the years ahead. As these entities integrate with the Internet servers, services, and solutions, the future Internet comprises servers, smartphones, and software services and all kinds of digitized elements. Empowered things join on the Internet to automate a multitude of business, social, and personal needs.

In summary, all kinds of digital data are then cleansed and subjected to a variety of investigations – this dedicated and more profound activity of analytics and mining results in actionable insights. The extracted information gets fed back into digital devices to exhibit adaptive behaviour, and those digital entities become smart and empowered digitized asset in their actions.

Intelligent and Real-time Applications

This is a contemporary twist and a paradigm shift. Private and or public clouds contribute as the highly optimized and organized IT infrastructure to host and run integrated analytics platforms and AI toolkits. These platforms come in handy in extracting insights out of data heaps. Subsequently, insights-driven decisions and actions by the devices become a reality. The point here is with such a traditional setup, the brewing needs of real-time data capture, analytics, knowledge discovery, and action could not be getting fulfilled. The network latency comes into consideration if we are using cloud-based platforms. What is the solution for this lacuna?

Edge AI

We have discussed Edge AI in the earlier chapters in detail. The lean and lightweight versions of data analytics platforms and AI toolkits directly deployed on resource-intensive IoT edge devices to facilitate real-time data capture, processing, knowledge extraction, decision-making, and action. As edge devices are there where everything happens, data can be gathered in nanoseconds and subjected to purpose-specific investigations through a single edge device or through a cluster/cloud of edge devices to emit out actionable insights in time. This better proximity data processing leads to real-time applications and services, which, in turn, facilitate the realization and sustenance of real-time enterprises and environments.

The Marriage of IoT and AI Paradigms

It is unmistakeably true that the IoT technology expands fast across and penetrates deeper into every aspect of our lives. With complete understanding and the need for strategic significance, most industry verticals have fully embraced this breakthrough phenomenon. It will place them ahead of their competitors and be relevant to their loyal and royal constituents such as customers, employees, and partners. IoT devices, applications, databases, middleware solutions, and enablement platforms in conjunction with cloud infrastructures are emerging as the prime ingredients in arriving and accentuating the much-desired IoT era. Fresh and versatile IoT sensors and actuators are being unearthed and deployed in important junctions to do more for people. IoT-enabled physical, mechanical, and electrical systems in our places emit out a massive amount of poly-structured data through their excellent interactions. Individual things and homes, hotels, hospitals, etc., are being IoT-enabled to visualize and realize new-generation context-aware services. A well-known example is that our smart cities, i.e. the cities are artistically empowered to be active, aware, and adaptive through the splurge of unique IoT techniques and tips. However, indeed, the actual transformation of world cities happens only if the IoT and AI concepts merge and meld voluntarily and vigorously.

Setting Up and Sustaining Smart Environments

Our everyday environments are all set to become intelligent through the seamless and spontaneous communication, collaboration, correlation, and corroboration of intelligent entities and networked embedded systems deployed in those environments. The IoT technologies simplify and streamline the accumulation of digitized assets and enable the devices with remote operations and management. Further on, digital entities can integrate and work with remotely held software applications and various platforms and databases. Increasingly digital data gets generated, accumulated, and processed to produce actionable intelligence.

Machine Learning (ML) Algorithms for the Cognitive World

In the last chapter, we have discussed a few supervised ML algorithms. In this chapter, we are to cover unsupervised ML algorithms.

Unsupervised Learning Algorithms

Let's try an analogy to start this section. While we take exams at school, there would be a question, and the grades are according to the answer key. Imagine there is no answer key to the questions, and the system needs to find the nearest answer and how it should find, which is unsupervised learning.

In our example, we only have input data X and no corresponding output variables. That is, there are no labelled data. The goal of unsupervised learning is to intelligently understand and construct the underlying structure or pinpoint the distribution in the data to learn more about the data deeply. Unsupervised learning algorithms come in handy in self-learning the data, discovering and disseminating the valuable structure and hidden facts in data.

Unsupervised ML is a grouping of ML algorithms. The commonality among the algorithms is that you must feed the input data (X) with no corresponding output variables. The unsupervised ML algorithms come out with a clustering or association model that clearly articulates the underlying structure or the distribution of the data. This clustering model helps the learning algorithm to learn more deeply and decisively about the data. As there are no correct answers for input data, these algorithms come under the unsupervised learning algorithm. That is, there is no supervisor to assist the algorithms in arriving at a decision. Algorithms have to leverage their intelligence to help identify and pinpoint any fact hidden in the data. Predominantly unsupervised ML algorithms focus on clustering and association problems. In short, **unsupervised learning** is an ML technique in which the users do not have any significant role, especially in supervising the model, which predicts based on new data points. Instead, it allows the model to discover undetected patterns on its own. It mainly deals with the unlabelled data. **Unsupervised learning algorithms** are famous for performing complex processing tasks and can be more unpredictable than supervised learning algorithms.

In other words, there are problems in which there is no target variable to predict. Such problems, without any explicit target variable, are known as unsupervised learning problems. We only have independent variables and no target/dependent variable.

Why Unsupervised Learning?

- Unsupervised ML can pinpoint all kinds of unknown patterns in data.
- Unsupervised methods can find features that are significantly useful for enhancing the quality of categorization.
- Unsupervised learning takes place in real time, so all the input data is getting analysed and labelled in the presence of learners.
- There is a large quantity of unlabelled data. There is a manual intervention to arrive at labelled data.

Types of Unsupervised Learning

Problems that need unsupervised learning can be of two types: clustering and another is association problems.

- **Clustering** – This is to discover inherent groupings of the data. For example, customers are grouped based on their financial clout/purchasing power and shopping behaviour. Clustering is a process of grouping objects into separate clusters, and those objects in a cluster are closer to each other in one or other aspects.
- **Association** – This is to identify the exact rules that clearly describe a large portion of the input data. For example, people who buy an item X buy an item Y. Association is primarily used to decide the probability of the co-occurrence of items in a collection. An association model might be used to determine customers' chances of buying eggs when they buy bread; say 80% of customers who bought bread also buy eggs.

Clustering

Any business focus is to understand its customers: who they are and what drives their purchase decisions?

There are different groups of users, and there are a few criteria for grouping activity in clustering. These criteria can be age and gender or personal trait and purchase process. Clustering algorithms will run through the data and find these natural clusters automatically if they exist. One set is with 30+ artists and another of millennials who own dogs.

- K-means clustering – It's a method of clustering data points into a K number of mutually exclusive clusters. Picking the optimum number of K involves complexity. However, direct and statistical testing methods help us choose the correct number K. We will discuss those methods and details in subsequent sections.

■ Hierarchical clustering – Clustering your data points into parent and child clusters. You might split your customers between younger and older ages and then break each of those groups into their assigned sets as well.
■ Probabilistic clustering – Clustering your data points into clusters on a probabilistic scale.

Clustering mainly deals with finding an appropriate and usable structure or pattern in uncategorized data points. Clustering algorithms will process data and try to find natural clusters (groups). The Figure 6.1 below tells it all.

The Clustering Types

Exclusive (partitioning): In this, datapoints get grouped so that one data point can belong to one cluster only. K-means clustering belongs to this category.

Agglomerative clustering: Agglomerative means clustered together but not coherent. And this method, from an ML standpoint, is the most common type of hierarchical clustering where the grouping of objects in a cluster happens based on similarity. Every data point is a cluster, and the unions occur between the two adjacent or nearest groups, thus reducing the number of clusters. The result of agglomerative clustering is a tree-based representation of the objects called a dendrogram. We will discuss agglomerative clustering and dendrogram with more details in later sections of this chapter.

Overlapping: In this technique, clustering happens using the concept of fuzzy sets. Each data point may belong to two or more clusters with separate degrees of membership, and the membership will have a value for each data point. Fuzzy C-means is the prime method.

Probabilistic: This technique uses probability distribution to create clusters. For example, the following sample keywords indicate the nature of inputs:

■ "men's clothing"
■ "women's clothing"
■ "women's shoes"
■ "man's shoes"
■ can be clustered into two categories "clothing" and "shoes" or "man" and "women"

Readers are encouraged to refer to the reference section for specific reading material on the above methods.

sample   Cluster/group

Figure 6.1   Clustering

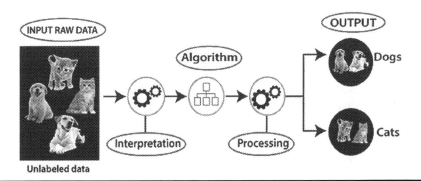

Figure 6.2   Clustering Flow

The working of unsupervised learning is depicted in the following Figure 6.2, and it may give readers a better understanding and a clarity.

Here, we have taken unlabelled input data. That is, the data is not categorized, and corresponding outputs are also not given. Now, this unlabelled input data is presented to the ML model to train it. It starts with interpreting the raw data to find the data's hidden patterns and then uses suitable algorithms such as K-means clustering, K-means ++, decision tree, etc. Once it applies the suitable algorithm, the algorithm divides the data objects into groups according to the similarities and difference between the objects.

The idea of clustering is that an entire data set subdivided into a set of groups. These groups are known as clusters. This technique is popular and widely used for clustering a population into different groups. A few more examples include segmenting customers, clustering similar documents together, recommending similar songs or movies, etc. Various algorithms help us to make these clusters. K-means and hierarchical clustering are popular, widely adopted, and most commonly used clustering algorithms.

Briefing the K-means Algorithm

The objective of K-means is simple. It is all about grouping similar data points together and discovers underlying patterns. The K-means algorithm starts with the first group of randomly selected centroids (processing the learning data), and the first group will act as the beginning points for every cluster. Then the algorithm performs iterative (repetitive) calculations and optimizes the positions of the centroids. The algorithm halts this process (creation and optimization of clusters) when

- The centroids have stabilized – there is no change in their values because the clustering has been successful.
- The process has reached or completed to the defined number of iterations.

K-means clustering is easy to understand, faster training, and quick results made this algorithm an extensively used technique and famous for data cluster analysis. However, there are cases where its performance is not as competitive as a few other sophisticated (K medoids, K-means ++) clustering techniques because slight variations in the data could lead to high variance.

Hands-On Lab

How Does K-means Clustering Work?

1. Decide and specify the number of clusters K
2. Initialize centroids
   a. Initialize centroids by shuffling the data set
   b. Select K data points randomly for the centroids without replacing them
3. Iterate them until no change to the centroids
   a. Assign all the data points to the closest cluster centroid
   b. Calculate the centroid of newly formed clusters

As discussed, this K-means clustering algorithm is an iterative process. It will keep running until either no more changes to newly formed clusters or the algorithm steps already iterated to the specified maximum number of iterations.

Once we have the K new centroids, a contemporary binding is a must, and this need to happen in between the same data set points and the nearest new centre. There needs a loop generation, and as a result of the generated loop, we can notice that the K centres keep changing the location step by step. This process will continue until there need no more changes or, in other words, can say the centres do not move anymore. Finally, this algorithm is always aiming at minimizing an objective function which is known to be a squared error function given and explained as

$$J(V) = \sum_{i=1}^{c} \sum_{j=1}^{c_i} \left(\left\| x_i - v_j \right\| \right)^2$$

Where "$\|x_i - v_j\|$" is the Euclidean distance between x_i and v_j., and "c_i" is the number of data points in the ith cluster, and "c" is the number of cluster centres.

Below is the sample python code using scikit cluster library for implementing K-means clustering. You may want to refer to the initial setup section from the earlier chapter and get hands-on with this algorithm by running this program with your laptop.

```
import numpy as npy
import matplotlib.pyplot as plt

# for 3D projection to work
from mpl_toolkits.mplot3d import Axes3D

from sklearn.cluster import KMeans
from sklearn import datasets

npy.random.seed(5)

# load iris data set
iris = datasets.load_iris()
X = iris.data
y = iris.target
```

```
# have the loaded data set
our_estimators = [('k_means_iris_8', KMeans(n_clusters=8)),
                  ('k_means_iris_3', KMeans(n_clusters=3)),
                  ('k_means_iris_bad_init', KMeans(n_clusters=3,
                      n_init=1, init='random'))]

our_diagrams_series = 1
our_headings = ['8 clusters', '3 clusters', '3 clusters, bad
  initialization']
for name, est in our_estimators:
    our_output_panels = plt.figure(our_diagrams_series, figsize=(4, 3))
    ax = Axes3D(our_output_panels, rect=(0, 0, .95, 1), elev=48,
        azim=134)
    est.fit(X)
    our_labels = est.labels_

    ax.scatter(X[:, 3], X[:, 0], X[:, 2],
        c=our_labels.astype(float), edgecolor='k')

    ax.w_xaxis.set_ticklabels([])
    ax.w_yaxis.set_ticklabels([])
    ax.w_zaxis.set_ticklabels([])
    ax.set_xlabel('Petal width')
    ax.set_ylabel('Sepal length')
    ax.set_zlabel('Petal length')
    ax.set_title(our_headings[our_diagrams_series - 1])
    ax.dist = 12
    our_diagrams_series = our_diagrams_series + 1

# plot Initial input
our_output_image = plt.figure(our_diagrams_series, figsize=(4, 3))
ax = Axes3D(our_output_image, rect=(0, 0, .95, 1), elev=48, azim=134)

for name, label in [('Iris Setosa', 0),
                    ('Iris Versicolour', 1),
                    ('Iris Virginica', 2)]:
    ax.text3D(X[y == label, 3].mean(),
            X[y == label, 0].mean(),
            X[y == label, 2].mean() + 2, name,
            horizontalalignment='center',
            bbox=dict(alpha=.2, edgecolor='w', facecolor='w'))

# Reorder the labels
y = npy.choose(y, [1, 2, 0]).astype(float)
ax.scatter(X[:, 3], X[:, 0], X[:, 2], c=y, edgecolor='k')

ax.w_xaxis.set_ticklabels([])
ax.w_yaxis.set_ticklabels([])
ax.w_zaxis.set_ticklabels([])
ax.set_xlabel('Petal width')
ax.set_ylabel('Sepal length')
ax.set_zlabel('Petal length')
ax.set_title('Initial Input')
ax.dist = 12

our_output_panels.show()
```

Sample output

Below depicted Figures 6.3 and 6.4 are the screenshots post-execution of our sample program. We can see the clustering and categorization stages of famous iris data sets. Run the code from the IntelliJ python console:

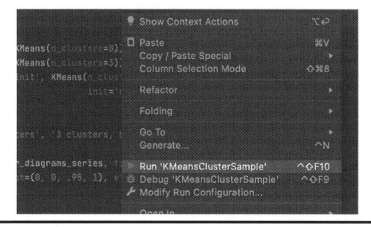

Figure 6.3   Run Your Sample

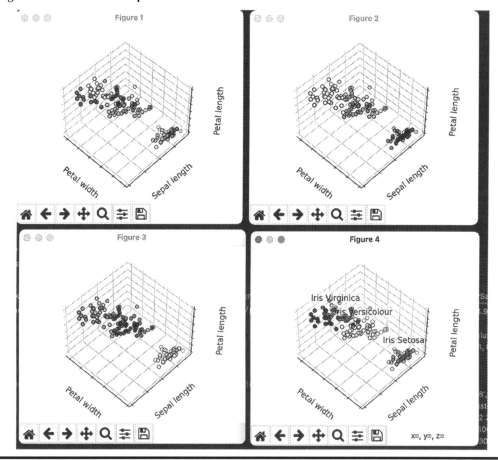

Figure 6.4   Sample Results

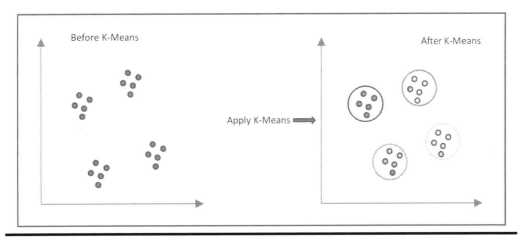

Figure 6.5   Sample Results Plot

The plotted outputs note each stage and the classification at the last figure by K-means.

The following Figure 6.5 is another sample depiction of before and after applying K-means to the data sets, which we can relate to the above sample code's results.

Before we move on to hierarchical clustering, let's summarize our understanding of K-means. K-means is an unsupervised and iterative algorithm that groups similar data into clusters by calculating the centroids of K clusters and assigns a data point to that cluster having the least distance between its centroid and the data point.

From the challenges with K-means implementation standpoint, we can quote the K-means always tries to make clusters of the same size, and the user has to specify the K (the number of clusters) in the beginning. Finding the optimum size of K is a challenge. Ideally, knowing how many clusters we should have at the beginning of the algorithm is challenging with K-means clustering.

Hierarchical Clustering – Agglomerative and Divisive Clustering

As we have touched upon earlier section, the hierarchical clustering algorithm falls into two categories: 1. agglomerative and 2. divisive. Agglomerative is a bottom-up approach where it first assigns every node as a single cluster, merges the closest (by distance) to another, and creates a hierarchical tree. This merge happens iteratively. Divisive is a top-down approach where it first groups all nodes into one cluster and then divide the clusters iteratively into a hierarchical tree.

As we see in the preceding Figure 6.6, the example elements are A, B, C, D, and E. As a bottom-up approach, the agglomerative process at step 0 assigns individual clusters and at step 1 finds the closest nodes. As A and B are closer to each other, the result of step 1 in the iterative method is AB, in step 2 we can see DE, step 3 its CDE, then step 4 its ABCDE and becomes root. In Hierarchical Clustering-Divisive, the divisive step 0 is all the nodes to one cluster ABCDE, then step 1 is division as per the closest that results in CDE, step 2 results in DE, and step 3 results in AB. The last step results in divided nodes with individual clusters and becomes a hierarchical tree, dendrogram.

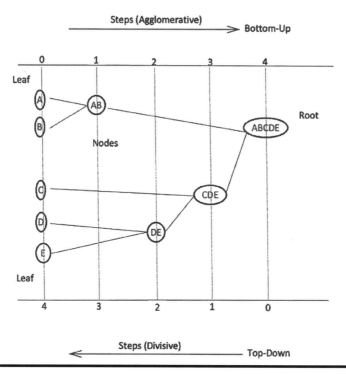

Figure 6.6 Agglomerative vs Divisive

The successive clustering process produces a binary clustering tree called dendrogram. The following Figure 6.7 is a sample depiction of nested clusters and their dendrogram.

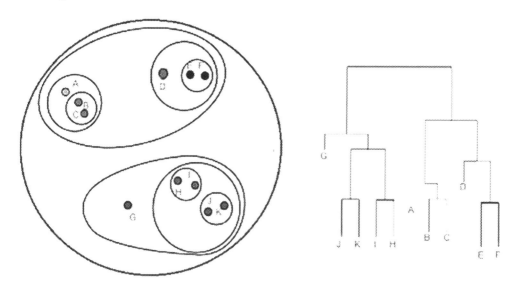

Figure 6.7 Successive Clustering
Source: https://www.statisticshowto.com/hierarchical-clustering/

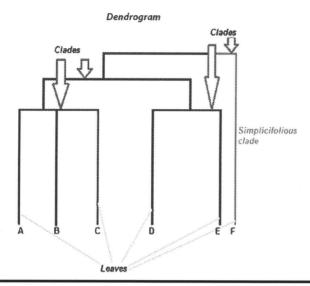

Figure 6.8 Hierarchical Clustering
Source: https://www.statisticshowto.com/hierarchical-clustering/

Dendrogram's root is the class that contains all the observations. This tree represents the hierarchy of partitions, and it is possible to choose those partition by truncating a tree at any given level. The user-defined constraints or more objective criteria drive the levels of dendrogram.

The following Figure 6.8 gives us a more detailed look at parts of the dendrogram.

Now, let us move on with how to decide the proximity or closeness or the criteria of determining which points are similar and which are not (recollect our earlier example).

Steps to perform hierarchical clustering – We need to decide which points are similar and which are not? The method to calculate similarity is as follows. Take the proximity between the centroids of these clusters. The data points having the least distance are considered similar in this case, and the way forward is to merge them. In this, there is a concept called a **proximity matrix**. Proximity metrics stores the distances between each point.

Association

Association rules allow one to establish associations amongst data objects inside large databases. As part of unsupervised learning, the association algorithm is about discovering common characteristics between variables in large databases.

The common characteristic is perhaps a relationship, connections, likelihood, etc. For instance, a customer who books a hotel would most likely need a rental car, so the chances of reserving a rental car are high. A few other examples could be

- A subgroup of diabetes patients grouped by their gene type and sequence
- Groups of online viewers based on their time spent on a page/product
- Music album ratings from music enthusiasts

Apriori algorithm for association rule learning problems – The Apriori algorithm is the first algorithm that is popular for frequent item set mining. It generates association rules by mining items, usually from a transactional database. As seen in the following Figure 6.9 this algorithm is beneficial for market-based analysis, where we need combinations of products that frequently co-occur in the database.

In general, we write the association rule for "if a person purchases item X, then he purchases item Y" as X -> Y.

If someone buys shoes and socks, then they more likely to buy a polish kit that keeps their boots clean and shiny. The association rule for the above sample may be {Shoe, Socks} -> Shoe Polish. Association rules always generated after crossing the threshold for support and confidence.

The support measure can help in pruning the number of sets during frequent itemset generation. This support measure is guided by the Apriori principle "if an itemset is frequent, then all of its subsets must also be frequent".

Understanding various buying patterns of consumers is essential and makes them useful for increased sales and revenues. The challenge is that each shopper has unique preferences with their purchases. Even the same buyer has different tastes at different times. Let's take a scenario where a supermarket manager needs to arrange the shopping items (frequently bought together) to increase the chances of the buyer picking up both. So preferences on a pair of things say X and Y, that is generally preferred together then the rules could be

■ Place the X and Y on the same shelf, and prompt the buyer who buys X to choose Y as well.
■ Provide promotional code and discount for one of the items.
■ Drive targetted marketing on Y to the buyer who buys X or vice versa.
■ X or Y can have a combined price or sell as a new combined product having one item have another flavour.

Association rules are not specific to retails but several other fields such as biology, insurance, meteorology, the Internet, etc. For instance, a medical diagnosis, understanding which symptoms tend to comorbid, can help improve patient care and medicine prescription. Millions and millions of document classification, clustering web log data to discover groups of similar access patterns in the Internet world are a few to quote.

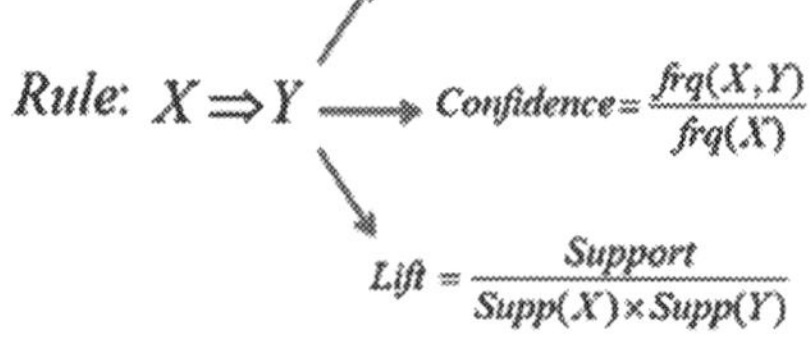

$$Rule: X \Rightarrow Y$$

$$Support = \frac{frq(X,Y)}{N}$$

$$Confidence = \frac{frq(X,Y)}{frq(X)}$$

$$Lift = \frac{Support}{Supp(X) \times Supp(Y)}$$

Figure 6.9   Apriori Algorithm

The Key Use Cases of Unsupervised Learning

Data Compression

As we all know, there are many noteworthy advancements in the IT landscape. The computing power has gone up sharply, and storage capacity also gets increased significantly through the pervasiveness of cloud computing. Still, there is a need to bring in substantial optimizations in data processing and storage aspects in the big data era. The optimization best practices called dimensionality reduction come in handy. This technique is an unsupervised learning technique, and we will discuss the same now in subsequent sections.

Dimensionality Reduction

Almost 90% of the data in the world that we have generated happened in just four years. However, visualizing and inferring information from such a massive volume of data is a real challenge with this growth rate. That's where dimensionality reduction plays a significant role. With the dimensionality reduction technique, most representations of information with just a fraction of actual content. Usually, there are many redundant data and too many factors for classification in any given data set collected and generated from devices. These factors are called features (aka variables). The higher the features and numbers harder it gets to visualize. So, the process of reducing the number of variables by obtaining a set of principal variables is essential. That is, represent most of the information in a data set with a fraction of the actual content.

- *Principal Component Analysis (PCA)* – This can find the linear combinations that communicate most of the variance in your data.
- *Singular-Value Decomposition (SVD)* – This factorizes your data into the product of three other, smaller matrices.

CV is a growing field of study and research, and dimensionality reduction is indeed essential. There are an enormous amount of static and dynamic images. There is a need to reduce the size of input images to lessen the load on compute, network, and storage powers. PCA or SVD algorithms usually run on images during pre-processing before applying machine and deep learning algorithms.

Generative Models

This is a class of unsupervised learning models. Herein, training data given and new samples generated from the same distribution. With the set of images as input, a generative model can create a collection of images very similar to the given set.

Unsupervised Deep Learning

Unsupervised learning in neural nets and DL space are getting momentum. A popular application of DL in an unsupervised manner is autoencoder, as depicted in the

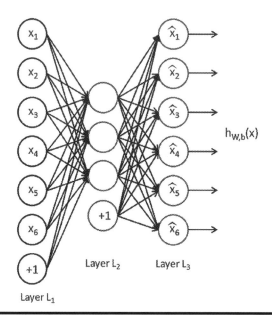

Layer L_1

Figure 6.10 Unsupervised Learning Algorithm
Source: http://ufldl.stanford.edu/tutorial/unsupervised/Autoencoders/

Figure 6.10 which uses a small subset of features to represent our original data. Autoencoder figures out how to best represent our input data as itself using a smaller amount of data than the original. An autoencoder uses weights to mould the input values into the desired output, like a neural net.

Autoencoder with as many n output units as input units has a minimum of one hidden layer (L2) with m units where m < n, and trained with the backpropagation algorithm. Backpropagation reproduces the input vector onto the output layer. It also reduces the columns in the data by using the hidden layer (L2) output to represent the input vector.

The first part of the autoencoder from the input layer to the hidden layer of m units is the encoder. The encoder layer is responsible for compressing the n dimensions of the input data set into an m-dimensional space. The second part from the hidden layer to the output layer is the decoder. The decoder is responsible for expanding the data vector from m-dimensional space back to the original n-dimensional data set and bringing it back to its initial values.

Applications of Unsupervised Machine Learning

Below are a few prominent applications of unsupervised learning that we will come across in our daily lives

■ **Clustering** – Split the data set into groups based on their similarities – Netflix recommendation systems groups viewers with shared audiovisual tastes.

■ In online transactions, anomaly detection to discover unusual data points in given data sets becomes necessary. It is critical to determine and **classify** transactions as correct or fraudulent using historical data collected as part of customer behaviour to detect fraud accurately.

■ Customer relationship management (CRM) – With CRM, banks try to determine preferences of different groups, products, and services customized to their liking to enhance the cohesion between credit card customers and the bank. So, essentially **association mining** helps determine sets of items that often occur together in the data set.

■ Latent variable models help in massive data pre-processing by reducing the number of features in a data set or make those data sets into multiple components by decomposition.

■ Psychometrics (psychology testing, measurement, assessment and related activities) of medical simulation – high-stakes US medical licensure exams using simulations for realizing the evidence-centred design. With simulations, based assessment can generate a wealth of real-time data. Latent variable models can be a good fit for those simulation-based applications.

Disadvantages of Unsupervised Learning

■ Accuracy and results
  – Getting precise information is not guaranteed as data sets in unsupervised learning are unlabelled. The less accuracy of the results is due to the input data being unknown and not labelled in advance. The machine requires to do this by itself.
  – Cannot ascertain the analysis results, as there is no prior knowledge, the number of classes also not known leads to the inability to confirm the results generated by the analysis.

■ It needs human intervention in interpreting and labelling the classes which follow that classification.

■ As properties of classes may change, it leads the algorithm not to rely on the same type while moving from one image to another.

In summary, unsupervised learning deals with problems involving the dimensionality reduction process for big data visualization, feature induction, or determining hidden structures. It can draw inferences from data sets consisting of input data without labelled responses.

We have discussed earlier clustering, a popular unsupervised learning technique and how it is helping in exploratory data analysis that can find hidden patterns in data. Also, it helps in the grouping of the data. Gene sequence analysis, market research, and object recognition are examples of applications that benefit from unsupervised learning.

This method finds its application in areas where data has no historical labels. So, the system can't have the "right answer", and the algorithm must identify what it is. The primary goal is to analyse the data and detect a pattern and hidden structure within the available data set. The transactional data may serve as a good source of data set for unsupervised learning.

Semi-supervised Learning Algorithms

There are scenarios/problems in which we need to deal with many input data points. Some data points are labelled, while the remaining data points are unlabelled. These problems are generally coming under semi-supervised learning problems. A good example is to photo-archive the places where only some of the images are labelled (e.g. dog, cat, person, etc.) and other captured images are unlabelled.

Many of the real-world ML problems fall into this category. This category of issues is quite expensive and time-consuming. To properly label the big data, there is a need for domain experts. The unlabelled data is cheap and comparatively easy to collect and store but labelling the unknown (unlabelled) data consumes precious time. The way forward is to use the above-mentioned unsupervised learning techniques to make sense out of unlabelled data. The supervised learning techniques provide the best guess predictions, which would belong to the unlabelled data. We can then feed that data back into the supervised learning algorithm as training data. The resulting model can be used to make correct predictions for new data points.

Research works have shown that using both labelled and unlabelled data offers the best long-term results for learning. The semi-supervised learning is a combination of the previous two categories. It works primarily unsupervised with the improvements that a portion of labelled data can bring. **Semi-supervised learning** fell between unsupervised **learning** (with no labelled training data) and **supervised learning** (with only labelled training data).

Why Is Semi-supervised ML Important?

Clustering, which is a popular unsupervised learning method, that homogeneity of data. That is, it partitions a data set into homogenous subgroups. Clustering generally takes place using unsupervised methods. Since its goal is to identify similarities and differences between any data points, it doesn't require any details about the relationships within the data to make decisions. However, there are situations where a few of the cluster labels, outcome variables, or information about relationships within the data are known to act as supervised. Semi-supervised clustering uses known cluster information to classify other unlabelled data. A text document classifier is an excellent example of semi-supervised learning. Firstly, it is a difficult task to find a large number of labelled text documents. It is not easy for a person to read through the entire text documents to assign a simple classification. So, semi-supervised learning learns from a small number of labelled text documents. In contrast, a large number of unlabelled text documents become classified training data. Below are the steps for semi-supervised learning.

- Start with a minimum training labelled data, train the model like supervised learning, and repeat the exercise until it gives good results.
- Then use it with the unlabelled training data set to predict the outputs, and they are pseudo labels since they may not give a preferred accuracy level.
- Link the labels from the labelled training data with the pseudo labels created in the previous step.
- Link the data inputs in the labelled training data with the information in the unlabelled data.
- Then, train the model as precisely as we did in the first step; however, with the labelled set in the beginning to decrease the error and improve the accuracy of the trained model.

We don't have enough labelled data in many real-time scenarios to produce an accurate model. Those situations use semi-supervised techniques as it helps in increasing the size of our training data. For instance, imagine that we are developing a model to detect fraud for a large bank. We know about some kinds of scams from historical records, and there are some other frauds unanticipated. You can label the data set with the known fraud instances. The unknown fraudulent transactions are still unlabelled. We can use a semi-supervised learning algorithm and label the data to retrain the model with the newly labelled data set. Once the model seems OK, you can supply new data to the retrained model to identify fraud using supervised ML techniques. Precisely speaking, semi-supervised learning is the type of ML that uses a combination of labelled and unlabelled data. Use a small amount of labelled data and many unlabelled data with semi-supervised learning models to train the models.

Reinforcement Learning

Reinforcement learning or RL is also an ML technique, and it has the potential to solve some tricky problems. As depicted in the Figure 6.11, RL goal is to find the best sequence of actions that will generate the optimal outcome. Here the optimal work happens by collecting the most rewards for the intended activities.

In RL, an agent learns in an interactive environment by trial and error using feedback from its actions and experiences. However, both supervised and RL uses mapping between input and output. It's not the same as semi-supervised learning. Unlike supervised learning, as depicted in the following Figure 6.12 RL uses rewards and punishments as signals for positive and negative behaviour, respectively.

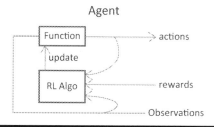

Figure 6.11   Reinforcement Learning

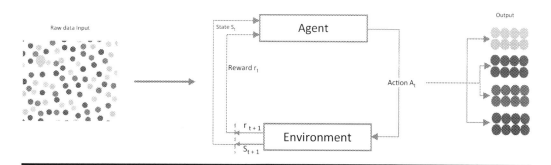

Figure 6.12   Reinforcement Flow

The agent in reinforcement algorithms aims to enforce and learn the best policy by interactions with the environment. Given any state, RL will always take the most optimal action and figure out the possible correct answer to take it to the further steps of the process, having the one that produces the most reward in the long run.

As we see in the preceding diagram, there are three main components in RL, namely agent, actions, and the environment. The agent a decision maker, the activities are what the agent does, and the environment is where the agent interacts with any underlying systems. Actions yield the best rewards enabled by algorithms that use trial and error methods. As stated earlier, the goal of the RL is to select the activities or actions that maximize the reward within a specified time. The purposes of RL get fulfilled by having the best policy or the method by the learning models. These ML models can develop thousands of such models in a week, unlike humans, as they can do only a handful of good models in that time.

Also, an interesting fact about RL is it is one of the most sophisticated algorithms that mimic the closest resemblance to how humans learn. This literary style of learning is an inspiration from game theory and behavioural psychology.

There is a lot of research and focus on RL in almost every field. Navigation, robotics, gaming, manufacturing, delivery management, power systems, healthcare, AI gaming, skill acquisition, robot navigation, and real-time decisions, and many more. RL is already made inroads into robotics and self-driving vehicles. However, it's usually deployed alongside other learning techniques such as supervised learning, creating an ensemble learning model. This combination of multiple algorithms is needed because otherwise, it becomes difficult to apply RL algorithms to scenarios where the environment, actions, and rules are variable. Also, artificial neural networks (ANNs) and DL make use of RL to the fullest extent.

Thus, ML algorithms are gaining surging popularity as they can solve most of the prediction and prescription problems across industry verticals.

The process for choosing the ML algorithm for a problem at hand – Several ML algorithms are emerging and evolving. Knowledge guides are accentuating on choosing ML algorithms that target classification, regression, clustering, and association problems. Finding and finalizing correct ML algorithms for solving problems at hand is not easy, even for seasoned talents. It needs many considerations as it involves many parameters and properties. Thanks to ML experts, as they have a jump starter pack for us with a set of questions that can help us not lose in numerous algorithms but focus on a specific algorithm set and arrive at correct algorithms. Those questions are as below.

- The size, quality, and nature of data;
- The available computational time;
- The urgency of the task;
- And what we want to do with the data.

Even hugely experienced data scientists face this intricate problem in their careers. Finding the most accurate and appropriate algorithms is not an easy task to be taken lightly. Further on, besides ML algorithms, there is a galaxy of ML libraries and frameworks. In the recent past, powerful chipsets are plenty to avail. The aspects of containerization and container orchestration platform solutions play a vital role in shaping data science projects. There are several enabling toolkits and platforms for lessening the workloads on data scientists.

- Data scraping, virtualization, and ingestion tools
- MLOps solutions
- Exposing ML models as microservices with REST APIs
- Containerizing and depositing models as container images
- Model repositories

As known widely, the success of the ML model relies upon the availability of big data. Today companies need to deal with a lot of multi-structured data. Data need cleansing to facilitate the realization of correct results. We have batch and real-time data processing techniques and platforms. However, ML platforms guarantee predictive, prescriptive, and prognostic outcomes. And hence the world is tending towards the ML paradigm. By consciously gleaning hidden insights from voluminous data (internal and external), businesses can increase productivity substantially. This technology empowerment helps them to yearn for a competitive edge in the knowledge-driven and cut-throat competitive environment. ML brings the automation in doing data analytics. For data analytics, we need to give input data and write the appropriate logic to process the data according to evolving needs. But with the spread of ML algorithms, just input data is enough. There is no need of writing the processing logic. Using ML algorithms, worldwide organizations gain premium and distinguished capabilities.

Further on, the ML domain comes in handy for any institution, individual, and innovator to explore, experiment, and expound on newer opportunities and possibilities. Suppose you are keen to steer the business in the right direction towards the targeted destination and leverage ML algorithms adroitly. In that case, the following things power the team and give a thrust to attain the intended success.

- Superior data preparation capabilities
- Knowledge of basic and advanced algorithms
- Cloud-native computing paradigm
- DevOps/GitOps
- Knowledge of ensemble modelling

For ably assisting data scientists and ML engineers in their everyday obligations, scores of automated toolkits, best practices, and guides are made available and marketed. We have discussed myriads of ML algorithms and provided insights that one can get the idea into which algorithm best fits what sort of problems.

Machine Learning Use Cases

Several industry verticals eagerly plan and leverage ML algorithms' unique competencies to be ahead of their competitors. Here are a few real-world applications. With the continuous rise in generating and garnering big data and in making it available across, ML became a lifeline for solving problems in areas such as

- Credit scoring and algorithmic trading in the financial industry
- Image processing and CV, for face identification and recognition, object/gesture/motion detection
- Tumour detection, drug discovery, and DNA sequencing in health science

■ Predictions for several tasks associated with establishing and sustaining smart grids

■ Predictive maintenance of assets and assembly lines across a variety of process industries

■ Enhanced user experience through HMI leveraging ML algorithms

Here are a few industry sectors and how they benefit from the advancements in the ML space. Today analytics is an inevitable supplement towards knowledge discovery. Hereafter, the core and central aspect of every business workload and IT service is none other than analytics. That means AI and data analytics platforms solutions will be an essential ingredient for the future of cognitive IT and business. Several industry verticals have fully embraced the vision of the combination of cognitive computing and the IoT to design, develop, and deploy more intelligent applications. In this section, we discuss a few business domains, which benefit immensely through the incorporation of ML capabilities.

Financial Services – ML algorithms are very much in demand across financial services providers. Especially pre-emptive and proactive fraud detection is essential for the survival of banks and insurance companies. Stock market professionals and investment bankers must go through a tremendous amount of data to take correct decisions. ML algorithms contribute immensely here in expertly simplifying and streamlining the whole process to give perfect and precise inputs/insights in time.

Marketing and Sales – Corporates must approach many to sell their products, solutions, and services. A lot of historical purchase data get decisively mined to understand bright spots and prospects efficiently. Insights-driven recommendations seem the way forward for companies to identify fresh avenues to substantial impact and increased revenue in the big data world. Personalization is one way to sell more products, and ML technologies come in handy here too.

Government – Government officials and administrators must strategically sound decisions on various matters directly affecting their constituents. Multiple data sources are multiplying the number of people and process data getting generated. ML algorithms accelerate data crunching to emit helpful information to drive informed decisions and improve the benefits of people. Smart cities are soon to be the reality through the extensive usage of ML solutions. Connected homes, hospitals, utilities, vehicles, etc., generate a massive amount of multi-structured data and this trending scenario enables several innovations and disruptions for institutions, individuals, and innovators.

Healthcare – The whole world witnessed the devastating impact of Covid-19. The virus mutations have instigated a considerable increase in the Covid +ve patients across. Numerous biosensors and wearables are being manufactured in large quantities to constrain the spread of this pandemic. These multifaceted sensors can cluster themselves to collect and aggregate sensor data to assist people and healthcare officials in strategizing with clarity and enthusiasm. Several healthcare-related activities are getting automated and accelerated with the proper usage of ML algorithms. Remote diagnostics and consultation happen real quick and provide insights from a combination of IoT and ML algorithms. A lot of clinical data are meticulously collected, cleaned, and curated to be used by data scientists to produce highly beneficial patterns, associations, and insights. ML algorithms are accelerating the widely popular process of converting data to information and intelligence. Ultimately the knowledge discovered and disseminated come in handy for multiple stakeholders in precisely predicting various things for patients, doctors, surgeons, molecular biologists, geneticists, virologists, and many specialized medical experts and so on. Automated fever detection, CT scan and voice-based disease identification, prediction of virus-affected people and places, etc., are the prominent use cases of the ML domain. In short, for the world infected with viruses and their variants, ML comes as a solace.

Oil and Gas – This is a prime industry vertical that needs the intelligent application of ML the most. The ML advancements greatly assist in deeply analysing underground minerals, pinpointing new energy sources, streaming oil distribution, etc. This business domain generates volume and volume of data, and ML contributes to realizing data-driven insights and insights-driven decisions and actions in time.

Thus, ML algorithms are greatly promising and path-breaking for myriads of business domains. With the sourcing of big data from different and distributed data sources and aggregators, the solidification of state-of-the-art data analytics platforms, the growing clout of AI algorithms, scores of cutting-edge technologies and tools, and IT infrastructures (public, private, and edge), newer ML applications across industry verticals emerge and get strengthened.

Conclusion

With the faster maturity and stability of ML algorithms, libraries, and frameworks, the adoption rate is going up fast. Many industry verticals have embraced the distinguished ML power to be adaptive, supple, and customer-centric. In this chapter, we have articulated the key unsupervised ML algorithms. Also, we have incorporated some of the popular business domains, which are thriving on ML technology.

References

Overlapping Hirarchical structuring: https://link.springer.com/chapter/10.1007/978-3-030-44584-3_21

An excellent online Guide for AI & ML: https://www.education-ecosystem.com/guides/artificial-intelligence/

Hierachical Clustering and Dendrograms: https://www.statisticshowto.com/hierarchical-clustering/; http://primo.ai/

https://www.xlstat.com/en/solutions/features/agglomerative-hierarchical-clustering-ahc

Agglomerative Clustering: https://www.datanovia.com/en/lessons/agglomerative-hierarchical-clustering/

Semi supervised learning: https://algorithmia.com/blog/semi-supervised-learning

Chapter 7

Deep Learning Algorithms for Cognitive IoT Solutions

Briefing Deep Learning

Artificial intelligence (AI) algorithms turn out to be the cornerstone of the next revolution in computing. These algorithms bring up the ability to recognize patterns based on data observed in the past. This knowledge comes in handy in predicting future outcomes. Amazon extends special offers as we shop online or Netflix recommends videos based on our preferences. These systems don't learn on their own. The intervention of human programming is necessary. Data scientists meticulously prepare the inputs and select the variables to be used for predictive analytics. Deep learning (DL) can do this job automatically.

DL is a field based on learning and improving on its own with powerful DL algorithms. While machine learning (ML) uses more straightforward concepts, DL works with artificial neural networks (ANNs), designed to imitate how human brains process a massive amount of multi-structured data and learn new things quickly. Forming and using neural networks (NNs) were greatly limited by the lack of appropriate computing power. But now, the situation is entirely different as we have robust processor architectures and massive storage along with high-bandwidth networks. Big data analytics (BDA) is becoming possible with the general availability of integrated analytics platforms and enormous computing power. Therefore, designing sophisticated NNs to process and extract accurate and actionable insights from big data is more straightforward and faster. Even with parallel and distributed computing facilities, computers can observe, learn and react to complicated situations better than human beings. DL helps in several areas including but not limited to language translation, speech recognition and image classification problems. It can solve any pattern recognition problem and without human intervention.

As ANNs are being stuffed with many internal layers to go deep into, the vocabulary of DL has gained prominence. Each layer can perform complex operations on an image, such as representation and abstraction found on images, sound, and text. With the faster maturity of DL algorithms and the emergence of supercomputers and clustered cloud servers, which are virtual and affordable supercomputers, the aspect of DL is bound to be phenomenal for worldwide business organizations in fulfilling their automation and acceleration requirements.

The Origin and Mesmerizing Journey of Deep Learning

The humble beginning for DL got a shape and phase in the year 2001. AdaBoost, an ML algorithm, detects faces within an image in real time. This ML algorithm meticulously filters images through decision sets. The decision set consists of rules such as "does the image have bright spots between dark patches, and is it possibly denoting the brßidge of a nose?" When the data gets moved further down the decision tree, the probability of selecting the right face from an image substantially grew. However, this process needs supercomputers. With the arrival of graphics processing units (GPUs), this complicated process started to happen in desktop computers.

Further on, with the setting up of ImageNet, a growing database of millions of labelled images captured from the Internet, the era of DL through breakthrough NNs started to flourish with the nourishment from worldwide researchers. Researchers continuously and consistently are delivering advancements to make DL pervasive and penetrative. There came several DL libraries and frameworks to make it easy to use. For example, Google had open-sourced its TensorFlow product, which is a modern DL library today. There are several other products in the market today.

Digital assistants like Alex, Siri, Cortana, and Google Now extensively use DL for speech recognition. Skype translates conversations to captions in real time. Several education portal video lectures provide transcripts on the fly. Many email platforms can identify spam messages before they land in their respective inboxes. An impressive achievement was from PayPal, that it has developed a DL algorithm to prevent fraudulent payments. Google DeepMind's AlphaGo computer program proved best among standing champions at the game of Go. DeepMind's WaveNet generates speech mimics human voice that sounds more natural than the currently available speech systems. Google Translate is a DL application, and it does image recognition to translate voice and written texts of different languages. Google Planet identifies the location where the photo was taken/captured.

As indicated above, robust NNs are the lifeline of self-driving cars. The NNs go through intense training to determine obstruction objects to avoid on the road, recognize traffic lights and lampposts in real time, and adjust the speed accordingly. NNs get into almost every field and becoming adept at forecasting everything from stock prices to the weather. Digital assistants could recommend when to sell shares or when to evacuate ahead of a possible hurricane. New DL algorithms and approaches are emerging and evolving fast. Thereby a variety of real-time and real-world applications could be articulated and accomplished through the power of DL, which has distinctly gained the ability to design even evidence-based treatment plans for medical patients and help detect cancers early.

How Deep Learning Works?

NNs represent layers of compute nodes as our brain, made of multiple neurons. Nodes within layers are connected to adjacent layers to continue with intensive and specific data processing/analytics. A single neuron of a human brain can receive and process thousands of signals from other neurons. Similarly, in an ANN, signals travel between nodes and assign corresponding weights. Heavier (weights) the node higher the exertion effect on the subsequent layers. The final layer assimilates and aggregates the weighted inputs to produce an output. As indicated above, DL systems require enormous computing power as they have to process big data and use complex mathematical functions to zero down on the correct outcome. Even with such a high-end computing facility, arriving at DL models can take weeks.

When processing the data, ANNs can classify data with the answers received from a series, with binary options (true or false) questions involving complex mathematical calculations. For example, a facial recognition program learns to detect and recognize edges and lines of faces, then essential parts of the faces, and the overall representations of faces. With more intense training, the probability of arriving at correct answers significantly increases. That is, machines can accurately identify faces with training and time.

For example, an NN can recognize photos containing a dog image with necessary training. There are varieties of dogs with their looks and poses different, images captured in various situations, lightings, indoors, outdoors, and settings. So, there is a growing set of images neatly depicting multiple aspects. Humans categorize many of the images as dogs and the remaining images as "not a dog" classification. The images fed into the NN gets converted to data. These data then moves through the networks, and various nodes assign different weights to multiple elements of those images. The last output layer in the array compiles the seemingly disconnected information and delivers the output (whether there is a dog image or not).

If the output is correct as certified by humans, then it is ok. If not, then the NN notes down the error and adjusts the weights. The NN always thrives on improving its recognition skills by repeatedly adjusting its weights again and again. This training technique is called supervised learning. The NN is not explicitly told what "makes" a dog. NNs have to recognize patterns in data over time and learn on their own.

Transfer Learning – Most DL applications use the transfer learning method. The transfer learning method involves fine-tuning a pre-trained model. We start with an existing network such as GoogLeNet and feed in new data to bring in appropriate refinements. These network refinements help to perform a few necessary tweaks to the NN. Once the model reached better accuracy, it can take a new task. The advantage of this learning is that there is no need to provide a large amount of data to arrive at competent models. When the amount of data is not massive, the time, energy, and space complexities are bound to be lesser. Transfer learning needs an exposed interface to the internals of the chosen existing network. These interfaces come in handy so that they can be modified and enhanced for the new task.

DL models generally use large sets of labelled data and NN architectures for their training needs. It can learn features directly from the data without the need for any manual feature extraction. Convolutional neural networks (CNNs) are popular NN types and famous for working with images. A CNN convolves features learned from the past with input data and uses 2D convolutional layers. These layers give CNN the best spot and make it suitable for processing 2D data such as images. With CNNs, there is no need to do manual feature extraction. That is, we do not need to identify the features that typically classify the images. The CNN functions by extracting features directly from photos. The relevant classes get necessary learnings automatically while the NN trains on a set of images. There can be hundreds of hidden layers depending upon the complexity of the problem at hand. This distinct capability leads to the fulfilment of computer vision tasks such as object classification.

DL, a grandiose subset of ML, is hugely distinct from ML. An ML workflow typically starts with relevant features, which are extracted from images manually. Then those extracted features used to create a model that primarily categorizes the objects in the embodiment. As indicated above, DL extracts features in an automated manner. Another noteworthy difference is that DL leverages big data. DL requires massive amounts of **labelled data**, such as millions of static and thousands of dynamic images. Besides, to achieve critical success, we need high-performance GPUs, tensor processing units (TPUs), and vision processing units (VPUs). The parallel architecture associated with the recent chipsets boosts DL. Also, we have cluster and cloud computing environments in plenty these days. Thereby, training DL models and refining them are being completed in a couple of hours rather than days and even weeks. The powerful chipsets in association with big data come in handy in fulfilling higher decision accuracy. DL needs such an enhanced accuracy, especially for safety-critical applications like self-driving cars. There are several noteworthy advancements in DL in automating most of the recognition, detection, vision, perception, and prediction activities.

The Deep Learning Use Cases

With the technologies and tools in place, the realization of DL applications is made swift and straightforward. In this section, we are to discuss a few famous use cases:

Automated Driving – Automobile manufacturing companies are focusing on producing self-driving cars and vehicles nowadays. Advanced and latest cars are empowered to collect and crunch various internal and external data to decide everything instantaneously so that they can steer in the right direction without any risk. The fully trained and optimized DL models can detect, predict, perceive, and decide several things for cars to smoothly tend towards the designated destination. Traffic lights, lampposts, pedestrians, objects, and other decision-enabling aspects rightfully are understood by cars through DL models.

Aerospace and Défense – DL models are used to accurately detect and predict objects of particular interest from satellite images in real time. This unique capability brings forth a variety of advantages and choices for troops operating in certain areas.

Medical Research – Detecting cancer cells precisely and perfectly is being accomplished through DL models. This detection capability goes a long way for surgeons and researchers to work out different things with clarity and confidence. Teams at UCLA have built an advanced microscope that provides a high-dimensional data set to train a DL model and find almost accurate cancer cells in patients' bodies.

Industrial Automation – A variety of tasks associated with industrial operations and manufacturing are getting automated profusely through the liberal usage of DL capabilities. Industries do product inspection, fake detection, and ensure an excellent level of worker safety through the intelligent use of DL algorithms and approaches.

Machine Vision – DL is expanding its scope as computer vision and machine vision competencies happening through DL. Face recognition, object detection, speech translation, video analytics, etc., are being facilitated through the power of DL. Home assistance devices, which are becoming prominent, penetrative, and pervasive, can understand our commands and respond accordingly.

In summary, DL is an ML field. DL and ANNs can complement each other to solve computer vision assignments such as image recognition, image classification, object detection, and pose estimation. There are different configurations of ANNs, such as CNNs, recurrent neural networks (RNNs), and deep neural networks (DNNs). These can automatically extract right and relevant features from data points and formats such as texts, static and dynamic images.

The Significance of Deep Learning Algorithms

The primary building block of DL is DNNs. This network has to process images and videos, and hence there are several layers in between the initial and the final layers. Typically, there are three different types of algorithms or problem classes for DL.

Classification

Here, you are processing the image at the whole image level. The algorithm is responsible for taking an image and then deriving a class from training data by learning on the entire image. For example, you are looking at a particular car model, and it identifies whether this is Model A or Model B. It takes the entire image as input and processes it to understand the difference between the two. You could have many different classes, and that makes it a multi-class architecture.

The typical application could be identifying a particular stock-keeping unit (SKU). You're doing incoming stock inventory and you're trying to determine which one of those incoming SKUs is coming into your material line. So, it takes an image, and from that entire image, it identifies that this belongs to SKU A. Suppose the feature within a photo or print is broad enough or visible enough concerning the whole picture. In that case, you could also use it for classifying whether something is defective or not defective. So, if the defect features are significant, that could also be an easy way to train an NN to identify whether something is good or bad.

Object Detection

And here it is a bit deep. That is, you are not trying to classify entire images, but you are going a little deep in pinpointing specific objects in the picture. The things could be the internal parts of a refrigerator like a shelf or a freezer compartment or a manual that's present. So here, it identifies the location as well as the presence of that object.

For object detection, a classic example could be assembly verification. It is all about identifying if all the engine parts within an engine body are present.

Segmentation

This is going a little bit deeper. And this is analysing the image at a pixel level. In segmentation, there are two types of segmentation problems: instance segmentation and semantic segmentation. In segmentation, analysis happens on each pixel to identify if they belong to a specific class. So, in this particular example, it could be whether each pixel is part of a vehicle, a part of the road, or a part of any other object present on the scene. So, you're going at not only just identifying the thing in a bounding box, but you're trying to classify every pixel present on this particular image.

The instance segmentation capability not only classifies whether a pixel belongs to a pedestrian but also tries to identify different instances of different pedestrians present in the image. So, if we have five other pedestrians or people, it classifies each of those five as separate instances and gives you that information. This information enables industrial machine vision and its use cases.

So, let's say you have a smooth surface and you're trying to identify a scratch or a dent. And the scratches and the marks can be pretty minor. So here, you have to determine which pixels of that entire surface in the image constitute a defect. For the ML algorithm or the NN to identify, you should have trained this algorithm to do this detection. And the process of training is called DL. And the training process involves a technique called supervised learning. The supervised learning technique is teaching by examples. So you give sufficient examples of the different types of classes or other varieties of images that you want it to identify. Then you teach it with those examples. The NN builds a specific model that helps you predict any kind of images that may come later (future) for recognizing or identification.

Classic ML algorithms work well for data sets with up to a few hundred characteristics. Many new technologies, like image recognition, are a different beast. A single RGB image of 1200 × 1000 pixel has 36 million qualities, and the classic ML approach to such data sets is insufficient. These drawback of inadequate data sets leads the world to explore DL and its enabling algorithms as its prime motivation.

The Top Deep Learning Algorithms

Several things are happening in parallel in the IT landscape. Without an iota of doubt, this is a big data era. With the exponential expansion of connected devices in everyday life, the world is emitting petabytes of digital data per day. Correspondingly we have parallel and high-performance server machines and storage appliances to collect and crunch digital data. There are BDA platforms.

Further on, we have promising machine and DL algorithms to purposefully analyse and mine digital data easily and quickly. In this section, we are to focus on the well-known and widely used DL algorithms. Let us start with some basic terms.

Modelled loosely after the human brain, the NNs are a set of algorithms. NN principles and design enforce the devices to recognize various trends and interpret sensory data through machine perception. NNs can also label or cluster raw input. The identified patterns are numerical and contained in vectors, into which all real-world data, be it images, sound, text, or time series, have to be transformed.

NNs typically help us with grouping and classifying data. NNs need to act on clusters and classification layer on top of any digital data collection. They can group unlabelled data according to some similarities among the example inputs, and they also can classify data on the training set when they have a labelled data set. NNs can also extract features that work as input to other algorithms for clustering and classification.

In short, an NN is a composition of perceptrons interconnected in different ways and that can operate on other activation functions. A perceptron is an algorithm used in the supervised learning of binary classifiers. A binary classifier is a function that decides whether an input (represented as a vector of numbers) belongs in one of two classes. A perceptron network is called a multilayer perceptron, as seen in Figure 7.1 also known as an artificial neural network (ANN).

Artificial Neural Networks (ANNs) – Generally, if there are more layers, then the model is deeper. That means we can attain higher performance.

DL uses layers of NN algorithms to decipher higher-level information at other layers based on raw input data. For example, in an image-recognition use case, one layer could identify features such as sharp edges or contrasts in light, while another could identify how different distinct shapes appear. Further, a third layer could decipher what the image is showing. All these are achievable by learning how information from previous layers understood together to form different objects.

NN algorithms designs recognize data patterns based on an early understanding of how the human brain functions. Visualization of DNNs as components of larger ML applications helps in involving algorithms for reinforcement learning, classification, and regression. The DL algorithm uses self-taught knowledge, and it constructs

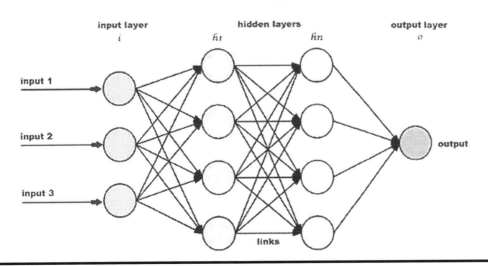

Figure 7.1   A Sample Artificial Neural Network Model

with many hidden layers, big data, and powerful computational resources. DL architecture implementation to social network filtering, fraud detection, image and video processing, audio and speech recognition, object detection, computer vision, bioinformatics, customer relationship management, etc., is getting pertinent focus for most industries' future strategy. Today's DL architecture primary constitution is based on ANN principles and characteristics that utilize non-linear processing (of multiple layers) to extract and transform features.

DL algorithms are feature self-learning representations. Those representations do depend on ANN's (the way they imitate the process of the human brain) method of processes information. Non-supervised learnings such as DL algorithms use unknown elements in the input data and extract insights, functional features, group objects and discover useful data patterns while training. All these happen at multiple levels using several algorithms to build the models. As indicated above, DL models make use of several algorithms. One single algorithm is perfect for all the requirements. Therefore, the trend is to leverage multiple algorithms together.

Let's gain a solid understanding of all primary algorithms from the below sections as we have touched upon a few critical ML algorithms. Also, please refer to the reference section should you need deeper details.

Multilayer Perceptron Neural Network (MLPNN)

The multilayer perceptron is a feed-forward supervised learning algorithm with a minimum of three layers of nodes, one for the input layer, one for the hidden layer, and one for the output layer. They are hidden layers because they are not directly exposed to the input and can generate outputs from a given set of information. As it indicates, this is composed of many perceptrons. They connect multiple layers of neurons in a directed graph to pass through the nodes in one direction. The output vector is computed with the inputs and a random selection of weights in the feed-forward computational network flow. The model trained to learn the correlation or dependencies between the given information and expected results from a training data set. It computes the error ratio between the desired outcome for a given input, and training involves tuning the weights and biases to reduce error at the output layer. Then repeat the process for hidden layers going backwards. Backpropagation makes the weight and bias adjustments relative to the error. We can measure those errors in a variety of ways, including with root-mean-squared error (RMSE).

MLPNNs can classify non-linearly separable data points, solve complex problems involving several parameters, and handle data sets with a large number of features, especially non-linear ones. MLPNN is used to solve problems that require supervised learning and parallel distributed processing.

- Image verification and reconstruction
- Speech recognition
- Machine translation
- Data classification
- E-commerce, where many parameters are involved

Backpropagation

The backpropagation algorithm is a supervised learning algorithm. It computes a gradient descent with the weights updated backwards (from output towards input) and hence termed as backpropagation. Initially, an NN consists of weights and biases. However, it goes through an imperfect calibration process to read data. An NN's interpretation of data and the physical world is made through the values of its weights and biases. Therefore, a poorly calibrated NN implies a flawed model. Whatever errors exist at the final prediction layer are sent back through the network to adjust the weights and biases so that future predictions have lower error values.

The algorithm calculates each neuron's error contribution using a delta rule technique or gradient descent optimization. The weight of neurons is adjusted to reduce the error at the output layer. Gradient descent implies a rate of change of a target marked as Y for change in a parameter marked as X. Here, Y would be the error produced in the NN prediction. X would represent various parameters in the data. Because there's more than one parameter, they use partial derivatives for each parameter. Also, because the layers of NNs operate sequentially, finding the derivatives at each layer establishes a relation of the change of error at each layer for parameters compared to its previous and subsequent layers.

Backpropagation lets developers know how the points of error contribute to weights, and with training, the network can map all those points while simultaneously adjusting all weights. It works well in error-prone projects and can be used to train DNNs. Backpropagation can be used in image and speech recognition to improve predictions and accuracy in data mining and ML and in projects where quick calculation of derivatives is necessary.

Convolutional Neural Network (CNN)

CNN, also known as ConvNet, is a multilayer, feed-forward NN that uses perceptrons for supervised learning and to analyse data. Its primary usage is with visual data, such as image classification. A deep convolutional architecture called AlexNet was the basis for the ImageNet Large Scale Visual Recognition Competition (ILSVRC). Its success was the primary reason for profound research in DL.

CNNs are not only for image recognition but also applied directly to text analytics. CNNs play a vital role in voice or sound as visual representation as a spectrogram and graph data using graph convolutional networks. To understand CNN architecture better, let us consider images as data. Typically, with computer vision, images are treated as two-dimensional matrices of numbers. However, in CNNs, an image is treated as a tensor or a matrix of numbers with additional dimensions. Tensors are arrays of arrays, the formation of tensors is nesting arrays, and nesting may be infinite.

Images, in particular, are considered as four-dimensional tensors. If a scalar is a zero-dimensional object, then a vector is one-dimensional. A matrix or collection of vectors is two-dimensional, and a stack of such matrices is the third dimension. Then a four-dimensional tensor is of multiple such three-dimensional objects where each object of the cube has a stack of feature maps connected to it.

The CNNs contain convolutional layers, normalization layers, pooling layers, and a fully connected layer, and they are hidden layers. It takes an image as input, assigns significant weights and biases to various aspects of the image to enable differentiation, and applies filters with minimum pre-processing. While the first convolution layer captures low-level features, the successive layers extract higher-level features, creating a network with a sophisticated analysis of the images in the data set. The CNN algorithm is highly efficient at recognition and highly adaptable. It's also easy to train because there are fewer training parameters and is scalable when coupled with backpropagation. CNN primary use cases involved where applications need

- Image processing, recognition, and classification
- Video recognition
- Natural language-processing tasks
- Pattern recognition
- Recommendation engines
- Medical image analysis

Recurrent Neural Network (RNN)

RNN recognize a data set's sequential attribute and use patterns to predict the next available best scenario in the sequence. It is a powerful approach to process sequential data like language, sound, time-series data, and written texts. The stochastic gradient descent (SGD), the randomness in gradient descent algorithm, is used to train the network along with a backpropagation algorithm.

In traditional networks, inputs and outputs are independent of each other. But in an RNN, the hidden layer needs to preserve the information from previous steps to use the same weights and bias for prediction. Preserving of information happens by saving output from an earlier stage and fed back to the current action from an in-built memory or storage. These layers with necessary data then combined to create a single recurrent layer. These feedback loops process sequential data, allowing information to persist, as in memory, and inform the final output. If an RNN needs to predict the subsequent letter of an earlier input letter, it is achieved by feeding letters of known words letter by letter in training to determine the relevant patterns. RNNs are layered to process information feed-forward and feedback loops. Feed-forward process data from initial input to final output and feedback loop use backpropagation, i.e. it loops the information back into the network.

RNNs are not feed-forward networks because feed-forward networks inputs are sequential, i.e. it accepts one input and one output at a time. RNN doesn't have this constraint as it can refer to previous examples from the built-in memory to form predictions. CNNs can learn the context in sequence-prediction problems, as well as process sequential and temporal data. They also can be used in a range of applications.

- Sentiment classification
- Image captioning
- Speech recognition

- Natural language processing
- Machine translation
- Search prediction
- Video classification

Long Short-Term Memory (LSTM)

This LSTM algorithm is a type of RNN that allows the training of deep recurrent networks without making the gradients that update weights become unstable. Patterns can stay in memory for more extended periods, with the ability to selectively recall or delete data. It uses backpropagation, but it can learn only the sequence data using memory blocks connected into layers instead of neurons. As the information processed through the layers, the architecture can add, remove, or modify data as needed. This algorithm is best suited for classification and prediction based on time series data. These enable data scientists to create deep models using large stacked networks and handle complex sequence problems in ML more efficiently. This algorithm is ideal for

- Captioning of images and videos
- Language translation and modelling
- Sentiment analysis
- Stock market predictions

Generative Adversarial Network (GAN)

GAN is a robust algorithm used for unsupervised learning. When given a training set, the network automatically discovers and learns regularities and patterns in input data to self-learn to generate new data. It can essentially mimic any data set with slight variations. GANs are deep neural net architectures comprising two nets, pitting one against the other and use two sub-models, one is called generators, and the other is discriminator. The generator creates new examples of data while the discriminator distinguishes between actual domain data and fake generated samples. As we repeatedly run algorithms, they become more and more robust with each repetition. The generative and discriminative algorithms differ in a few fundamental ways.

- Discriminative algorithms separate a data set into distinct classes based on similarities in their features, like classifying emails into spam and not spam. You could say the likelihood of a data point being class Yi given features Xi – p(y|x) in terms of conditional probability.
- Generative algorithms try to determine the likelihood of a set of features in a data point that is already classified. For example, the generative algorithm finds out how likely the actual words present in the email are to be present in a non-spam-type message to help determine and categorize the email as not spam. Say the classification Yi – p(x|y)0 in terms of conditional probability, the probability of features x and i are existing for a data point p.

GANs can capture and copy variations within a given data set, generate images from a given data set of images, create high-quality data, and manipulate data. GANs are useful for

- Cybersecurity
- Health diagnostics
- Natural language processing
- Speech processing

Deep Belief Network (DBN)

DBN is a probabilistic DL algorithm, and its network has a generative learning model. We have discussed the generative learning is a process of constructing interpretations through generating relationships and associations between the current data set (knowledge), assumptions, etc. It is a blend of directed and undirected graphs (network), with the top layer an undirected RBM and the lower layers directed downward. These layers enable a pre-training stage and a feed-forward network for the fine-tuning stage. The DBN has multiple layers of hidden units connected, and the learning algorithm is "greedy" from the stacked RBMs, meaning there is one layer at a time, sequentially from the bottom observed layer. DBNs offer energy-based learning and can benefit from unlabelled data.

The applications include:

- Image and face recognition
- Video-sequence recognition
- Motion-capture data
- Classifying high-resolution satellite image data

Hands-On Lab

A Sample Implementation of CNN Image Classification with Python

As we have discussed many of the DL process and algorithms earlier, having a sample implementation of anyone DNN algorithm (CNN image classification) would opt to conclude this chapter, so go ahead and try your hands on the given sample implementation.

> *This chapter source code is available at the repository*
> https://github.com/mybookssamplecode/dnn-samples/tree/master/ch-6-dnn

The folder structure of the sample python code is as depicted in the Figure 7.2

Preceding python code examples implement a CNN, a most popular image classification ANN model. CNN models are prevalent in healthcare, automobiles, and many

master ▾   dnn-samples / ch-6-dnn /

..

🖿 model

🖿 test-images

🗋 evaluateCNNModel.py

🗋 finalModelCNN.py

🗋 sampleImageClassificationWithCNN.py

🗋 testMyModel.py

Figure 7.2   Project Folder Structure

more fields. For instance, healthcare professionals can predict Covid-19 or common flu from the patient X-Rays. Automobile engineers may able to find damaged automobile/machinery parts from the images and so on.

The preceding Figure 7.3 represents a CNN architecture and how the CNN picks up pixel positions and neighbourhood semantic meanings and elements of interest from any part of the image.

Here in this section, we cover a primary example (yet most important for a hands-on) model predicting a hand-written digit from an input image using CNN. CNN image classification layers as depicted in the preceding Figure 7.4 involve convolution, pooling, flattening, and full connection.

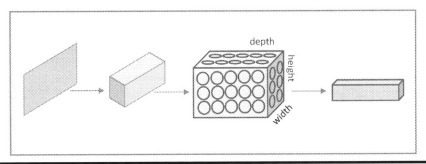

Figure 7.3   CNN Model

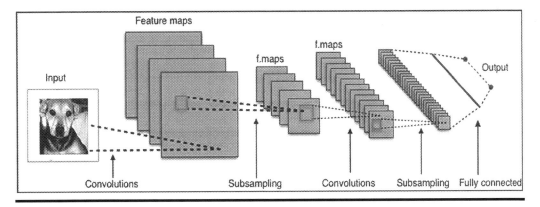

Figure 7.4   CNN Stages

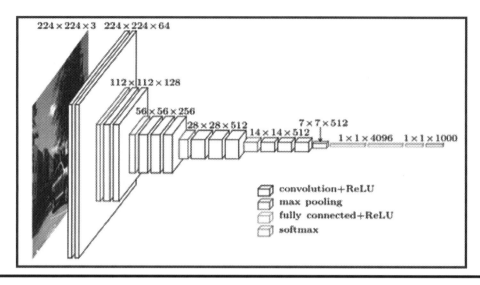

Figure 7.5 CNN Layers

The preceding Figure 7.5 provides more details of each layer of CNN; we will get into a primary sample, yet critical for us to get heads-around on CNN with code. Please note that our example uses Kera library, ReLU (rectified non-linear unit), the most successful in combat the vanishing gradient issues, and easy to compute and generate sparsely;

Please note that we will continue to use the PyCharm IDE for running the sample for this CNN example. But later, we will introduce readers with more powerful online tools to run more complex models online without the need to download high volume and install powerful software to local machines for faster results.

Importing necessary libraries

```
from numpy import mean
from numpy import std
from matplotlib import pyplot
from sklearn.model_selection import KFold
from keras.datasets import mnist
from keras.utils import to_categorical
from keras.models import Sequential
from keras.layers import Conv2D
from keras.layers import MaxPooling2D
from keras.layers import Dense
from keras.layers import Flatten
from keras.optimizers import SGD
```

Convolution

```
model = Sequential()
model.add(Conv2D(32, (3, 3), activation='relu',
```

Pooling

```
model.add(MaxPooling2D((2, 2)))
```

Flatten

```
model.add(Flatten())
```

We have different Python source code for the readers to execute and see the output one by one. We will discuss some of the results of SampleImageClassificationWithCNN in the below section.

Please note that the execution takes several minutes. However, we don't need to run all the code again and again, and with finalModel.py we will save the model, and so with testMyModel.py we would be able to input images of hand-written digits and quickly predict the number from the saved model.

```
2020-07-26 09:57:37.619634: W tensorflow/stream_executor/platform/default/dso_loader.cc:55] Could not load dynamic library 'cudart64_101.dll'; dlerror: cudart64_101.dll not found
2020-07-26 09 57 37.620040: I tensorflow/stream_executor/cuda/cudart_stub.cc:29] Ignore above cudart dlerror if you do not have a GPU set up on your machine.
2020-07-26 09:57:41.526975: I tensorflow/stream_executor/platform/default/dso_loader.cc:44] Successfully opened dynamic library nvcuda.dll
2020-07-26 09:57:42.543196: I tensorflow/core/common_runtime/gpu/gpu_device.cc:1561] Found device 0 with properties:
pciBusID: 0000:01:00.0 name: Quadro P1000 computeCapability: 6.1
coreClock: 1.5185GHz coreCount: 4 deviceMemorySize: 4.00GiB deviceMemoryBandwidth: 89.53GiB/s
2020-07-26 09:57:42.544815: W tensorflow/stream_executor/platform/default/dso_loader.cc:55] Could not load dynamic library 'cudart64_101.dll'; dlerror: cudart64_101.dll not found
2020-07-26 09 57 42.546035: W tensorflow/stream_executor/platform/default/dso_loader.cc:55] Could not load dynamic library 'cublas64_10.dll'; dlerror: cublas64_10.dll not found
2020-07-26 09:57:42.547242: W tensorflow/stream_executor/platform/default/dso_loader.cc:55] Could not load dynamic library 'cufft64_10.dll'; dlerror: cufft64_10.dll not found
2020-07-26 09:57:42.548434: W tensorflow/stream_executor/platform/default/dso_loader.cc:55] Could not load dynamic library 'curand64_10.dll'; dlerror: curand64_10.dll not found
2020-07-26 09:57:42.549638: W tensorflow/stream_executor/platform/default/dso_loader.cc:55] Could not load dynamic library 'cusolver64_10.dll'; dlerror: cusolver64_10.dll not found
2020-07-26 09:57:42.550849: W tensorflow/stream_executor/platform/default/dso_loader.cc:55] Could not load dynamic library 'cusparse64_10.dll'; dlerror: cusparse64_10.dll not found
2020-07-26 09:57:42.552063: W tensorflow/stream_executor/platform/default/dso_loader.cc:55] Could not load dynamic library 'cudnn64_7.dll'; dlerror: cudnn64_7.dll not found
2020-07-26 09:57:42.552449: W tensorflow/core/common_runtime/gpu/gpu_device.cc:1598] Cannot dlopen some GPU libraries. Please make sure the missing libraries mentioned above are installed properl
Skipping registering GPU devices...
2020-07-26 09:57:42.553590: I tensorflow/core/platform/cpu_feature_guard.cc:143] Your CPU supports instructions that this TensorFlow binary was not compiled to use: AVX2
2020-07-26 09:57:42.581100: I tensorflow/compiler/xla/service/service.cc:188] XLA service 0x134bc3d37b0 initialized for platform host (this does not guarantee that XLA will be used). Devices:
2020-07-26 09:57:42.561431: I tensorflow/compiler/xla/service/service.cc:196]   StreamExecutor device (0): Host, Default Version
2020-07-26 09:57:42.563224: I tensorflow/core/common_runtime/gpu/gpu_device.cc:1102] Device interconnect StreamExecutor with strength 1 edge matrix:
2020-07-26 09:57:42.563588: I tensorflow/core/common_runtime/gpu/gpu_device.cc:1108]
```

Ignore the warnings as we don't use the Nvidia GPU processor; however, if readers wish to have GPUs (parallel processing) in their execution environment, please follow the Nvidia CUDA toolkit installation.

Run the SampleImageClassificaitonWithCNN.py and observe the below output; our console will display accuracies as and when we train the model with images from the MINST data set.

> 98.567
> 98.592
> 98.542
> 98.733
> 98.767

Plots for the classification accuracy and loss as depicted in the Figures 7.6 and 7.7.

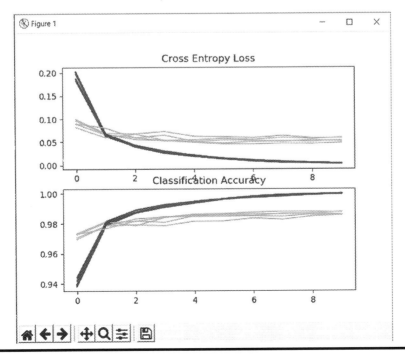

Figure 7.6   CNN Output Plot

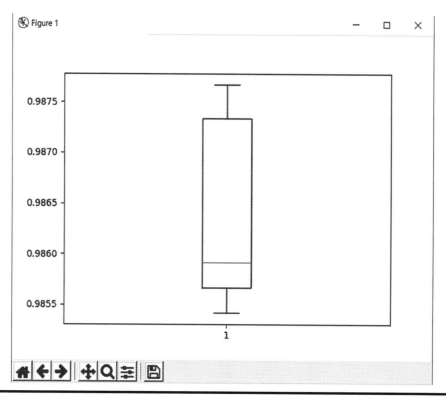

Figure 7.7   CNN Accuracy plot

Also, observe the below accuracy and the exit code to assert our code created the model.

```
Accuracy: mean=98.640 std=0.092, n=5

Process finished with exit code 0
```

Save the Model

So, far we haven't saved our model, so let's run finalModel.py, and after several minutes, please observe we have the model created and saved in the same folder (final_model.h5).

Evaluate and Test

Let's run the evaluateCNNModel.py and observer the below output in your PyCharm console.

```
2020-07-26 15:20:56.217820: I tensorflow/core/common_runtime/gpu/gpu_device.cc:1102] Device :
2020-07-26 15:20:56.218249: I tensorflow/core/common_runtime/gpu/gpu_device.cc:1108]
> 99.300

Process finished with exit code 0
```

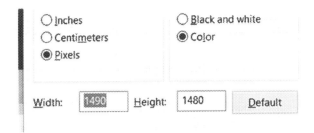

Figure 7.8   Sample hand written digit

Now time to test with our input images, so run testMyModel.py and witness your input images** reflect as a digit

** Note that you can download different images of digits and ensure the background of the image is black and the numbers are in white pixels; also, the size of the image represented in pixel 1490 × 1480. We can modify it with simple paint/png tools; below Figure 7.8 is the screenshot of MS Paint and a sample image when viewing in 25% zoom; and you can also create hand-drawing images as well.

Also, we encourage readers to visit 3-D and live explanation of the CNN algorithm at the below website: https://www.cs.ryerson.ca/~aharley/vis/conv/

Summary

DL is an essential artificial intelligence (AI) function that typically mimics the workings of the human brain in processing data for use in detecting objects, recognizing speech, translating languages, and making decisions. DL AI is distinct because it can learn without human supervision. DL can happen by generating insights out of multi-structured data.

There are powerful DL algorithms facilitating computers, communicators, and edge devices to learn from data automatically. This self-learning empowers systems and machines to discover, detect, and perceive something valuable and unique without any intervention, instruction, and involvement of humans. Ultimately all kinds of personal, social, and professional devices will become intelligent in their actions and reactions by embedding DL capability. This chapter discussed each of the popular DL algorithms and how they contribute to visualizing and realizing next-generation AI products, platforms, solutions, and services.

References

Deep Learning Inroduction: https://www.mathworks.com/discovery/deep-learning.html
https://www.ibm.com/cloud/learn/deep-learning
Deep Learning Algorithm and architectures: https://ieeexplore.ieee.org/stamp/stamp.jsp?arnumber=869478
Recurrent Neural Network: https://machinelearningmastery.com/an-introduction-to-recurrent-neural-networks-and-the-math-that-powers-them/
Deep Belief Network: https://ieeexplore.ieee.org/abstract/document/7111524

Chapter 8

Computer Vision (CV) Technologies and Tools for Vision-based Cognitive IoT Systems

Introduction

Computer vision (CV) trains computers to interpret and understand the world visually. Today, a number of innovations and disruptions have converged together to bring in a real renaissance in the field of CV. Smartphones with built-in cameras have saturated and stuffed the world with photographs and videos. Computing power has become affordable and accessible. Powerful chipsets are being produced in plenty. There are pioneering processor architectures. New algorithms such as convolutional neural networks (CNNs) and recurrent neural networks (RNNs) have emerged and solidified to take instantaneous and intrinsic advantages of high-performing hardware and software modules promising better future for the total human society. The effects of these distinct advancements in the CV field have been astounding thus far. Accuracy rates for object identification and classification have gone up significantly. The much-worried accuracy level is easily touching 99% these days. And today's systems are more accurate than humans at quickly detecting and reacting to visual inputs.

For a computer, an image is just an array of pixels, which are numerical values that represent shades of red, green, and blue. The longstanding challenge is how to enable our computers and electronic gadgets to quickly and accurately make sense out of photos and videos as we do in our everyday lives. Software engineers could create software solutions to perform such a thing. That is, software can precisely and concisely receive, process, perceive, and describe the specific content of any visual data. But crafting such a challenging software package for pinpointing specific objects in a photo or in a video has inspired many to visualize and realize a host of

DOI: 10.1201/9780429328220-8

machine and deep learning (DL) algorithms to artistically replicate this fundamental function of the human brain in a simplified manner. Machine learning (ML) has enabled machines to identify interesting patterns and objects in image files. DL went one step ahead and has brought in a series of automations in processing and analysing images and videos. The deeper and decisive automation brought in by DL is being perceived and proclaimed as the real game changer. CV thereafter thrived and today with all the technological advancements and the ready availability of necessary computer infrastructure, resources, and algorithms, it reached 99% accuracy from 50% a decade ago.

Image Processing vs Computer Vision – Image processing is a shallow processing of images just like raw data is conventionally getting collected, cleaned, stored, processed, and presented in an informative fashion. Searching, querying, manipulation, and visualization of data become possible with the stability of databases, query languages, and business intelligence (BI) tools. In the same way, images are captured, pre-processed, stocked, and processed to serve users' requests. Image processing is something closely associated with smoothing, sharpening, contrasting, stretching, etc. It makes the image more enhancive and readable That is, there is no deeper and decisive analytics and mining of image files with the intention of extracting useful and usable insights out of them. With the penetration of analytics tools, slowly images are getting analysed in a deeper and decisive manner. Not only images but also videos are subjected to a variety of investigations in order to squeeze out actionable insights in time.

That is, CV is the advanced version of image processing. A CV system collects a lot of images and videos and analyses them in order to discover useful patterns and objects hidden inside the images and videos. Ultimately, the goal of CV is to empower computers, robots, drones, consumer electronics, and machines to emulate human vision. That is, computers and communicators and other edge devices are able to do self-learning to make correct inferences and take actions based on visual inputs. CV is not limited to pixel-wise operations and is more advanced. The input can be images and videos and the output can be any quantitative or qualitative information. Precisely speaking, CV is to recognize distinct objects of any image or video and recommend something useful for people or actuation systems to factor the next and best course of actions with all the clarity and confidence.

In the past, even supercomputers might take days or weeks to chug through all the calculations required to finish a CV task. Today's ready availability of ultra-fast and specialized chips along with the speedy and reliable Internet makes this process lightning fast. Nowadays there are powerful DL algorithms and hence many real-world applications of CV get done in microseconds. Real-time CV use cases are being unearthed and popularized due to the noteworthy advancements in the field of CV. Not only computers but also machines in homes, hospitals, hotels, manufacturing floors, retail stores, and entertainment plazas are enabled with vision capability. Before the advent of DL, CV tasks were not that advanced. Further on, even a simple CV task required a lot of manual coding and the effort needed were very huge. For instance, if you wanted to perform facial recognition, you would have to do the following.

- **Create a database** – Capture and store all the right and relevant images in a specific format.

- **Annotate images** – Then for every individual image, there is a need to add several key data points, such as distance between the eyes, the width of nose bridge, distance between upper-lip and nose, and other fine-grained details in order to unambiguously define the unique characteristics of each person.
- **Capture new images** – Capture new images from photos or videos and repeat the process.

A new image has to be compared with the ones stocked in the database to tell whether it corresponds with any of the profiles. This is a time-consuming, error-prone, and manual process. Therefore, automation is mandated to simplify and speed up the recognition process.

ML has brought in a delectable breakthrough in accelerating CV needs. With ML, developers need not manually code every single rule in their vision applications. Instead they programme "features", which are smaller applications that could detect specific patterns in images. Then a statistical learning algorithm such as linear regression, logistic regression, decision trees, or support vector machines (SVM) is used to detect patterns and classify images and detect objects in them. Thus, the ML approach has solved many problems of classical software development and maintenance. The speed and accuracy are better with ML methods. For an example, ML developers could create a software package that could predict breast cancer survival windows better than medical doctors. However, building and optimizing features through feature extraction/engineering from data points turn out to be a difficult proposition. There is a need for cancer specialists and an army of software developers to meticulously come out with a competent feature set. Thus, again automation is sought out.

DL automates several aspects being associated with ML. DL extensively relies on neural networks (NNs), which is a general-purpose function that can solve any problem representable through examples. When you supply an NN with many labelled examples of a specific kind of data, it is able to extract common patterns between those examples and transform it into a mathematical equation, which comes handy in accurately classifying and categorizing future data points.

Creating a facial recognition application with DL only requires you to develop or choose a preconstructed algorithm and train it with examples of the faces of the people it must detect. Given lots of examples, the NN will be able to detect faces without further instructions on features or measurements. DL is a very effective method to do CV. In most cases, creating a good DL algorithm comes down to gathering a large amount of labelled training data and tuning the parameters such as the type and number of layers of NNs. Compared to previous types of ML, DL is both easier and faster to develop and deploy. Most of current CV applications such as cancer detection, self-driving cars, and facial recognition use DL algorithms. DL and deep NNs have moved from the conceptual realm into practical applications thanks to the ready availability of cloud resources and scores of AI services.

How Does Computer Vision Work?

Generally speaking, CV is all about discovering hidden patterns such as objects in any image. A large number of images, which can be labelled or not, have to be sent to a computer and the idea is to arrive at a competent detection, recognition, and prediction model with the help of machine and DL algorithms. With additional data, the model arrived can be further fine-tuned to guarantee better accuracy in making correct inferences. So, for example, if you feed a computer with a million images of cats, it will subject them all to algorithms that let them analyse the colours in the photo, the shapes, the distances between the shapes, where objects border each other, and so on. The model generated clearly helps to identify a profile of what "cat" means. When the training gets fully finished, the computer, which is supplied with new and unlabelled images, will be able to use its model to pinpoint the images that are of cat.

COMPUTER VISION TASKS

Object Classification – What broad category of object is in this photograph?

- Labelling an X-ray as cancer or not (binary classification).
- Classifying a handwritten digit (multi-class classification).
- Assigning a name to a photograph of a face (multi-class classification).

Image Classification with Localization – This involves assigning a class label to an image and showing the location of the object in the image by a bounding box (drawing a box around the object). Some examples of image classification with localization include

- Labelling an X-ray as cancer or not and drawing a box around the cancerous region.
- Classifying photographs of animals and drawing a box around the animal in each scene.

Object Identification – Which type of a given object is in this photograph? There can be multiple objects in an image. This insists not only for localization but also classification. Some examples of object detection include

- Drawing a bounding box and labelling each object in a street scene.
- Drawing a bounding box and labelling each object in an indoor photograph.
- Drawing a bounding box and labelling each object in a landscape.

Object Verification – Is the object in the photograph?

Object Detection – Where are the objects in the photograph?

Object Landmark Detection – What are the key points for the object in the photograph?

Object Segmentation – What pixels belong to the object in the image? This is called as semantic segmentation, which is the task of object detection where a line is drawn around each object detected in the image. Image segmentation is a more general problem of spitting an image into segments. However, unlike object detection that involves using a bounding box to identify objects, object segmentation identifies the specific pixels in the image that belong to the object. It is like a fine-grained localization. That is, "image segmentation" might refer to segmenting all pixels in an image into different categories of object.

Object Recognition – What objects are in this photograph and where are they?

Video motion analysis uses CV to estimate the velocity of objects in a video or the camera itself.

Style Transfer – This (alternatively referred to as neural style transfer) is the task of learning style from one or more images and applying that style to a new image. This task can be thought of as a type of photo filter or transform that may not have an objective evaluation. Examples include applying the style of specific famous artworks (e.g. by Pablo Picasso or Vincent van Gogh) to new photographs.

Image colourization or neural colourization involves converting a greyscale image to a full colour image. This task can be thought of as a type of photo filter or transform that may not have an objective evaluation. Examples include colourizing old black and white photographs and movies.

In **image segmentation**, algorithms partition images into multiple sets of views.

Image reconstruction and image in painting is the task of filling in missing or corrupt parts of an image. This task can be thought of as a type of photo filter or transform that may not have an objective evaluation. Examples include reconstructing old, damaged black and white photographs and movies (e.g. photo restoration). In **image restoration**, noise such as blurring is removed from photos using ML-based filters.

Image super-resolution is the task of generating a new version of an image with a higher resolution and detail than the original image. Often models developed for image super-resolution can be used for image restoration and inpainting as they solve related problems.

Scene reconstruction creates a 3D model of a scene inputted through images or video. Image synthesis is the task of generating targeted modifications of existing images or entirely new images. It may include small modifications of image and video (e.g. image-to-image translations), such as

- Changing the style of an object in a scene.
- Adding an object to a scene.
- Adding a face to a scene.

In short, any application that involves understanding pixels through software can safely be labelled as CV. For more details, please refer the page https:// towardsdatascience.com/everything-you-ever-wanted-to-know-about-computer-vision-heres-a-look-why-it-s-so-awesome-e8a58dfb641e

Computer Vision Applications

With the faster maturity of CV technologies and tools, there are a number of easy-to-use CV applications emerging and evolving. Vision-based systems are being developed and used across industry verticals. Not only computers but also handhelds, wearables, and other edge devices are also empowered to gain the vision capability so that a variety of people-centric use cases can be envisaged and fulfilled. With the device ecosystem grows rapidly, the scope of CV services is bound to expand broadly and deeply. A couple of well-known and renowned CV applications are as follows. Google uses the power of CV to help you to search for objects (dog) and scenes (sunset) in our image repository. Facial recognition has turned out to be a dominant use case of CV. Latest smartphones use this aspect of face recognition to accurately recognize us thereby the automatic unlocking of phones is being facilitated. Security and surveillance activities are being accelerated and automated through face recognition. There may be some downsides too. Facebook is using this functionality extensively. Facebook has to review billions of posts, images, and videos and this automation capability helps Facebook to remove any insidious, illegal, and indecent content fast.

CV is therefore turning out to be an extremely versatile and indispensable technology for the connected era. DL algorithms are increasingly vital for healthcare services. The increased and impressive accuracy demonstrated by DL algorithms at recognizing, detecting, and analysing medical images is being applauded by the medical fraternity across the world. As we all know, CV helps in predicting different types of cancer. X-rays and MRI scans are being examined deeply and decisively through the power of CV. The scanning machines are being embedded with CV capability not only to capture images but also to decide the thing precisely. Last year during the pandemic, lung images of people are automatically analysed through the CV feature to decide whether he or she is affected with the virus. The widely tested self-driving cars and vehicles also rely heavily on CV to make sense of their surroundings in real time. DL algorithms are highly advanced nowadays and hence they are capable of appropriately analysing video feeds from multiple cameras installed on the vehicle. This helps to detect people, cars, lampposts, traffic signals, and other critical objects to help the car navigate its complex environment in an intelligent manner.

As indicated above, consumer, social and industrial machines and devices are increasingly mounted with sensors/cameras in order to have the CV capability, which can spot defects in products getting manufactured. Further on, it is able to pinpoint early signs of plant diseases in trees and plants.

Today's AI systems are powerful and can take additional actions based on an understanding of the image as given below.

- Image segmentation partitions an image into multiple regions or pieces, which can be examined individually and deeply.
- Object detection identifies a specific object in an image. Advanced object detection recognizes many objects in a single image: a football field, an offensive player, a defensive player, a ball and so on. These models use X and Y coordinate to create a bounding box and identify every object inside the box separately.
- Facial recognition is a kind of object detection. It can recognize a human face in an image and identifies a specific individual.

- Edge detection is to identify the outside edge of an object or landscape to better identify what is in the image.
- Pattern detection is for recognizing repeated shapes, colours, and other visual indicators in images.
- Feature matching is a type of pattern detection to match similarities in images. This capability is to help classify images.

These are all simple applications of CV. In the recent past, there are advanced applications of CV. One of them is self-driving cars, which leverage multiple CV techniques together. Generally, a computer is often fed with hundreds or thousands of related images. We have been supplying hundreds and even thousands of images to computers to arrive at a competent model, which can recognize specific object(s) in a new image. This is a tedious process. Now with noteworthy advancements in the field of CV, there is no need for training computers to look for whiskers, tails, and pointy ears to recognize a cat. Programmers just upload millions of photos of cats and then the model automatically learns the different features that make up a cat. This is being extended to other real-world requirements such as processing the live action of a football game. Interestingly CV rivals and surpasses human visual abilities in many areas.

CV is an interesting field of computer science. The goal is to replicate the distinct capability of human vision system into computers and machines. Such an empowerment enables computers and communicators to identify and process objects in images and videos in the same way that we normally do. CV is being facilitated due to the fast stability and maturity of multiple realization technologies and tools. Today we have a greater number of images (static as well as dynamic) readily available. Another key driver is the emergence of powerful chipsets. Thanks to a series of such technological advances, the CV field has been able to surpass humans in some tasks in detecting and labelling objects.

A New Era of Cancer Treatment

Traditional methods of evaluating cancerous cells or tumours are incredibly time consuming. With less data, such methods may lead to erroneous decisions. Working with SAS (https://www.sas.com/en_in/home.html), Amsterdam UMC (https://www.vumc.com/) has transformed tumour evaluations through the smart leverage of AI capabilities. Using CV technology and DL models, UMC could increase the speed and accuracy of chemotherapy response assessments. Doctors can quickly pinpoint cancer patients who are candidates for surgery faster, and with lifesaving precision.

Self-driving cars is one of the prime applications of CV. Face recognition, inspecting bottles in a manufacturing production line, controlling robots, and organizing information are some of the widely articulated CV use cases. CV enables self-driving cars to make sense of their surroundings. Multifaceted cameras fitted in the car capture and collect videos from different angles in and around the car and then feed the captured to CV software, which is made to run in one of the electronics devices inside the car. The videos are getting subjected to a variety of investigations to identify and understand the extremities of roads, read traffic signs, detect lampposts, other vehicles, objects, and pedestrians. Everything happens instantaneously so that real-time decision making and action are getting accurately activated so that self-driving cars can steer in the right direction towards the preferred destination through streets and highways without any problem by smartly avoiding hitting obstacles.

Waymo (https://waymo.com/) is in the business of optimizing transportation. It is equipping cars with multifaceted cameras and CV systems in order to provide a 360-degree view around the car. This sensor-enabled CV system helps the vehicle to identify pedestrians from around 300 yards. By precisely spotting potential hazards, car can take the evasive action. Generally fatigued drivers may be a bit slower to identify and react to potential hazards. However, by enabling vehicles with the competent CV system, cars can identify and react to any impending danger proactively. This ultimately drives down accident rates. With the power of machine and DL algorithms, all kinds of roadside objects, people, and scenes can be trained comprehensively so that any CV-enabled vehicle can safely and securely navigate through any chaotic traffic.

Autopiloting Cars

Tesla is a highly popular name these days with the much-debated autopilot capability. Tesla car is extensively leveraging CV and DL for its special autopilot features. The car is fitted with multiple cameras in order to gain 360-degree visibility at a distance of 250 metres. The car also has ultrasonic sensors and this allows the car to detect both hard and soft objects accurately. Additionally, Tesla's forward-facing radar allows the car to see much ahead even in hazardous and haphazard weather conditions such as heavy rain or fog.

Face Recognition

CV is an important ingredient for achieving face recognition. As indicated above, there are several use cases emerging for face recognition. Faces in images can be detected, recognized, and compared with databases of face profiles. Social media and law-enforcement authorities greatly use this face recognition to visualize and realize futuristic things.

Augmented and mixed reality (AR/MR) technologies are increasingly being implemented in smartphones, wearables, and tablets. In the recent past, we hear and read more about smart glasses, which are intrinsically supported through the distinct advancements of AR/MR technologies. These products require the power of CV to pinpoint the location, detect objects and establish the depth or dimensions of the virtual world. CV enables computing and communication devices to overlay and embed virtual objects on real-world imagery.

Computer Vision in Healthcare

We know that there are a lot of image data getting generated and stocked in the healthcare field. Therefore, in order to make sense out of healthcare data, CV algorithms gained prominence and dominance. The CV technology can detect abnormalities in imagery derived from MRI and CAT scans with better accuracy. With the unique ability to detect early-stage tumours, arteriosclerosis and thousands of other conditions, radiologists, cardiologists and oncologists have fully embraced the CV domain. The CV technology is being used in operations including caesarean births. With deeper automation being facilitated through CV, the field of medical imaging is growing rapidly.

The CNN algorithm, which is more appropriate to play around with image data, is prominently used one for empowering CV. CNNs are used to detect diseases from MRI.

Computer Vision for Defect detection

Traditionally, detecting defects in manufactured goods is manual. With CV, this time-consuming and tedious task is increasingly getting automated. That is, CV comes handy in detecting defects such as cracks in metals, paint defects, bad prints, etc. CV can give a better result than human eyes. CV algorithms power up cameras as the intelligent brain, which is able to perfectly differentiate what is a defect and what is not. CV allows consumers to find safe products. Hyperspectral cameras are able to differentiate a stone from a fruit, a plastic from a metal, or other combinations while the material is different.

Computer Vision for Assembly Verification

Today complex assemblies are being made with more dynamic parts. CV helps to verify whether each piece/part of an assembly is in its place and also whether the final assembly is correct. This is highly useful for the assembly of machinery, equipment, electronic boards, etc. This speeds up the product development.

Computer Vision and Robotics for Bin Picking

We have advanced robots in the form of industrial and service robots. **Collaborative robotics** enabled with CV is capable of performing bin picking of pieces placed disorderly. The robot needs the CV capability to tell it what a piece is and where it is. This enables the robot to decide what is the best way to pick up the piece.

CV applications in the financial sector – CV is already impacting on the banking and finance industry. Mitek Systems (https://www.miteksystems.com/) develops CV-driven image recognition applications. This is for checking passports, driver's license, and ID cards. It also allows customers to use their mobile device to take a photograph of their ID. This can then be sent to the bank where CV software verifies the authenticity of the document. This does away with the need for a customer to visit a branch to verify their identity to open an account. This, in turn, speeds up business processes and financial transactions.

Assisting in Diagnostics

CV is assisting medical doctors in identifying and detecting diseases at their earliest stage. The ChironX software (https://tracxn.com/d/companies/chironx.ai) uses CV to read retinal fundus images. The software solution is able to detect eye disease at its earliest stage. It is able to predict the risk of eye disease and systemic diseases such as cardiovascular ailments. AWS DeepLens (https://aws.amazon.com/deeplens/) helps put ML in the hands of developers, literally, with a fully programmable video camera, tutorials, code, and pre-trained models designed to expand DL skills. It can accurately detect and recognize objects, classify your food as either hot dog or not, recognize more than 30 kinds of actions such as brushing teeth, applying lipstick, and playing guitar, detect faces of people, and detect nine different head pose angles, etc. DeepLens is being adopted and adapted to power up several new applications. One such application is DermLens which is a simple and sagacious solution empowering patients with psoriasis to monitor and manage their condition.

CV in the retail industry – There are many business-to-consumer (B2C) electronic commerce applications for enabling online across the globe these days. Besides there are off-line retailing. Amazon is one of the pioneers in popularizing e-commerce activities. Recently Amazon has unveiled a smart store and is named as Amazon Go. This store facilitates checkout-free shopping experience for its customers. The implementation technologies include CV, sensor fusion, and DL. Shoppers can just walk in, pick the required items, and walk out. There is no need to stand in queue to get billed for the items picked in and packed out. The technology automatically detects when products are taken from or returned to the shelves and keeps track of them meticulously in a virtual cart. When you're done shopping, you can just leave the store. Later, you will get a receipt and your Amazon account gets accordingly updated. CV augments, accelerates, and automates a number of manual activities in any critical and crowded environment.

Personalized Experience

Retail shops use CV-driven facial recognition software to identify valued customers the moment they enter a store. An integrated application immediately informs the sales associate of the customers purchasing history, preferences, and other decision-enabling information. This AI-driven application is to deliver a series of personalized and preferred services. Lolli & Pops sweet store uses facial recognition capability to readily recognize valued customers. Neutrogena (https://skin360.neutrogena.com/) has developed a skin assessment application (Skin360). This application uses decades of Neutrogena expertise and a breakthrough technology to assess your skin and creates a custom skincare routine that fits your needs.

Reducing In-store Theft

StopLift by NCR (https://www.ncr.com/) is a powerful anti-theft solution for self-checkout. This extensively uses CV to guarantee its promise. Their ScanItAll system detects checkout errors and also identifies cashiers who avoid scanning products. ScanItAll can also be easily installed into the stores' existing video cameras and point-of-sale (PoS) systems, making integration easy.

Industrial Applications of Computer Vision

CV software is proving useful in many sectors. Especially it has an immense potential in minutely monitoring industrial sites such as manufacturing floors, oil wells, and factories. In manufacturing, machine vision is being used for enabling automated inspections, identifying defective products/parts on the production and assembly lines and also for remote inspections of pipelines and equipment. Computer and machine vision technologies and tools are being piloted and proceeded to decisively automate and optimize operational and control processes. By flagging irregular events or inconsistencies, it is being tested how these technologies contribute for the ultimate goal. Experts have insisted that CV can be effectively and efficiently leveraged for predictive maintenance, product assembly, package inspection, barcode reading for effective tracking, text analysis, and control of robotic workers. For example, Osperity (https://ospreyinformatics.com/) provides AI-driven intelligent visual monitoring and alerting for industrial operations and cut costs and mitigate risks.

Predictive Maintenance

This is an often-repeated use case. Vision-based systems and sensors are set in place to monitor the health of the critical structures, infrastructures, and assets. Shell (https://www.shell.com/) is using CV to keep their equipment in prime condition.

Computer Vision for Automating Inventory Management

Inventory tracking, management, and replenishment in retail stores are being facilitated through CV. For example, intelligent robots such as Bossa Nova Robotics' shelf-scanning robots (https://www.bossanova.com/) are gaining traction these days. The world's largest retailers use Bossa Nova, which is substantially enabled through CV, to provide insights 3x faster with double the accuracy of their manual processes. These robots are able to identify products with missing labels as well as items that are out of stock or incorrectly priced.

Warehouse Management

Management of warehouse inventory is becoming a tough and time-consuming activity as the warehouses are becoming bigger. Gather (https://gather.ai/) is a software-only autonomous inventory management platform for modern warehouses. They are developing autonomous drones to conduct warehouse inventory management. These operate autonomously and are able to integrate with existing warehouse management systems and devices such as motion sensors. Gather makes use of CV in autonomous drones to conduct warehouse inventory management. CV systems then scan the recorded images, allowing for an accurate record of available inventory to be created. Warehouse automation is being accelerated through the liberal usage of software-defined robots and drones.

Helping Business to Optimize Marketing

Marketing campaign has to be accomplished and sustained through new content. As we know, Generative Adversarial Networks (GANs) are NNs that utilize AI tools such as CV to help the user to create realistic visual content.

Branded Object Recognition

CV and image detection allow established brands to monitor various online channels including social web sites. This monitoring helps them to keep their edge and dominance for long by identifying any tangible threat from their competitors and start-ups, who may suddenly and surprisingly bring in innovative and disruptive products and services into the market. GumGum (https://gumgum.com/) is perfected a contextual intelligence platform that scans text, images, videos, and audio when evaluating online content. This platform solidly uses the distinctions of DL.

Optimizing Agriculture with Computer Vision

Increasingly farmers are looking for powerful digitization and digitalization technologies to automate and accelerate agriculture activities. In the recent past, the AI digital technology is being seen as the silver bullet. In the agriculture section, a number of pioneering technologies are being meticulously used in order to increase productivity through efficient methods and technology-enabled solutions. CV is all set to impact the agriculture domain decisively. SlantRange (https://slantrange.com/) is mounting CV-enabled cameras onto drones, which, then scan crops. Based on the data gathered, SlantRange delivers accurate and timely insights on crop performance to guide precision management.

Crop and Livestock Monitoring – Healthy crops and livestock are vital for any farm. Dublin-based Cainthus (https://www.cainthus.com/) is using sophisticated technologies to help farmers monitor the health condition of their crops and livestock. Cainthus uses CV expansively. Their smart cameras observe nutritional, behavioural, health, and environmental activities that can impact production. This visual information gets converted into actionable insights that enable the farmer to make data-driven decisions to improve their farm operations and animal health.

Encouraging Citizen Scientists

Computer vision is extremely beneficial for crowdsourcing programs such as iNaturalist, which is a social network of naturalists, citizen scientists, and biologists built on the concept of mapping and sharing observations of biodiversity across the globe. iNaturalist encourages people to use their mobile phones to take pictures of flora and fauna. ML classifiers and CV help the photographer to identify the species in their photograph by suggesting matches. These images are then submitted to iNaturalists where biologists can process them quickly and usefully.

Assisting Law Enforcement – The police departments across the USA use licence plate detectors to identify drivers with suspended licenses, catch stolen vehicles, or issue traffic citations. CV plays a very vital role here. Axon cameras are stuffed with CV capability to ensure public safety.

Military – Military needs such as situational awareness, are comfortably achieved through competent image sensors. This discovered knowledge creates and delivers battlefield intelligence, which can be used to take tactical decisions with all the clarity and confidence. As articulated above, the CV capability is leveraged for autonomous vehicles, which navigate challenging terrains and detect adversaries.

Remote Visual Assistance & Self-service

Multifaceted IoT devices are being bought and used in our everyday environments such as homes, hotels, etc. We have smart home devices to assist us in our everyday assignments and obligations. Devices are enabled to be interactive and instructive with human-device interfaces. Through standards, IoT devices are interoperable to find and interact with one another on need basis. However, installing, updating, securing, and maintaining personal, social, and professional devices turn out to be a difficult affair. Self-service is being increasingly insisted in order to mitigate the device operational complexity. CV plays a significant role in accomplishing the much-needed self-service. Bots with the power of sight can easily understand the customer's issue and decide the path to resolution. CV-enabled bots can provide clear and concise visual instructions in the form of augmented reality (AR) pointers on the customer's smartphone screen. The bot can then confirm whether the correct set of actions have been taken in the desired sequence. Also, they verify whether the issue is solved and settled amicably to the fullest satisfaction of the customer. There are massive visual repositories of devices and their issues and how those got resolved. Bots powered by DL-enabled CV can leverage that knowledge to optimize self-service interactions from start to finish.

There are several disruptive start-ups concentrating on CV products, solutions, and services. CV is augmenting and automating activities that need human vision. CV brings in the much-needed accuracy and precision. Path-breaking industrial use cases will be unveiled with the continued maturity and wider adoption of CV technologies and tools.

Vision-enabled Machines

CV capabilities are being methodically replicated in machines so that machines employed in our backyards, manufacturing floors, and other important places can see and perceive what is happening there. With ML and DL libraries getting embedded in machineries, vision-based machines are being produced and realized in order to replace human vision for applications like welding. Machine vision also ensure that there is a correct relationship between tool and workpiece. Further on, it assists in the assembly of parts to analyse the position of the parts so that other parts can be correctly aligned for insertion or some other form of mating.

There are other prominent use cases for vision-enabled machines. Machine vision systems are frequently used for printed circuit board inspection to ensure minimum conductor width and spacing between conductors. Machine vision is being used for weld seam tracking, robot guidance and control, inspection of microelectronic devices and tooling, on-line inspection in machining operation, on-line inspection of assemblies, monitoring high speed packaging equipment, etc.

The ability of an automated vision system to recognize well-defined patterns and to determine if they match up with those stored in the memory contributes immensely for a variety of manual activities such as the inspection of parts and their assemblies. The inspection includes both the quality and quantity checking. Machine vision systems are able to perform 100% on-line inspection of parts at high speeds and they work in rough and tough environments with the much-needed accuracy. Another important application of vision-enabled machines is for the recognition of an object from its image (object detection and recognition). These systems are designed to have strong geometric feature interpretation capabilities and are used in conjunction with part-handling equipment like robots.

Deep Learning for Machine Vision

We have detailed the important aspects of DL in the previous chapters. There are a number of research accomplishments in the DL space and they bring in a number of newer use cases in designing and deploying vision-based machines in our everyday environments. As indicated above, there are highly powerful chipsets from various chipmakers These multifaceted and miniaturized chipsets have eased and fast-tracked the journey towards DL models and applications. Increasingly these powerful chips are easily fit in personal and professional devices and machines. Further on, the ready availability of large-scale images and videos contributes for the intended success of DL.

The emergence of GPU hardware has totally changed the scenario. A GPU chip typically comprises thousands of relatively simple processing cores. The GPU architecture looks like NNs and hence is primed to precisely mimic the human brain. By using such a deep yet sophisticated architecture, DL accomplishes specific tasks without being explicitly programmed to do so. Conventionally we need to write the logic and supply input data in order to get the required output. But DL uses input data (images, videos, speeches, texts, numbers, etc.) and trains it via NNs. The process actually starts with a basic logic, which is developed during the initial phase through training data and then the logic gets continuously refined and advanced through checking their performance with test and new data.

DL is based on detecting differences. It permanently looks for alterations and irregularities in a set of data. DL is extremely sensitive/reactive to unpredictable defects. Humans also conventionally follow the same process and pattern. In daily life, the widely used applications of DL are facial recognition (we could unlock our phones, homeland security teams use it for …). DL also articulates its accurate recommendations to streaming video/music service providers and also empowers retail store managers to provide a memorable shopping experience to their customers in their stores. Increasingly DL is being primed for disease diagnostics. The practical use cases of DL are fast evolving to be people-centric in their daily activities and assignments. For manufacturing businesses, DL contributes immensely in product quality checking. Generally speaking, DL is predominantly leveraged for extracting predictive and prescriptive insights. Pattern detection and recognition in static as well as dynamic images can be fully realized through the power of DL. Further on, it can detect and pinpoint variance and anomalies. Based on the insights gained, timely and trustworthy decisions can be taken by machines and decision-makers.

How Does Deep Learning Contribute for and Complement Machine Vision?

A machine vision system typically leverages rule-based algorithms to accomplish what it has to deliver. Based on those rules, machines do things in different environments. Cameras are attached in industrial machines in order to empower them to see around and act. Traditionally, cameras capture and transmit images and videos to compute machines to do image and video analytics to extract timely insights, which eventually help systems and people to take correct decisions in time with alacrity. Such machine-vision systems perform reliably with consistent and well-manufactured parts. They operate via step-by-step filtering and rule-based algorithms.

On a production line, a rule-based machine-vision system can inspect hundreds of parts per minute with high accuracy. This is definitely a cost-effective approach when compared to human inspection. On a factory floor, traditional rule-based machine vision is great for guidance (position, orientation, etc.), identification (barcodes, data-matrix codes, marks, characters, etc.), gauging (comparison of distances with specified values), inspection (flaws and other problems such as missing safety-seal, and broken part). Coding simple rules is easy to implement. But visualizing all kinds of simple as well as complex rules and programming them is quite a tedious and tough job to do. When things are not clear, producing and sustaining rule-based machine-vision systems are beset with challenges and concerns. Herein, the power of DL comes in. Feature extraction and engineering are quite easily automated through DL. A typical industrial example is as follows. Looking for scratches on electronic device screens is quite challenging. Those defects generally differ in size, scope, location, and varying when the background changes. Forming rules for an unpredictable situation is quite a difficult proposition. DL can quite easily tell the difference between good and defective parts. DL networks can be trained for a new target.

Further on, DL comes handy in inspecting visually similar parts with complex surface textures and variations in appearance. Due to multiple variables that can be hard to isolate (lighting, changes in colour, curvature, or field of view), some defect detections are difficult to program and solve with traditional machine-vision systems. Here too, DL comes to the rescue.

In short, traditional machine-vision systems perform reliably with consistent and well-manufactured parts. But when exceptions and defect libraries grow up, programming CV applications becomes a hard nut to crack. Thus, empowering vision-based systems to learn accordingly is the way forward. The faster maturity and stability of DL algorithms is being seen as a positive step in the right direction. For the complex situations that insist for human-like vision capability and computer-like reliability, DL turns out to be a solace.

It is, therefore, going to be the much-anticipated hybrid model of rule-based machine vision and DL-based image analysis. For some applications such as measurement, rule-based machine vision is the correct route. For complex inspections involving wide deviation and unpredictable defects, DL-based machine vision systems are preferred.

The Limitations of Computer Vision

Definitely CV is emerging as one of the challenging fields in computer science. Enabling a machine to see and process what it sees, like a human, is definitely difficult. Firstly, for CV to be hugely successful, the object recognition ought to be fast and robust. This involves resolving issues such as object classification, identification, verification, and detection. Additionally, a successful CV solution will be able to identify the key points or landmarks in a photo image. Object segmentation and identifying the pixels in an image is also vital for successful object recognition. Once recognition is achieved, CV systems must also correctly analyse the image. If applied to a video, this requires accurate motion analysis. This allows the system to estimate the velocity of objects in the video. Other applications such as scene reconstruction, the creation of a 3D model via the inputting of 2D images or video, are also challenging. These problems have to be resolved if CV is to continue growing in importance and value.

Current computer-vision systems do a decent job at classifying images and localizing objects in photos if they're trained with a large number of labelled data. The DL algorithms that power CV applications are able to match pixel patterns. However, they do not understand what is really going on in the images. It is important to gain a correct understanding the relations between different objects in images and videos. What the visual data convey has to be precisely captured by DL algorithms. The contextual knowledge has to be cleanly gleaned and articulated for the intended success of the CV technologies and tools. This is a grave challenge at this point of time. For example, CV is not able to clearly understand the difference between safe nudity (breastfeeding) and banned content such as pornography. Likewise, the DL algorithms struggle to tell the difference between extremist propaganda and a documentary about extremist groups.

Therefore, unlike humans, CV algorithms need to be thoroughly instructed on the types of objects they must detect. As soon as their environment contains things that deviate from their training examples, they start to behave in irrational ways. For example, CV algorithms are unable to detect emergency vehicles parked in odd locations. The only way out is to train CV algorithms with more and more examples to accommodate as many situations and scenes. This huge lacuna clearly tells us that vision-based systems have to be empowered with real human intelligence through the AI technologies and tools. Precisely speaking, it will take some time before the world experiences and enjoys real-time and real-world CV solutions. In the section below, we are to see a sample example and its implementation.

Hands-On Lab

Computer Vision Sample Code Implementation

This section intends to help the readers visualize the concept through hands-on programming with a few samples that we have discussed in this chapter. Getting started and installations to jump into coding have been given in the earlier chapter, and you may please follow the installation and tools setup given in the earlier chapter and run the samples to run in your local computer. Also please note that there are numerous online labs such as Google's code lab, code geeks, Kaggle, and many such cloud-based online programming lab can also be very useful if you don't want to install and download the libraries.

Image Detection with OpenCV

In this hands-on section, lets discuss how we realize the CV with OpenCV library.

OpenCV

OpenCV is an open-source library for CV, ML, and image processing. It's prevalent and widely used across ML enthusiasts. It supports many programming languages and available for different OS platforms, exposing many CV plug-and-play libraries as APIs. Started at Intel in 1999 by Gary Bradski, OpenCV was released by 2000. Since then, OpenCV has massively evolved and supported many algorithms related to CV and ML, and it is expanding day by day.

OpenCV-Python is the Python API of OpenCV. It combines the best qualities of OpenCV C++ API and Python language, and our hands-on is using OpenCV Python API. With OpenCV libraries, image and video analysis, like facial recognition and detection, license plate reading, photo editing, advanced robotic vision, and optical character recognition, we can do a lot more implementation.

Python and OpenCV libraries combine computationally intensive codes in C/C++ and Python code as wrappers. Also, the support of NumPy makes the OpenCV implementation easier as NumPy is a highly optimized MATLAB style syntax numerical operations library and combining the NumPy operations with OpenCV makes it more attractive. OpenCV-Python is an excellent tool for fast prototyping CV problems; we choose to use OpenCV Python libraries for this hands-on exercise.

Haar Cascade Classifier

Haar Cascade is an object detection method based on the research paper "Rapid Object Detection using a Boosted Cascade of Simple Features" by Paul Viola and Michael Jones. Haar cascade classifiers are an ML-based approach where a cascade function is trained from a few positive and negative images. Our example uses two feature sets (trained models) from OpenCV, and these XML files make life merrier for object detection examples. OpenCV library has many trained feature sets as XMLs come in handy for anyone who wants to learn CV and apply ML for object detection.

Installing OpenCV Python

Windows OS
    pip install numpy
    pip install matplotlib

Linux/Mac OS
    apt-get install python3-OpenCV
    pip3 install numpy or apt-get install python3-numpy
    pip3 install matplotlib or apt-get install python3-matplotlib

With IDEs (IntelliJ in our example), by right click and install the necessary packages for this example is possible.

Detect cat face from the image (sample) with Haar Cascade Classifier

Our example program will detect cat faces from the given images, with Haar codes feature set available. Below is the step-by-step guide for you to get your code ready for the experiment.

- Download the following files from https://github.com/opencv/opencv/tree/ master/data/haarcascades haarcascade_frontalcatface.xml, and haarcascade_ frontalcatface_extended.xml
- Download images that you want to detect cat faces and have them under images folder
- Copy the below source code and save it as a .py file

```
import argparse
import cv2
from matplotlib import pyplot as plt
from PIL import Image

my_argparser = argparse.ArgumentParser()
my_argparser.add_argument("-i", "--image", required=True,
  help="Please provide path to the input image")
my_argparser.add_argument("-c", "--cascade", default="cv-models/
  haarcascade_frontalcatface.xml", help="Please provide the path to Open
  CV haar cascade model")
given_args = vars(my_argparser.parse_args())

image = cv2.imread(given_args["image"])
gray = cv2.cvtColor(image, cv2.COLOR_BGR2GRAY)

# let's display the loaded image properties to validate the code loading
  the image

print("Loaded Image Properties")
print("- Number of Pixels: " + str(image.size) + " - Shape/Dimensions: " +
  str(image.shape))
print("- Gray scale info: Pixels " + str(gray.size) + " and Size :" +
  str(gray.shape))

# now loading the Harr codes
cat_face_cascade = cv2.CascadeClassifier(given_args["cascade"])

newsize= (600, 600)
imager = Image.open(given_args['image'])
imager = imager.resize(newsize)
imager.save("images/image_resized.jpg")
imager = imager.convert('L')
imager.save('images/image_ready.jpg')

image_to_detect = cv2.imread(given_args['image'], cv2.IMREAD_GRAYSCALE)
```

```
# play around with different images by changing the scale factor/min
  neighbors detected = cat_face_cascade.detectMultiScale(gray,
  scaleFactor=1.2, minNeighbors=3, minSize=(75, 75))

# loop over the cat faces and draw a rectangle surrounding each
for (i, (x, y, w, h)) in enumerate(detected):
    cv2.rectangle(image, (x, y), (x + w, y + h), (0, 255, 0), 2)
    cv2.putText(image, "detected #{}".format(i + 1), (x, y - 10),
      cv2.FONT_HERSHEY_SIMPLEX, 0.55, (0, 0, 255), 2)
    cv2.imwrite('images/image_detected.png', image)
    # show the detected image
    cv2.imshow('Faces', image)
    # Press ESC or any key to close the window
    cv2.waitKey(0)
    cv2.destroyWindow('Faces')
```

So, you will have sort of the following folders and structure as found in the following Figure 8.1 for the sample program.

Ensure your libraries within Python code are downloaded (by right click and install the package within IDE or by using pip-install commands). With our samples CV2 (for OpenCV), Matplotlib, PIL for image utils.

■ Download images for your testing and place them in images folder.

Sample Code Walk Thru

```
Packages to install/download.

import argparse // for inputs
import cv2 // open CV
from matplotlib import pyplot as plt
from PIL import Image

inputs through argument
```

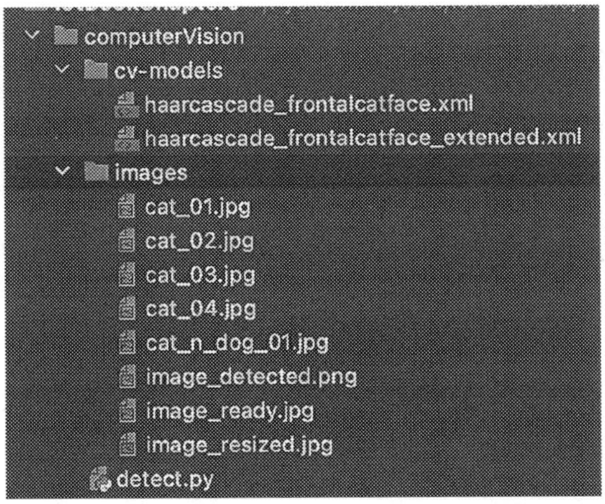

Figure 8.1   Sample code folder structure

```
image = cv2.imread(given_args["image"])
gray = cv2.cvtColor(image, cv2.COLOR_BGR2GRAY)
```

The preceding Figure 8.2 depicts a screen capture shows the arguments through IntelliJ input and we are using image/cat_n_dog_01.jpg.

Load the Haar Cascade classifier feature set

```
# now loading the Harr codes
cat_face_cascade = cv2.CascadeClassifier(given_args["cascade"])
```

Input image to detect the cat face

```
image_to_detect = cv2.imread(given_args['image'], cv2.IMREAD_GRAYSCALE)
```

Grey image as we need only necessary information for each pixel

```
gray = cv2.cvtColor(image, cv2.COLOR_BGR2GRAY)
```

Extract bounding boxes of the face identified with detectMultiScale

```
detected = cat_face_cascade.detectMultiScale(gray, scaleFactor=1.2,
minNeighbors=3, minSize=(75, 75))
```

Arguments/parameters to the detectMultiScale function
   Image name: image to detect (the grey image in our case).
   ScaleFactor: image size is reduced at each image scale (>1).
   minNeighbors: number of neighbours each rectangle should have to retain.
   maxSize: Maximum possible object size. Objects larger than that are ignored.
   minSize: Minimum possible object size. Objects smaller than those are ignored.

The ScaleFactor and MinNeighbors need various tunings, so in case if you don't get desired results, you may want to try different values for both arguments.

   ■ Run the sample and see the results as below samples

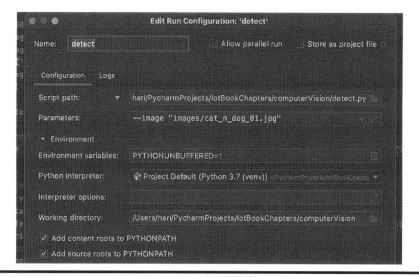

Figure 8.2   IDE Settings for Sample code

Sample Output

At your terminal/console, you will see the properties of the given image.

And we will see the cat's face marked with a green rectangle, as shown in preceding Figure 8.3 and the OpenCV detection output finds the cat's face drawn.

You will also see multiple images created within your images folder, as depicted in the Figure 8.4 including the above-detected pictures in the same folder.

```
Loaded Image Properties
- Number of Pixels: 3383628 - Shape/Dimensions: (914, 1234, 3)
- Gray scale info: Pixels 1127876 and Size :(914, 1234)
```

Figure 8.3   Sample image to process

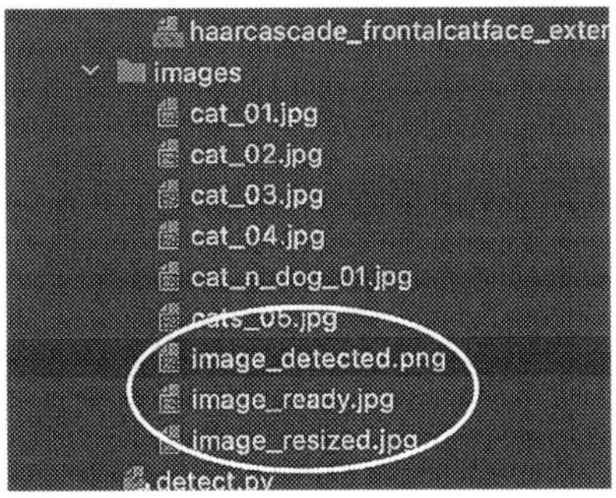

```
haarcascade_frontalcatface_exte
images
    cat_01.jpg
    cat_02.jpg
    cat_03.jpg
    cat_04.jpg
    cat_n_dog_01.jpg
    cats_05.jpg
    image_detected.png
    image_ready.jpg
    image_resized.jpg
detect.py
```

Figure 8.4   Image output

Canny Edge Detection Algorithm with OpenCV

Edge detection is an image processing technique with which we can find boundaries of objects within images, which is critical in CV, machine vision, and image processing. A practical algorithm called the Canny Edge Detection Algorithm can sketch the edges of any object present in the picture, and the algorithm's implementation is simple with the OpenCV library. The below example depicts the sample code and a sample output as found in the following Figure 8.5:

```
import argparse
import cv2
from matplotlib import pyplot as plt
from PIL import Image

my_arg_parser = argparse.ArgumentParser()
my_arg_parser.add_argument("-i", "--image", default ="images/cats_05.
  jpg", help="Please provide path to the input image")
my_arg_parser.add_argument("-c", "--cascade", default="cv-models/
  haarcascade_frontalcatface.xml",
    help="Please provide the path to Open CV haar cascade model")
given_args = vars(my_arg_parser.parse_args())

image = cv2.imread(given_args["image"])
gray = cv2.cvtColor(image, cv2.COLOR_BGR2GRAY)

# Apply canny edge detector algorithm on the image to find edges
canny_edges = cv2.Canny(gray, 100, 200)

# Plot the original image against the edges
plt.figure(figsize=(16, 16))
plt.subplot(121), plt.imshow(image)
plt.title('Original Gray Scale Image')
plt.subplot(122), plt.imshow(canny_edges)
plt.title('Canny Algo Edge Image')

# uncomment and see the edges plot with Canny edge detector Algo
plt.show()
```

Sample Output

 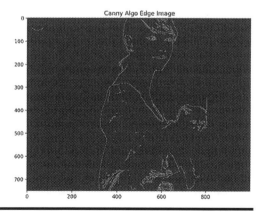

Figure 8.5   Sample Input and Output for Canny Algorithm

Conclusion

CV is an important technical domain for automating a variety of everyday tasks. Manufacturing, supply chain, warehousing, retailing, defence, surveillance, and security domains are incredibly benefited out of the improvisations being accomplished in the CV field. Simple detection, recognition, tracking, etc., are being implemented through traditional rule-based software. But with the emergence of software-defined dynamic environments, the traditional method may fail. Also, CV capabilities are being replicated in machineries, equipment, appliances, and instruments. Also, the wider adoption of artificial intelligence (AI) technologies, the CV domain is also all set to flourish in the days to come. Complex situations and requirements are being attended through the immaculate power of DL algorithms, which occupy an important portion in the AI field. The aspect of edge AI is growing fast and resource-intensive edge devices will be empowered with AI-enabled vision power to see, perceive, understand, and act.

With the focus turned towards CV technologies and tools with the consistent contributions from the research community, we can expect grandiose things in the near future. With the ready availability of enabling frameworks, libraries, accelerators, and platforms, software engineers can build sophisticated and sagacious CV applications. The phenomenon of CV has the required wherewithal to open up fresh possibilities and opportunities. Having understood the strategic significance of CV systems, path-breaking products, solutions, and services are being built and deployed by start-ups and established companies.

References

Computer Vision Introduction: https://towardsdatascience.com/everything-you-ever-wanted-to-know-about-computer-vision-heres-a-look-why-it-s-so-awesome-e8a58dfb641e

Deep Learning In Computer Vision Principles and Applications Mahmoud Hassaballah and Ali Ismail Awad

Deep Learning for Computer Vision: A Brief Review Athanasios Voulodimos: https://www.hindawi.com/journals/cin/2018/7068349/

Chapter 9

Natural Language Processing (NLP) Methods for Cognitive IoT Systems

Natural language processing (NLP) is one of the prime ingredients in the flourishing field of artificial intelligence (AI). The primary job is to empower our everyday computers and communicators to purposefully and intelligently understand and process human languages. As we all know, our spoken languages are typically informal. However, on the other side, we have a variety of formal programming languages. Due to the casual nature of human communication languages, computing machines are at loggerheads with human speeches. Therefore, the challenge is to bring forth viable methods to enable our everyday devices to unambiguously understand and act on human instructions with precision and perfectness.

Without an iota of doubt, NLP is an interdisciplinary field that comprises proven and potential techniques to process, understand, and analyse human languages. NLP enables most current state-of-the-art AI applications by providing intelligent algorithms that convert the data humans understand (e.g. speech, tweets, texts, emails, etc., in human languages) into data computers can operate upon with all the confidence and clarity. With this unique capability, several business operations get automated, adding huge value addition to worldwide businesses.

There are a humungous amount of texts, and they have to be processed quickly to come out with proper and perfect answers for a series of pertinent questions. Thus, besides speech recognition, text classification acquires special significance. Text classification is all about assigning categories to text data according to its content. Different techniques are emerging to extract information from raw text data and train a classification model. There are many techniques such as Bag-of-Words (used with a simple machine learning (ML) algorithm), the word embedding model (combined with deep learning neural network), and the language models (used with transfer learning from attention-based transformers). NLP breaks down words into

DOI: 10.1201/9780429328220-9

their simplest form and identifies patterns, rules, and relationships between them. It uses proven computer algorithms to parse and interpret written and spoken natural language to allow systems and devices to learn and understand human languages. NLP uses translation and language generation for summaries, annotation, or even explaining other ML models, classification and clustering, sentiment analysis, and other information extraction. The simplest forms of NLP are spell-checking, suggested email and messaging responses, and virtual assistants and chatbots.

On the enabling platforms, algorithms, toolkits, and frameworks, there are many positive things and trends. There are many algorithms for constructing your NLP tasks along with frameworks such as Python NLTK, Sanford CoreNLP, and Apache OpenNLP. At this point, Microsoft's 17-billion parameter Turing natural language generation model is the largest ever published. And BERT and GPT-2 also have billions of parameters. The leading NLP services providers are Microsoft, Amazon, Google, and IBM. Telefonica uses Microsoft's Power platform to enable business users with no developer expertise to create their tools with services such as Q&A Maker. Chatbots are a key NLP solution. Chatbots can take orders and supply answers from FAQs, route inquiries, book meetings, and handoff conversations to humans when necessary. In short, NLP is also a powerful tool for gaining customer insight from the growing volume of text and voice data companies already have.

Businesses often now hold over 100 terabytes of unstructured data – everything from call centre notes and customer emails to comments in surveys. Any customer-focused enterprises aiming to improve their customer experience or deliver more detailed insight about their brand can use NLP to sift through vast quantities of data and find the nuggets of valuable data safely hiding within. Any company dealing with clients can leverage NLP to gain insights from their interactions. Topic clustering, which uses NLP techniques like sentence embedding rather than just keyword extraction, is more accurate at grouping issues that customers may report using different terms. Highlighting those clusters in a dashboard can help reveal trending issues or repeated problems. Signoi aims to tackle open-ended comments in surveys by surfacing frequently used words, highlighting positive and negative terms and aggregating them by demographic group. The independent UK transport user watchdog "Transport Focus" used Signoi to see the biggest concerns for commuters and leisure passengers on various train services. Business travellers were angry about overcrowding on one line; those taking the train for leisure wanted better car parking and more space for luggage and bikes. NLP can generate language to explain results appropriately. Microsoft's Power BI business analytics service and Salesforce.com's Tableau offer features that enable users to type in questions about their data and get charts or automated analysis in response.

Prominent NLP Use Cases

NLP gracefully manages natural human languages like speech or text with many ML algorithms. NLP comes in handy in automating many day-to-day activities. Several industry verticals embrace this strategically sound technology.

- NLP helps enable the recognition and prediction of diseases based on electronic health records (EHRs) and patient's speech. This capability vehement exploration in health conditions goes from cardiovascular diseases to depression and even schizophrenia. Amazon Comprehend Medical service vigorously uses NLP and extracts ailment conditions, necessary medications, and treatment outcomes from clinical trial reports, patient records, and other vast general EHRs.
- As indicated elsewhere, worldwide service providers, product vendors, government organizations, and other establishments instantly hook up social media sites to source users' views on various offerings. This sentiment analysis provides a great set of information about user's choices and their decision-enabling sentiments.
- Some virtual cognitive assistants work as a personalized search engine by learning all about the users and then remind them of a name, a song, or anything that they can't remember the moment they need it.
- Email service providers filter and classify out emails with NLP. It happens by analysing the emails for specific texts that flow through their servers and stop them from spamming before they even enter our inbox. Similar to spam email identification, fake news identification is also being accomplishing NLP.
- Voice assistants are prominent examples of intelligent voice-driven interfaces that use NLP to respond to vocal prompts and do everything like finding a particular shop, telling us the weather forecast, suggesting the best route to the office, or turning on the lights.
- NLP continuously penetrates new domains. Financial investors and investment managers are getting the relevant and correct insights in time as NLP is rigorously used to track news, reports, comments about possible mergers between companies. Everything can then be incorporated into a trading algorithm to generate massive profits.
- NLP is also being used by hiring managers to identify potential hires' skills and spot prospects proactively.
- LegalMation developed a tool, an IBM Watson–based platform, to automate routine **litigation tasks** and help legal teams save time, drive down costs, and shift strategic focus.

For the healthcare industry, NLP technology is improving care delivery for sure, diagnosing ailments, and bringing down the costs while healthcare organizations are going through an exponential adoption of EHRs. Companies like Winterlight Labs are making considerable improvements in treating Alzheimer's disease by monitoring cognitive impairment through speech. They can also support clinical trials and studies for a wide range of central nervous system disorders. Stanford University has developed Woebot, a chatbot therapist, to help people with anxiety and other ailments.

Other Use Cases

Smartphones with voice and virtual assistants embedded use the NLP capability extensively. Human-machine interactions happen naturally. For this, smartphones intrinsically leverage NLP to understand, learn, and answer accordingly. The prominent use cases of NLP improve the consumer end-user experience, democratizing access or providing autonomy to big data in organizations, speech recognition (translating speech to text), and sentiment analysis.

With NLP, we can make any software application easier for users to interact with it. For instance, it is very tedious and time-consuming filling out a long and lengthy online form. We used to do this for downloading white papers from corporates' websites. So, instead of spending time trying to understand the online form, we can engage an automated toolkit such as chatbots, which comes in handy in the entire process of completing the form. NLP can auto-correct misspellings or misinformation. If desired, a chatbot can replace the complete online form, and it engages the end-user in conversation to extract the information needed.

Getting access to specific data sets from a web-scale company is notoriously time-consuming. Advances in NLP can help these business analysts go straight to the source and query the database in natural language – asking the computer questions like "What region performed best last quarter?" or "Compare store x and store y revenue in 2010 and 2012".

NLP also facilitates the translation of speech to text. In the business context, translating speech to text results in automating a variety of manual business activities. For instance, in healthcare, auditing clinical trial interviews used to be a very lengthy task. With several noteworthy advances in NLP, these audio interviews can convert to text or captions, and consent determination happens with a simple search ("crt+f") operation.

Finally, companies sell their products and provide solutions and services based on different products. Consumers express their opinions, feedbacks, comments, clarifications, compliments, etc., on social web sites about the solutions and services received. Herein, sentiment analysis of the text can help businesses tap into the human-generated text to understand the consumers more profoundly. As consumers voice their viewpoints on the public platforms, companies can easily collect and subject them through a host of deeper investigations using NLP to gain a better and deep understanding of people and their leanings and likes. This understanding of people's likes and dislikes empowers businesses to tweak their product strategy, engineering, and management positively.

Natural Language Processing (NLP) towards Cognitive IoT Solutions

Applying NLP in IoT systems helps address different challenges and bring forth newer possibilities and opportunities. One prominent capability derived from the application intelligence of NLP in IoT devices is the use of hands-free operation. For instance, let's take a driving a car situation. Let's assume while driving, you notice a warning sign on the vehicle dashboard. Instead of stopping and reading the manual, the driver can ask the car about its severity and if they need to stop immediately at a service station to have that warning signal investigated. Another example is the maintenance of machinery. A technician uses his hands and tools to work on an asset, but at the same time, he needs to check the device or the system about how to do a specific task or would like to know if anyone else reported a similar kind of noise.

A fascinating example of this capability is applied in a real-world situation. Imagine a technician working on a power line or wind turbine above the ground and in the air, with a strong wind blowing, carrying a set of tools on their belt. He needs to fix any issues, if there are any and on the spot. In this situation, the technician on site is performing regularly scheduled maintenance at the wind farm. But imagine he hears a subtle vibrating sound from the motor – and he thinks that's something irregular and never experienced that before. Then the technician performs a few routine diagnostics to determine the root cause. With no success in determining the root cause of diagnostics, he connects a mobile device such as a smartphone to the wind turbine network to review the data from the past two months to get more insights.

NLP Can Improve Many Different Processes

For example, manufacturers can predict device failures before they occur by just collecting data. Data here means it is the performance of a device in a system, including various conditions and parameters under which it fails – applying advanced analytics to this stored information in a database that helps to predict the failures. An airline can combine data from sensors and stress on aircraft with turbulence data in flight. The technicians may try to optimize maintenance schedules and eliminate expensive repairs, including failures in flight.

IBM WATSON NLP PLATFORM USE CASES

With Watson's suite of NLP offerings, including Watson Natural Language Understanding, you can surface concepts, categories, sentiment, and emotion and apply knowledge of unique entities in your industry to your data, no matter where it lives.

Using the "Ask Watson" feature of the Watson NLP toolset, the technician describes the noise to Watson. Watson's replies displayed on the technician's phone, with certainty percentage and potential cause. Watson understands the verbal communication of the issue and momentarily searches historical data of sensors, maintenance records, and logs for information about that specific turbine and other turbines of the same model. In seconds, Watson provides many potential root cause and potential solutions as well. The technician logs his report on his mobile device. Recording the actual root cause of the problem and the solution makes Watson learn from that solution. The next time a technician may face an identical situation, Watson knew what to answer and will always be ready to have a similar question.

Watson IoT generates conditions for any device failures and enables manufacturers to avoid them before they occur in real time. Similarly, by engaging a deep level of data processing in real time on information gathered from field technicians, engineers, customers, and sales representatives, Watson IoT can help companies create innovative products and services. Organizations engaged in constructing a safe, energy-efficient building can combine their experience with Watson's analytical abilities and ready to deliver energy-efficient, reliable, environment-friendly, cost-optimized, and sustainable buildings. Another scenario might involve a technician who can access help on a service call and is asked to fix a problem with the home power supply, washing machine, or elevator. Using a large amount of scanned and filtered information based on the context or state of the device, the technician can quickly access and review the most relevant information based on context. As a result, it can make more accurate decisions and faster.

The ability to analyse a massive volume of literature and texts, then extract knowledge and semantic out of it in addition to goalpost, is what IBM has been striving to achieve. An organization can create applications and continue its innovation using these new technologies. IBM is enabling these capabilities by making them available and consumable through APIs.

Before we conclude Watson's use cases, let's see another exciting example about self-driving shuttle. A self-driving cognitive shuttle brought to market by Local Motors, a fascinating example of devices using NLP. Olli uses natural language recognition that enables the passenger to have a virtual assistant relationship between him and the car. The potential use case for machines to understand human language – Imagine you get in your car and say, "Take me to work", and it's taking you to work is the proverbial tip of the iceberg. In the instance of Olli, the vehicle relies on more than 30 sensors that pick up environmental cues that enable autonomous driving and to interact with the passenger. Olli uses streams of data from connected devices that are in turn connected to the IBM cloud. Through Watson, passengers can interrogate the vehicle asking how Olli works, where are they going, how Olli is deciding on a route or speed and so on. The passenger can get suggestions for popular restaurants or historical sites according to their personal preferences.

Creating an Evolving Knowledge Base

To achieve a successful implementation of NLP applications, the developer creates a knowledge base on which an intelligent system can confidently rely to extract applicable intelligence. The noteworthy aspect here is that an NLP system is supposed to regenerate itself as it continuously learns. There is a kind of continuous learning of new things with the accumulation of advanced knowledge. To create a knowledge base, developers first need to understand the cognitive system and its relevance to IoT. They have to know how human beings process things like nuances in language, considering variations in conditions relative to specifics like weather or mood.

Human Decision-processing Simulation by Systems

Human decision including logic and emotions by the system? Is it real? Yes, it is. One takes any decision – be it a simple decision to take the stairs or the elevator or make a complex decision. It involves evaluating a set of criteria. For example, he has to select a new car model or find his favourite destination across the globe. The human decides observation and information inputs. We rely on facts to rationalize decisions to weigh up alternatives by looking for evidence in artefacts. We take and justify our choices through the lens of our values – what we care about, how we think, what motivates us, etc. Emotional response to situations plays a significant role in human decisions, especially when making choices. Many studies indicate that humans tend to make emotional decisions first and then use facts and statistics to rationalize their options, the main reason for the surging popularity of sentiment analysis.

Common Examples of Human and System Interactions

The interaction between a human and a device or thing gives them a hands-free experience. A good example could be where the user is not just a consumer sitting in an office or home sending commands to a microphone or a speaker. But he/she could be a driver in a vehicle and interact with it through NLP, or a passenger of a train, travelling in a bus, an employee on a production floor, or a doctor in a surgery room or a patient hospital room.

Thomas Jefferson University Hospital has formulated an idea around the future of healthcare with IBM Watson. The hospital setting is where patients can speak to a cognitive concierge and get answers to their questions, or adjust their environment based on personal preferences, and anticipate their needs. Then the teams got to work on a pilot project to produce a working prototype of a health care app deployed in a cognitive environment. Via a speaker-based interface, the hospital's room can answer questions and execute requests specific to the user's context. The information across the building (devices and systems), patient records, CRM systems, and administrative records collected and collated to draw patterns remembers patients' preferences and allows for a personalized, engaging, and interactive patient experience.

The office supply giant Ricoh is embedding cognitive capabilities into its whiteboards with the help of IBM Watson. Ricoh uses cognitive capabilities into whiteboards using Watson's NLP Classifier API to enable an interactive cognitive ability by capturing and translating speech in real time.

Facilitating the Ability to Interrogate a System

It is interesting to see the possibilities of NLP conjunction with text analytics capabilities. There is a chance to examine a system with a person's ability by giving individuals the ability to ask questions without typing into a search engine. The Internet enables contextual information to help find an answer or solution. However, the Internet searches lack the context for that specific IoT device. The benefit is that being able to "interrogate" a system becomes relevant because it can interpret its current state data and offer suggestions based on just learned knowledge. What's gone wrong? What's the error code? These are the knowledge gained by the system. Also, it can scan the history from the messages sent over in the past from their devices. All this information provides a context to help to understand why something might not be functioning in the present.

In summary, organizations and individuals can reach new levels of efficiency, create unique customer experiences, and offer more opportunities for businesses to grow. Cognitive computing gives incredible opportunities for unparalleled, customized experiences for customers by taking full advantage of data streaming from all connected devices and the Internet of things. It includes the automobile's various sensors and systems. NLP solutions in IoT starts from simple command-response exchanges in a given domain to the level of rationalizing a user's location, IoT data, and third-party data to truly understand a user's context is in and is asking questions about them. Cognitive IoT areas represent two significant training spectrums and correlated intelligence that requires a reasonable degree of planning and training.

The Future of Smart Devices

NLP technologies enable contextual understanding and allow devices actually to solve our problems. The IoT paradigm and AI are deeply connected. IoT systems produce big data, which gets converted into information and knowledge through the distinct capabilities of ML and DL algorithms. NLP recognize human voices, and it's the way to implement voice control over different systems.

In complex systems, it is harder to implement a user-friendly mobile or web interface to control it. The voice interface, in turn, is intuitive by its nature and doesn't require a significant learning curve. The voice control capabilities of the devices are also growing, especially in consumer sectors. This phenomenon change resulted in the increased number of consumer electronics activated by voice becomes a critical step for the upcoming technological revolution.

Thanks to translation capabilities by machine, it powers up the localization features. And with the current growth of market globalization, the localization explodes beyond translations resulted in reaping benefits of transcreation (creative translation). Machine translation is exemplary for any IoT devices or products with enabled speech recognition if the product focuses on distribution. A Tokyo-based start-up called "ili" created a wearable that can translate simple common phrases for travellers without access to the Internet. A tool called "Pilot" is another connected device that enables translation on the go. Unlike "ili", it facilitates a two-way conversation; the Pilot understands various languages and can synthesize a relevant response in a foreign language.

Indispensable Assistants

Speech recognition goes hand in hand with the other NLP concept – question and answer. It's all about answering questions given in a natural language. Nowadays, more and more devices get enabled with speech recognition to use question and answer to provide feedback to user input. The most familiar and popular home assistants, such as Amazon Alexa, Google Home, and Apple HomePod, are good examples of virtual assistants. All these devices get activated and controlled over voice recognition, and they can answer our various questions. As a result, voice assistants enhance user productivity as they help people get relevant information quickly on the go. In many industries, especially healthcare, the voice recognition and voice assistants with these NLPs will be phenomenal and may get a rousing welcome. Thanks to NLP and ML improvements, the automotive landscape changes fast and provides drivers with intelligent navigation, high safety features, and voice controls for cars.

In summary, the noteworthy improvements in the NLP space have led to the realization of many robust offerings. Especially the IoT sensors, devices, networks, systems, and environments are all set to experience cognitive behaviour due to the close relationship with the NLP algorithms. The following section is to enumerate and elaborate on the popular NLP algorithms.

The Prominent NLP Algorithms

NLP usually signifies the processing of text or text-based information (audio, video). Text representation generally happens in the form of mathematical equations, formulas, paradigms, and patterns. This structuring facilitates understanding the text semantics (content) for further processing steps such as classification, fragmentation, etc. An essential step in this process is to transform different words and word forms into one speech form. Also, we often need to measure how similar or different the strings are. Usually, in this case, we use various metrics showing the difference between words.

One of the simple and easily usable metrics is edit distance (also known as Levenshtein distance). Levenshtein distance is an algorithm for estimating the (cosine) similarity of two string values (word, words form, words composition) by comparing the minimum number of operations to convert one value into another. Below are the popular NLP applications for edit distance

- automatic spell-checking (correction) systems;
- in bioinformatics – for quantifying the similarity of DNA sequences (letters view);
- text-processing – define all the proximity of words that are near to some text objects.

Cosine similarity is a metric used for text similarity measuring in various documents. Calculations for this metric is based on the measures of the vector's similarity by the well-known cosine vectors formula:

You can use various text features or characteristics as vectors describing this text, for example, by using text vectorization methods. For example, the cosine similarity calculates the differences between such vectors. The calculation result of cosine similarity described the similarity of the text and presented it as the cosine of angle values. The cosine value tends to reach one and angle to zero when the texts match. The cosine similarity values are helpful for simple semantic text pre-processing.

Vectorization

The text vectorization method is a transformation of the text to numerical vectors. A procedure for converting words (text information) into digits and extract text attributes (features) can feed into NLP/ML algorithms. The most popular vectorization method is "Bag of words" and "Term Frequency – Inverse Document Frequency (TF-IDF)".

Bag of Words (BoW)

This is a commonly used model that allows you to count all words in a piece of text. Typically, it creates an occurrence matrix for the sentence or document, disregarding grammar and word order. The occurrence matrix is then used as features for training a classifier. This approach may reflect several drawbacks like the absence of semantics, its meaning and context. The stop words (like "the" or "a") add noise to the analysis, and some words are not weighted accordingly.

Term Frequency – Inverse Document Frequency (TF-IDF)

It's an approach to solve the noise reduction and rescale the frequency of words by how often they appear in all texts so that the scores for frequent words like "the" get penalized. This scoring approach is TF-IDF, and it improves the bag of words by weights. i.e. rewarded when it appears frequently but punished if it appears in other texts within the same context. In contrast, this approach highlights and rewards rare and unique words considering all texts.

Tokenization

The process of segmenting running text into sentences and words is called tokenization. Tokenization creates tokens. So, tokenization is the task of splitting a text into pieces called tokens and at the same time discarding certain characters, such as punctuation. However, it may seem essential and separate words by a blank space like in English (called segmented languages). However, not all languages behave the same. Thinking about this process, even for English, just not all the empty spaces are sufficient for the tokenization process. Splitting into blank spaces may break up to one token.

Removing Punctuation

Tokenization helps remove punctuations, resulting in ease of proper word segmentation, but may trigger possible complications. Take the case of Dr.; the period following the abbreviation must be part of the same token, and it should not take it. The tokenization process is not a complete fool-proof, primarily when it deals with biomedical text domains containing lots of hyphens, parentheses, and other punctuation marks.

Stop Words Removal

It is a process of getting rid of typical language articles, pronouns, and prepositions such as "and", "the", or "to" in English. In this process, some prevalent words appear to provide little or no value to the NLP algorithm objective and filters (removes) those non-informative but widespread and frequent texts. A full lookup in a predefined list of keywords can safely ignore the stop words; additionally, it's freeing up database space and improving processing time. It would be great if there are universal stop words across languages, but of course, there is none. These stop words are built from scratch or can be pre-selected, and a potential approach is to begin by adopting pre-defined phrases to the list later on.

Nevertheless, the general trend over the past time has been to go from the use of sizeable standard stop word lists to the use of no lists at all. The thing is stopping words removal can wipe out relevant information and modify the context in a given sentence. For example, if we perform sentiment analysis, our algorithm for removing a stop word like "not" goes off-track. Under these conditions, we select a minimal stop word list and add additional terms depending on our specific objectives.

Text Normalization

To process and pre-process the text, words, and documents, use text or word normalization methods in the NLP. Such procedures are usually used for the correct text (words or speech) interpretation to acquire more accurate NLP models.

- Context-independent normalization: removing non-alphanumeric text symbols.
- Canonicalization: convert data to "standard", "normal", or canonical form.
- Stemming: extracts the word's root.
- Lemmatization: transforms word to its lemma.

Stemming

Stemming refers to the process of slicing the words either at the beginning or at the end of it, intending to remove affixes (lexical additions to the root of the word). Affixes that are at the front of the word are called prefixes (e.g. "Ortho" in the word "Orthopedic"), and the ones attached at the end of the term are called suffixes (e.g. "less" in the word "restless"). Now let's consider walk, walks, walking, and walked. The affixes like -s and -ed are inflexional. It creates a problem, as those affixes can expand to any new forms of the same expression or even create new words and entirely different meaning (called derivational affixes).

Say If we add the derivational prefix "un-" to the adjective word "happy", also "unhappy" is an adjective. So unhappy remains an adjective, but the meaning is completely changed, and that's a derivational affix. Prefix and suffix, eco is a prefix and derived from the word ecosystem, 'ist is a suffix and derived from guitarist, 'er is also a suffix; however, it is an inflexion to form a new word. In English, prefixes are derived from the words (eco from ecosystem), but suffixes are derivations ('ist from guitarist) or inflexions ('er from faster).

A potential approach is to consider a list of common affixes and rules and perform stemming based on those affixes, but of course, this approach presents limitations. Since stemmers use algorithmic techniques, the result of the stemming process may not be an actual word or even a modified word (or sentence). We can offset this limitation by editing those predefined methods by adding or removing affixes and rules. Still, we must consider that we improve the performance on one side while producing a degradation on another side. So it's critical that we look at the entire picture and test the model's performance as a whole and not in chunks.

First of all, stemming indicates and helps correct spelling errors from the tokens. Stemmers are simple, easy to use, and run very fast (they perform simple operations on a string), and if speed and performance are essential in the NLP model, then stemming is undoubtedly the way to go. Remember, we use it to improve our performance, not as a grammar exercise.

Lemmatization

This is for reducing a word to its base form, also grouping its different forms. For example, verbs in the past tense to the present (e.g. "stand" is changed to "stood"), and synonyms are unified (e.g. "best" is changed to "good"). Standardizing words with the same meaning to their root is challenging. Although it seems closely related to the stemming process, lemmatization uses a different approach to reach the root forms of words. Resolve words to their original dictionary form (known as lemma) is lemmatization. So it does require detailed dictionaries for the algorithm to look into and link the corresponding words to their related lemmas. For example, "running", "runs", and "ran" are all forms of the word "run", so "run" is the lemma of all the words.

Lemmatization also considers the word's context and helps to disambiguate the texts, i.e. it can discriminate between identical words that have different meanings depending on the specific context. Think about "ball" (which can correspond to many interpretations such as tennis ball, cricket ball, and so on) or "banks" (corresponding to the financial institution or lands along with the river flow or water body). By providing a part-of-speech parameter to a word (whether it is a noun, a verb, and so on), it's possible to define a role for that word in the sentence and remove disambiguation.

Lemmatization is a much more resource-intensive task than performing a process called stemming. At the same time, since it requires more knowledge about the language structure than a stemming approach, it demands more computational power than setting up or adapting a stemming algorithm.

Topic Modelling

The process of uncovering hidden structures from a group of texts or documents is called topic modelling. It clusters texts and finds latent topics based on their contents. It processes individual words and assigns them values based on their distribution by making reasonable assumptions about various topics. Each group includes a set of words by spotting hidden topics and unlock the meaning of texts.

Latent Dirichlet allocation (LDA) is one of the most commonly used NLP modelling techniques. It's relatively a new algorithm that works as an unsupervised learning method by discovering different topics from underlying a collection of documents. In unsupervised learning methods, no output variable can guide the learning process, and the algorithms do the data exploration and find the patterns by assigning and labelling the entire documents.

1. Assigning: Assigning each word to a random group, where the user defines the number of topics it wishes to uncover. We don't limit the groups for topics by themselves (but we just indicate the number of topics). Then the assignment approach of the algorithm will map all of the documents to those groups so that those imaginary groups mainly capture words from each document.
2. The algorithm goes through every word iteratively and reassigns the word to a topic, assuming the term belongs to a probable topic group and generate documents. These probabilities are calculated multiple times until the convergence of the algorithm.

Unlike other clustering algorithms like K-means that perform hard clustering (where topics are entirely disjointed), LDA assigns each document to a mixture of topics. One or more topics can describe each document (e.g. Document 1 is characterized by 70% of topic A, 20% of topic B, and 10% of topic C), and this setup reflects more realistic results. Topic modelling is beneficial for classifying texts, building recommender systems (e.g. recommending books based on past readings), or even detecting trends in online publications.

In general, the operation of systems using NLP as depicted in the following Figure 9.1 is described as the following pipeline

1. Enter the text (or sound converted to text).
2. Perform segmentation of text into components (segmentation and tokenization).
3. Do text cleaning (filtering from "garbage") – removal of unnecessary elements.
4. Perform text vectorization and feature engineering.
5. Lemmatization and stemming – reducing inflexions for words.
6. Use ML algorithms and methods for training models.
7. Interpret the result.

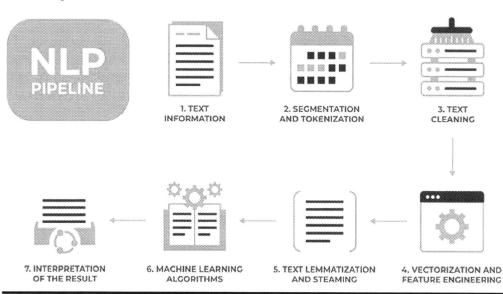

Figure 9.1   NLP Pipeline

Naive Bayes Algorithm

Naive Bayesian Analysis (NBA) – NBA is a classification algorithm based on the Bayesian theorem, with the hypothesis on the feature's independence. The NBA assumes the existence of an element in the class doesn't correlate with any other feature. The advantage of the NBA classifier is the low data volume for model training, parameters estimation, and classification. NBA algorithm text classification (clustering) is prominent in most cases, and spam detection filter is its most common use case. This approach advantages include:

- Classification and multi-class classification are quick and straightforward.
- On the assumption of words independence, NBA performs better than other simple ones.
- The NBA works better with categorical features than with continuous ones.

Below are the few most popular applications for text analysis:

- Text classification, aka text categorization or text tagging, is the task of assigning predefined categories to the open-ended text.
- Spam filtering is a well-known application across emails and other digital communication mediums.
- Text tonality analysis is a part of sentiment analysis and detects joy, fear, sadness, anger, analytical, confident, and tentative tones found in the text.

Word Embedding

Word embedding is a learned representation for text where the words are with the same meaning. It's a set of various methods, techniques, and approaches for creating NLP models to associate words, word forms, or phrases with number vectors.

Word Embedding Principles

The embedding principle works based on words that appear in the same context and have identical meanings. In this case, finding the similarity is the algorithm principle, and it locates only similar words near each other (within a context).

The trained model will predict the probability of a word by its context. So, the NLP model will train vectors of words so that the chance assigned by the model to a text will be close to the probability of its matching in a given context (Word2Vec model). Generally, the likelihood of the word's similarity by the context is calculated with the softmax formula. This similarity in context is necessary to train the NLP model and the backpropagation technique, aka backward error propagation. The below lists a few most popular word embeddings:

- Word2Vec – This is an NN (neural network)–based word embedding that calculates the similarity in words' context.
- GloVe – Based on the combination of word vectors and the probability of co-occurrence words in the text.

- FastText – Similar principle as Word2Vec, but uses parts and symbols, not the words like Word2Vec, and as a result, the word found becomes its context.

Long Short-Term Memory (LSTM)

LSTM is a specific type of neural network architecture capable of training long-term dependencies. Frequently, LSTM networks are used for solving NLP tasks. LSTM network includes several interacting layers. The prominent NLP tasks accomplished through LSTM are

- Question answering.
- Sentiment analysis.
- Image to text mappings.
- Speech recognition.
- Part of speech tagging.
- Named entity recognition.

Machine Learning (ML) for Natural Language Processing

ML for NLP involves statistical techniques for identifying parts of speech, entities, sentiment, and other aspects of a text. The methods are expressed as a model, and those models then applied to other classes (text). These supervised algorithm models work across large data sets to extract meaning and be treated as unsupervised ML. ML for NLP makes data analysts' tasks easy by turning unstructured text into usable data and insights.

Text data requires a unique approach to ML because text data can have many dimensions, maybe even thousands of words and phrases and very sparse. For example, English alone has around 100,000 common words in use. But we don't witness those many at any given social media or such platforms, and they only contain a few dozen of them. However, other digital media, books, video content, where we have very high dimensionality. Still, we have oodles and oodles of data to work with whilst it's not relatively as sparse.

A batch of text documents is annotated with examples of texts that the machine should interpret or match that aspect in supervised algorithms. These documents are used to "train" a statistical model, an untagged text to analyse. Later, we can use larger or better data sets to retrain the model. For example, we can use supervised learning to train a model. It knows more about the documents it analyses to analyse hotel reviews and then later introduce it to factor in the reviewer's score eventually to a star rating of the hotel.

Named Entity Recognition (NER)

Lexalytics uses supervised ML and improves text analytics functions and NLP features.

People, places, and things (products) represented as text in a document are named entities. Unfortunately, these named entities can also come as a hashtag, emails, mailing addresses, phone numbers, and Twitter handles. Anything can be an entity if we look at it the right way. And don't get us started on tangential references. At Lexalytics, they have trained supervised ML models on large amounts of pre-tagged entities. This approach helps them to optimize for accuracy and flexibility. They have also trained NLP algorithms to recognize non-standard entities (tree species or types of cancer). It's also essential to note that NER models rely on accurate PoS tagging from those models.

Part-of-Speech Tagging (PoS Tagging)

Part-of-speech tagging (PoS-Tag) is a process of finding tokens from the part of speech (noun, adverb, adjective, etc.) and tagging. PoS tagging forms the basis of many essential NLP tasks. There need clear findings on parts of speech to recognize entities, extract themes, and process sentiment. Lexalytics has a highly robust model that can PoS-tag with >90% accuracy, even for short, gnarly social media posts.

Natural Language Processing and Text Analytics from Unsupervised ML

With splendid improvements in ML processing abilities, unsupervised ML involves training a model without annotations or tagging. Below are a few quick overviews for the same.

Clustering

Grouping similar documents into groups or sets is clustering, and the grouped clusters are then sorted according to their importance and relevancy (hierarchical clustering).

Latent Semantic Indexing *(LSI)*

LSI is another type of unsupervised learning that identifies frequent words and phrases in the given text. Data scientists make use of LSI for faceted searches or return search results that aren't the exact search term.

Sample Code Implementations

This section intends to help the readers visualize the concept through hands-on programming with a few samples discussed in this chapter. Getting started and installations to jump into coding has been given in the earlier chapter. You may please follow the installation and tools setup provided in the earlier chapter and run the samples from your local computer.

Also please note that there are numerous online labs such as Google's code lab, code geeks, Kaggle, and many such cloud-based online programming lab can also be very useful if you don't want to install and download the libraries.

Hands-On Lab

NLTK Naïve Bayes Sample Implementation

Before moving to other sample implementation, let's have a quick look at NLTK, a Natural Language Toolkit platform that provides 50+ corporate and linguistic resources. We have a Naïve Bayes algorithm implementation as below (check out the code ntlk_naive_bayes_movie_sentiments.py):

■ Import nltk library and movie data set

```
import nltk
nltk.download('movie_reviews')
from nltk.corpus import movie_reviews
```

■ frequency distribution with nltk is as simple that as below

```
# FreqDist class for encoding "frequency distributions", to count the
number of times of occurrences (of executions)
all_the_words = nltk.FreqDist(word.lower() for word in
movie_reviews.words())
word_features = list(all_the_words)[:2000]
```

Make sure you change the range of word_features and re-run to see different results

■ Naïve Bayer classifier for prediction

```
# naive bayes classifier to predict the sentiments of new movie
feature_sets = [(doc_features(doc),cl) for (doc,cl) in documents]
train_set, test_set = feature_sets[100:], feature_sets[:100]
classifier = nltk.NaiveBayesClassifier.train(train_set)
```

■ The accuracy rate;

```
# see the accuracy without any tweaking or fine-tuning the inputs
print(nltk.classify.accuracy(classifier, test_set))
```

■ As found in following Figure 9.2 it is the output (and not a code); it's amazing (82%) for the first run.
■ Display all the classifier

```
# display the features as interpreted by Naive Bayes
classifier.show_most_informative_features(10)
```

The complete code is as below

```
import nltk
nltk.download('movie_reviews')
```

Figure 9.2   Sample accuracy output

```
from nltk.corpus import movie_reviews
import random
documents = [(list(movie_reviews.words(fileid)), category)
             for category in movie_reviews.categories()
             for fileid in movie_reviews.fileids(category)]


random.shuffle(documents)

# FreqDist class for encoding "frequency distributions", to count the
number of times of occurrences (of executions)
all_the_words = nltk.FreqDist(word.lower() for word in
movie_reviews.words())
word_features = list(all_the_words)[:2000]

def doc_features(document) :
  doc_words = set(document)
  features = {}
  for word in word_features:
    features['contains({})'.format(word)] = (word in doc_words)
  return features

# naive bayes classifier to predict the sentiments of new movie
feature_sets = [(doc_features(doc),cl) for (doc,cl) in documents]
train_set, test_set = feature_sets[100:], feature_sets[:100]
classifier = nltk.NaiveBayesClassifier.train(train_set)

# see the accuracy without any tweaking or fine-tuning the inputs
print(nltk.classify.accuracy(classifier, test_set))

# display the features as interpreted by Naive Bayes
classifier.show_most_informative_features(10)
```

Run the above code as we generally run the Python code with our PyCharm or in terminal. Please note the imports in nltk library (it's needed only for the first time, subsequent run it doesn't need to import)

Once we run the code, you will see the below output as depicted in the Figure 9.3:

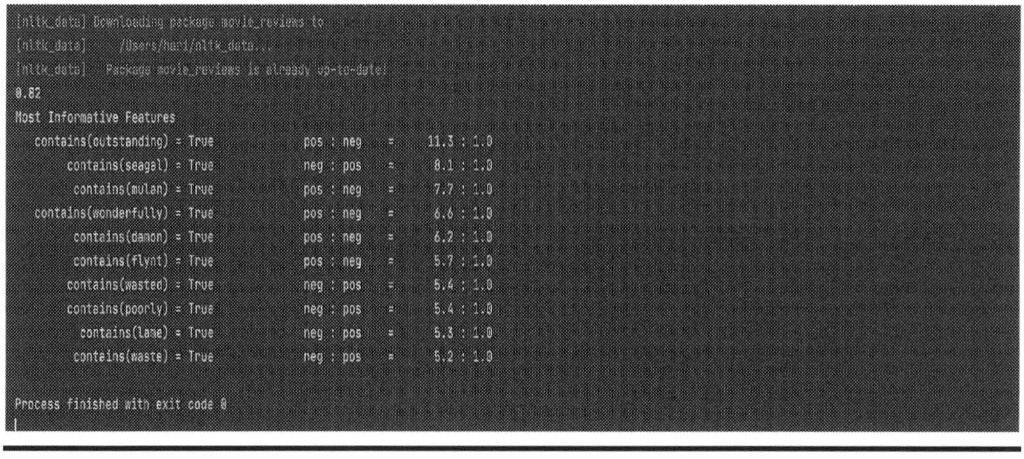

```
[nltk_data] Downloading package movie_reviews to
[nltk_data]     /Users/hari/nltk_data...
[nltk_data]   Package movie_reviews is already up-to-date!
0.82
Most Informative Features
     contains(outstanding) = True           pos : neg    =   11.3 : 1.0
         contains(seagal) = True            neg : pos    =    8.1 : 1.0
          contains(mulan) = True            pos : neg    =    7.7 : 1.0
    contains(wonderfully) = True            pos : neg    =    6.6 : 1.0
          contains(damon) = True            pos : neg    =    6.2 : 1.0
          contains(flynt) = True            pos : neg    =    5.7 : 1.0
         contains(wasted) = True            neg : pos    =    5.4 : 1.0
         contains(poorly) = True            neg : pos    =    5.4 : 1.0
           contains(lame) = True            neg : pos    =    5.3 : 1.0
          contains(waste) = True            neg : pos    =    5.2 : 1.0

Process finished with exit code 0
```

Figure 9.3   Sample output

spaCy Libraries for Out-of-the-Box NLP Implementation

In this section, our samples explore enterprise-grade Python NLP library (framework) spaCy. An industrial-strength NLP framework provides simple APIs to create products or gather insights with ease and faster.

We will use spaCy (spacy.io) Python modules to explore the NLP concepts. spaCy provides out-of-the-box implementation for NLP processing and algorithms.

Quick spaCy Setup

As we have installed PyCharm and executed other samples from earlier chapters, let's use the same for NLP examples. Below are the steps to get spaCy to your computer/ laptop and run a quick sample before move on to advanced use case.

- Create a new file – name it helloworldNLP
- Type or copy and paste the following lines into your helloworld

```
import spacy
nlp = spacy.load('en_core_web_sm')
```

PyCharm may complain that it doesn't recognize the first line import spacy. We need to install the spaCy into our laptop by following either one of the approaches below. If you already have installed spaCy, you can directly jump to the next section; Also, please ensure you have installed Python 3> and use PyCharm's venv to refer to your Python 3> installations.

Install spaCy through a Terminal (Command Prompt)

We can use PyCharm terminal for installation; use the following command:

```
Pip install spacy
```

or (upgrade)

```
pip update -U spacy
```

Install directly with PyCharm

Right-click and install the package, wait for your IDE to download, and we will see the alerts disappear once the installation is done.

We also need to download the language model, and our examples use en_core_ web_sm, so they need to be loaded for our examples.

Run the following command in the terminal:

```
python -m spacy download en_core_web_sm
```

Hello NLP

Once the download completes, we are ready to move ahead with other examples, but before that, ensure you run the helloNlp and see no compiler errors or any other errors.

helloNlp source codes as below:

```
import spacy

nlp = spacy.load('en_core_web_sm')

test_txt = 'this is a test input text for hello world of nlp with spacy'
nlp_doc = nlp(test_txt)

print([token.text for token in nlp_doc])
```

As we use tokenizing of spaCy in our helloNlp, we would see the output of tokens as depicted in the Figure 9.4 for the given text as follows:

Entity Linking or Entity Relation

Another interesting example that we will see in this section is an entity-relationship prediction with spaCy and how simple to write a code for the same.

spaCy Pipeline

As we see with the preceding Figure 9.5, spaCy pipeline for NLP involves tokenizer, tagger, parser, and so on. However, how can we ground that information into the real-world knowledge base?

What are all millions/billions/trillions of means in the below-given texts?

■ "Net income was $9.4 million compared to the prior year of $2.7 million".
■ "Revenue exceeded twelve billion dollars, with a loss of $1b".
■ "Revenue continues to gain, major loss of $5 Trillion across the world due to COVID-19 situation".

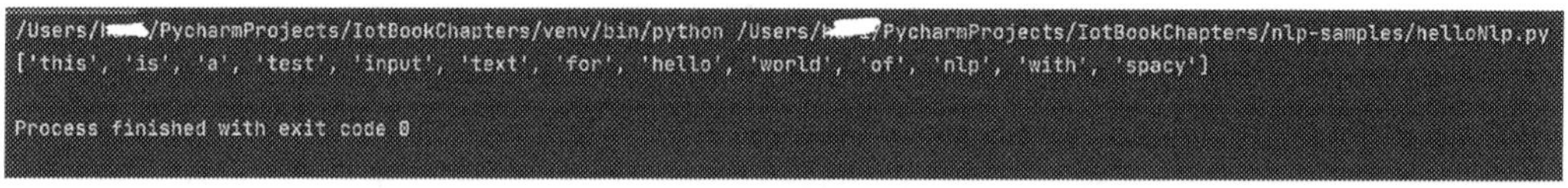

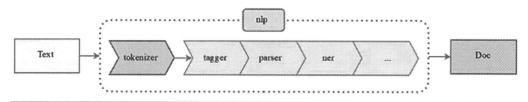

Figure 9.4   Sample SpaCy output

Figure 9.5   SpaCy Pipeline

Yes, the entity linking to the accurate word for those million/trillion is money. The cool part is spaCy provides out-of-the-box implementation for entity linking. The following Figure 9.6 gives more clarity on the spaCy entity linking flow.

As entity linking (EL) happens on the overall text, the context of the given text is probed with CNN models of spaCy.

We will see a sample implementation of entity relations with the spaCy library and how the context of the given text is predicted in the next section.

The below example picks up various texts (given inside the code) that grounds the context as MONEY.

```
from __future__ import unicode_literals, print_function

import plac
import spacy

TEXTS = [
  "Net income was $9.4 million compared to the prior year of $2.7
million.",
  "Revenue exceeded twelve billion dollars, with a loss of $1b.",
  "Revenue continue to gain, major loss of $5 Trillion across the world
due to COVID-19 situation"
]
@plac.annotations(
  model=("Model to load (needs parser and NER)", "positional", None, str)
)

def elmain(model="en_core_web_sm"):
  nlp = spacy.load(model)
  print("Loaded model '%s'" % model)
  print("Processing %d texts" % len(TEXTS))

  for text in TEXTS:
    doc = nlp(text)
    relations = extract_currency_relations(doc)
    for r1, r2 in relations:
      print("{:<10}\t{}\t{}".format(r1.text, r2.ent_type_, r2.text))
```

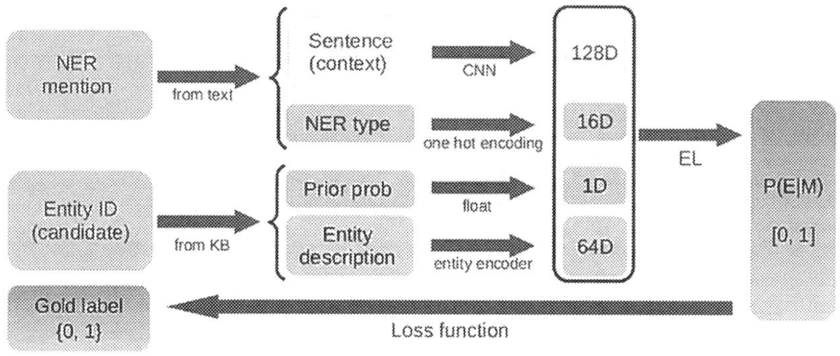

Figure 9.6 SpaCy Flow

```
def filter_spans(spans):
  # Filter a sequence of spans so they don't contain overlaps
  # For spaCy 2.1.4+: this function is available as spacy.util.
filter_spans()
  get_sort_key = lambda span: (span.end - span.start, -span.start)

  sorted_spans = sorted(spans, key=get_sort_key, reverse=True)
  result = []
  seen_tokens = set()
  for span in sorted_spans:
    # Check for end - 1 here because boundaries are inclusive
    if span.start not in seen_tokens and span.end - 1 not in seen_tokens:
        result.append(span)
    seen_tokens.update(range(span.start, span.end))
  result = sorted(result, key=lambda span: span.start)
  return result

def extract_currency_relations(doc):
  # Merge entities and noun chunks into one token
  spans = list(doc.ents) + list(doc.noun_chunks)
  spans = filter_spans(spans)
  with doc.retokenize() as retokenizer:
    for span in spans:
      retokenizer.merge(span)

  relations = []
  for money in filter(lambda w: w.ent_type_ == "MONEY", doc):
    if money.dep_ in ("attr", "dobj"):
      subject = [w for w in money.head.lefts if w.dep_ == "nsubj"]
      if subject:
        subject = subject[0]
        relations.append((subject, money))
    elif money.dep_ == "pobj" and money.head.dep_ == "prep":
      relations.append((money.head.head, money))
  return relations

if __name__ == "__main__":
  plac.call(elmain)


  # end of code
```

and observe the below results/output depicted in Figure 9.7 by running the above code with your PyCharm.

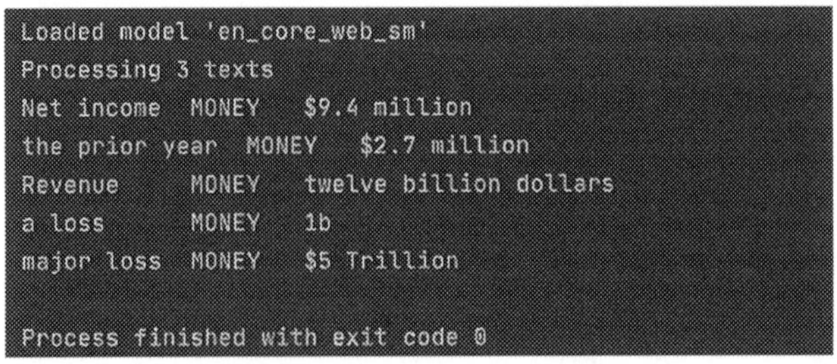

```
Loaded model 'en_core_web_sm'
Processing 3 texts
Net income   MONEY   $9.4 million
the prior year  MONEY   $2.7 million
Revenue      MONEY   twelve billion dollars
a loss       MONEY   1b
major loss   MONEY   $5 Trillion

Process finished with exit code 0
```

Figure 9.7 Sample results

So, we can see the texts linked with money. Change the texts or add more texts with context to money and see the output from your model.

Sentiment Analysis Sample Code

Another fascinating use case is sentiment analysis, and we will have a quick look at how to implement the same with spaCy and sklearn toolkits. The sample code classifies good or not good for the given sentence as seen in the following Figure 9.8.

So for the above text, the first sentence reflects good sentiment, and the second and third ones are not. Then the last one reflects it is good. When we run the sample, we would see the below results:

As we see in the preceding Figure 9.9, it correctly reflects the sentiment good or not good. Our sample uses three data sets of reviews and sklearn library.

Please note that as we have discussed the pipelines of case normalization, removing stop tokens, lemmatization, PoS tagging, entity linking/detection, and so on, we skip those explanations and list the source code as below:

```
import pandas as pd

from sklearn.feature_extraction.text import TfidfVectorizer
from sklearn.pipeline import Pipeline
from sklearn.model_selection import train_test_split
from sklearn.metrics import accuracy_score, classification_report,
confusion_matrix

data_yelp = pd.read_csv('my_datasets/yelp_labelled.txt', sep='\t',
header=None)
data_imdb = pd.read_csv('my_datasets/imdb_labelled.txt', sep='\t',
header=None)
```

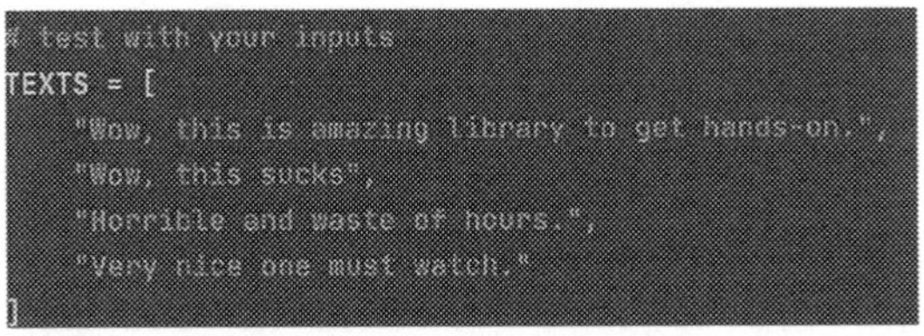

```
# test with your inputs
TEXTS = [
    "Wow, this is amazing library to get hands-on.",
    "Wow, this sucks",
    "Horrible and waste of hours.",
    "Very nice one must watch."
]
```

Figure 9.8 Sentiment Analysis Sample Input

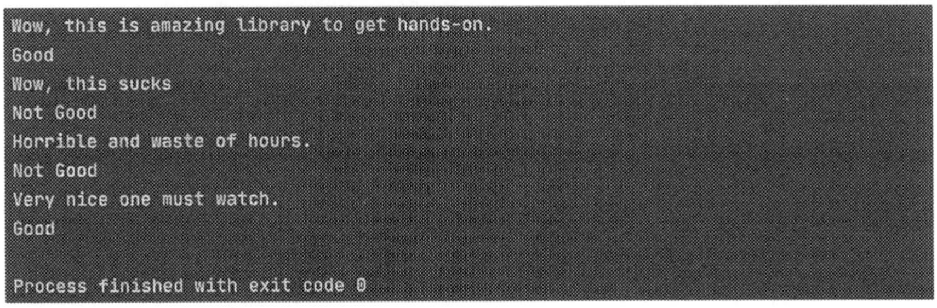

```
Wow, this is amazing library to get hands-on.
Good
Wow, this sucks
Not Good
Horrible and waste of hours.
Not Good
Very nice one must watch.
Good

Process finished with exit code 0
```

Figure 9.9 Sentiment Analysis output

```python
data_amazon = pd.read_csv('my_datasets/amazon_labelled.txt', sep='\t',
header=None)

columns_name = ['Review', 'Sentiment']
data_yelp.columns = columns_name
data_amazon.columns = columns_name
data_imdb.columns = columns_name

# combine all

data = data_yelp.append([data_amazon, data_imdb], ignore_index=True)
print(data.shape)
print(data.head())
print(data['Sentiment'].value_counts())
print(data.isnull().sum())

import string
import spacy
from spacy.lang.en.stop_words import STOP_WORDS

nlp = spacy.load('en_core_web_sm')
punctuations = string.punctuation;
print(punctuations)

stopwords = list(STOP_WORDS)

def text_data_cleaning(sentence):
  doc = nlp(sentence)
  tokens = []
  for token in doc:
    if token.lemma_ != "-PRON-":
      temp = token.lemma_.lower().strip()
    else:
      temp = token.lower_
    tokens.append(temp)

  cleaned_tokens = []
  for token in tokens:
    if token not in stopwords and token not in punctuations:
      cleaned_tokens.append(token)
  return cleaned_tokens

print(text_data_cleaning("Hello how are you doing. are you learning new
code"))

# TF-IDF
from sklearn.svm import LinearSVC
tfidf = TfidfVectorizer(tokenizer = text_data_cleaning)
classifier = LinearSVC()
X = data['Review']
y = data['Sentiment']
X_train, X_test, y_train, y_test = train_test_split(X, y, test_size =
0.2, random_state = 42)
```

```
print (X_train.shape, X_test.shape)

clf = Pipeline([('tfidf', tfidf), ('clf', classifier)])
clf.fit(X_train, y_train)
y_pred = clf.predict(X_test)

# wait for sometime to compute while you run you will see this display
after a few seconds
print(classification_report(y_test, y_pred))
print (confusion_matrix(y_test, y_pred))

# test with your inputs
TEXTS = [
  "Wow, this is amazing library to get hands-on.",
  "Wow, this sucks",
  "Horrible and waste of hours.",
  "Very nice one must watch."
]
for text in TEXTS:
  print(text)
  if clf.predict([text])== 1 :
    print('Good')
  else :
    print('Not Good')
```

Download the necessary data set, modify the source code accordingly, and run with PyCharm. Once run the code observe below results as depicted in the Figure 9.10; observe each step, tokenization, clean up, accuracy, etc.

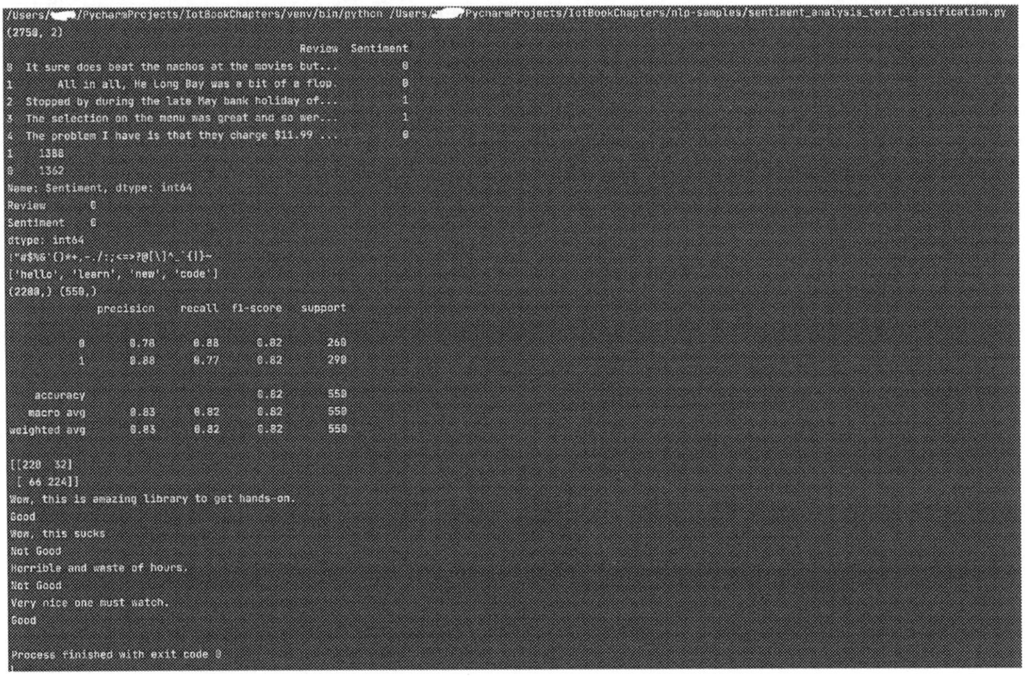

Figure 9.10   Sample output

Conclusion

NLP is a part of the AI domain. The main contribution is empowering handhelds, smartphones, machines, portables, instruments, equipment, appliances, wares, utensils, drones, robots, gaming consoles, consumer electronics, etc., the much-needed ability to read, understand, and derive meaning from human languages. Today, NLP is booming thanks to the enormous improvements in access to data and the increase in computational power, allowing practitioners to achieve meaningful results in areas like healthcare, media, finance, and human resources, among others.

References

Natural Language Processing https://surface.syr.edu/cgi/viewcontent.cgi?article=1043&context=istpub
NLP Tasks: https://www.ibm.com/cloud/learn/natural-language-processing
Text Mining, Text Analytics and Natural Language Processing: https://www.linguamatics.com/what-text-mining-text-analytics-and-natural-language-processing
Latent semantic indexing: https://nlp.stanford.edu/IR-book/html/htmledition/latent-semantic-indexing-1.html

Chapter 10

Design of a Secure Infrastructure for Cognitive IoT Platforms and Applications

Introduction

Information and communication technology will be the key foundational component of cognitive IoT ecosystem. These information and communication technological components are closely interconnected using various networking technologies in order to facilitate efficient co-ordination amongst the various components which are part of the cognitive IoT ecosystem. A cognitive IoT ecosystem can have huge number of interconnected components which are exchanging data in real time. For this communication and collaboration to happen effectively, the safety and security of the underlying cognitive IoT infrastructure is very important.

In this chapter, we will identify the security challenges and the security requirements to be kept in mind for the design of cognitive IoT infrastructure. These challenges are based on the generic cognitive IoT platform which is outlined in the next section. The main layers of the reference cognitive IoT platform are the following:

- Data layer and its components
- Network layer and its components
- Knowledge management layer and its components
- Intelligent services layer and its components

DOI: 10.1201/9780429328220-10

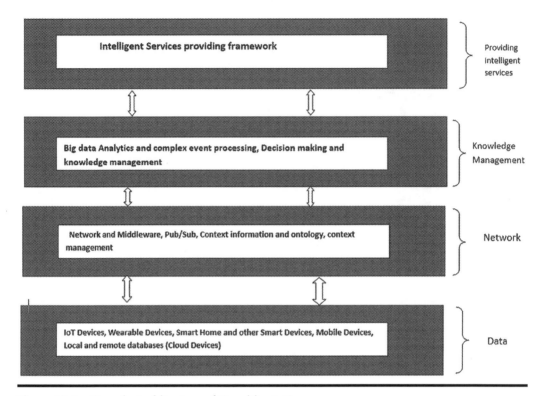

Figure 10.1   Generic Architecture of Cognitive IoT

Generic Reference Architecture for Design of Security of a Cognitive IoT Platform

The generic architecture of cognitive IoT which we use as a reference in this chapter is depicted in the following Figure 10.1; this has been explained in greater detail in one of the previous chapters in this book.

Security in the Data and Network Layer of Cognitive IoT Framework

The key security aspects which need to be kept in mind for the security of information technological components which are applicable to a cognitive IoT infrastructure are discussed in this section.

■ **Confidentiality, Integrity, and Availability (CIA) triad:** The three fundamental requirements which need to be kept in mind during the design and development phase of the underlying cognitive IoT infrastructure are depicted in the following Figure 10.2 which is given below:

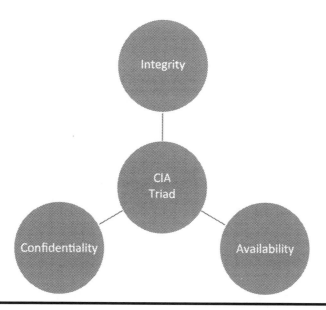

Figure 10.2   Cognitive IoT Infrastructure Phases

Confidentiality: It protects the data by ensuring that only authorized users will have access to it. In other words, it ensures security of data by preventing unauthorized access to data and information which is created, transferred, and stored within an underlying cognitive IoT infrastructure. Data is the most important component when it comes to a cognitive IoT infrastructure/ecosystem. Hence, it is very important to ensure that the data is safe and secure.

Integrity: It ensures that only authorized users will have the right/ability to modify the underlying information which is stored in the cognitive IoT infrastructure. It ensures that unauthorized users will not have capability to alter the stored/transmitted information in any manner. Modification in this context refers to write, delete, and update operations on data.

Availability: In addition to protection of information, it is also important to ensure availability of information to the authorized users at the correct point in time as and when it is needed. This includes ensuring the fact that the cognitive IoT infrastructure has fault tolerance and fault resilience capabilities built into them. One of the important aspects which needs to be kept in mind in order to ensure availability of information is elimination of single points of failure in a cognitive IoT infrastructure. When you talk about a cognitive IoT infrastructure there could be several single points of failure like data centres, storage servers, interconnecting networks, and so on. This needs to be carefully identified and appropriate steps should be taken to ensure business continuity in case of failure of any component.

Fault tolerance/fault resilience can be built into the cognitive IoT infrastructure by ensuring that backup components are present for each of the IoT infrastructure components namely servers, storage, and networks. Server backup can be ensured by clustering the servers in order to provide a high availability environment. It is also important to ensure that the backup server is an identical copy of the primary server and can take over the role of the primary server immediately upon the failure of the primary server. Storage backup can be ensured by using the highly scalable RAID architecture for hard disks in which same data is striped and mirrored across multiple hard disks so that even if one hard disk fails, data will not be lost as it will be stored in the other disks of the array. Fault tolerance in networks can be ensured by providing multiple switches, multiple ports, and multiple cables between the two connecting endpoints in order to ensure that the failure of any network component will not hamper the transfer of data through the network.

These components confidentiality, integrity, and availability are commonly referred to as CIA triad.

Authentication, Authorization, and Audit Trial Framework (AAA)

AAA framework is a security requirement which is of paramount importance for the cognitive IoT infrastructure. As depicted in the following Figure 10.3, the various components of the framework are:

Authentication

This process ensures that a user with only valid credentials is able to access the infrastructure and the underlying information. The simplest way to implement authentication is with the help of user names and passwords. But as hacking techniques are evolving day by day, it is very important to ensure that sophisticated authentication techniques are in place. One straightforward technique which could be implemented is

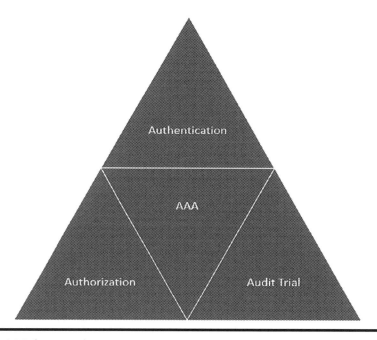

Figure 10.3 AAA framework

the usage of strong passwords. What is the meaning of strong passwords? Strong passwords are very difficult to be guessed or interpreted by a third-party agent or malicious user who is trying to access the system in an unauthorized manner. One important rule to be kept in mind to create a strong password is that it should not be pertaining to any personal information of the user and should have minimum eight characters which should ideally contain a mix of letters, numbers, and alphanumeric characters.

Another authentication mechanism which is commonly used is called multi-factor authentication. Multi-factor authentication is a special authentication technique which uses a combination of multiple parameters to verify a user's credentials. An example of multi-factor authentication mechanism is described below:

First factor: A user name and password which will be unique for the specific user. In some cases, it will be unique for the specific session under consideration as well.

Second factor: A secret key which is generated by a random number generator or it could be something like an OTP (one-time password) which is sent only to the registered mobile device of the user. Some other examples are secret key phrases known only to the user or answer to a secret question which varies from one user to another for sure.

Third factor: This could be any biometric parameter of the user which could be used as the user's biometric signature. This could include aspects like face recognition, voice recognition, iris recognition, fingerprint recognition, and so on.

A multi-factor authentication uses one or a combination of all the parameters mentioned above in order to verify a user's credentials. In some cases, only two factors mentioned above may be used for authentication, then it is called a two-factor authentication.

Authorization

Authorization is a process which ensures that a specific user has rights to perform only certain kinds of operations on a specific object. This is generally implemented by granting different types of permissions to different types of users based on their roles and the operations they are expected to perform as part of the role. Authorization of data is implemented using a component called access control list (ACL). ACL specifies different types of permissions for different users on different objects. These permissions are mapped and stored in the form a table. The different types of permissions which are given for users are classified as the following:

- Read only: The user has permission to only read the object. The user cannot delete or edit the object. These types of permissions are granted to staff who are not required to perform any alteration on the data.
- Read and write: The user has permission to read and alter the object. These types of permissions are granted to authorities who have the overall authority and discretion to validate the rights and access permissions of other users.

Audit Trial

Audit trial is an activity which is conducted periodically to assess the effectiveness of the security measures which are implemented in the cognitive IoT infrastructure.

Audit trial is performed with the help of audit logs which tracks the operations which are performed by different users.

Defense-in-Depth

This is a mechanism which should be used to provide high level of security to the cognitive IoT infrastructure. This mechanism ensures that multiple levels or layers of security are offered to a cognitive IoT infrastructure to ensure that even if security at one level gets compromised due to some reason, security at other levels should be able to safeguard the underlying cognitive IoT infrastructure. As multiple levels of security are provided in this approach, it is also called a layered approach to security implementation. It gives enhanced security to the IoT infrastructure by providing multiple layers of security and more time to officials to react to a security breach which has happened in one layer where the other layer security measures will be working to protect it. A high-level architecture of the Defense-in-Depth approach is given as depicted in the following Figure 10.4:

Layer 1

Physical or perimeter refers to the physical safety of the underlying cognitive IoT infrastructure. This includes ensuring the safety of the building by protecting from intentional or unintentional attacks by man, animals, and other elements pertaining to nature. Layer 1 security can be implemented by having a well-secured building/ room for the infrastructure. Security of the building can be implemented by having security personnel or by using technologies like video surveillance or monitoring of the building. Another important aspect to ensure level 1 security is the choice of building location away from natural calamities like earthquake, volcanoes, etc.

Layer 2

This layer of security can be implemented by restricting direct access to the underlying infrastructure. Direct access can be restricted by having controls like virtual private network and firewalls which will protect the infrastructure from malicious and third-party attacks.

Layer 3

Some of the techniques to implement Layer 3 security are outlined in this section. They are:

Figure 10.4   Defense-in-Depth Approach

Trusted Computing Base (TCB)

This defines the boundary for the critical information components which form a part of the cognitive IoT infrastructure. Any security breaches which happen within the TCB boundary will affect the entire IoT infrastructure in an adverse manner. This helps to establish a clear definition between the critical and non-critical components of the IoT infrastructure. For example, if we take an example of a PC or tablet, operating system and configuration files will be a part of the TCB as any security breaches to the operating system will corrupt the entire PC. It is very important for TCB to be defined for the IoT infrastructure. It helps to provide multiple additional levels of security for the components which fall under the TCB of the IoT infrastructure.

Encryption

It is the process of converting data into a format which cannot be interpreted easily and directly by unauthorized users. It is very important to ensure that data which is stored in the IoT infrastructure and the data which is transmitted via the networks are in encrypted form. This is very helpful to prevent unauthorized deception of data by third-party agents. the process of converting the data back to its original form is called decryption. Several encryption software are available in the market.

PRETTY GOOD PRIVACY (PGP)

Pretty Good Privacy (PGP) is a strong data encryption and decryption program which is widely used by federal government for protecting all types of government data like mails, files, and entire disk partitions of computers.

Most of the cognitive IoT applications use cloud platform. Hence, all common security concerns of cloud platforms will pose security threats for IoT components as well. In the next section, we will examine some of the security concerns of cloud platforms.

Security Concerns of Cloud Platforms

As per a recent study as shown in the following Figure 10.5, majority of web traffic and the resulting security threats are due to cloud.

Figure 10.5   Security concerns of Cloud Platform

Ensuring security of cloud-based cognitive IoT applications is the need of the day. The architecture which is outlined in the next section talks about cloud security architecture.

Cloud security architecture as depicted in the following Figure 10.6 has three different layers: software applications layer, platform layer, and infrastructure layer. Each layer has its own set of security concerns. We will discuss some of them in the context of cognitive IoT components which would mainly rely on public cloud for its IT requirements.

One of the main concerns of cloud is multitenancy. Multitenancy refers to the fact that cloud infrastructure, because of the underlying virtualization platform, provides features to service multiple independent clients (tenants) using same set of hardware and (or) software resources. This consequently increases the risks for breach of data confidentiality and integrity. These risks are especially more prominent in case of public cloud environment. This is because, in public cloud, services can be used by competing clients as compared to private clouds and number of cloud users are much higher in public clouds.

Some of the countermeasures to tackle security issues arising out of multitenancy architecture (MTA) of cloud are the following:

Separation of Duties (SoD)

Separation of Duties (SoD) as per the definition refers to the system's ability to split a single task, function, or component into multiple areas of responsibility. These areas are then assigned to different roles or individuals. The key goal of SoD is to prevent conflicts of interest by offering guarantee that no individual can perform actions beyond those defined for his or her role. The risks surrounding SoD implementation in the context of cloud computing are mostly focusing on role definition and

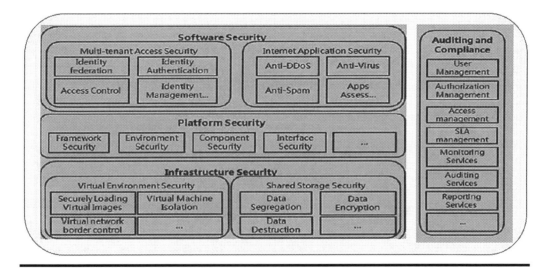

Figure 10.6 Cloud Security Architecture Layers

clarification. Due to the quick evolution of cloud technologies, and the rapid increase in cloud service provider offerings, there has been very little time available to stabilize and develop SoD into standard roles.

A typical example of this scenario is the CSP role. This is more prominent in case of administrative access and security policy creation. In these scenarios, it is necessary for CSP's need to secure the services they offer, without compromising their customer's authorities in any resource or data domain.

This scenario is applicable to MTA environments. In an MTA setup, multiple tenants may not have the same level of reliance on the CSP's role in security management, or similar capability to take the security role in-house. This leads to confusion around the CSP's role definition and gives rise to SoD concerns. One emerging cloud standards body, the Cloud Security Alliance (CSA), specifies that the CSP assumes maximum security responsibility in SaaS, and least possible responsibility in IaaS, with focus on PaaS when it comes to fine-grained control.

SoD as a concept is added to many commercial security products, including the ones which offer Enterprise Single Sign-On (ESSO) and Identity and Access Management (IAM) capabilities. In general, security products which are currently available in the market do not support adequate SoD separation for cloud environments. This is because they have been designed for single security domain in which the ownership is primarily with IT team.

Multi-Tenancy Trusted Computing Environment Model (MTCEM) implements the Trusted Computing Group's (TCG: http://www.trustedcomputinggroup.org) Trusted Computing Platform (TCP). TCP is a set of standards that enable a data owner to implicitly and explicitly "trust". This is done by holding accountable, the underlying computing infrastructure on which the applications which create data operate. TCP contains two basic assertions, they are:

- Transitive trust
- Platform assertion

Transitive Trust

In transitive trust mechanism, a platform can only boot or initialize from a Core Root of Trust Measurement (CRTM). CRTM could be anything like a microcode, ROM module, or a hardware chip or any other encrypted firmware which is certified by an authority to be a trustworthy source. This initialization from CRTM ensures that right from the bootstrap process, there is a pathway of trust which is followed. Using this mechanism, one level of initialization can trust that the previous level has also undergone a similar level of trust validation mechanism.

Platform Assertion

Platform assertion is a mechanism using which a platform proves its trustworthiness to a third party. Using the platform attestation capability, a system should deem itself to be trustworthy by other systems with which it will interact. The key aspect here is to determine and define a set of metrics that can be used to establish trustworthiness of computing platform. Several attestation prototypes have been built in the area of cloud computing which uses multiple parameters to establish trustworthiness. One of the prominent ones is to establish trustworthiness based on behaviour history. Behaviour history refers to conformance of patterns of normal or expected computing behaviour when a system request is received.

Virtualization is one of the key topics to be kept in mind for all the IaaS offerings. Implementation of virtualization opens lot of security threats and concerns which becomes more prominent in the context of multitenancy.

Some of the ways to overcome these virtualization-related security concerns which arise in multitenancy-based cloud environment are:

■ Virtual machine segmentation
■ Database segmentation
■ Virtual machine introspection

Virtual Machine Segmentation

Virtualization forms the basis of most of the IaaS offerings. There are many virtualizations software available in the market like VMware vSphere, Citrix XenServer, and Microsoft Hyper-V. This software provides the capability to convert a physical machine into multiple virtual machines. These virtual machines serve as databases, web servers, and file servers. These components which run on virtual platforms are provided to customers as a part of IaaS. The main component of virtualization platform is hypervisor which acts as operating system for the virtual machines and provisions all the resources required for the operation of virtual machines. The major security concerns in virtualized infrastructure is due to the fact that virtual machines owned by multiple customers reside on the same physical machine. This aspect places the virtual machines in a privileged position with respect to one another. This can introduce several types of security risks like unauthorized connection, monitoring, and malware induction. In order to prevent occurrence of such security concerns, it is very important to ensure that VMs which contain confidential customer data should be segmented and isolated from one another. This process of ensuring that virtual machines are isolated or separated from one another is called virtual machine segmentation.

Database Segmentation

In IaaS, infrastructure resources are offered as a service. In SaaS, apart from software applications, database is also offered as a service. This will introduce a scenario that multiple customers will store their data in the same database as multiple rows which are differentiated based on customer ID which will be assigned to customers. In some situations, like application code errors or access control list errors, there is a lot of risk for customer data. For controlling access to database data, there are quite a few tools and technologies available. In order to prevent the occurrence of such situations, there are many tools which are available in the market. These tools work on the basis of a system for authentication and authorization which ensure that only some rows are only modifiable based on certain predefined security policies which ensure that access to data is warranted. Another technique which could be used to reduce security threats in this situation is the encryption of data which is stored in the database. This ensures that even if the security of the data is compromised, it would be difficult to decrypt it.

VM Introspection

Another important technique which could be used to eliminate the risks of multitenancy is VM introspection. VM introspection is a service which is provided by the hypervisor. This service examines the internal state of each VM which runs on top of the hypervisor. There are many tools available in the market which leverage the benefits of this service to provide VM segmentation and isolation. VM introspection provides the following details of each VM:

- Applications and services which are present
- Configuration details

With the help of these details of VMs, it is possible to create and implement custom security policies on each VM. An example of a policy could be to ensure that no other VM should join a specific VM group until it has some matching OS configuration parameters. This ensures that in a multitenant environment, VMs remain segmented and isolated.

Distributed Denial of Service (DDoS)

In a cloud system, if a host of messages attack all nodes of the cloud system and overutilize the server resources, making the resources unavailable for actual requirements, then it is called a DDoS attack. There are multiple versions of DDoS attacks which are available: simple and complex. Examples of simple DDoS attack tools are X-DoS (XML-based Denial of Service) and H-DoS (HTTP-based Denial of Service). Example of complex DDoS attack tools are Agobot, mStream, and Trinoo. H-DoS is used by attackers who are interested in using less complex web-based tools for attack. One additional advantage of these simple tools is the ease of implementation of attacks. DX-DoS occurs when XML-based messages are sent to a web server in such a way that it will use up all their resources. Coercive parsing attack is an X-DoS attack in which web content is parsed using SOAP to transform it into an application. A series of open tags are used by coercive parsing attack to exhaust the CPU resources on the web server. In case of an H-DoS attack, a series of about 1000 plus threads are started to create HTTP simultaneous random requests to exhaust all the resources. There are several tools available in the market to detect and eliminate

DDoS attacks. The cloud service provider can use these tools at their discretion. One such example is discussed below.

REAL-LIFE EXAMPLE OF DDOS ATTACK

Bloomberg News reported that hackers used AWS's EC2 cloud computing unit to launch an attack against Sony's PlayStation Network and Qriocity entertainment networks. The attack reportedly compromised the personal accounts of more than 100 million Sony customers.

Steps to Prevent DDoS Attack

DDoS attacks can create lot of panic in the system and hence having a DDoS mitigation plan in place is the need of the day for all organizations. Some of the key steps to be followed in order to create a DDoS mitigation plan are outlined in the following Figure 10.7:

These points are explained in greater detail below:

1) Anticipate single points of failure: Typically, there are many single points of failure components which exist within an organization; they are generally the first ones which are targeted by the attackers. Some of the common single points of failure in an organization are the following:
   ■ APIs
   ■ DNS and origin servers
   ■ Data centre and related network infrastructure

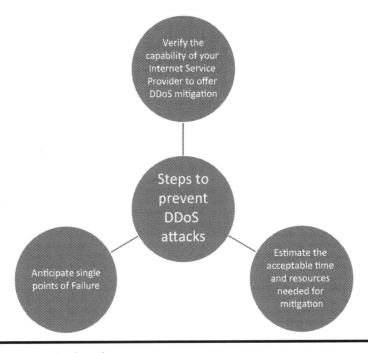

Figure 10.7 DDoS Mitigation Plans

■ Website and other web applications

For each of these single points of failure, it is important to have a backup mechanism to ensure business continuity in the event of a failure. Some common business continuity measures which are deployed by the organization could be something like having a continuous mechanism to take backup of data, deploying a secondary infrastructure as a backup in case of failure of primary infrastructure and so on.

2) Verify the capability of your Internet service provider to offer DDoS mitigation:

Some of the key questions which should be asked to the ISP could be the following:

■ Scale of DDoS attacks which can be prevented

■ Requirements to restore continuity of internet service

■ Capability to decrypt TLS/SSL to find out application DDoS attacks in SSL sessions

■ Capability to block DDoS sources using an ACL mechanism considering all possible scenarios.

3) Estimate the acceptable time and resources needed for mitigation:

There are different types of DDoS protection services which are available. Some of them are always running and some others are activated based on manual request after a DDoS attack is detected. There are two types of DDoS:

■ CDN-based DDoS protection services: They are always running and can start providing DDoS services instantaneously; however, they do not offer protection to network infrastructure and data centre.

■ DDoS scrubbing services: They are usually on-demand services and require specialized network infrastructure with high bandwidth availability and flow monitoring capabilities. If this service needs to be used, appropriate infrastructure must be planned.

Imperva SecureSphere Web Application Firewall to Prevent DDoS attacks

The Imperva SecureSphere Web Application Firewall as depicted in the following Figure 10.8 is a security appliance which is capable of preventing DDoS attacks in a cloud infrastructure. In addition to DDoS, this software also has the capability to prevent several types of web attacks like SQL injection.

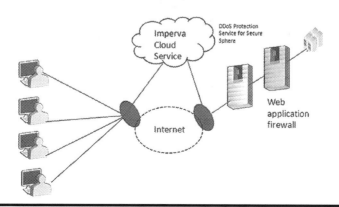

Figure 10.8   Imperva SecureSphere Web Application Firewall

The tool uses the following features to prevent DDoS attacks on cloud infrastructure:

- **ThreatRadar Reputation:** This service keeps track of users who are attacking other websites. By using this information, it will filter off any request from those users and prevent them from getting into the cloud system.
- **Up-to-Date Web Attack Signatures:** This service helps to monitor and keep track of bot user agents and DDoS attacks vectors.
- **DDoS Policy Templates:** This service helps to detect users who have the pattern of generating and sending HTTP requests with long response times.
- **Bot Mitigation Policies:** This service has the capability to sends a JavaScript challenge to users' browsers. This JavaScript challenge has the capacity to detect and block bots.
- **HTTP Protocol Validation:** This service monitors and records buffer overflow attempts and other intrusion techniques.

Virtual Machine/Hypervisor-based Security Threats

The virtual machines which form the basis of cloud infrastructure are also subjected to various types of vulnerabilities. These pose severe threats to the cloud infrastructure. Some of them shown in the following Figure 10.9 and discussed in details in subsequent sections.

Unauthorized Alteration of Virtual Machine Image Files

Virtual machines are susceptible to security threats when they are running as well as when they are powered off. When a VM is powered off, it is available as a VM image file. This image file is exposed to several security threats like malware infections. Apart from that, if appropriate security measures are not in place, VM image files can be used by hackers to create new unauthorized VMs. It is also possible to patch

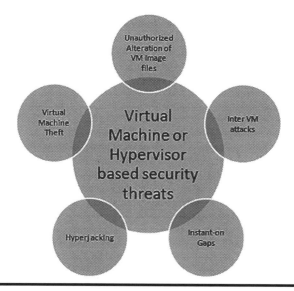

Figure 10.9   Types of Vulnerabilities of Virtual Machines

these VM image files so as to infect the VMs which are created using these image files. VM security can be compromised even during VM migration. At the time of VM migration, the VMs are exposed to several types of network attacks like eavesdropping and unauthorized modification. One technique which could be used to protect the VM image files is to encrypt them when they are powered off or being migrated.

VM Theft

VM theft enables a hacker or attacker to copy or move a VM in an unauthorized manner. This is mainly made possible because of the presence of inadequate controls on VM files. These inadequate controls will allow the unauthorized copy or movement of VM files. VM theft could prove to be very fatal if the VM that is stolen contains confidential data of a customer.

One way to restrict VM theft is to impose required level of copy and move restrictions on VMs. Such restrictions effectively bind a VM to a specific physical machine in such a way that even if there is a forceful copy of the VM, it will not operate on any other physical machine. A VM with required level of copy and move restrictions cannot run on a hypervisor installed on any other physical machine.

Apart from VM theft, another threat which can happen at VM level is known as "VM escape". Normally, virtual machines are encapsulated and isolated from each other and from the underlying parent hypervisor. In normal scenarios, there is no mechanism available for a guest OS and the applications running on it to break out of the virtual machine boundary and directly interact with the hypervisor. The process of breaking out and interacting with the hypervisor is called a VM escape. Since the hypervisor controls the execution of all VMs, due to VM escape, an attacker can gain control over every other VM running on it by bypassing security controls which are placed on those VMs.

Inter-VM Attacks

Multiple VMs run on the same physical machine. So if the security of one VM is compromised, there is a very easy possibility for the security of other VMs running on the same physical machine to be compromised. In one scenario, as shown in the Figure 10.10 it is possible for an attacker to compromise one guest VM which can then get passed on

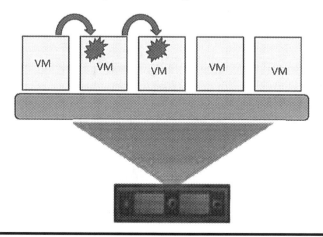

Figure 10.10   Inter-VM Attacks

to the other VMs which are running on the same physical machine. In order to prevent the occurrence of such scenarios, it is very important to have firewalls and intrusion detection systems which have the capability to detect and prevent malicious activity at the VM level.

Instant-on Gaps

Virtual machines have some vulnerabilities which are not present in physical machines. This is mainly due to the techniques which are used to provision, use, and de-provision them. Sometimes these cycles are repeated very frequently. This frequent activation and deactivation of VMs can pose challenges to maintain their security systems constantly updated.

After some time, these VMs can automatically deviate from their defined security baselines and this in turn can introduce significant levels of security threats. This will give lot of options to attackers to access them. As shown in the Figure 10.11, there is also a possibility that new VMs could be cloned and created out of these VMs which have vulnerabilities. If this is done, the security threats will get passed on to the newly created VMs and this will increase the area of the attack surface. It is very important to ensure that VMs possess a security agent which has all the latest security configurations update.

When a VM is not online during an antivirus update, that VM will have vulnerabilities when it comes online as it would not have got the latest security updates. One solution to this problem could be to have a dedicated security VM in each physical machine to automatically update all VMs running in that physical machine with all latest security updates.

Hyperjacking

Hyperjacking enables an attacker to install a rogue hypervisor that has the capability to take complete control of the underlying physical server. This is a rootkit level vulnerability. A rootkit is a malicious program which is installed before a hypervisor fully boots on a physical server. In this manner, the rootkit is able to run in the server with privileged access and remains invisible to the system administrators. Once a rootkit is installed, it gives permission to an attacker to mask the ongoing

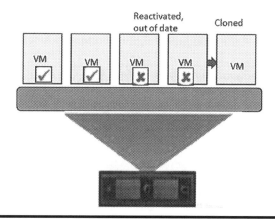

Figure 10.11   Dedicated Security VM and Auto Update

intrusion and maintain privileged access to the physical server by bypassing the normal authentication and authorization mechanisms which are employed by an OS.

Using such a rogue hypervisor, an attacker can run unauthorized applications on a guest OS without the OS realizing the presence of such an application. With hyperjacking, an attacker could control the interaction between the VMs and the underlying physical server. Regular security measures are ineffective against this rogue hypervisor because:

■ Guest OS is unaware of the fact that underlying server has been attacked;
■ Antivirus and firewall applications cannot detect the presence of the rogue hypervisor as it is installed directly over the server itself.

Measures against hyperjacking include:

■ Hardware-assisted secure launching of the hypervisor so that rootkit level malicious programs cannot launch. This would involve designing and using a TCB for the hypervisor getting support at the hardware level.
■ Scanning hardware level details to assess the integrity of the hypervisor and locate presence of rogue hypervisor. This scanning may include checking the state of the memory as well as registering in the CPU.

Security in the Knowledge Management Layer of Cognitive IoT Framework

Big data is huge volumes of constantly changing data which comes in from a variety of different sources. The constantly changing nature of big data introduces a variety of security threats for big data platforms. Some of the key challenges are summarized in the following Figure 10.12.

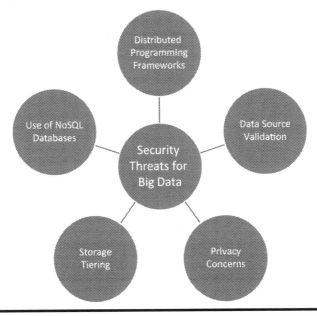

Figure 10.12   Security Threats of Big Data

Distributed Programming Frameworks

Many programming frameworks which process big data use parallel computation to process huge amounts of data quickly. One such example is the MapReduce framework which is used for processing big data. This framework splits the data into multiple chunks. The mapper then works on each chunk of data and generates key/value pairs for each chunk. In the next step, the reducer component combines values which belong to each key and then generates a final output. In this framework, the main security threat is with regard to mappers. Mappers can be hacked and made to generate incorrect key value pairs. This in turn will lead to the generation of incorrect final results. Due to vast amounts of big data, it is impossible to detect the mapper which generated the incorrect value. This in turn can affect the accuracy of data which may adversely affect data rich computations. The main solution to this problem is to secure mappers using various algorithms which are available.

Use of NoSQL Databases

NoSQL databases which are designed to store big data scale well to store huge amounts of data. But they do not have any security controls/policies embedded in them. The security controls are designed and incorporated into the middleware by the database programmers. There is no provision to include security practices as a part of NoSQL database design. This poses significant threat to the big data which is stored in the NoSQL databases. A solution to this problem is that organizations should review their security policies thoroughly and ensure that appropriate levels of security controls are incorporated into their middleware.

Storage Tiering

Most of the present-day organizations have a tiered approach to store data. Tiered approach consists of multiple tiers of heterogeneous storage devices each of which vary in terms of cost, performance, storage capacity, and security policies which are enforced. In normal scenarios, data is stored in different tiers based on their frequency of access, cost, volume, or any other parameter which is of importance for the organization. The tiering of data is done manually. However, with the ever-increasing volumes of big data, it is becoming very difficult for the storage administrators to do tiering of such huge amounts of data manually. Hence, many organizations now have automatic storage tiering which is done with the help of some preconfigured policies. This might ensure that some data like R&D data which is not frequently used may be stored in the lowest tier as it may not be frequently used as per the policy. But it might be an important data from the context of organizations and storing such data in the lowest tier which has less data security may expose the data to security threats.

Data Source Validation

As per the 3V's of big data, i.e. volume, velocity, and variety, input data can be collected from diverse kinds of sources. Some sources may have data validation techniques in place and some other sources will not have data validation. This is more prominent when the input comes in from mobile devices like tablets and cell phones. Since many of the present-day organizations are promoting bring your own device concept (BYOD), the possibility of threats which are likely to creep in from the mobile devices are still higher. Some examples of mobile device threats are spoofed cell phone IDs.

Privacy Concerns

In an attempt to perform analytics to derive insights, lot of activities of the users are being tracked without their knowledge. This data which is tracked by organizations for deriving various types of insights could prove to be extremely harmful for the users if it gets passed on to some untrusted third party.

PRIVACY CONCERN OF BIG DATA ANALYTICS

A recent event which was news recently is an eye opener on how big data analytics could intervene into the privacy of an individual. An analysis which was done by a retail organization for marketing purposes was able to inform a father about his teenage daughter's pregnancy.

Requirements of Security Management Framework for Big Data

Big data involves data of huge sizes, different types which are constantly changing in nature. In order to design a security management framework for big data, the three key parameters to be kept in mind are summarized in the following Figure 10.13:

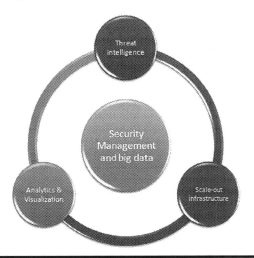

Figure 10.13   Security Management Framework Key parameters

Agile Scale-out Infrastructure

In order to manage huge amounts of constantly changing data, the IoT infrastructure of organizations should have agility and scale-out capabilities. Apart from storing and managing huge amounts of big data, organizations also use this data to support a plethora of new delivery models like cloud computing, mobility, outsourcing, and so on. The security management infrastructure should have the capability to adapt quickly to collect and secure this type of data. The underlying security infrastructure should be able to expand and adapt easily to facilitate easy identification of new threats which evolve continually with each new type of data and the associated delivery mechanism.

Security Analytics

Many data analytics and visualization tools exist in the market. They support analytics for wide range of activities and device types. But the number of tools which provide security analytics capabilities are limited in the market. Security management officials require many types of sophisticated analytical tools which can provide them diverse kinds of security analysis insights and visualization capabilities. Security management in enterprises covers a wide range of functions which include security analysis of networks, security analysis of databases, and so on. Each type of security analysis requires different type of data. For example, in order to perform security analysis of networks, logs and network information pertaining to specific sessions of activity are required. Software which supports the analytical and visualization requirements of diverse types of security personnel in an organization should be present in the organization. For example, in order to perform security analysis of log information, there are a separate category of tools available which come under the broad umbrella called as " Machine to Machine (M2M)" analytics.

IBM ACCELERATOR FOR MACHINE DATA ANALYTICS

Machines produce large amount of data. This data contains a wealth of actionable insights. However, in order to extract and perform analysis on such huge amount of data, tools with large scale data extraction, transformation, and analysis capabilities are required. IBM® Accelerator for Machine Data Analytics provides a set of diverse applications which helps to import, transform, and analyse this machine data for the purpose of identifying event and pattern correlations and use them to make informed decisions based on the data which is present in the log and data files.

IBM Accelerator for Machine Data Analytics provides the following key capabilities:

- Search within and across multiple log entries using text search, faceted search, or a timeline-based search in order to find specific patterns or events of interest.
- Enrich the context of log data by adding and extracting log types into the existing repository
- Link and correlate events across systems

Threat Monitoring and Intelligence

Diverse types of threats for data exists within an organization and outside as well. To add on to this, new types of threats are evolving every day. It is very important for organizations to stay updated on the threat environment so that the security analysts can get a clear picture of the various types of threat indicators and the security prejudice which is inflicted by them.

All the mobile applications and use cases of intelligent cities which was discussed in the previous chapter are designed with respect to smartphones. In the next section, we will examine some of the security threats for smartphones and also some mechanisms which can be used to secure smartphones.

SAMPLE IMPLEMENTATION OF SECURITY IMPLEMENTATION IN BIG DATA ENVIRONMENT

We will take an example of Law Enforcement Agencies (LEA) of the USA which has launched the INDECT project. The main objective of this project is to implement a secured infrastructure for a secured data exchange between agencies and other members. The solution includes the following:

■ A public key infrastructure (PKI) with three levels of security. They are the following:
  – Certification authority
  – Users
  – Machines
■ The PKI access control works based on a multi-factor authentication mechanism which considers security level required for each data type. For example, access to highly confidential applications is provided using a valid certificate and a password.
■ Another concept which is used by INDECT is Federated Identity Management. This is used to enhance access control and security. This type of federated identity management is implemented by delegating to an identity provider (IdP) which is placed within a monitored trust domain. Security tools used in this case are the following: certificates and smart cards. The function of these tools is to store user certificates issued by the PKI to encrypt and sign documents and emails.
■ An INDECT Block Cipher IBC algorithm is a new algorithm for implementing asymmetric cryptography. This algorithm was developed and used to encrypt databases, communication sessions (TLS-SSL), and VPN tunnels. The goal in this scenario is to ensure a high level of data confidentiality

---

Security Threats in Smartphones

Smartphones have the capability to connect to various types of external systems like internet, GPS, and other different types of mobile devices using wireless networking technology. This is the key feature of smartphone which makes it one of the most widely used and popular devices. Many cognitive IoT applications which are run using smartphones store personal data like address book, bank account details, meeting and appointment details, and so on, in the smartphones. Proliferation of technologies like near-field communication (NFC) for various purposes makes it very critical to ensure security of the smartphone and the data which is stored in the smartphone. A smartphone is exposed to a lot of vulnerabilities which can compromise its security.

The vulnerabilities in smartphones can be classified into two broad categories: internal and external. Internal vulnerabilities exist within the smartphone and external vulnerabilities creep into smartphones from the external systems to which they are connected. Some of the internal vulnerabilities are:

■ Operating system implementation error: This error will happen due to the presence of some erroneous code in the operating system of mobile devices. Usually, these types of errors are not introduced by the end users and they creep into the mobile devices due to fault of the mobile OS owning organizations. It is very common to have such errors in the new version or version upgrades of mobile operating systems. These OS errors can easily provide lot of options to the attackers to hack the operating system and gain illegitimate access to the smartphone or install rogue applications which can track and retrieve the details of the user from the smartphone. One way to avoid this could be by installing only version upgrades which have been fully tested and corrected and to defer from installing beta versions of operating systems.

■ End user unawareness error: The smartphone end user can compromise the security by one or all of the following actions which are mainly due to the lack of awareness of the end user. Some of the common errors which are introduced by the end users are the following:
  – Use untrusted wireless networks to connect to the internet
    • Install mobile applications from untrusted sources
    • Connect to untrusted web sites using mobile phones which can inject some malware into the device
    • Improper configuration settings in the mobile device browser
  – Loss of mobile devices which can pose a serious security threat for the user's personal information which is stored in the mobile device

Some of the external vulnerabilities are the following:

■ Wireless network threats: The attacker could hack the wireless network to which the smartphone is connected and thereby gain access into the mobile device of the user.

■ External websites: If the external website to which an end user is connected is hacked by an attacker, it is also possible for the attacker to gain access to the mobile device of the user with the help of the details which are gathered from that specific web site. It is also possible that a malware which is present in an external website can get automatically installed in the mobile device if security mechanisms in the mobile device is not properly configured like unavailability of anti-virus software in the mobile devices.

■ Other wireless devices: Smartphones have the capability to connect and communicate with a wide range of other wireless devices. Such wireless devices are subject to security vulnerabilities like tampered or fake wi-fi access points, packet sniffing, evil twin, and so on.

Security Solutions for Mobile Devices

Many measures can be adopted by the user to enhance the security of the mobile devices. But none of these measures will offer complete security to mobile devices as threats are getting added day on day and it is impossible to devise solutions at the pace at which threats are being created. Some of the possible security solutions which can be adopted by the users are:

■ System add-on: This refers to system updates which are periodically made available to the smartphones. This will include platform updates which will provide enhanced features and, in some cases, enhanced security as well. It is the responsibility of the user to ensure that the system updates are installed periodically.

■ System configuration: This is a very expensive and time-consuming activity as this process involves modification of the mobile OS code in order to add enhanced security features at the kernel level. This approach is rarely adopted by the users because of the huge amount of cost and time involved in it.

■ Anti-virus, spam filter: In order to protect the smartphones from virus attacks, anti-virus software which is available for specific mobile OS. Also, some attacks from rogue websites can be prevented by turning on the spam filter in the smartphones.

■ Cryptographic security mechanisms: Cryptographic techniques are available to ensure confidentiality and integrity of the data which is stored in the smartphone. Cryptography can be implemented in smartphones in two ways: mobile applications and mobile platform APIs. Cryptographic techniques use various mechanisms to ensure security of data which is stored in the smartphone. One such mechanism is used to encrypt the data which is stored in the smartphone so that even if it is hacked by a third party, the information cannot be deciphered without the availability of the key which will be known only to the smartphone user. Most of the mobile platforms make several APIs for use by the developers. Some of these APIs can be used to access the mobile OS-specific security library. This way, the developers can develop specialized mobile security applications for various mobile platforms.

Apart from these methods, several mobile security applications are available in the mobile application store. It is the responsibility of the user to check and install the appropriate applications. In addition to this, in order to protect the information stored in the mobile devices, users can lock the mobile phones using strong passwords. Another option is to make a note of the IMEA number of the mobile device so that if the mobile device is lost/stolen, the International Mobile Equipment Identity (IMEA) number can be deactivated which will disable all the functionalities of the mobile device automatically.

Security Concerns in IoT Components

An IoT platform will contain hundreds of sensors and other different types of devices which are sending data to a public or private cloud or some big data platform using a wired or wireless network through a gateway as shown in the following Figure 10.14 which is given below. The gateway for some devices will be present within the device itself, and for some other devices, gateway will be present externally.

In cognitive IoT platforms, all types of platforms and technologies which were discussed previously in this chapter are used. So, the security concerns which are present in each of them are applicable to IoT platform as well. In addition, because of huge number and types of devices and the plethora of technologies which are used by them for communication, it is necessary to adopt a multifaceted and multi-layered approach in order to ensure appropriate security for all components which are part of the IoT platform. The diverse aspects of this multifaceted approach should start right from the booting of the devices and should continue at each phase of the device lifecycle in order to build an IoT ecosystem which cannot be tampered. Some of these security measures are discussed below.

Security Measures for Cognitive IoT Platforms/Devices

In order to ensure security of various devices and platforms which are a part of the IoT network, it is essential to ensure adopt a holistic mechanism which spans across all the phases of a device's lifecycle. Some such mechanisms are discussed below:

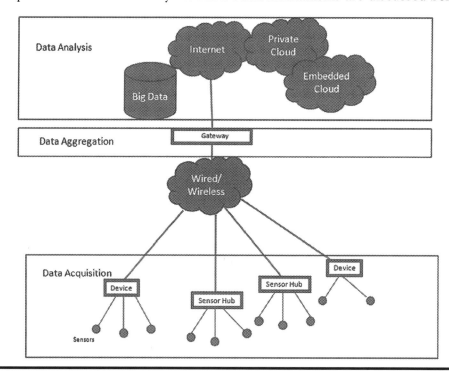

Figure 10.14 Security Concerns

Secure Booting

When a device powers on, there should be an authentication mechanism to verify that the software which runs on the device is a legitimate one. This is done with the help of cryptographically generated digital signatures. This process ensures that only authentic software which have been designed to run on the devices by the concerned parties will run on the devices. This establishes a trusted computing base for the devices upfront. But the devices still need to be protected from various kinds of run time threats.

Mandatory Access Control Mechanisms

Mandatory access control mechanisms should be built into the operating system of the devices in order to ensure that the various applications and components will have access only to those resources which they need for their functioning. This will ensure that if an attacker is able to gain access to any of those components/applications, they will be able to gain access only very limited resources. This significantly reduces the attack surface.

Device Authentication for Networks

A device should get connected to some kind of a wired or wireless network in order to begin transmission of data. As and when a device gets connected to a network, it should authenticate itself before it starts data transmission. For some types of embedded devices (which operate without manual intervention), the authentication can be done with the help of credentials which are maintained in a secured storage area of the device.

Device-specific Firewalls

For each device, there should be some kind of firewall which will filter and examine the data which is specifically send to that device. It is not mandatory for the devices to examine all types of traffic which traverse through the network as that will be taken care of by the network security appliances. This is required also because of the fact that some specific types of embedded devices have custom-made protocols which are different from the common IT protocols which are used by organizations for data transmission. One classic example is the smart grid which has its own set of protocols for communication. Hence it is very essential for the device to have firewalls or some such mechanism in place which is intended to filter the traffic which is intended specifically for that device.

Controlled Mechanism to Ensure Application of Security Patches and Upgrades

Once devices are connected to the networks, they start receiving security patches and upgrades. It so happens that in some situations, these patches and upgrades consume a whole lot of network bandwidth making it unavailable for other devices or applications which are a part of the network. Operators need to ensure that patches, upgrades, and authentication of the devices should be planned in such a way that it should involve minimum bandwidth consumption and it should not impact the functional safety of the device.

In short, for a cognitive IoT network's security, the traditional safety measures which are typically adopted are not sufficient. It is mandatory to inject security measures starting from the operating system of the participating devices.

Security Threats in Different Use Cases of Cognitive IoT

Some of the key cognitive IoT use cases are summarized in the following Figure 10.15:

Next, we identify key security threats which are present in these IT infrastructure components along with some measures to curb them.

Security Threats in Smart Transportation Systems

Smart transportation systems enhance the quality of life by tracking and monitoring the transportation services. Sensors can capture data about the real-time status of transportation services and send the data to a centralized control centre or dashboard which can then use the data to co-ordinate transport services. Tracking and monitoring of transportation services requires a highly sophisticated IoT infrastructure and close co-ordination between the various components in order to avoid disruptions. The different types of security threats which are possible in a smart transportation system are the following:

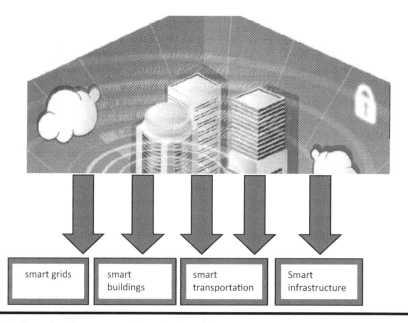

Figure 10.15 Security Threats use Cases in Cognitive IoT

- Hacking the travel navigation systems to misguide vehicle drivers into wrong routes by providing erroneous information about the traffic volume at various routes.
- The data transmitted to or from mobile devices may be subjected to spoofing.
- Unencrypted traffic reports can be attacked by hackers who can inject incorrect or false traffic-related data or reports into satellite-based navigation devices.

ATTACK OF A PUBLIC TRANSPORT SYSTEM IN EUROPE

A teenager in Europe was able to attack the public transport systems with the help of a modified television remote control. He was able to cause severe traffic disruption in the city and he was even able to cause a tram derailment by forcing a vehicle to take an abrupt turn when it was travelling at high speed.

Security Threats in Smart Grids and Other Cognitive IoT–based Infrastructure Components

The different components of smart grids are the following:

- Smart meters: Digital meters which can track user consumption in real time and provide alerts to user end-point devices.
- Networks with two-way communication capabilities.
- Meter data acquisition and management systems: Software which collects data from the smart meters, calculates bill value, and analyses usage metrics.

The security of each of these components can be compromised. Smart meters may be hacked to steal energy or to tamper consumption data. Meter data acquisition and management systems can be hacked by the attackers using some of the vulnerabilities which may be present in the system and this can severely hamper the transmission of data to the end users. White listing techniques which can ensure that only certain applications or processes are active at specific points in time are effective in some situations. However, there are no solutions to zero-day vulnerabilities. Zero-day vulnerabilities are those which no security patches are available.

Networks used by smart grids and other infrastructure components can be hacked by the attackers by installing some malwares which are capable of tracking sensitive network-related information. This sensitive information can be later used by the attackers to create Denial-of-Service attacks. These network-related threats can be eliminated to a great extent by using intrusion prevention techniques combined with some robust security practices to handle aspects like browser patches, end-user awareness creation, and network usage tracking.

One of the best possible ways to prevent tampering of smart meters and meter data acquisition and management system is the use of PKI. PKIs can be directly implemented on smart meters. This will ensure authentication and validation of meters in a connected network. It is also important to ensure that keys and certificates pertaining to a PKI environment are guarded appropriately using an appropriate management solution.

Conclusion

The cognitive IoT infrastructure is a conglomeration of technologies like cloud, big data, mobile devices, and Internet of Things. It is very essential to ensure that each of this component is safe and secure in order to ensure continuous availability of services. The security requirements of the cognitive IoT infrastructure components were examined in detail in the first section of the chapter.

Each component of the cognitive IoT infrastructure is subjected to diverse types of vulnerabilities and threats. The vulnerabilities and threats which exists in each of these platforms were examined in detail. The techniques to safeguard the IT infrastructure components from these threats and vulnerabilities were also discussed in this chapter.

The different smart applications of cognitive IoT are smart grids, smart transport systems, smart water systems, smart buildings, and so on. The security concerns of these applications and the different ways to tackle them were also discussed in this chapter.

References

http://www.imperva.com/docs/SB_DDoS_Protection_Service.pdf

http://www.symantec.com/security_response/publications/threatreport.jsp?inid=us_ghp_thumbnail1_istr-2013

http://www-01.ibm.com/support/knowledgecenter/SSPT3X_2.0.0/com.ibm.swg.im.infosphere.biginsights.product.doc/doc/acc_mda.html

Multitenancy - Security Risks and Countermeasures Wayne J. Brown, Vince Anderson, Qing Tan

Chapter 11

Revolutionizing Manufacturing Using Cognitive IoT Technologies

In this chapter, we broadly categorize these technology trends into two types, and they are

- Industrial Internet of Things (IIoT)
- Industry 4.0

Accordingly, this chapter is divided into two parts: The first part focuses on IIoT and the second part focuses on Industry 4.0. We discuss the generic architecture of IIoT and the various related frameworks in this chapter. Also, we learn some of the key enabling technologies of IIoT and their challenges in this chapter. The key technologies in the context of IIoT that we will discuss in subsequent sections are below

- 3D Manufacturing
- Artificial intelligence and Automation
- Robotics

The second part of the chapter focuses on Industry 4.0, which is a subset of IIoT. The main components of Industry 4.0 are the following:

- Smart buildings
- Smart homes
- Smart grids
- Business web
- Social web

We also elaborated each of the components of Industry 4.0 in detail, along with their architecture and various features.

DOI: 10.1201/9780429328220-11

Introduction

The gamut of technology-driven improvements has been happening in the manufacturing sector. Increasing customer expectation is one of the main motivations for these improvements. These trends have paved the way for large-scale automation, which has, in turn, increased the quantity and quality of outputs generated by the manufacturing units. In a recent survey, it came out that an hour of shop-floor downtime could cost a minimum of USD 300,000. In some cases, it could be as high as five million USD. Many research and reports found that the production disruption is primarily due to process inefficiencies. In most of the scenarios, actions taken to handle production disruption are reactive and not proactive.

Lack of suitable connectivity options and obsolete manual processes are the most important reasons for shop floor downtime. A deeper analysis of shop floors reveals that most of the machines on the shop floor are isolated and disconnected. According to an unpublished research study, 39 per cent of manufacturers state that one of their key challenges in achieving intelligent automation is the misalignment of processes and workflows that could support automated decision making.

These non-suitable connections and shopfloors shutdown situations are where connecting Internet of Things (IoT) devices and using cognitive capabilities (CIoT) to align workflows and processes of intelligent manufacturing plants could prove extremely useful. But these factories/plants don't rely on just one or two technologies to enhance efficiency. Smart factories amalgamate several automation technologies like artificial intelligence (AI), the IoT, edge computing, cloud, and 5G.

The results of automation using all these technologies can fetch a lot of good outcomes. Intelligent manufacturing using CIoT technologies can improve defect detection by as much as 50 per cent and improve yields by 20 per cent.

In this chapter, as depicted in the preceding Figure 11.1, the CIoT technologies which contribute to smart or intelligent factories are grouped into two broad categories, and they are:

- IIoT (Industrial Internet of Things): IIoT refers to the interconnection of manufacturing devices and other devices which are present within the factory. They are distinguished clearly from other consumer devices.
- Industry 4.0: This refers to the importance of having lean, efficient, and effective operations which in turn help in the setup of sustainable and advanced manufacturing practices. Industry 4.0 is a subset of IIoT.

Chapter Organization

The chapter has two parts as indicated in the following Figure 11.2:

Industrial Internet of Things (IIoT)

IIoT is a network of connected industrial components that are highly intelligent and deployed at shopfloors to achieve a high production rate. Another main objective of IIoT is to reduce operational costs using several mechanisms like:

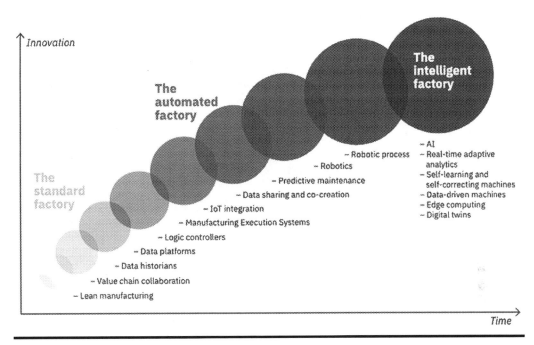

Figure 11.1   Evolution of IoT in Manufacturing Industries
Source: IBM Institute for Business Value.

Figure 11.2   Chapter Organization

- Real-time monitoring
- Efficient management
- Industrial processes, assets, and operational time controls

IIoT is, in fact, a subset of IoT. The main differentiator of IIoT is the increased need for safety, security, and reliable communication. Since most of the industrial operations happen in mission-critical environments. One of the key focus areas of IIoT is efficient management of industrial assets and functions along with predictive maintenance. Industry 4.0 is a subset of IIoT, which focuses on safety and efficiency in manufacturing. IIoT is marching to revolutionize the future of manufacturing in the years to come. IIoT will help to narrow the gap between humans and machines in future. Some of the recent research figures show that there will be 70 billion Internet-connected devices by 2025, and in 2023, the share of IIoT in the global market will be approximately 14.2 trillion US dollars. Some of the main differences of IoT are summarized in the following Table 11.1:

Table 11.1 IIoT vs IoT

Topic	IIoT	IoT
Area of focus	Industrial applications	General applications
Focus of development	Industrial systems	Smart devices
Security and risk measures	Advanced and robust	Utility centric
Scalability	Large-scale network	Low scale network
Precision and accuracy	Synchronized with milliseconds	Critically monitored
Programmability	Remote and on-site programming	Easy off-site monitoring
Output	Operational efficiency	Convenience and utilization
Resilience	High fault tolerance required	Not required
Maintenance	Scheduled and planned	Consumer preferred

In the next section, we will understand more details about the IIoT system.

Generic Architecture of an IIoT System

The generic layered architecture of an IIoT system as depicted in the following Figure 11.3 and the details of major components are discussed in the subsequent sections:

The bottom-most layer (Layer 1) consists of several industrial data sources which generate vast amounts of data. The edge and cloud servers are layers 2 and 3, respectively. Their role is to empower IIoT applications. Layer 4 has enterprise applications. The architecture also shows the flow of data and information which happens amongst the various layer. Some other aspects as well depicted in the IIoT devices and industrial data sources generate continuous data streams at Layer 1 while the edge servers and cloud computing systems empower IIoT applications at Layer 2 and Layer 3, respectively. The enterprise applications are at Layer 4. The diagram also shows the flow of data and information among different layers. Another aspect in the above image is the orchestration flow for various aspects of resource management and operational flow for managing assets present in the industrial networks.

However, the architecture depicted is interpreted differently based on various design variation parameters. And a few of the critical design variation parameters that every cognitive, IIoT application must consider are in the below list:

- Location awareness
- Communication paradigms
- Computational assignments
- Execution paradigms
- Resource management schemes
- Safety, security, and privacy
- Resilience

Several architectural variants exist for the proposed generic IIoT architecture. One of the proposed solution frameworks is called Wireless Evolution for Automation

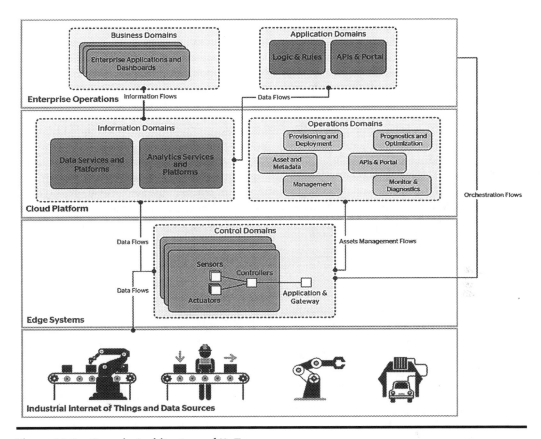

Figure 11.3   Generic Architecture of IIoT

(WEVA). WEVA follows and adheres to open-source software and communication protocols. Some of the components of WEVA architecture are the following:

- Sensor actuator boards
- Motes and operating system
- Protocols
- Access gateway
- Services and applications

Moreover, WEVA uses Easy Wireless Sensor Network as a graphical management tool. Mostly, it is suggested that IPv6 is an essential requirement for the implementation of IIoT as it offers a lot of flexibility. However, there is always a tradeoff that needs implementation to achieve high performance for IIoT.

We discuss and learn a few of the other prominent trends in smart manufacturing/Industry 4.0 in the upcoming section.

3D Manufacturing

3D manufacturing is an area that is evolving rapidly nowadays. One of the main drivers for this trend is the rapid advances in the field of material science. Advances in printing technologies have opened a wide gamut of opportunities in the areas of conformable electronics and physical components, which are applicable even for subsystems and various embedded devices in 3D structures used as part of the manufacturing process. The past 20+ years have seen rapid advancements in the area of 3D additive manufacturing technologies. Some of the critical applications of these technologies are conventional prototyping, rapid tooling, medical implants, aerospace, automotive manufacturing, 3D electronic devices, and micro-systems. The technologies have a very high accuracy rate with features ranging from micron-sized to building size. The process and advancements in 3D printing technology remove the barriers on part geometry. This improvement, in turn, leads to faster production of components with less material and energy. In addition to this, there is a possibility to combine precision modelling and simulation with additive manufacturing to create complex parts that are otherwise impossible to manufacture today.

Some of the essential and enabled features in 3D printing technology are the following:

■ Durable latticework
■ Intricate textures
■ Organic shapes
■ Extensions and optimization of existing parts

The reduction in the weight of printed devices can lead to vast improvements. For example, 3D printing antenna-reflector becomes light, i.e. reduced the weight from 395g to around 80g, which is four times better. 3D printing offers a plethora of benefits. One of the key points to be considered in 3D printing is the security concern.

It is crucial to ensure that the engineers who use the technology have deep knowledge about cybersecurity concepts to protect the outputs of 3D printing from its security threats. It is critical to saving the 3D printing processes from hacks and other model corruptions. There is also a possibility that a malicious component can attack the system and network help in 3D printing needs. These dangerous components can track and capture a lot of information about designs, future component plans, and the design plans which a supplier sends to a customer. Some of the critical security attacks which are possible in 3D printing technologies are the following:

■ Deception
■ Denial of service
■ Disruption
■ Degradation and disruption

Automation and Artificial Intelligence

The increase in the number of sensors and end devices in an IoT used for one of the following purposes:

- Reduce operating cost
- Increase process efficiency

One of the key tactics to achieve both the purposes listed above is to reduce manual processes and increase automated processes. One of the primary goals of IIoT is to be "self-organizing, self-configuring, self-healing, scalable to larger sizes, with low energy consumption, low cost, simple to install and based on global standards". Vendors across the globe are working together to achieve this so that incorporating new sensors and other software components without any proportionate increase in manual effort becomes a reality.

One of the main challenges in implementing IIoT is the lack of hardware and communication interoperability and presents a significant roadblock to the realization of advanced automation in factories. An increase in the automation of feedback collection from sensors and higher fidelity of sensor readings can offer many benefits to a factory setup.

Automatic analysis of the enormous amount of data collected from sensors and other devices can offer massive reductions in waste, energy cost, and manual effort. A few exciting examples of cost optimizations in a factory due to the implementation of IIoT could be the following:

- Machine's function monitoring and turning off the power automatically when the devices are not in use.
- In a factory, auto-switching off HVAC, lights, etc., when humans are not around or working.
- Do charging of electric vehicles at a point in time and during the day when power is most cheaply available.
- Improve the efficiency of automatic braking and collision avoidance systems in automotive

One of the most compelling use cases of the IoT involves rapid sensing of unpredictable conditions in real time and provides instantaneous responses guided by automated systems that mimic human reactions. A few of the valuable parameters for comparison could perhaps consider the rate at which the human eye sensors record (perhaps megabits per second), the transmission of an appropriately reduced amount of visual information to the human brain, and the complex function and processing utility of the human brain in this automated process.

All these aspects of the various capabilities (sensing, data reduction, process, archival storage) of the human process of seeing will need better understanding in the new era of the future IoT.

Advances in robotics, AI, and implementing machine learning algorithms will be vital for the efficient interoperability of a self-organizing IoT system. One of the downsides of this automation is that it reduces security due to a lack of manual intervention. Hence, it becomes necessary to implement software to enhance security. Will it be possible to test all security vulnerabilities which may happen due to IoT-related automation in factories? These are all open points that need to be addressed in the future before all the factories entirely adopt the Industry 4.0 framework.

Robotics

Industrial robots have tremendous potential to alter production processes comparable to the automation introduced by computers in offices. Some of the key benefits of using robots in factories are the following:

- Increase the speed of performing operations
- Increase the accuracy of performing an operation
- Improve the quality of tasks such as carrying heavy loads or weights by robots than by humans

These activities performed by robots have added tremendous value to manufacturing processes. One example could be the petrochemical industry which has used robots extensively to improve the safety and efficiency of performing operations that are otherwise very difficult to be done by humans. Some examples of such tasks are maintenance, inspection, repair, etc. The downside of using robots in some environments is that it could give rise to a breach of trust and accountability.

Another aspect to be considered while using robots is that how they will fit into the organizational structure. An essential factor is that any distributed system will introduce vulnerabilities in the network layer. These vulnerabilities could compromise the server security or the security of any other component present in the communication network.

At the latest, robots can operate autonomously with little to no human intervention. A few of them are remotely operatable as well. However, there are challenges with autonomous robots when it comes to practical usage. First and foremost, it must be highly predictable to operate under complex and dynamic conditions with high confidence levels, instantly interruptable by human operators.

Fixing the level of autonomy in a human-robotic interaction also needs to be considered. For example, robots with too little independence may lead to a situation in which human operators need to attend to robots instead of doing their work. It will also demand a new skill set for future human operators to maintain robots in their work environments if they are skilled enough to fix or maintain robots in their manufacturing environments. The primary purpose of the autonomous capabilities of a robot should be to extend and complement human capabilities. They should not replace the human workforce but a complement to their work efficiency and improve the human kinds. Some experts advise that even if robots are in a manufacturing environment, the control of those robots should be with humans. Humans should be allowed to monitor and modify the behaviour of the robot as per the situation.

Mobile robots can operate a crewless aerial vehicle, work in disaster response, inspect infrastructure, decommission nuclear plants, etc. A key technology that makes this implementation possible for the robots is teleoperation: a more significant reason to enable humans to control robots remotely. In manufacturing industries, primarily transporting parts within factories uses autonomously guided vehicles. Autonomously driven vehicles in many other robotics applications for logistics are in the current strategic focus of the logistics landscape. Robots can unload and move parts from trucks to the plant supply rooms while simultaneously maintaining inventory accountability and control. This role of robot systems is likely to increase in years to come.

Nanobots

Nanobots are a type of microscopic robot. A nanorobot is any artificial machine with overall size on the order of a few micrometres or less in all spatial directions and constituted by nanoscopic components with individual dimensions in the interval between 1 and 100 nm. A nanobot device has shown to have the capability to move quite freely through the entire human body circulatory system. One can envision a future where these nanobot technologies could be used in a manufacturing process, for example, to provide a microscopic view into the process conditions critical to certain bio-pharmaceutical or nuclear facilities. The idea of surveying the state of fluid suspension with swarms of nanobots could be demonstrated in the bloodstream. A nanobot in a capillary has demonstrated the ability to feel the metabolic pattern of the family of cells fed by the capillary itself, thus surveying the cells contained within a given length of the tube. Each nanobot is a self-propelled machine, obtaining energy from the environment, and can recognize and dock to the components within their process. They can sense membranes and subsequently recognize the state of health of its environment. They also may be used to store the information, to transfer it to the central unit, and eventually take actions which may influence the overall process conditions. Within a swarm of nanobots, each bot stores specific chemicals to be released for detection by other nanobots. This could also be used in a manufacturing setting to transfer information from one location in the process to the other. Ensuring that nanobots and nanobot swarms are operating securely is a complicated matter. Nanobots are extremely small and are therefore very difficult to monitor for individual malicious behaviours, especially if a large swarm of nanobots is deployed. If individual nanobots are programmed with software, how might one scan the nanobot operating code for infections? If nanobot swarms are programmed with chemical means, would there be a means to ensure that the function and control of the swarm not be overtaken by a malicious actor, in the same manner that viri and bacteria affect human biological receptors? How will the health monitoring and maintenance of the nanobot swarm be performed? When nanobots reach the end of life, how are they disposed? As with other aspects of innovative IoT devices, nanobot systems offer incredible utility but have not been yet designed or analysed for safety and security.

Industry 4.0

Industry 4.0 is an umbrella term which is used to refer to the plethora of technologies which describe the strategic approach adopted towards digitalization in the manufacturing sector. Industry 4.0 was a term coined in Germany which is the manufacturing hub of the world. Various transformation journeys which are happening in the manufacturing sector are depicted in the following Figure 11.4:

Though there are a plethora of technologies, the two key technologies which are linked to Industry 4.0 are Internet of Things (IoT) and Cyber Physical Systems (CPS). IoT refers to the larger ecosystem of physical devices and objects which can communicate with each other using inbuilt communication devices, internet connectivity, and other types of hardware components which enable communication.

CPS refer to the group of systems which represent an integration of networking, computation, and physical processes. In a CPS, physical processes are driven by embedded computer systems along with networks which enable communication. These embedded computer systems monitor and control the physical processes. The physical processes have feedback loops which in turn affect the computer systems and vice versa. In short, CPS link information technology to the mechanical and electronic components present in the manufacturing unit and communicate with them via network.

In short, the combination of IoT and CPS together with the communication networks plays a major role in converting the factories into automated smart factories. In the next section, we will examine the IoT-enabled smart ecosystem which is present in smart factories.

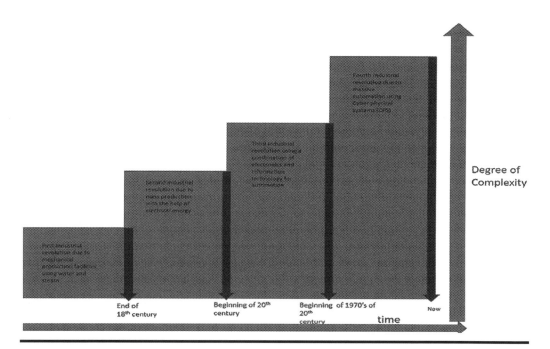

Figure 11.4 Transformation Journey of Manufacturing Sectors

Ecosystem of Smart Factories

The various components of smart factories are summarized in the following Figure 11.5:

The main components which we will cover in this chapter are the following:

- Smart buildings/homes
- Smart grids
- Smart homes
- Social web
- Business web using mobile devices

Smart Buildings/Homes

Smart buildings are those where information technology is used to integrate all aspects of the building, like lighting, water, ventilation, temperature, and security. Usage of smart buildings as smart factories helps in enhancing the quality of life of the factory workers and provides lot of cost savings by ensuring efficient utilization of the various resources. This is more justified by some facts and figures which are given below:

- Worldwide, buildings consume 42 per cent of all electricity – more than any other asset
- Commercial buildings lose as much as 50 per cent of the water that flows into them

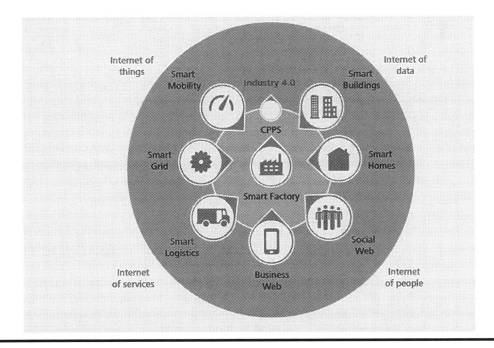

Figure 11.5   Components of Smart Factories

If we are making buildings smart by adding various IoT-enabled components like sensors and actuators, we will be able to reduce the wastage of resources significantly.

LOGISTICS – SMART CONTAINER SOLUTION

Smart container and logistics solution enables container location tracking and monitoring key parameters (e.g. temperature, humidity, etc.). It also provides ability to analyse and predict exceptions.

Components of Smart Buildings/Homes

Buildings are complex entities with multiple interconnected systems such as control and maintenance systems, heating, lighting and cooling systems, and security systems. These systems need to communicate and coordinate with one another for the buildings to work efficiently. In most of the traditional buildings, these systems exist in silos, leading to lot of energy wastage. It is possible to convert these buildings into smart and energy-efficient buildings by infusing sensors, actuators, and CCTVs that sense and respond intelligently to the needs of the building occupants. Smart buildings have been found to help save up to 30 per cent of water usage, 40 per cent of energy usage, and thereby help reduce building maintenance costs by 10 to 30 per cent. The Smart Building Management Systems market is around $621 million and is expected to reach $1,891 million by 2016. Now, let us look at the various systems present in smart buildings:

Security and surveillance systems: Security sensors for windows, doors, motion, and smoke detection can provide critical security information about buildings. IP-enabled security and surveillance cameras are very important for ensuring tight, unbreakable, and impenetrable security for buildings. The camera feeds can be analysed to take proactive and reactive security measures. Video analytic technologies, which have the capability to generate real-time alerts when specific objects of interest are identified in camera feeds, are now available in the market. These video analytic technologies will go a long way in providing proactive security capabilities to buildings, which are equipped with CCTVs. Another important aspect of security for smart buildings is access control mechanisms that can be customized according to the type of area in the building. For example, occupants can be given smart cards to access specific floors in the building as per their identity.

Heating, Ventilation and Cooling (HVAC) systems: It is a very critical component of any building as it makes it healthy and comfortable for its occupants. For a smart building, HVAC systems should be able to automatically detect and respond intelligently to several aspects such as weather conditions, time of the day, occupancy of the building, and so on, with the help of sensors and other data gathering equipment. For example, HVAC systems in smart buildings should be able to automatically switch off lights in the room of the building where there are no occupants or adjust temperature of a room automatically as per the prevalent weather conditions and the number of occupants in the room.

Water management systems: These systems use smart meters to automatically regulate or stop water supply to various parts of the building based on occupancy data obtained from other building systems.

Parking management systems: These systems automatically detect empty parking slots in various parking areas and guide vehicles appropriately to optimize time for occupants.

- **Computing and Communications Devices** – A wider variety of compute machines ranging from personal computers (PCs), notebooks/laptops/tablets, Wi-Fi routers & gateways, wearables, and smartphones are being extensively used in home environments these days. With the seamless convergence, computer and communicator are often interchanged.
- **Entertainment, Edutainment, and Infotainment Media Systems** – There are several notable innovations in media technologies and products. Today we boast about fixed, portable, mobile, and handheld devices for ubiquitous learning. IP-enabled television sets are being produced in mass quantities sharply increasing our choice, convenience, and comfort considerably. Web, information, and consumer appliances are plentiful and pioneering. Technologies for social sites (Web 2.0) are on the climb facilitating higher productivity for humans and for forming digital communities for real-time knowledge sharing. Home theaters, hi-fi music systems, DVD devices, game consoles, etc., are for entertainment.
- **Home Networking** – All passive, numb and dumb items are getting transformed into digitalized objects. These are being wirelessly and wisely networked with all sorts of household electronics in order to connect and communicate (directly (peer-to-peer) or indirectly (through a middleware)) to derive competent people-centric, networked, and embedded e-services. Home networking infrastructures, connectivity solutions, bridging elements, and other brokering solutions are being found more in numbers these days. Home network also can connect with the outside world via the pervasive Internet. This enables remote monitoring, management, and maintenance of home devices. Car multimedia, navigation and infotainment systems, and parking management systems, etc., too gets connected to household systems directly or via a box-based middleware for real-time connectivity and interaction.
- **Home Access Control** – E-locks are emerging as a crucial security measure for home access control.
- **Kitchen Appliances, Wares & Utensils** – Modular kitchen comprising all kinds of electronics emerges as a key factor for smarter homes. Coffee makers, bread toasters, electronic ovens, refrigerators, dish washers, food processors, etc., are being enhanced to be smarter in home environments.
- **Relaxing and Mood-creating Objects** – Household items such as electric lamps, cots, chairs, beds, wardrobes, window panes, couches, treadmills, tables, and sofas besides the objects in specific places such as gyms, spas, bath rooms, car garages, parking slots, etc., are being linked together in ad hoc manner in order to greatly enhance the experience of users.
- **Healthcare Systems** – Medicine cabinets, pills and tablets containers, humanoid robots, etc., are occupying prime slots in guaranteeing good health for home occupants.

There are statistical estimates and forecasts that there will be hundreds of micro-controllers in any advanced home/office environments in the days to emerge. The much-touted edge technologies such as cards, chips, labels, tags, pads, stickers, smart dust and motes, specks, etc., are enabling the onset of powerful environments. That is, our everyday places are going to be stuffed and saturated with a growing array of event producing and consuming entities, environmental monitoring and measurement solutions, controlling, actuation and notification systems, integration fabrics, hubs and buses, and visualization displays and dashboards, networking and automation elements, scores of handhelds, wearables, portables, implantables, etc., to make our lives and locations lovable and liveable.

These are only some basic elements of smart buildings. Nowadays, many of the features required by buildings are provided by an integrated software called building management system (BMS), instead of disparate systems that communicate with one another using diverse protocols. However, the technology which forms the foundation of present-day smart buildings is IoT. IoT is a technology that is used to interconnect embedded objects/devices such as sensors, mobile devices, and so on, and facilitate communication among them without the need for any human intervention.

The increased proliferation of smart phones, rapid advances in IoT technology, and emergence of 6LoWPAN (a standard for low power wireless networks) will enable networks of sensors and actuators natively to use Internet Protocol V6 and allow smart buildings to rapidly go to the next level of automation. In the next level of smart buildings, the following could be some of the interesting features:

- Automatic functioning of various components in the kitchen such as coffee maker, toaster, and microwave oven based on the time of the day and food patterns of the occupants. Food patterns can be uncovered by tracking and analysing the data generated by the kitchen equipment.
- Automatic watering of plants in the garden based on the water content present in the soil and the surrounding weather conditions.
- Automatic mood-based adjustment of lighting in the rooms that will detect the mood of the occupants and adjust the intensity of light accordingly. This is done with the help of communication between the wearable used by the occupant and the sensors present in the building.
- Automatic adjustment and volume control of various electronic gadgets in the room based on various situations of the occupant. For example, if the occupant receives a call on the mobile phone, the television volume will get automatically reduced until the mobile conversation is over.

Smart buildings have already seen some level of traction in a few Indian cities. To ensure the success of the smart building concept in India, it is important to ensure that the government supports smart building initiatives by providing tax subsidy. It will, in turn, reduce the total cost of ownership of smart buildings, making it a lucrative option for the common man. The government should also provide special funding schemes to attract a lot of public-private partnerships for smart building projects.

The role played by buildings in the everyday lives of people is getting redefined. They are no longer mere physical structures but are slowly starting to define the quality of life of the citizens and the entire city. Given the anticipated rise in urbanization in the coming decades, cities are expected to transform to a place where many different people and companies collectively work to make our lives better and more sustainable. The shift to smart buildings has only just begun and will now accelerate very quickly if we make the citizens aware of the benefits of smart buildings and also make it a cost-effective option for them.

Smart Grids

Smart grid is an advanced electricity transmission and distribution network (grid) that uses robust two-way communications, smart sensors, and centralized software applications to improve the efficiency, reliability, and safety of power delivery. Smart grids comprise a range of emerging and evolving technologies that can be applied along the end-to-end electricity supply chain from power generation plants through transmission, distribution to end-users (homes, apartments, hospitals, hotels, commercial buildings, factories, etc.). The key feature of a smart grid is its capability to distribute power to various sites/buildings as per their requirements at a specific time. It also provides features to integrate other energy sources such as solar panels, wind mills, etc., to the grid to cater to the ever-increasing demands of consumers.

According to a GTM Research report published in 2013, the value of the smart grid market is expected to surpass $400 billion by 2020. Also, the market is growing across the world at a rapid pace with an average compound annual growth rate of over eight per cent. Moreover, smart grids will be mandatory for establishing and sustaining smart factories. This is mainly due to the flexibility offered by them to distribute power as per the varying needs of various sites/plants which are present in a factory or also present across factories. The high-level diagram of a smart grid is as depicted in the following Figure 11.6:

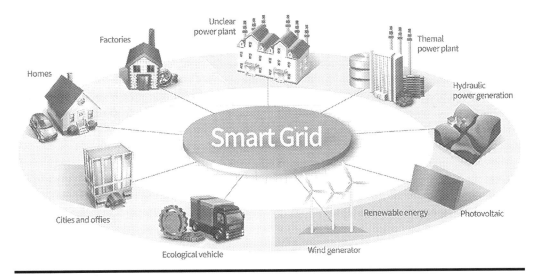

Figure 11.6   Smart Grid

The key infrastructure components needed for building smart grids in smart factories are the following:

■ Smart meter: These are digital meters capable of capturing consumption-related information and transmitting it using different kinds of networks to the utility and billing device which keeps track of usage and pricing. Smart meters are also equipped to receive data from utility and billing devices and transmit that in real time to consumers so that they know their consumption and bill amount.
■ Network: The networks which are used for smart grids should be equipped with sophisticated two-way communication capabilities.
■ Meter Data Acquisition and Management Systems: These are software applications which can acquire data from smart meters, store, and analyse them. These analyses will help factories get a fair idea about the power consumption patterns.

The smart grid in the context of smart manufacturing has several advantages over the traditional grid system, the high-level benefits are the following:

■ High efficiency
■ Reliability
■ Economics

High Efficiency

High levels of efficiency are very essential for factories and this is enabled by smart grids because of their capability to monitor and adjust distribution of power. This will enable factories to reduce excessive consumption of power. Another aspect which will increase the efficiency is the capability of smart meter component of smart grids to track and record the energy consumption precisely. The data collected by smart meters can be used to optimize the scheduling process which greatly enables factories to be energy efficient.

Reliability

The capability of smart grids to implement estimation and automation in the power transmission system offers the capability to isolate and identify possible faults in an electric network. As the networks in a smart grid system have self-healing capability, it helps to increase the reliability of power supply. The self-healing capability also resists the damages which are caused by natural disasters such as earthquake. Smart grids also reduce situations like power blackouts. All these capabilities of smart grids will go a long way in making the factory infrastructure and ecosystem more reliable.

Economics

The capability of smart meters to track energy usage helps the factories to monitor and arrange energy-intensive tack in the low energy usage time. This helps factories to save both energy and cost. The real time tracking and reporting capability of smart meters also helps energy generators in factories to arrange power plants more adaptively, which in turn will help in the reduction of costly power plants.

Social Web/Social Internet of Things (SIoT)

IoT plays a major role in Industry 4.0 which is expected to revolutionize the manufacturing operations. Social media networks like Facebook and Twitter generate huge amounts of valuable data. The integration of the data generated by social media networks and the data generated by the entities which are a part of IoT concept/network provides valuable use cases in areas like traffic route management, manufacturing, etc. The integration of social media and IoT gives rise to an important concept called as Social Internet of Things (SIoT). In this section, we will explore some of the interesting use cases of SIoT in the manufacturing sector with a prime focus on industrial revolution which is triggered by Industry 4.0.

One of the important aspects about the manufacturing process is asset maintenance and management. Proactive maintenance and management of assets is a very critical aspect of the manufacturing process. This is very important as it plays a very important role in reducing the cost of ownership of assets by ensuring the following aspects:

- Increased machine availability
- Improved security
- Increased productivity

The conventional asset management techniques used in manufacturing sector have the following drawbacks:

- Focus of the asset management techniques are on individual assets and not the interconnected group of assets which would be present in the manufacturing plant. Nowadays, most of the manufacturers outsource the maintenance of their assets to their original equipment manufacturers (OEMs). Since the OEMs will have a view/visibility only of the assets supplied by them, they will never be in a position to do maintenance which will deliver system-level optimization to the manufacturers. System-level optimization will offer lot of value and cost savings to the manufacturer than individual asset maintenance and management.
- Maintenance plans are devised mostly considering the decision making associated with maintenance. There is no correlation between the operation of the assets and the maintenance strategies. If there is appropriate synchronization between the operational data received from the assets to their maintenance plan, the maintenance strategy would offer much higher returns.

SIoT enables assets to share their data via social media platforms and this enables cooperation among assets and helps in maintenance strategies considering the entire system rather than stand-alone components. The assets which are part of such an ecosystem are referred to as social assets. In the next section, we will examine more about the SIoT.

Social Internet of Things (SIoT)

Assets and equipment which are used nowadays in manufacturing plants are smart assets. Smart assets are equipped with sensors which continuously track and monitor their operations thereby generating huge amounts of data. This data can be collected and analysed further to derive useful insights about the assets. SIoT with reference to industrial plants is called Social Internet of Industrial Things (SIoIT).

The main feature of SIoIT is that the network consists of social assets which share their data and status via a social network to achieve very high levels of system performance. This data sharing also helps to achieve system optimization. In SIoIT, assets or machines can provide updates of their status to the social network. This helps the machines or assets to share their condition and related details to other assets which have subscribed to that network.

In SIoIT, there are lot of possibilities to use machine learning and other optimization techniques to analyse the collected data and plan performance optimization and management. SIoIT enables performance optimization and management at three different levels, they are the following:

- Machine level
- Production plant level
- Network level

Machine-level performance optimization: The data collected from SIoIT helps manufacturers to analyse the reliability parameters of machines. This in turn will help them to find out the root cause for performance difference and degradation.

Production plant–level performance optimization: Analysis of data collected from the machines by social network will help manufacturer to identify system-level bottlenecks. This in turn will help to devise measures which will enhance the productivity of the overall system.

Network-level performance optimization: The data which are generated by the machines which are part of an SIoIT network helps all the parties involved: OEMs, manufacturers, and other service providers to derive useful and meaningful insights regarding the machines, their reliability, performance bottlenecks at the system and at the network level. This will go a long way in the design and implementation of fault tolerant systems with very high levels of performance.

Characteristics of Social Assets

The characteristics of social assets are depicted in the following Figure 11.7:

Identity: For any asset to be referred in a network, a unique identifier is required.
State Awareness: Smart assets should have the capability to sense their status and measure some parameters like temperature, pressure, vibration, etc., and use them for future references. Hence state awareness is a necessary characteristic of all smart assets.

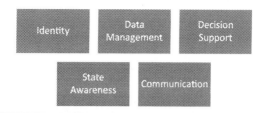

Figure 11.7   Basic Characteristics of Social Assets

Communication: The assets should possess the capability to exchange information with other assets which are part of the network and with other entities like OEMs and human operators.

Data Management: It is necessary to classify and store measurements possibly made by sensor transducers associated with the assets, while removing some history data, if appropriate.

Decision Support: Smart assets should have a decision support mechanism to generate apt actions in response to different situations that have arisen. Moreover, they should be able to exhibit opportunistic, goal-directed behaviour and act proactively.

Business Web Using Mobile Devices

Mobile networks already offer connectivity to a wide range of sensors and other smart devices which has opened new realms of service and connectivity options both for the service providers and for the end users. One type of service which is very important in the context of Industry 4.0 is M2M (Machine 2 Machine) service. M2M is a term used to describe solutions that focus on remote collection and transfer of data from embedded sensors or chips placed on remote assets which are fixed or mobile. This use case is very prominent in smart factories where mobile devices are used extensively to interact and control various machines, and hence, they are excellent candidates to perform communication with remote devices using M2M technology.

Architecture for Mobile-enabled Industry 4.0 Communication

An architecture for IoT services using mobile devices is depicted in the following Figure 11.8:

Figure 11.8   Generic Communication Architecture for Mobile Enabled Industry

Figure 11.9   Data collection Stages

The main components of the preceding Figure 11.9 are explained as follows:

1. Data is collected from a wide range of sources including machines and other equipment using mobile phones. This data includes both the data which is collected from remote sensors and other electronic devices, and the data which is generated by various infrastructure components like factories and buildings, water networks, transportation systems, and other smart sensor–enabled components.
2. This data is transferred using the various wired and wireless networking options. They are then collected and stored in a database or a data warehouse. Analytics is applied to this data in order to derive meaningful insights which define the future course of action.
3. This data is used as input for service delivery platform ("SDP") which runs several IoT application services. These services span across all domains like transportation, healthcare, water networks, healthcare, and so on. These SDPs will provide open APIs which will help the developers to design new value-added services.

Some of the interesting use cases of mobiles in the context of Industry 4.0 in factories are the following:

■ Intelligent Energy Conservation: This helps the officials in factories to track and manage energy consumption in real time. It also helps officials to track aspects like energy theft and energy leakage.
■ Wireless Fleet Management: Mobile-based intelligent fleet management system which enables tracking and monitoring of fleet using embedded telematics. This is helpful to track and monitor the vehicles which are used to deliver materials to factories.
■ Analytics and Commercial Insights: Mobile business intelligence platforms that offer real-time insights for factory officials.

Wireless Technologies for Mobile-enabled Industry 4.0

In this section, we examine some core wireless technologies which support mobile device usage and their implementation in Industry 4.0. Some of the core technologies which support implementation are 5G and UWB.

5G Technology

The key features of 5G which makes it a preferred choice for mobile devices in Industry 4.0 implementation are the following:

- Support for massive number of devices (10-100 times more device support than the existing networks).
- Support for high data rate (increase the existing data rate 10-100 times).
- Reduce the latency between end-to-end devices. Ideally the latency should be less than 5ms.
- Provide consistent Quality of Experience (QoE).
- Reduce capital and operations cost.

Ultra-Wide Band (UWB) Technology

Ultra-Wide Band (UWB) is a technology which is used for communication amongst low range and low power sensors and mobile devices which require very low power and high bandwidth. UWB has a lot of features which make it suitable for IoT communication, they are:

- Possibility of high accuracy transmission even indoors.
- Resistance to multipath fading.
- Good scalability in dense deployment.
- Low power consumption.
- High bandwidth transmission.

UWB acts as a complementing technology to other existing wireless radio technologies like Wi-Fi and WiMAX. UWB provides very cost-effective, power-efficient, and high bandwidth solution for data communication amongst devices which are within 10 metres or 30 feet.

How UWB Works

UWB works differently from conventional narrowband radio frequency (RF) and spread spectrum technologies (SS), such as Bluetooth* Technology and 802.11a/b/g. The UWB transmitter works by sending billions of pulses simultaneously across a wide range of frequencies which are several GHz in bandwidth. The UWB receiver which receives these pulses then translates these pulses into data by listening to a familiar sequence of pulses sent by the UWB transmitter. UWB's combination of larger spectrum, lower power, and pulsed data improves speed and reduces interference with other wireless spectrum. The high-level architecture of UWB is depicted in the following Figure 11.10:

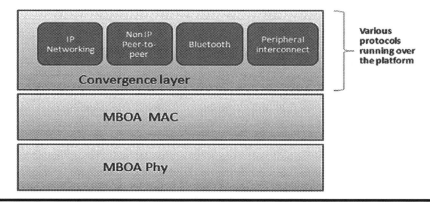

Figure 11.10   General Architecture of Ultra Wide Band (UWB)

The key technology which is used in UWB is Multiband Orthogonal Frequency Division Multiplexing (MBOA). The benefits of MBOA are the following:

■ Flexibility to configure spectrum using software-configurable emissions.
■ Capability to adopt easily to different worldwide regulatory bodies.
■ Future scalability and backward compatibility.
■ Use of standard CMOS technology which helps to speed up development and also provides advanced performance.
■ Very robust in multi-path environments.

ISO 18000 7 DASH7

This standard was developed by DASH7 Alliance. This is a low power, low complexity radio protocol for all sub 1 GHz radio devices. It is a non-proprietary technology for an open standard and the solutions which use this protocol may contain a pool of technologies which operate in their own ways. Common for these technologies are that they use a Sub 1GHz Silicon radio as their primary communicating device. The main application use cases of DASH7 are the following:

■ Supply chain management, inventory/yard management, warehouse optimization, smart meters, commercial green building development.

Summary

The chapter was split into two parts focusing on the two important aspects of technology automation which is happening in the manufacturing sector. The focus areas were:

■ IIoT
■ Industry 4.0

The architecture of IIoT and the key components of IIoT were discussed in the first part of the chapter. Second part of the chapter focused on Industry 4.0. The key components of Industry 4.0 are the following:

■ Smart buildings
■ Smart homes
■ Smart grids
■ Business web
■ Social web

Each of the components and their architecture was discussed in the second part of the chapter.

References

https://www.ibm.com/thought-leadership/institute-business-value/report/smart-manufacturing

Industrial Internet of Things: Recent Advances, Enabling Technologies, and Open Challenges November 2019 Computers & Electrical Engineering 81(2)

The Future Internet of Things and Security of its Control Systems Misty Blowers, USAF Research Laboratory Jose Iribarne, Westrock Edward Colbert, ICF International, Inc. Alexander Kott, US Army Research Laboratory

http://ecee.colorado.edu/~ecen4242/marko/UWB/UWB/wireless_pb.pdf

Chapter 12

Edge AI: The Consumer, Social, and Industry Use Cases

Introduction

Due to the surging popularity of digitization and edge technologies, there will be trillions of digitized entities (alternatively referred to as sentient materials, smart objects, IoT sensors and actuators, etc.). Digitized entities/IoT sensors are typically not empowered with much processing, memory, and storage power to do real-world data processing. Increasingly electronics devices are being instrumented to enable seamless and spontaneous connectivity with one another and with remotely held applications, services, and databases. Thus, instrumentation and interconnectivity are the prime characteristics of today's devices, machinery, equipment, home appliances, medical instruments, robots, drones, consumer electronics, kitchen utilities, etc. Many studies reveal that there will be billions of such IoT devices on the planet earth soon. In contrast to digitized entities, IoT devices do have some processing, memory, and storage power, and hence they can do data processing individually and collectively.

When IoT devices and sensors interact, there will be many multi-structured data getting generated and garnered. The challenge here is to subject all kinds of IoT data to various investigations to produce actionable insights that can be looped back to IoT devices and sensors to decide the next course of actions in time with all the clarity, enthusiasm, and care. Thus, data analytics capability results in intelligent machines. That is, instrumented devices, interconnected and getting cleverer in their operations, offerings, and outputs. One direct challenge is that the massive amount of data IoT devices getting generated could easily cripple IT infrastructure. Thereby digital infrastructure is being recommended for the digital era. Software-defined cloud infrastructure has taken a pivot role as the next-generation IT infrastructure to handle big data. Cloud infrastructure is the highly optimized and organized IT infrastructure to host and run digital platforms and applications with ease and elegance.

DOI: 10.1201/9780429328220-12

As connected technologies such as road sensors and navigation systems communicate with each other, they generate data that has to be quickly captured and processed to emit actionable insights. Usually, the data needs to pass through a mediator such as IoT gateway/hub/connector/broker/adaptor/bus before reaching its destination. Cloud storage is the mainstream storage place these days. For real-time computing, the concept of edge or fog computing getting its share faster as the cloud-hosted database data transit depends on its hosted regions/locations that are remote more the distance more the latency. Data analytics capability in edge devices closes the latency gap, and the data analysis happens at the edge devices itself. So, real-time data analytics can lead to more meaningful and real-time insights fed back to edge devices to exhibit a self-adaptive behaviour.

Together, the digitized entities and IoT devices can bring in scores of delectable automation, acceleration, and augmentation. Productivity across industry verticals is bound to go up fast. The convenience, choice, comfort, and care for people are to see a paradigm shift. Ambient intelligence (AmI), pervasive computing, adaptive communication, ubiquitous sensing, natural interfaces, machine vision, and perception will see a grand reality soon. Knowledge discovery and dissemination, factory automation, process excellence, context-awareness, people IT, intelligent systems and environments, cognitive applications, intelligent services, virtual, augmented, and mixed reality (VR/AR/MR) solutions realization happens in an accelerated manner.

With the surging popularity of artificial intelligence (AI) capabilities (machine and deep learning algorithms, computer vision and natural language processing (NLP)), edge devices inbuilt with AI toolkits emit out predictive insights in time. Thus, there is a rush and reward for AI-enabled edge devices. That is, edge devices are gaining real-time intelligence through AI capabilities.

Pushing Intelligence into Edge Devices

Arriving in an accurate data model from complete data sets or their subset is essential for machine and deep learning (ML/DL) algorithms. Their use cases ability to access data stored in data warehouses or data lakes is paramount. Cloud infrastructures and platforms contribute to enabling the AI/ML infrastructure to efficient data access and process-intensive data activities. The above approach works well when the data doesn't change frequently. But the reality is it does change frequently. Therefore, real-time data capture, processing, and analytics gained momentum. Real-time analytics is also essential in many industries, such as but not limited to healthcare, financial services, manufacturing, and advertising. In general, the real-time data analytics and insights are even more critical where even a tiny change has significant impacts like health sectors, transportation, financial sectors, safety and security systems, etc.

Edge computing is emerging as a powerful and futuristic paradigm that brings the much-insisted decentralized computing capability. The distance between edge devices and edge data processing centres has to be very minimal so that real-time action can be initiated and fulfilled in a hassle-free manner. In other words, the networking architecture for edge computing has to be built in such a way to close down the distance between edge devices and edge cloud environments, wherein device data gets collected and processed. For real-time data capture, storage, and analytics, we need edge device clusters/clouds setup comprising many heterogeneous networked edge devices. Edge clouds are near to edge devices, which are owned and operated by users. Edge clouds accomplish real-time computing, analytics, decision making, and action.

Edge data from digitized entities gets captured and transmitted to edge devices and their clouds to be processed immediately. That is, intelligent edge devices will become the new normal. Incorporating AI into edge devices is getting simplified and speeded up with the general availability of AI-specific chipsets. Lately, edge devices are equipped with higher computational capability along with higher storage capacity and larger memory capacity. There are lightweight versions of AI toolkits to easily fit in edge devices, allowing edge devices to be cognitive in their actions and reactions.

Intelligent edge devices can collect, communicate, store, process, mine, and analyse edge data in real time. For example, cameras, actuators, single-board computers (SBCs), drones, humanoid robots, self-driving cars, GPS receivers, navigation systems, point-of-sale (PoS) devices, etc., are becoming smart edge devices. To be categorized as smart edge, the devices need certain specific components, and the below list provides those with a brief overview:

- **Connectivity** – Devices ought to be interconnected to the other devices in the vicinity and with cloud-hosted applications, services, and databases through any network, including the Internet, the world's most giant information superhighway, open, public, and affordable communication infrastructure.
- **Computing** – As discussed in many sections, the edge devices are equipped with computational power. It all started with the generic CPU, and today they are with powerful processors such as GPUs, TPUs, VPUs, etc. As recent, AI-specific chipsets are emerging and evolving, which makes edge computing at a greater level soon. With the arrival of versatile databases, data analytics platforms, and AI toolkits with non-volatile memory for edge devices, edge devices' data storage and processing capabilities will soon increase exponentially.
- **Observability and Controllability** – Edge devices ought to be remotely monitored, measured, and managed. Edge devices and their capabilities are made accessible (interface) through API-driven microservices that are visible to facilitate inter-device interactions. Containerization, the latest cloud paradigm of bundling all in one technique, including OS, software, and configurations that the application needs to run, comes in handy in helping heterogeneous device operation as good as homogenous devices. As the edge devices are programmable, the devices' control vicinity becomes a more straightforward choice on the controllability of the device; otherwise, it is not feasible or scalable in managing multiple devices in an ecosystem.
- **Cluster Formation** – Devices must form ad hoc and purpose-specific device clusters/clouds to accomplish more extensive assignments. With more digitized entities joining mainstream computing, the amount of digital data generated and collected increases significantly. So, we need multiple and heterogeneous edge devices to sync up with one another; the cluster comes to the rescue and helps gather and crunch all the data from the heterogeneous devices to bring forth valuable insights.

AI is systematically embedded into almost everyday thing to be AI-enabled. Therefore, our wearables, handhelds, implantable, and fixed, portable, nomadic, mobile, and wireless devices gain distinct capabilities such as image recognition, NLP for speech recognition and synthesis, pattern and anomaly detection, etc. In short, edge devices are getting connected and enhanced with AI capabilities to contribute to devising multi-device, process-aware voluntarily, and people-centric services, highly configurable, customizable, and composable.

The Recent Developments in Edge AI Space

Edge AI space comprises hardware, network protocols, and software. Many companies focus on IoT edge hardware. BrainChip Akida Neuromorphic System-on-Chip, CEVA, Google Edge TPU, GreenWave, Huawei Ascend Chips, Nvidia Jetson, Qualcomm Vision Intelligence Platforms are to name a few.

Some other companies focus on IoT edge software. Ekkono, FogHorn, and Swim, a cloud-based PoS system, Renesas (e-AI) are the leading ones. Some companies develop software with both capabilities, such as Amazon's AWS Greengrass ML Inference model, BrainChip (Studio Software), Google (Cloud IoT Edge), Huawei (Atlas platform), and IBM (Watson IoT Platform). Large technology companies are building ecosystems to empower developers to create industry and scenario-specific solutions.

A few other IoT players such as Softeq, ScienceSoft, Oxagile, Style Lab, PTC (Boston based) are already in the IoT game. Few other popular companies like Cisco, GE Digital, Bosch, Siemens are also venturing into the IoT space is an encouraging sign for the IoT arena.

TensorFlow, Caffe, and PyTorch are the most popular, open-source AI development frameworks. Support for CPU and GPU designs as native integration into the backend of these frameworks; however, many new AI processors are not yet integrated. What does that mean? The software stack for many AI processors needs to depend on these frameworks' output as the input of their custom compiler and uses it to create the binary executable file. In some cases, data scientists have to switch from the development framework to the custom compiler and back to the framework until they achieve desired performance results.

With new types of ML algorithms and AI-specific chipsets such as GPUs, TPUs, and VPUs, the field of edge AI started to flourish. Another noteworthy phenomenon is the open ISA (Instruction Set Architecture), RISC-V, which provides another option beyond traditional general-purpose architectures, such as x86 or Arm. With RISC-V, it is possible to customize the instruction set for specialized or extreme application demands, such as AI/ML. In the widely quoted surveillance example, it is possible to reduce the amount of data (video frames) transfer needed to the cloud by correctly designing the application and specialized processor. AI gives the necessary intelligence to choose the relevant decision-enabling video frames and help in the reduction of transmission size of data to the cloud.

The new variety of AI-focused semiconductor components and the latest AI/ML algorithms, along with the speedy and low-cost local storage offered by flash memory, facilitate powerful computing to be accomplished in edge devices.

Benefits of Intelligent Edge Devices

In this section, let us discuss a few key benefits of the edge devices that are smart. When we have an in-memory database inside an edge device, edge devices need not do the long-distance transfer of data with remote cloud storage servers. Businesses can extract actionable insights immediately from the local databases for perfect real-time analytics, proximate processing, ultra-low latency, and bandwidth efficiency. Unified protection is another critical benefit. Cyberattacks are exponentially growing in the connected era. So, suitable or coordinated security management systems can provide integrated threat detection and protection for edge devices and edge clouds.

Digital data generated by digitized entities and edge devices are being aggregated and subjected to various investigations to emit usable intelligence to arrive at intelligent devices. Having AI capability at edge devices, the widely anticipated real-world and real-time data analytics can see a glorious reality. ML models can be created in traditional and large-scale cloud environments and used in edge devices to infer new data items. Sufficiently powered by in-memory databases and AI, edge devices can set the ball rolling for visualizing and realizing next-generation sophisticated applications. With 5G communication capabilities and the proliferation of edge clouds, last-mile connectivity is becoming simpler and speedier. Newer possibilities will emerge with edge computing. Image classification, face recognition, object detection, machine vision and intelligence, outlier identification, etc., can be facilitated at the edge.

Precisely speaking, a successful edge solution comprises resource-intensive and AI-enabled edge devices, local edge clouds, and integration with traditional clouds, as pictorially represented in the following Figure 12.1.

In summary, edge computing can bring cloud services closer to edge devices. It will significantly lower latency and lay down a stimulating foundation to envisage newer applications and services. Edge computing is predominantly a distributed computing. AI applications being built and run on large-scale cloud environments are slowly yet steadily moved to edge devices with the faster maturity and stability of

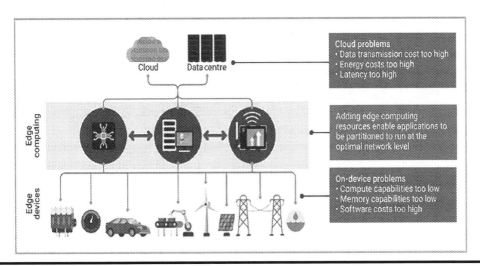

Figure 12.1   Intelligent Edge Devices and Cloud computing Integration

edge technologies and tools. That means the buzzword edge AI will gain prominence in the years to unfurl. Without an iota of doubt, it will be hybrid computing, which combines the traditional and next-generation edge cloud environments.

Latency-sensitive applications need to be at the edge. Computing at the edge dramatically reduces the data transfer size over the network, thus reducing network congestion, saving bandwidth, speeding up operation, and reducing costs. Further on, the performance is comparatively better as the processing occurs at the edge devices. That is, the processing happens where the real action is. Also, as the processing gets performed very near the data source, network latency is almost nil. In the case of surveillance, real-time analysis helps in understanding the difference between safety and disaster. Practically speaking, instead of having a security camera streams, the content of its video feeds up to the cloud for analysis for specific requirements such as face recognition, object detection, etc., at the edge devices themselves, i.e. the possibility of recognition, detection, and decision can happen in the camera and no need to transfer those data back and forth in the network.

Proximate Processing Saves a Lot

IoT edge devices installed in any environment such as hospital, hotel, manufacturing floor, warehouses, retail stores, etc., can collect, store, and process a tremendous amount of edge data emitted from edge sensors. By logically processing data directly at the edge, organizations achieve a lot of cost savings. All the irrelevant data gets filtered out locally. Only decision-enabling data is transmitted over the Internet to cloud storage to be stocked and processed conveniently and comprehensively. Cloud platforms make big data processing and historical analytics conducive.

For example, take monitoring vibrations in an electrical motor where the vibration readings are measured at different intervals. If motor vibration metrics are consistent, measuring the metrics once every minute instead of every second makes sense. If not, the readings need intervention more frequently, i.e. less frequent data to the cloud leads to network efficiency and, of course, results in cost savings.

Security

As data collection, storage, and processing happen within an edge environment, edge device and data are comparatively secure and safe. When edge devices are connected directly to the cloud via the Internet or when edge devices are connected to the cloud through one or more IoT gateways via the Internet, the security scene is bound to change. Real-time analysis of security data plays a very vital role here. If there is any misadventure from somewhere, security insights discovered in time come handy in proactively eliminating any security attack. The ability to find anomalies by immediately detecting a perceptible change in the device behaviour (without going back to the cloud for processing) clearly shows the value of training at the edge.

Edge AI guarantees a high level of safety and security. Data getting streamed via cloud-connected devices are highly vulnerable to snooping, hacking, and breaching. So it's evident that the edge devices need bolstering with internal and external security mechanisms. Through real-time security analytics, AI-enabled devices can come to know if there is any deviation and accordingly eliminate any security flaw before any disaster happens.

Performance

Industrial assets and machinery integrated through a local network. For example, manufacturing floors occupied with several machines, appliances, equipment, instruments, tools, etc. These devices need to integrate with cloud-hosted manufacturing execution system (MES), asset management system, device management system, etc. Industry applications, which comprise different and distributed industrial assets, should be high performing and highly available. Connecting and sharing data with remotely held applications and services is a time-consuming affair. That is, latency is a serious problem to be surmounted. However, the latency is almost nil through edge computing, so accomplishing the much-required high performance is naturally elegant. If industrial sensors see any sign of slowdown or breakdown by processing data at the edge, it can send a real-time alert to people in charge, or even it can generate an API call to switch off the machine as well.

Neural Network (NN) Precision

It is essential to review the precision requirements carefully. Otherwise, one may have to spend more time and waste resources for retraining the NN. Today most of the accelerators for edge inferences work with reduced precision. The reason is the need to convert the NN to lower accuracy, as it simplifies the hardware implementation and dramatically reduces the power consumption, which is incidentally critical for an edge application. While CPUs/GPUs make calculations at 32-bit with floating point precision, the current accelerators working at INT8/INT12/INT16 precision is a trade-off otherwise.

Accuracy

Due to the distinct improvements in NN development, it is possible to maintain high accuracy though there is a possibility for precision getting damaged a bit. However, these gaps reduce with the participation of many NNs. Also, better and much-needed accuracy is achievable with training and retraining.

Energy Efficiency

Power consumption is a critical factor for edge devices. Low-end edge devices are mainly battery-powered, and this is a definite challenge. Thus, power preservation methods are sincerely sought for edge computing to survive and thrive. Therefore, for industry IoT solutions, the thermal design power (TDP) of the chip is a critical factor. With less power consumption, the amount of heat getting dissipated to the environment, fragile, is also less. Chip manufacturers are therefore investing their time, treasure, and talent on engineering power-efficient chips towards embedding in edge devices.

We all know that AI and edge computing domains are individually prevalent and path-breaking. With their strategically healthy convergence, the combination brings in delectable and ground-breaking innovations and inventions. The idea behind the massive success of edge computing is about distributing computing capability spread across the whole network instead of centralizing it in the cloud.

Context-aware applications development will be made accessible through multi-device computing. Software applications will be bolstered with context details to produce and supply timely and relevant services to people. Event-driven applications will get a substantial boost with devices becoming self-contained and intelligent. Devices will become an event producer and processor. Event data and messages are accordingly unwrapped and analysed to squeeze out valuable intelligence in time. Device clouds/clusters will be quickly realized through the voluntary participation of heterogeneous devices to solve more significant problems locally. Real-time enterprises will see the grand reality with edge AI.

Edge AI Is Known for Its Flexibility

The edge devices ecosystem is in a rapid expansion phase. With the arrival of slim and sleek, trendy, and handy, purpose-agnostic and specific, resource-constrained and intensive devices across industry verticals, the days to come will positively impact the edge AI space. Various engineering and business domains, including healthcare monitoring, building energy management, Industry 4.0 use cases, etc., will immensely benefit from edge AI-enabled edge devices. Edge AI devices contribution to making intelligent applications is immense. These devices are incredibly beneficial to commoners, travellers, field service professionals, etc. It's not just the information, transactional, analytical, and operational applications, but situation-aware physical services through smart-edge devices are already in progress in many areas.

Fascinating and Famous Use Cases for Edge Intelligence

Any new technology will go through stringent evaluation for its unique contributions, and edge IoT is no exception. In that view, several use cases and their evaluation boost users' confidence in expressing the power of technology.

In the following sections, we will brief a few famous consumer and industry use cases. As the changing situations warrant, business logic for data processing and AI models for classification, regression, clustering, association, and anomaly detection must happen at the edge.

As we have emphasized earlier, sending edge data to the faraway cloud is not recommended to get a real-time response. In other words, the long-standing goals of real-time data capture, storage, processing, analytics, knowledge discovery, decision making and action need to happen in edge environments through edge analytics. Taking edge data to faraway cloud environments may result in many limitations and risks. Real-time computing is one of the prime requirements for establishing and sustaining intelligent enterprises. Pushing computation and intelligence to the edges leads to real-time decision making, and these computational aspects are certain in many industrial and consumer IoT applications.

Tech-savvy fast-food restaurants are moving towards more automated kitchens to ensure food quality, reduce employee training, increase operational efficiency, and ensure customer experiences meeting expectations. A great practical example of edge computing in retailing is the fast-food chain (Chic-fil-A (https://www.chick-fil-a.com/)). They deployed a Kubernetes cluster in each of their 2000 restaurants for real-time analytics at the edge without an Internet connection. The hardware is pretty tiny and provides an Intel quadcore processor with 8 GB RAM and SSD.

In the consumer world, features like facial recognition or iris recognition on the latest smartphones are well-known examples of local ML capability. Modern phones can learn specific details of your unique identity by training. ML algorithms running locally on the phones then verify your identity every time you sign in to your device. Local recognition and verification become essential for many reasons. Without any external world connectivity, such empowered edge devices can instantaneously do most of the necessary and repeatable activities. Second, the sign-in process occurs frequently, and hence it has to be fast and frictionless. Finally, biometric data has to be secure, and therefore local storage and processing is a must. Also, avoiding sending personal and private data over the Internet is always preferable and less risky than being stored and processed in the cloud.

Humans communicate in different ways: natural languages, gestures, tones, facial expressions, voice recognition, etc. Using edge-based inference, devices in our every-day environments (personal, social, and professional) can pick up these signals to provide next-generation natural experiences.

Smart Cities

The faster maturity and stability of digitization and digital technologies has brought in a series of hitherto unheard changes in our cities. Breakthrough AI techniques are deftly beefing up homes and buildings, medical facilities, hospitality sectors, and social, cyber, and connectivity infrastructures. This strategically sound transition is intrinsically able to automate most of city dwellers' everyday activities and needs. The IoT, AI, 5G, and blockchain technologies are cognitively empowering every article and asset in our operating environments to be aware of people and their requirements. The proliferation of AI-enabled devices ably assists people to take their decisions ingeniously and embark on the right deals and deeds. Data trustworthiness and timeliness are essential for these devices to make the right decisions almost every time. Government agencies show interests in steady adopting such futuristic technologies to fulfil their promises and obligations to their citizens. Digital technologies willingly participate in lessening loads of people in their official, personal, and family assignments and commitments with utmost dedication, discipline, and determination. The intelligent edge helps to manage garbage, traffic, drainage, water, and other utilities. Edge AI is the way forward to produce people-centric, event-driven, service-oriented, knowledge-filled, process-aware, technology-enabled, and cloud-hosted applications.

For example, assume a situation 10,000 lightbulbs deployed in a single area and the IoT application, running in a cloud environment, continuously monitors and manages its energy usage. Each lightbulb is sending data to the cloud-based IoT application on a per-second basis. The remote application empowered with analytics capability is keenly looking for any worthwhile anomaly. An anomaly could be energy levels going up above a certain amount. The brewing trend is that instead of leveraging cloud applications and platforms, it is prudent to use AI toolkits locally to train and predict any outlier time, i.e. make AI toolkits run on edge devices IoT gateway, which is interacting with deployed lightbulbs.

Inertial/Environmental Sensor Analytics

Inertial and environmental sensors are essential to smartwatches, buildings, factories, homes, and even fitness bands. An edge AI supports in analysing the local situations swiftly and provides a fast response.

Pilot AI has developed an algorithm suite that guides moving AI inference workloads from the cloud to the edge and provides a private, secure, and fast way to make decisions close to the data source. This transformation is becoming more relevant in places like retail stores, factories, buildings, and offices. With the Qualcomm chipset QCS610, Pilot AI can follow the movement and aggregate inputs from multiple cameras in a three-dimensional (3D) space onto a two-dimensional (2D) map. One timely application of this futuristic technology is in addressing the current coronavirus pandemic. AI cameras and wireless communication have an indispensable role in upholding and managing social distancing, which remains indisputable for public and private entities. Analysing traffic, office managers and employee's footfall, work area or assembly area of a retail store, shop floors in manufacturing plant and many such sites can determine how proximity the people are moving and trigger social distancing breach alerts. That is especially useful in cafeterias, hallways, or doorways, where people naturally gather and mingle together.

The ability to trace the origin and path of a person with suspected body temperature can help manage affected areas. Insights generated by pilot AI are used for sending real-time alerts; also, in the longer term, for assisting companies in rearranging floor plans based on where people tend to congregate.

AI dashcams from an IoT organization called Samsara helps several companies improve their vehicle (fleets) safety, security, and visibility. Dashboard-mounted cameras use AI and edge processing for the real-time event and object detection, intending to reduce vehicle accident rates. A dual-facing dashcam that uses AI and edge computing to analyse driver behaviour (paying attention, dozing off, taking eyes off the road, etc.) and street conditions in real time results in lowering the accidents and risk of accidents. AI dashcams also detect events and send alerts if the vehicle operator is driving haphazardly, not stopping at a red light, changing lines without indicators, changing multiple lines at once and many more that otherwise punishable acts. As a critical part of a platform for fleet management and driver safety, the dashcam records and persists the footage of the events such as sudden accelerations, unexpected braking, and collisions. The device can automatically upload footage to the cloud for batch processing.

There are several practical uses of artificial intelligence of things (AIoT) for setting up and sustaining smart cities. Monitoring drone traffic is one such use case artistically accomplished through AI. Vehicle traffic movements and traffic congestion are hated among drivers, and they do need an innovative solution. With AIoT monitoring, traffic movements in real time and diverting the traffic flow adjust according to the congestions will soon be a reality as drones can monitor a large area and transmit traffic data. AI then can analyse the data, and the knowledge discovered helps make timely decisions on how to alleviate traffic congestion with proper adjustments to speed limits. The timing of traffic lights also can be adjusted without any human involvement, interpretation, and instruction.

Autonomous vehicles were in the papers a few years back, and now it's a prominent use case for edge intelligence. Vehicles, which are connected, have to intelligently and immediately adapt to changes in the road environment. A variety of environmental data has to be meticulously collected and crunched in milliseconds to empower the car components and owner/operator with all the valuable insights to reach the destination without any hitch or hurdle. What does it mean? Modern cars, which are software-defined, need high computational power and innate intelligence. Hundreds of purpose-specific sensors, microcontrollers, SBCs, cameras, actuators, radar, lidar, etc., to generate a lot of poly-structured data, garner, analyse, and produce real-time intelligence. DL-inspired computer vision capability is the need of the hour for self-driving vehicles.

Toyota is a company that is keeping pace with technology advancements. Taking advantage of the AWS cloud, they now use video-based tools to perform analytics at the edge. All vehicle data are collected from various car sensors. Then, the insights extracted are used for deftly automating a variety of manual activities, thereby addressing and achieving high standards of car safety.

Further on, with path-breaking digital technologies, the convenience, care, choice, and comfort for car driver and occupants are innately enabled. The power of ML at the edge allows detecting and alerting drivers about tornadoes or other lurking dangers. Updating maps in real time, optimizing transportation routes and emergency services can be intelligently accomplished through the golden combination of AI, edge computing, unified communication, ubiquitous sensing, and perception.

It's not just the young generation, but any generation's interest lies in Formula 1 car racing. AI has an interesting use case for the same. Yes, race cars on the track and off the track can generate 100 gigabytes (GB) data per car over a race weekend. There will be more than 100,000 data points getting streamed from a single McLaren track car per second. Tire change, safety, and gear change analysis and insights drive critical decisions that have to be taken in real time by the engineers at the trackside or mission control.

As discussed earlier on dashcams, AI edge computing helps analysing videos from the vehicle and the roadside cameras to cogently monitor a driver's behaviour. Longer drives make driver behaviours change. Imagine systems on the roads and cameras working together to collect metrics about how fast the driver drives the vehicle. The level of driver's distraction, their postures at the driver seats, and other such details can be minutely captured and analysed to extract timely insights to alert drivers and even alert nearby patrolling vehicles. Captured videos then made subject to various investigations towards guaranteeing safe, less stressful, sweet memorable drive, travel, and trip.

Incorporating predictive maintenance in vehicles by tracking the performance/health condition of the vehicle's parts and sending information regarding performance to the vehicle infotainment system to do the right analytics in time is another excellent use case. The performance data at the network edge processing helps sharply reduce backhaul. For example, edge computing filters out critical measures like "tyre pressure" and its condition like optimum, flat, low, etc., while letting through any alert indicates an unusual vehicle performance.

AIoT is extensively used to monitor a fleet of vehicles to reduce fuel costs, track vehicle maintenance, and identifying unsafe driver behaviour. Through IoT devices such as GPS and other sensors and an intelligent AI system, companies can manage their fleet better thanks to AIoT. Next-generation cars can use radars, sonars, GPS, and cameras to gather data about driving conditions and hand them to an AI system to make the right decisions.

Autonomous Delivery Robots

The use of AIoT with autonomous vehicles and autonomous delivery robots is another example of AIoT. Robots have sensors that collect details about the environment where the robot is traversing and then make moment-to-moment decisions about responding through its onboard AI platform.

Smart Homes

These come under the domain of smart cities. In digitally transformed homes and apartments, it is possible to use the GPS data from your smartphone or connected car to trigger the smart thermostat at home when you approach as configured. Using visual recognition, new smart locks in conjunction with doorbells can also recognize you, unlock the front door, trigger the lights and even start playing music. All these happen automatically in a discreet manner. What is adorable is that the combination and coordination among these edge devices guarantees a scintillating and sparkling experience.

Intelligent edge devices can significantly enhance safety. For example, one can train a smart home edge kit to recognize danger signals such as alarms going off, a person's fall, glass breaking, or a tap left dripping. The kit could then alert the house owner and occupants immediately and act or react accordingly on sensing the precarious situation. Ambient Intelligence (AmI) is another area that can benefit from edge-based data. AmI refers to the deployment of edge devices sensitive and responsive to people's presence and needs. AmI can facilitate people and environments to have fruitful interactions with each other. Daily activity monitoring for elderly, diseased, debilitated, and bed-ridden people is a prime example of AmI. The main objective of these intelligent environments for enabling ambient-assisted living (AAL) is to detect anomalies quickly, such as a fall or a fire and take immediate action by informing caregivers.

Some companies choose to deploy a network of smart environmental sensors in their office premises. These interconnected sensors can detect what personnel are present and adjust temperatures and lighting accordingly to improve energy efficiency. A building can control building access through face-recognition technology. The combination of connected cameras and AI can compare images taken in real-time against a database to determine who should be allowed and who should not, i.e. grant access to individuals to a building is AIoT at work.

Predictive Maintenance in Industrial Environments

Industrial assets and machinery need to be continuously monitored for wear and tear. Their health condition, performance level, and other functional parameters need to be checked programmatically to decide whether one or more assets need some shutdown, suspend, or repair. All kinds of operational, security, performance, and log data have to be therefore sincerely collected and subjected to a variety of deeper investigations. ML algorithms are now playing a more significant role in assets' maintenance in an optimal and organized manner and predicted through ML models. Manufacturing processes also need to be optimized to increase productivity. By smartly leveraging ML algorithms on edge devices, industry houses can quickly lookout for any potential warning signs to accomplish timely maintenance to avoid any slowdown or breakdown. Edge AI sensors attached to a machine can measure its temperature, vibration, and noise levels to detect anomalies.

Augmented Reality (AR) and Virtual Reality (AR)

These are pretty recent developments. AR and VR tools require high-end graphic processing capabilities to cleanly provide immersive reality experiences for users. With the general availability of powerful GPUs to be fit in edge devices, the era of AR and VR are all set to bloom beautifully. Such powerful GPUs are already available in cloud servers. But the network latency is a primary deterrent for a real-time experience.

Edge AI in Retail

Edge computing, in conjunction with ML algorithms, opens up a series of hitherto unheard opportunities and possibilities. Some cutting-edge store capabilities such as trying on clothes or make up virtually by leveraging cameras and AR–type applications let potential customers visualize their choices real quick. The customers can see how different colour combinations, patterns, and fabrics look on them via monitors or smart mirrors. Instead of going through the traditional trial process of physically trying out new choices, the new computer vision–based and ML-driven services are enabling consumers to find what they want quickly. On the other side, sellers can complete sales more quickly.

As personalization is an ever sought and evolving trend, advertisement and other industries always look for opportunities to personalize as much as possible towards ads, targeted marketing to increase sales prospects. The digital-out-of-home (DOOH) advertising uses data on individual needs and traits by capturing and processing in real time to deliver advertisements, and they are context-aware. By pushing this processing to the edge, either on-site (e.g. in a shopping centre/retail store) or on the network, this personal data can be analysed locally and generate real-time and relevant advertising. This local processing of data is in contrast to aggregating personal data and processing it in the cloud.

A camera with computer vision capabilities can use facial recognition to identify customers when they walk through the door in a smart retail environment. The system gathers intelligence about customers, including their gender, product preferences, traffic flow, and more. Then analysis happens on the collected data and results in the prediction of consumer behaviour. The predicted information helps make decisions about store operations from marketing to product placement and other decisions such as inventory and replenishment management. For example, if the system detects that most customers walking into the store are millennials, it can push out product advertisements or in-store specials that appeal to that demographic. Smart cameras could identify shoppers, and they can skip the checkout queue like what happens in the Amazon Go store.

Real-time Tracking of Inventory

The increase in online shopping and demand for super-fast delivery has resulted in unique challenges for logistics and retail companies. Keeping track of what inventory is in the warehouse or in store helps businesses to make informed decisions. The optimal management of products, bundles, packages, and pallets needs an effective process in place. And so the company effectively needs to gather volumes of data on the real-time position and the goods conditions (e.g. monitoring the temperature of fresh produce throughout the supply chain).

Pallet and Product Matching

To improve accuracy and speed up warehouse processes, smart cameras can scan barcodes on each pallet to know stock levels in every micro-location. Robotic workers (or robots) can lift boxes, holding them within view of the cameras, which in turn reads the barcode metadata and provides a cue to indicate whether the package has been placed on the correct pallet. The metadata is then analysed in real time, and the analytics platform can alert staff of fraudulent barcodes or if pallets landed in the wrong place. Data is then streamed between the edge devices, the warehouse management system, ERP software at cloud, and warehouse employees.

Robots (Picking/AGV Navigation)

Deploying robots can lead to more efficient warehouses by reducing error rates, higher customer satisfaction, and improved warehouse safety. Furthermore, using IoT edge analytics, robots can autonomously navigate the warehouse and collect the items that need to be managed. These analytics happen in real time, particularly in robot navigation, where robots steer and navigate the warehouse and avoid other automated guided vehicles (AGVs).

Edge AI for Real-time and Precision Healthcare

In this Covid time, the concept of the Internet of Medical Things (IoMT) is acquiring special significance. All kinds of medical instruments, equipment, robots, drones, and devices connected to cloud-hosted healthcare applications, services, and databases.

Healthcare sensors and actuators in association with the devices, as mentioned earlier, generate a lot of data, which must be collected and crunched by the machines that are having high processing capability, high memory capacity, and higher storage space. Especially during the lockdown period, it is pretty difficult to physically and personally meet doctors and specialists to get medical options and opinions. Therefore, everything becomes virtual. That is, remote monitoring and measurement, telediagnosis, consultation, and care have become the new normal. The interconnected nature of all healthcare entities comes to the rescue. Not only edge devices are computational and communicative, but also, they are sensitive, perceptive, and responsive with the embedding of the right intelligence into them.

For instance, recently, GE Healthcare has introduced a virtual care solution, which aggregates data from several systems and devices, including ventilators, patient monitoring systems, electronic medical records, labs, and other systems. The solution allows one clinician to monitor several patients simultaneously. Smartwatches, fitness bands, and such wearable devices collect and record any data about the user's location, activity, heart rate, the sugar level in the blood, and other health-related data. These details are helpful to keep track of the health, diet, or other necessary activities.

Intensive care is an area that can positively exploit the edge-based ML, where real-time data processing and decision making are critical for closed-loop systems. The intensive care units or devices must measure and maintain vital physiological parameters, such as blood glucose level or blood pressure, within the prescribed threshold. As hardware and ML models become more sophisticated, parameters indicating more complex operations and gets involved in monitoring and analysing with edge devices, like neurological activity or cardiac rhythms.

Image Analytics

Every minute, still, and dynamic image is captured by smartphones and cameras installed not just a few but many in essential junctions. Edge AI enables real-time recognition and detection of something influential in those images and video streams. Edge AI can comprehensively understand the scene by doing real-time and deeper context analysis. The knowledge discovered gets disseminated to concerned systems, and executives may ponder the next course of action with all the confidence and clarity. However, sharing image and video files over the Internet wastes a lot of network bandwidth and delays the process. That is, the much-required real-time action is not possible with data analytics at remote cloud environments.

Audio Analytics

Earlier, we have discussed real-time image and video analytics where an audio frame divided into small parts by DL. Edge AI recognizes an audio/voice among overlapping sounds swiftly and effectively. It detects baby's sounds, glass falling and breaking sounds, the screeching sound of a car wheel from several other overlapping voices and sounds. MS team meetings are enabled with noise-cancelling levels where one can suppress almost all the surrounding noises when you attend a meeting.

Mining, Oil, and Gas and Industrial Automation

The business value of edge-based ML becoming evident in the oil, gas, or mining industry is growing steadily. People work in harsh and rough environments. Connectivity is also a tricky thing in such places. Power-efficient sensors on edge devices such as robots can capture large amounts of data and accurately predict things like pressure across pumps or operating parameters outside their normal range of values.

Predictive machinery maintenance in a manufacturing establishment can reduce unnecessary costs and extend the life of industrial assets. Typically, as part of maintenance, the factories take machinery offline at regular intervals, and they conduct complete inspections as per the specifications of the equipment manufacturers. Understandably, it is not efficient, and it can become an obsolete process with edge AI. Machines inside the factory or warehouse may come with the embedded sensors that can read and identify patterns indicating any potential breakdown by applying DL to still images, audio, or video.

As we have discussed in another chapter, the device-to-device (D2D) and device-to-cloud (D2C) integration led to the realization of sophisticated use cases for people, business behemoths, and governments. The adoption of 5G in IoT is bringing several benefits. The prominent one among them is ultra-low latency. The AI domain is seeing numerous noteworthy advancements. Thus, with faster and reliable connectivity, IoT devices are presented as the new operating environment. The much-published and propagated combination of AI, 5G, IoT, and blockchain facilitates more innovative applications for the next era of knowledge.

Edge AI: The Challenges

The first and foremost challenge is **processing and power consumption**. AI consists of training and inferencing software. Training trains a model to identify many relevant parameters so that it can interpret the incoming data. Inferencing is when the model makes learning-based predictions. The data and process-intensive training occur at the traditional clouds, and then the trained model is deployed to the edge. Inferencing (prognosis) is a relatively low-energy and more straightforward action. For IoT devices, the increased energy consumption poses a more significant problem and this mandates for a rebalancing process capacity versus the power requirements.

Data storage and security represent the second challenge with many IoT sensors and devices generating various data, so the data storage in edge devices becomes risky. When edge devices deal with more digital data, the challenge of data security and privacy comes up. Thus, edge devices have to have more processing, memory, and storage power. Further on, their energy consumption while doing data processing has to be a lower side for the idea of edge computing and analytics to flourish consistently.

Indisputably edge computing and AI-enabled edge devices together can bring many innovations and disruptions. However, they also get some unwanted security and privacy risks. Security issues, holes, threats, and vulnerabilities must be proactively and pre-emptively pinpointed and surmounted to thwart malicious attacks. Malware and bugs have to be identified and eliminated. AI-enabled edge devices with fool-proof security can bring about cost savings, process optimization, productivity improvement, service delivery efficiency, real-time computing, etc. This enablement will pave the way for hitherto unexplored avenues for new and sustainable revenue.

The Cybersecurity Concerns with Edge Devices

With the explosion of connected devices, device and data security aspects are becoming a more significant concern for security experts and architects. With the data storage, processing, and analytics fervently and frequently happening at the edge, cybersecurity risks correspondingly go up. Edge devices may directly hook to cloud assets or indirectly connected to cloud resources through intermediaries such as IoT gateways/hubs/brokers/buses. If an intermediary is compromised, then all the edge devices sitting behind the gateway will also subject to risk and compromise. With cyberterrorism, edge devices are vulnerable and prone to the threat of losing confidential and company data.

AI is used extensively to unlock phones with facial recognition technology and is also being used to control data access. If there is any security lapse, such edge devices can be compromised. Then there may be irreparable losses. Surveillance cameras, access control systems (ACSs), and voice assistants are increasingly fit with AI capabilities to perform proximate processing to emit out actionable insights in time. If there is any untoward break-in, then the damage may be enormous. The way forward is to stringently lockdown ML models and treat them as prime assets.

The Security Standards for Edge Devices

Having understood the cybersecurity implications, the worldwide standard organizations and agencies are seriously considering bringing forth competent security standards for adequately securing edge devices. Companies can follow the specifications towards incorporating unbreakable and impenetrable security mechanisms in edge devices by creating benchmarks.

However, edge devices are heterogeneous, distributed, and decentralized. Hence the optimal distribution of data processing tasks across a network of edge devices presents a challenge. Further on, efficient task and resource scheduling are vital for optimally finishing ML jobs.

With the faster proliferation of AI-specific chipsets, lightweight AI toolkits, in-memory databases, and other automated toolkits, edge computing marching towards increase operational reliability, bring forth real-time insights and improve data security. 5G, which promises lower latency and accommodates more edge devices per square kilometre, billions of resource-intensive connected devices, and quantum computing, the efficacy of edge computing is bound to go up remarkably.

Edge AI – The Best Practices

Several noteworthy developments are happening in the promising edge AI space. Experts have come out with a list of best practices based on their experience and education.

- Most ML models need the corresponding ML frameworks such as TensorFlow, PyTorch, etc., to run. Readers are encouraged to look at resources in the other exclusive chapter for IoT tools and frameworks.
- Use ONNX – ONNX is an open format built to represent ML models. ONNX defines a standard set of operators – the building blocks of ML and DL models. This set of operators enables AI developers to use models with various frameworks, tools, runtimes, and compilers.
- When selecting edge hardware for running an ML model, the ML model configuration must go together with a hardware configuration. That is, there may be a need for more processing power.
- ML models may be very resource-hungry, and hence the selection of edge hardware platform has to be made carefully.
- Many popular ML libraries depend on low-level ones that are available for Intel architectures only. For instance, NumPy is a Python library that works well with Intel architecture.

Compression of AI Algorithms and Data

Compressing AI algorithms and data will prove pivotal to mass adoption. There are research works initiated to explore and speed up compressing NNs. Such optimization results in using less powerful processors, less memory, less storage, and less bandwidth at the device level. The approach prunes the "unimportant" neural connections, reweighting the connections and applying a more efficient encoding model.

Data-compression schemes will enable endpoint-embedded NNs to continue to ingest necessary and sufficient sensor data to detect subtle patterns. These techniques will also help endpoints rapidly consume cached training data for continual fine-tuning of the accuracy of their core pattern-discovery functions. And superior data compression will reduce solid-state data-caching resource requirements at the endpoints.

Researchers have concluded that minimizing the number of parameters in deep neural network (DNN) models helps decrease the need for computational resources for model inference. A few well-known models which have used such techniques with minimum (or no) accuracy degradation are YOLO, MobileNets, Solid-State Drive (SSD), and SqueezeNet.

Thus, model compression is emerging as a viable technique to execute models at the edge device. We need to understand a trade-off; compared to the original model, the compressed model may lose accuracy. However, in most of the situation, it is acceptable. Using several compression techniques and caching intermediate outputs to reuse iteratively, researchers have improved the execution speed of DNN models. DeepMon (https://nsr.cse.buffalo.edu/mobisys_2017/papers/pdfs/

mobisys17-paper07.pdf) which is an ML framework continuous computer vision application at the edge device is one such example. TensorFlow Lite uses similar techniques (https://www.tensorflow.org/lite) to run models at the edge.

Applications in IoT, industrial, supplier, and consumer segments generate a colossal amount of data from their sensors to make decisions faster based on commands from human-machine interfaces (HMIs). Fusion sensor technology makes obtaining data on edge devices more accessible, accurate, and fast. HMIs help human interactions more adaptive by making them user friendly. So it makes processing data in the ML computing engine closer to its origin a natural pattern.

While MCU power consumption stays relatively flat, the number of transistors, clock speed, and parallel cores trend. As more high-performance and low-power MCUs become available, edge computing can help build an intelligent and user-friendly system. These improvisations mean supporting commonly used surveillance cameras, dashboard cameras, and video conferencing devices with applications like object classification, segmentation, vehicle's license plate recognition, human face recognition, body detection, and people footfall counts. Moving AI workloads from cloud locations to IoT devices is the next important step in computing at the network edge. When ordinary, camera-driven devices deliver more inferences per second, innovative applications are bound to increase.

Kafka at the Edge: Use Cases, Scenarios, and Architectures

Event streaming with Apache Kafka **and Kafka** at the edge becomes an essential thing and no longer a mere hype. To have the same, Kafka's primary characteristics of open, flexible, and scalable architecture are at the edge of the cloud. The possible locations for a Kafka edge deployment include retail stores, cell towers, trains, small factories, restaurants, etc.

Edge Kafka is an essential ingredient of a streaming nervous system that spans IoT environments (offices, warehouses, airports, buildings, etc.) and non-IoT environments (private, public, and hybrid clouds). Kafka clients and the Kafka brokers **are available and** run on the edge **devices**. So Kafka enables better edge processing, integration, decoupling, low latency, and cost-efficient data processing.

More giant factories can provide competent infrastructure to deploy a reliable Kafka cluster with stable network connectivity to the cloud. Unfortunately, many IoT projects require **more pragmatic** edge capabilities. The edge projects present the following distinctions.

- Offline business continuity is important because the connection to the cloud is not continuous and not guaranteed all the time. Therefore, the viable option is proximate processing, real-time analytics with low latency, and only online from time to time or low bandwidth.
- Often edge solutions need to deploy Kafka brokers across hundreds of locations. A single broker is usually good enough without high availability. But for back pressure and local processing, there is a need for many brokers. Many real-time scenarios in retail stores, trains, restaurants, cell towers, small factories, etc., will use brokers.

■ Low-footprint, low-touch, little-or-no-DevOps-required installations of Kafka brokers are mandatory for many of these use cases. Hence, certified OEM hardware usage is undoubtedly a better option to install and operate Kafka at the edge.

■ **CioT or consumer IoT** – Use cases fall under smart home, ride-share, retail store, etc. And Industrial IoT (IIoT) use cases always have good tangible factors for sectors such as vehicles, food, etc.

■ Many edge use cases are all around sensor and telemetry data. An application that processes millions of messages per second is acceptable to lose a few of the messages as it does not ultimately affect the calculation outcome.

Architectures and use cases include data integration, pre-processing, and replication to the cloud, big and small data edge processing and analytics, disconnected offline scenarios, shallow footprint scenarios with hundreds of locations, and situations without high availability and others.

Scenarios for Edge Computing with Kafka

■ **Public Sector** – Smart city applications such as public transportation, traffic management, integration of various connected car platforms from different carmakers, cybersecurity, etc., are to benefit from edge processing.

■ **Transportation/Logistics/Railway/Aviation** – Edge computing empowered through Kafka in the trains for offline and local processing/storage, traveller information (delayed or cancelled flight/train/bus), real-time loyalty platforms (class upgrade, lounge access, etc.), etc., are getting momentum and widely discussed in latest edge AI developments.

■ **Manufacturing (Automotive, Aerospace, Semiconductors, Chemical, Food, and others)** – Edge computing enabled by Kafka is very prevalent in these scenarios: IoT aftermarket customer services, OEM in machines and vehicles, embedding into standard software such as ERP or MES systems, cybersecurity, a digital twin of devices/machines/production lines/processes, production line monitoring in factories for predictive maintenance/quality control/production efficiency, operations dashboards and line wellness (on-site for the plant manager, and aggregated global KPIs for executive management), track & trace and geofencing on the shop floor, etc.

■ **Energy/Utility** – Smart home, buildings, smart meters, monitoring of remote machines (e.g. for drilling, windmills, and other energy sectors), pipeline, and refinery operations (e.g. predictive failure or anomaly detection) strengthen through Kafka-inspired edge computing.

■ **Telecommunications/Media** – Comes under OSS real-time monitoring analysis and metrics reporting, root cause analysis, and response to the underlying network devices. Also, the infrastructure (routers, switches, other network devices), BSS customer experience and OTT services (mobile app integration for millions of users), and 5G edge (e.g. street sensors) are the widely known use cases and part of Kafka integration with edge computing, where Kafka enhances the experience.

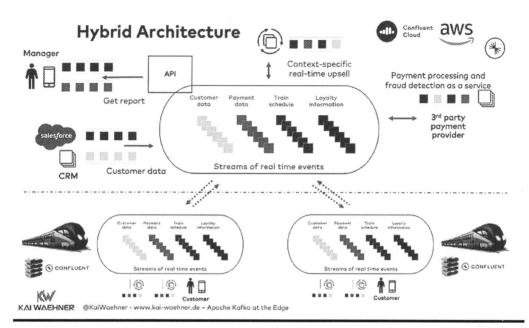

Figure 12.2   Hybrid Architecture from Edge to Cloud

■ **Retailing/Food/Restaurants/Banking** – It's so common that we witness almost every day many scenarios on customer communication, cross-selling, up-selling, loyalty system, payments in retail stores. The perpetual inventory, PoS integration for (local) payments and (remote) CRM integration, EFTPOS (electronic funds transfer at point of sale) are the widely reported use cases of edge computing, which Kafka is significantly bolstering.

The following example shows an edge and hybrid solution for railways to improve the customer experience and increase the **railway company's revenue**. It leverages offline edge processing for customer communication, replication to the cloud for analytics, and integration with third-party interfaces and APIs from partners.

Hybrid Architecture from Edge to Cloud

As depicted in the following Figure 12.2 the local processing of data at the edge is happening on the trains. However, the replication of relevant data is also happening in real time, data sent to the cloud in real time when there is Internet connectivity and free network resources. If not, Kafka is handling the backpressure and replicating to the cloud when internet connectivity is available again.

It's not only the great benefit that Kafka has at the edge and real-time messaging for handling backpressure, but it also opens several potential avenues of integration with other heterogeneous systems as depicted in the following Figure 12.3. For example, restaurants, traveller information, hotels, car rentals, loyalty system, and so on, integrate with it and do data processing for the plethora of ideas as cross-selling, up-selling, real-time delay information, etc., at the edge. This way, only one single platform is required to solve all the different and varieties of problems.

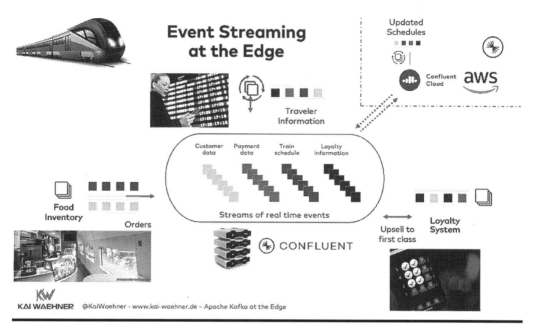

Figure 12.3   Event Streaming at the Edge

In summary, Kafka turned out as an excellent solution for the edge as that enables deploying the same open, scalable, and reliable technology at the edge and the cloud.

Conclusion

With more IoT sensors and devices joining mainstream computing through digitization and edge technologies, a humungous amount of data gets generated, collected, and stocked. IoT device data gets processed to extract actionable insights with the broader acceptance and adoption of digital technologies. Cloud platforms have been the prime component in IoT data processing. However, due to network latency, the real-time processing of IoT data is facing the problem. To overcome the above limitation and to perform intelligent processing of IoT data, the concept of edge AI is gaining prominence and dominance. Instead of sending all IoT edge data to cloud environments, local processing is prescribed and promoted. Besides considerably reducing the network latency, the other benefits include bandwidth saving, data security, faster response, etc.

In the next few years, we will see many path-breaking IoT products, solutions, and services coming to market that leverage this increasingly capable intelligent edge. Future innovations could include in-memory computing and quantum AI. These will speed up the leverage of machine and deep learning (ML/DL) algorithms at the edge. The software and hardware limitations of edge devices will be completely wiped out to make edge AI normal. The computing will be more tuned for commoners. Real-time computing will flourish with the nourishment of technology product and tool vendors.

References

https://brainchipinc.com/

https://www.ceva-dsp.com/

https://cloud.google.com/edge-tpu

https://greenwaves-technologies.com/

https://e.huawei.com/en/products/cloud-computing-dc/atlas/ascend-910, https://www.nvidia.com/en-in/autonomous-machines/embedded-systems/, https://www.qualcomm.com/products/vision-intelligence-400-platform

https://ekkono.ai/, https://www.foghorn.io/, https://www.onswim.com/

https://www.renesas.com/us/en/solutions/key-technology/e-ai.html

http://pilot.ai/

https://www.edureka.co/blog/top-10-machine-learning-frameworks/

https://onnx.ai/

https://www.kai-waehner.de/blog/2020/10/20/apache-kafka-event-streaming-use-cases-architectures-examples-real-world-across-industries/

Index

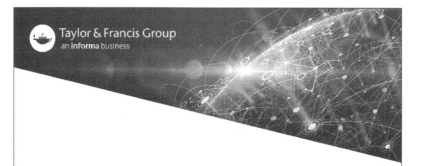